Guesses at Truth, by Two Brothers.

Third Edition.   First Series, 6s.;   Second Series, 7s.

Reader, if you weigh me at all, weigh me patiently; judge me candidly; and may you find half the satisfaction in examining my Guesses, that I have myself had in making them.—*To the Reader*.

Dr. Schmitz's History of Rome,

From the Earliest Times to the Death of COMMODUS, A.D. 192. One thick volume 12mo. Second Edition. 7s. 6d. cloth, or 8s. 6d. strongly bound in leather.

THE immense progress made in investigating Roman history and antiquities within the last thirty or forty years, having materially altered the whole complexion of that study, has rendered indispensable a new manual, for the use of schools, removing the old errors and misconceptions which have long since been exposed and exploded by scholars. This compendium is designed to supply the want, by condensing and selecting out of a voluminous mass of detail, that which is necessary to give rather a vivid picture of the leading epochs of the history, than a minute narrative of the particulars recorded in the authorities. The author has availed himself of all the important works on the whole Roman history, or portions of it, which have appeared since Niebuhr gave a new life and new impulse to the subject. A copious table of chronology and indexes are added.

Dictionary of Greek and Roman Antiquities.

By various Writers.   Edited by Dr. WILLIAM SMITH.   Second Edition.   One thick vol. 8vo. with several hundred Engravings on Wood.   2l. 2s.

THIS work, written by the editor in conjunction with seventeen other gentlemen, embodies the results of the latest investigations of the distinguished German scholars whose labours, within the last half century, have shed an entirely different light on the history, the private life, and the political relations of the Greeks and Romans. It comprehends all the topics of antiquities properly so called, including the laws, institutions, and domestic usages of the Greeks and Romans; painting, sculpture, music, the drama, and other subjects on which correct information can be obtained elsewhere only by consulting a large number of costly or untranslated works.

The dictionary is illustrated by numerous wood-cuts, made under the superintendence of the writers of the several articles. They are chiefly representations of costumes, weapons, ornaments, machines, implements, utensils, money, plans of buildings, and architectural embellishments.

Subjoined are tables of Greek and Roman measures, weights, and money: with full indexes, Greek, Latin, and English.

Dictionary of Greek & Roman Biography & Mythology.

Edited by WILLIAM SMITH, LL.D.   Medium 8vo.   Illustrated by numerous Engravings on Wood.   Complete in Three Volumes 5l. 15s. 6d.   Each volume may be had separately.

THE period comprehended in this history of remarkable individuals, real or ideal is from the earliest times to the fall of the Eastern Empire, in 1453. The work is the result of the joint labours of twenty-nine writers, whose names are attached to their respective articles,—the divisions of subjects having been severally allotted to such of the contributors as had made them more or less their peculiar study. Copious accounts are given of the writings of mathematicians, jurists, physicians, historians, poets, philosophers, and orators. The Latin and Greek Christian fathers also occupy considerable space; and the lives of painters, sculptors, and architects, contain details, useful to the artist, of all their works still extant, or of which there is any record in ancient writers. In fact, the work exhibits a view of the whole circle of ancient history and literature for upwards of two thousand years. It is embellished, whenever possible, by wood-cuts, taken from ancient coins. Extensive chronological tables of Greek and Roman history are added; and a table exhibiting at a glance the years B.C. or A.D. corresponding to any given A.U.C. or olympiad.

LECTURES

ON

THE HISTORY OF ROME,

FROM

THE EARLIEST TIMES TO THE FALL OF THE
WESTERN EMPIRE.

BY

B. G. NIEBUHR.

EDITED BY

DR. LEONHARD SCHMITZ, F.R.S.E.,

RECTOR OF THE HIGH SCHOOL OF EDINBURGH.

Second Edition.

WITH EVERY ADDITION DERIVABLE FROM DR. ISLER'S GERMAN EDITION.

IN THREE VOLUMES.

VOL. I.

LONDON:

TAYLOR, WALTON, AND MABERLY,

UPPER GOWER STREET, AND IVY LANE, PATERNOSTER ROW.

M.DCCC.L.

LONDON
PRINTED BY J. WERTHEIMER AND CO.,
CIRCUS PLACE, FINSBURY CIRCUS.

PREFACE.

WHEN in 1844, I published the Lectures of Niebuhr, embracing the History of Rome from the commencement of the first Punic war down to the death of Constantine, I entertained a strong hope that Niebuhr's friends in Germany would be roused to a sense of duty, and no longer withhold from the world his valuable relics in his own language. In that hope I was, for a time, disappointed; for no sooner were the Lectures published in this country than there appeared, at once, advertisements of two German translations of them. The idea of translating from English into German a work of which there existed in Germany numerous manuscripts containing the very words and expressions of Niebuhr, and which required only the careful and conscientious supervision of an editor, seemed to be a somewhat preposterous undertaking. If the Lectures were to be published in Germany, assuredly the German public had a right to expect that the exact language of the historian should be scrupulously preserved, which is an impossibility in a re-translation, in the execution of which, moreover, no use was to be made of the manuscript notes taken by the students

during the delivery of the Lectures. Only one of the adver-
tised translations, however, made its appearance; and that
was more than enough, for it bore so many marks of careless-
ness, and displayed so flagrant a want of knowledge of the
English language, that even the most moderate expectations
were disappointed. As there was reason for believing that
every succeeding volume of Niebuhr's Lectures which might
appear in this country would meet with the same fate in
Germany as the first two, and that an unpardonable wrong
would thus be done to the memory of the author, M. Marcus
Niebuhr, the son of the historian, and some of the more
intimate friends and pupils of Niebuhr issued an announce-
ment, that they would forthwith set about preparing
a German edition of all Niebuhr's Lectures, on the only
principle that could secure for his memory that honour among
his own countrymen to which he is so justly entitled. Thus
the very circumstance which at first had seemed to thwart
my hopes contributed in reality to their speedy realisation.

The task of preparing the German Edition was undertaken
by M. Marcus Niebuhr, Dr. Isler of Hamburgh, and Professor
Classen of Lübeck. My co-operation also was solicited ;
but other engagements prevented my accepting the honourable proposal; and it was finally arranged that I should undertake the Editorship in England of the whole Series of
Lectures. The first volume, containing the Lectures on the
History of Rome from the earliest times down to the commencement of the first Punic war, edited by Dr. Isler,
appeared at Berlin in 1846. Of this a translation is now presented to the English public. As to the materials of which
the German editor has made use, and the plan he has followed,
I shall do best to let him speak for himself. " The History
of the Roman Republic," he says, " is one of those few subjects

on which Niebuhr gave two courses of Lectures in the University of Bonn; the first in the winter of 1826-7, and the second during the winter of 1828-9. In the summer of 1829, he lectured on the history of the Roman Emperors down to the overthrow of the Western Empire. In the course of 1826, he did not carry the History further than to the time of Sulla; but in many parts of it he entered more minutely into the criticism and analysis of the existing materials; and this circumstance prevented him from carrying the History as far down as in the latter course of 1828. What is here presented to the reader, consists essentially of the latter course of Lectures; but all that is of interest or importance in the earlier one of 1826 has been incorporated, wherever it seemed appropriate. This combination of the two courses of Lectures into one, though it does not always preserve the exact form and order in which Niebuhr related the History, yet does not contain a single idea, nay hardly a single word, which was not actually uttered by him. If this should be thought an arbitrary mode of proceeding, the editor takes the responsibility upon himself; but he must at the same time state, that he considered this to be the way in which the treasures entrusted to his care could be disposed of in the most careful and conscientious manner. A considerable number of manuscripts have been collated, and all the available materials have been scrupulously sifted and weighed, in order to ensure the value of the work as much as possible. The editor's labour has been of a purely philological nature, inasmuch as it was necessary to form, as far as it could be done, a genuine text out of a mass of notes presenting such discrepancies and inaccuracies as naturally occur in notes hurriedly made by students in the lecture-room. Those who are acquainted with such matters know that the formation of the text consists not only in restoring the exact expressions of the Lecturer, but also in tracing the facts stated to their respective authorities, wherever practicable."

Dr. Isler further states, that when his manuscript was ready for the press, it was revised by Professor Classen; and that M. Marcus Niebuhr, who afterwards undertook the revision of the proof-sheets, also suggested several improvements. From these statements, the reader will see that the German editor had greater advantages than could have fallen to the lot of any one undertaking the task in this country; for he not only had notes from two distinct courses of Lectures on the same subject, one of which was supplementary to the other, but he was assisted by those most deeply interested in the work. As, moreover, the three volumes of Niebuhr's immortal History treat of the same period as that contained in these Lectures, the former always served as a corrective, wherever the manuscripts of the latter were obscure or imperfect.

Under these circumstances, I might have confined myself to the mere translation of the present Lectures; but as I possessed some very excellent manuscripts, I thought it right to institute a careful collation of them; and my labour has been amply rewarded, for I found a considerable number of most interesting remarks and statements which do not occur in the German edition, so that in many respects the present volume is more complete and perfect than the work on which it is founded. Dr. Isler has not divided his edition into Lectures, because the Lectures in the two courses did not always correspond, or treat of the same subject; but in the present work the Lectures have been kept distinct, partly because I consider that division to be essential to a right understanding of the work, and partly for the sake of consistency, the same plan having been adopted in the two volumes published in

1844. In doing this, however, I was under the necessity of making some Lectures disproportionately long, as passages of considerable extent or even entire Lectures from the course of 1826 had to be inserted in Lectures of the course of 1828; while, by the transference of passages from one Lecture to a more appropriate place in another, some Lectures will appear rather short.

It may perhaps be asked, What is the use of publishing the Lectures on that portion of Roman History on which we possess the author's own elaborate volumes? To this it may be replied, that the present Lectures contain a more popular and familiar exposition of the subject, which in the three volumes is treated in a severe style, little calculated to attract ordinary readers. They, therefore, may be used as an introduction to, or as a running commentary on, Niebuhr's great work. I also agree with the German editor in thinking that it does not seem right to suppress any part of the Lectures on Roman History, one of the objects of their publication being to give as vivid a picture as possible of the extraordinary personal and intellectual character of Niebuhr; an object which can be attained only by the complete and entire publication of all that he has ever said on the history of Rome. These Lectures, moreover, as Dr. Isler remarks, " distinctly show the different objects which Niebuhr had in view in preparing a work for the press, and in lecturing from the professorial chair; each, in his opinion, demanded a totally different mode of treatment, whence many points are set forth in these Lectures more clearly and distinctly, nay sometimes even more minutely than in the larger work. The reader need only be reminded of the Introductory Lectures on the Sources of Roman History, of the Discussion on the Saturnian verse, and the like. Lastly, it must not be forgotten, that on many subjects these Lectures contain the latest and most matured opinions of Niebuhr. The revision of the last edition of the first volume of his History was finished by him, chiefly, in the year 1826; and the additions to the third edition belong to the year 1827. A mind like that of Niebuhr never ceased acquiring fresh stores of knowledge, and making new inquiries, although the principal results were already firmly established. Sundry new fragments of ancient writers also were discovered after the publication of the last edition, which led him to modify the views he had expressed in his printed work. In regard to the period treated of in the third volume, the reader will find in these Lectures many additions and corrections; for the greater part of that volume was composed as early as 1812, and if Niebuhr had lived to prepare a new edition of it, he would undoubtedly have introduced many important alterations. Hence even those who by a careful study have acquired a thorough familiarity with the three volumes of the Roman History, will find in these Lectures much that is new and striking."

L. SCHMITZ.

Edinburgh, November, 1847.

CONTENTS.

LECTURE XXXIII.

LECTURE XXXIV.

LECTURE XXXV.

LECTURE XXXVI.

LECTURE XXXVII.

LECTURE XXXVIII.

THE HISTORY OF ROME

FROM

THE EARLIEST TIMES TO THE FIRST PUNIC WAR.

————◆————

LECTURE I.

AT the time when Fabius began to write the history of Rome, his materials consisted of the *annales pontificum,* the *fasti,* the *libri pontificum* and *augurales,* the *laudationes,* and poetical lays. Of the meagreness of these materials we have already satisfied ourselves; but what was their authenticity? They might have been not less authentic than our Merovingian and other ancient annals; nay, as the *annales pontificum* began *ab initio rerum Romanarum,* or at least from the time of Numa, *they* might have been very authentic; in them, as we are informed by Dionysius, the pontiffs had recorded with the utmost accuracy every year of the kingly period; and the triumphal *fasti* even mentioned the very days on which the kings had triumphed over their enemies.

But the consideration that the early history, such as it has come down to us, is impossible, must lead us to enquire whether the earliest annals are deserving of credit. Our task now is to prove that the earliest history does contain impossibilities, that it is poetical, that the very portions which are not of a poetical nature, are forgeries, and, consequently, that the history must be traced back to ancient lays and to a chronology which was invented and adapted to these lays at a later period.

The narrative concerning the primitive times given by Livy differs considerably from that of Dionysius; Livy wrote his first book without assigning the events to their particular years, and with an extraordinary want of criticism; he here evidently followed Ennius, as we may see by comparing the fragments of the poet's writings with the statements of Livy; compare, for example, Livy ii. 10 with the fragment of Ennius:

Teque pater Tiberine tuo cum numine sancto. Dionysius, attempting to make out a true history, proceeds on the supposition
that the detail of Roman history can be restored, and that the
historical ground-work is only overgrown with legendary tales;
he endeavours to reconstruct the former in an arbitrary manner, and inserts his pragmatical speeches in his account of the
mythical ages, whereby he often makes himself truly ridiculous.
Livy, on the other hand, wrote the history such as he found
it in the most ancient books and as it appeared to him the
most beautiful; he gives it in its ancient form before it was
artificially corrupted; and hence his narrative is the purest
source for the history of those times.

The story of the miraculous conception of Romulus is an
historical impossibility; although in the school of Piso it was
metamorphosed into an history: the same must be said of the
account of the rape of the Sabine women, whose number was
thirty in the original tradition, and also of the ascension of
Romulus during an eclipse of the sun.[1]   Such also is the character of the long reign of Numa with its uninterrupted peace,
and of his marriage with the goddess Egeria, which among the
contemporaries of Scipio was as implicitly believed as the
history of the Punic wars.   The story of the combat of the
Horatii and the Curiatii, who were born on the same day of
two sisters has a very ancient poetical character.[2]   We next
come to Tarquinius Priscus, who was already married to
Tanaquil when he migrated to Rome in the eighth year of the
reign of Ancus (which lasted twenty-three years).   Tarquinius
himself reigned thirty-eight years and was at his death upwards
of eighty years old, leaving behind him children under age
who were educated during the forty-three years of Servius's
reign, so that Tarquinius Superbus must have been at least
fifty years old when he slew his father-in-law.   Tanaquil lived
to see this crime, and required Servius to take an oath not to
resign his crown: at that time she must have been 115 years
old.   One of the first features in the story of Servius is that on
one occasion in his infancy his head was encircled with a flame,
which Dionysius attempts to explain in a natural way.   Collatinus is said to have been the son of a brother of Tarquinius

---

[1] The moment at which Mars overcame Ilia was likewise marked by an
eclipse of the sun.—N.
[2] Livy's account is already somewhat disfigured.—N.

Priscus, and this brother, it is stated, was born previously to the migration of Tarquinius Priscus to Rome, that is, 135 years before the expulsion of Tarquinius Superbus; and Collatinus is described as being a young man thirty years old, at a time upwards of 120 years after his father's birth. Brutus is said to have been *Tribunus celerum*, which was the first place in the equestrian order, in which he represented the king, assembled the senate, and was obliged to perform the most important sacrifices; and this place the king is stated to have given to a man, whom he thought to be an idiot and whom, for this reason, he had deprived of the management of his own property! Brutus, the story goes on to say, feigned idiocy for the purpose of escaping the envy and avarice of the king. He is described as the son of a daughter of Tarquinius Priscus, and as dreading to enrage the king by taking possession of his own property:—but Tarquinius did not even belong to the same gens. At the beginning of the reign of Tarquinius Superbus, Brutus was only a child, and immediately after the king's expulsion he appears as the father of sons who have attained the age of manhood.

All these chronological points, to which many others might be added, even down to the time of Camillus, bear so much the character of absurdity and historical impossibility, that we are obviously entitled to criticise. Now let us remember the two-fold sources of the earliest history of Rome, namely, the chronological: the *fasti* and *annales pontificum;* and the un-chronological: the lays, *laudationes*, the *libri pontificum* and *augurales*. As regards the chronological sources, in the most ancient account, that of Fabius, we find 360 years reckoned from the building of Rome to its destruction by the Gauls, exactly the number of the γένη in Attica, which number was declared, even by the Greeks, especially by Aristotle, from whom the grammarians Pollux, Harpocration and others derived their information, to be that of the days in the solar year. But the number 360 if accurately examined will be found to be the mean number between the days of the solar and those of the lunar year, and the nearest to each that can be conveniently divided. Of this period of 360 years, the time assigned to the kings was, according to the earlier calculation, 240 years, and that to the republic 120 years. This number has as much of a mathematical character as that of the

Indian ages of the world, the Babylonian and other Oriental numbers. The 120 years assigned to the republic is adopted even by those writers who calculate the whole period at 365 years. Whether 120 years be correct, must be determined according to the view respecting the time at which the Capitol was consecrated. That the *annales pontificum* were destroyed in the Gallic conflagration is strongly confirmed by Claudius (undoubtedly Claudius Quadrigarius) as quoted by Plutarch, and indirectly by Livy, who could not state it directly, since he would thereby have declared the first books of his own work valueless; it is moreover confirmed by the fact, that the eclipse of the sun in the year A.U. 350, the first which was actually observed, was mentioned in the annals, whereas the earlier ones were subsequently calculated, and, as we may safely infer, considering the means of the science of that time, were, of course, calculated wrongly. For the first 240 years we have seven kings, whose reigns are said to have been of extraordinary length, for the most part somewhere about forty years each. Even Newton expresses his opinion of the improbability of a succession of princes reigning for so long a period, and assigns to the reign of a king as a mean number, seventeen years. But the truest parallel is to be found in the case of the doges of Venice, who like the kings of Rome were elective princes; in a period of 500 years (A.D. 800—A.D. 1300) Venice had forty doges, so that there were eight in each century. Now if we closely examine the number of the Roman kings, we shall find a numerical artifice just as among the Orientals. I shall premise the following considerations to illustrate what I mean.

The Etruscans had, as the foundation of their chronology, two kinds of *saecula*, physical and astronomical; the latter contained 110 years, as the supposed mean number of the physical; and by a double intercalation the calendar was restored so as to leave a wonderfully small difference. 110 of these years were nearly equal to 132 years, of ten months each, and this consequently formed an astronomical period. The physical *saeculum* was thus defined by the Etruscans: the first *saeculum* was determined by the life-time of the person who lived the longest, of all those that had been alive at the foundation of a state, the second was indicated by the longest life of the persons living at the conclusion of the first *saeculum*, and so on. Now we find an ancient tradition in Plutarch and Dion Cassius

(Dionysius has at least an allusion to it) that Numa was born on the day of the foundation of Rome, so that probably his death in the year A.U. 77, determined the first *saeculum* of Rome.[3] If this was the case we see the reason why thirty-eight years (the number of the *nundines* in a year of ten months) were assigned to Romulus and thirty-nine to Numa. In regard to the last five kings there existed historical traditions, but they were not sufficient for the whole period. It was certain that Rome had had far more than five kings, and as there were still wanting one as the founder of the Ramnes and another as that of the Tities, a number was chosen which had a sacred meaning, namely, the number of the planets, etc. The first half of 240 years is the end of the 120th, that is exactly the middle of the reign of the fourth among the kings, manifestly an artificial invention; twenty-three years were assigned to him in order to make them begin with the year 110, some striking number being always desired for the beginning of a reign and 110 being the secular number. The ancient year had ten months, and 132 of such years are equal to 110 of the later ones; it was therefore necessary to place the reign of Ancus between 110 and 132. The period between 77 and 110, or thirty-two years, was naturally assigned to Tullus Hostilius. Tarquinius Priscus reigned until A.U. 170, half a century being added to half the years of the kingly period, and his reign accordingly lasted thirty-eight years. The twenty-five years of the last king may be historical; but it is possible also that a quarter of a century was assigned to him. The period from A.U. 170 to A.U. 215 was left for Servius Tullius. But now, supposing that the two reigns of Tarquinius Priscus and Servius Tullius did not last so long, all absurdity disappears, and the ancient unanimous account that Tarquinius Superbus was a son of Tarquinius Priscus is restored to its full right. We see then how the greatest nonsense arises from chronological restorations; the forgery is manifest.

Now although the other sources of the earliest history, the ancient lays, were not falsified, they are nevertheless entirely insufficient. We have a parallel to this in our own lay of the *Nibelungen;* its authors have no intention to deceive and do not pretend to give an annalistic history; historical persons

[3] T. Tatius is said to have given him his daughter in marriage, and yet Tatius dies in the fourth year after the foundation of Rome.—N.

occur in it such as Theodoric, Attila, the Burgundians, and yet no one portion of the whole poem belongs to history. In like manner, history cannot claim Romulus and Numa, they belong to the sphere of the gods, Romulus as the son of Mars, and Numa as the husband of Egeria; Romulus is only a personification of Rome. Other poems of a similar kind contain more of historical substance, such as the Spanish Romances of the Cid; in this the fundamental features are indeed historical, but they form only a line, whereas the substance as given in the poem is a surface. It is the same with many portions of Roman history, and whoever entirely rejects the early history of Rome does not know what he is doing. Romulus and Numa, then, form the first *saeculum*, because they do not belong at all to history; they form a *saeculum* by themselves, as it were a totally different period; and whatever ancient traditions were found respecting the succeeding kings and their period (and many such traditions were current) were inserted in the chronological outline. Any who may think this criticism dangerous, would cease to do so, were they better acquainted with events nearer our own time. It is well known that the middle-age romances about Charlemagne and his Paladins are based upon Latin chronicles ascribed to archbishop Turpinus; these we now look upon as romance and allow them to stand by the side of history; but who would believe that scarcely 150 years after Charlemagne, in the reign of Otho the Great, when not even the remotest idea of a crusade existed, the chronicle of Benedictus of Soracte gives a detailed account of an expedition of Charlemagne to Jerusalem, and without any suspicion of its not being true. Even before the Carlovingian race was extinct, we find wholly fabulous features in the history of Charlemagne, such as his journeys across the Alps, etc., related in the chronicles with the greatest possible assurance. These we can now refute, as we have contemporaneous annals and the biography of Eginhard; the expedition to Jerusalem is disproved even without these by Oriental annals. It is the same in Ireland, for there too we find annals in which a series of kings is given, and among them Niall the Great, a contemporary it seems of the emperor Theodosius; he conquered Britain, Gaul and Spain, crossed the Alps and threatened the emperor in Rome. The most positive evidence can be adduced against this entirely fabulous account, for the authentic history of that period is generally known.[4]

We might with the same facility prove that the early history of Rome is not authentic, if we had earlier historical books to correct the legends. But where are we to find them? The Greeks did not come in contact with Rome till long afterwards, and although they possessed information about the Romans at an earlier period than is commonly supposed, they nevertheless gave themselves no concern about them, just because they did not come in contact with them. The case might be different in regard to the Greeks of the south of Italy and the Siceliots, but none of their writers have come down to us: neither Herodotus nor Thucydides could make mention of the Romans. But there still exists an isolated fragment of Etruscan history, which gives us an opportunity of seeing the manner in which the history of Rome was told among other nations. The emperor Claudius, who was so unfortunate in his early youth and so ill used by his mother, and whose weak mind, although he was possessed of many amiable qualities, was entirely misguided by bad treatment, seems to have excited the sympathy of Livy, who instructed and encouraged him in historiography. He accordingly wrote several works in the Greek language, Καρχηδονιακά in eight and Τυρρηνικά in twenty books, the loss of which we have great reason to regret. Even Pliny does not notice the last named work. But in the sixteenth century there were found two tables, containing fragments of a speech of the emperor Claudius, in which he proposes to the senate, to grant the full franchise to the Lugdunensian Gauls and to admit them into the senate as had long been the case in the *provincia Romana*. The inhabitants of Gaul were Roman citizens and had Roman names, but they had not the right to be admitted into the senate; and it was this right that the emperor Claudius conferred upon the Lugdunensian Gauls. Of the several brass tables which contained the speech mentioned by

---

[4] The old Irish tradition, as far as I can ascertain, differs somewhat from the statement made in the text. It was not Niall the Great who advanced as far as the Alps, but his successor Dathy, who was struck dead at the foot of the Alps by a flash of lightning A.D. 427. Comp. Keating's General History of Ireland, translated by Dermod O'Conor. Lond. 1723, fol. p. 319; M'Dermot's History of Ireland, London, 1820, 8vo. vol. i. p. 411. The accounts of Roman writers on Ireland, are collected in O'Conor's *Rerum Hibernicarum Scriptores*, v. i., Prolegom. p. 1.—ED.

Tacitus two still exist; they do not contain a continuous portion of the speech unless a considerable piece is wanting at the bottom of the first table. Previous to the French revolution, they were kept in the town hall of Lyons, but whether they are still there I cannot say.[5] They give us an idea of Claudius's stupidity and we must acknowledge that the ancients did not wrong him in this respect. In this speech he says in detail what Tacitus has compressed into a few words. " It ought not to be objected," says the emperor, " that this is an innovation, since innovations have been made ever since the beginning of the state; strangers have always been admitted, as for example the Sabines of T. Tatius; strangers have even been made kings, to wit Numa, Tarquin the Etruscan, a descendant from Greece, and Servius Tullius, who according to our annals was a native of Corniculum, and according to those of Etruria an Etrurian of the name of Mastarna, and a follower of Caeles Vibenna. He migrated, settled on the Caelian hill, which was thus called after his leader, and there called himself Servius Tullius." This then is a direct proof of what the Roman annals were in those days. For nothing that is related of this Etruscan Mastarna can be applied to Servius Tullius, the son of a female slave.

There is therefore no doubt that the earliest history of Rome arose out of lays. Perizonius mentions similar instances among other nations: even in the historical books of the Old Testament such lays are to be found; in reference to the Romans he quotes as a proof Cato's testimony, to which Cicero refers in two passages: " Would," says Cicero, " that those lays were extant, which Cato in his Origines states used many ages before his own time to be sung at repasts by the guests in praise of illustrious men." A third mention of them is found from Varro in Nonius Marcellus to the effect that *pueri honesti* sang at repasts songs in praise of deceased great men, sometimes with and sometimes without the accompaniment of the flute. Every one must consider these testimonies to be valid. Among all nations with whose early national literature we are acquainted, we find either long historical poems of an epic character or short ones in praise of individual men. Now previously to making and proving the assertion, that fragments of both kinds

---

[5] They are printed in Lipsius' edition of Tacitus and in Gruter's *Corpus Inscriptionum*, but are little read.—N.

have come down to us in Roman history, I must make some remarks upon the oldest metre.

The Ancient Romans, before their adoption of Greek poetry, used the Saturnian verse, of which Horace speaks;

Horridus ille defluxit numerus Saturnius,

and which several ancient grammarians have explained. Atilius Fortunatianus and others among them, being ignorant of its real nature, confined their remarks to a couple of lines that were extant, especially to the following:

Malum dabunt Metelli Naevio poëtae,

in which according to the opinion of the time a hypercatalectic senarius appears. Terentianus Maurus, who belongs to the end of the third century, speaks of it in treating of the Anacreontic verse, because the first part of the Saturnian resembles it. But the true Saturnian verse is quite different, as I intend shortly to show in a separate treatise. It is capable of a variety of forms and is quite independent of Greek metres. The Latin expression for rhythm, which was not applied to Greek metres till a later time, is *numeri*. The Greek metre is based upon music and time, but the Romans actually *counted* the syllables and rarely if at all measured them; a certain number of syllables was necessary to constitute rhythm. Our forefathers too had no idea of long or short syllables after the Greek fashion; in the old hymns of the Latin Church likewise short syllables are used as long and *vice versa*. Plautus and Terence in their iambic and trochaic verses in reality observe the rhythm only and not the time. The same is the case with all Northern nations. The prevailing character of the Saturnian verse is, that it consists of a fixed number of feet of three syllables each. The number of feet is generally four, and they are either bacchics or cretics, alternating with spondees. Sometimes the cretics predominate and sometimes the bacchics; when the verses are kept pure the movement is very beautiful, but they are generally so much mixed that it is difficult to discern them.

These verses, in use from the remotest times, are quite analogous to the Persian, Arabic, the ancient German, Northern and Anglo-Saxon verses, and in fact to all in which alliteration prevails. The old German verse is divided into two halves, an alliteration occurs in the first half twice and in the second

half once; it has four arses.   The same fourfold rhythm occurs
in the old Saxon harmony of the gospels, in Otfrid and others,
but five or even six rhythms may occur; in the Persian we find
generally four feet of three syllables, in the Arabic frequently
the same, but often also feet of four syllables.   The Spanish
coplas de arte major which were common previous to the
adoption of the Alexandrines, and which were introduced into
Flanders, also are of exactly the same kind.   It is probable
that the same metre is found in the longer Provençal poems.
This ancient Roman metre occurs throughout in Roman poetry
down to the seventh century.   I have collected a large number
of examples of it and discovered a chapter of an ancient grammarian with most beautiful fragments especially from Nævius.
I shall publish this important treatise on the Saturnian verse,
for the grammarian really understood its nature.[6]   In Plautus
it is developed with great beauty.

There were also smaller ancient poems in this metre.   At
the funerals of Romans *naeniae* were sung with the accompaniment of the flute, and these were not melancholy and soft
dirges, but must have had the same character as the *laudationes;*
the dead had passed to their illustrious ancestors, their glory
was made use of as a show and as an encouragement, and for
this reason simple praise was bestowed upon them in these
naeniae.   The words of Horace, *absint inani funere naeniae,* etc.,
refer, if songs were sung at all at funerals, to the lamentations
of later times; for the Romans originally were not tender-
hearted: they made use even of a dead man for the good of the
republic; from his grave he continued to call upon the living
to follow in his footsteps.   *Naeniae* and *laudationes,* therefore,
were certainly quite plain and simple, according to the ancient
style in which periods were not yet known, and bore no

---

[6] The grammarian, whose fragment on the Saturnian verse is here mentioned,
is Charisius.   Niebuhr took a copy of it from a Neapolitan manuscript in 1823,
and his copy has been entrusted to Prof. Lachmann of Berlin, who is preparing
its publication.   Prof. Schneidewin of Göttingen published it in 1841 in a pro-
gramme, "Flavii Sosipatri Charisii de versu Saturnio commentariolus ex codice
Neapolitano nunc primum editus," from a copy taken by O. Müller, and severely
criticised Niebuhr's expressions respecting the Saturnian verse; but a glance at
the fragment, as it is there printed, shews, that Müller's copy is very imperfect,
and it would have been more becoming accurately to examine the copy taken
by Niebuhr, before criticising him in a manner, which does not indeed injure
the memory of Niebuhr, but certainly does not place the modesty of Schneidewin
in the most favourable light.—ED.

resemblance to the λόγοι ἐπιτάφιοι of Thucydides and the later
Greeks. Two poems evidently of this kind are still extant on
the tombs of the Scipios, which were discovered in 1780 on
the Appian road; the upper compartment, which contained the
sarcophagus of the younger Africanus and the statue of Ennius,
had disappeared, but the lower one was worked into the rock
and was found filled with rubbish. The latter contained the
sarcophagus of L. Scipio Barbatus, who was consul in the year
A.U. 454. Persons had descended into this tomb from above
long before[7], and had taken out one of the slabs, which is now
fixed in the wall of the palace Barberini, but it was forgotten
again.[8] These magnificent sarcophagi bear inscriptions in
verse, which are written like prose it is true, but the verses
are divided by lines; on the sarcophagus of the son the verses
are even marked, and that they are verses may be seen from
the unequal length of the lines, for otherwise the Romans always
wrote their lines to the end of the slab. These are quite plain
and simple verses but still there is rhythm in them—

> Cornéliu' Lúciu' Scípio Barbátus,
> Gnáivo prognátu', fortis vír sapiéns que —
> Consúl, censor, aédilis, quí fuit apúd vos, etc.

—These are certainly the *naeniae* which were sung at the time
and were afterwards inscribed on the tomb. The ancient songs
at repasts were for the most part just as simple.

Now these *naeniae*, which together with the *laudationes* were
kept in the atrium, are sources of the earliest history. But
besides these there also existed longer epic poems among the
Romans no less than among other nations such as the Servians;
the songs of the modern Greeks are of a purely lyrical character,
but those of the Servians are a combination of epic and lyric.
I think I have discovered in Livy a fragment of such an heroic
epic, on the fight of the Horatii and Curiatii. Now we cannot
indeed suppose that Livy saw these ancient epics and wrote
his history from them, but he wrote in part directly and in part
indirectly through the medium of Varro, from the books of the
pontiffs and augurs, which contained a great many fragments
of such ancient epics, some of which may have been as old,

---

[7] In the year 1616.
[8] The bodies of the Cornelii down to the time of Sulla were not burned
according to the Pelasgian and Greek fashion, but were buried in coffins.—N.

even as the time of the taking of Rome by the Gauls. In the passage of Livy in which he relates the trial of Horatius, which he took from those books, he speaks of a *lex horrendi carminis;* the formulae of that time were called *carmina* and were in the ancient metre. That Livy drew his materials from those books either directly or indirectly becomes the more certain from Cicero's statement, that the formula of the *provocatio ad populum* was contained in the *libri augurales.* The formula is—*Duúm-viri pérduelliónem júdicent, etc.,* in which the ancient metre is still discernible.

I have elsewhere observed that Cicero's statement: *lauda-tionibus historia nostra facta est mendosior,* is also acknowledged by Livy: as every thing good may easily acquire a tendency to evil, so also could the beauty of Roman family pride dege-nerate into falsehood, and there is no reason for disbelieving the assertion.

After the first scanty records of the early times had for the most part been destroyed in the Gallic conflagration, they were restored according to certain schemes from the songs of the *vates;* the poems became altered as they passed from mouth to mouth, and they, combined with the *laudationes,* form the groundwork of our history—the material which Fabius found when he began to write.

If we look at the tenth book of Livy, we find in it a disproportionate minuteness in his account of the campaigns of Fabius Maximus Rullianus, and this minuteness arises from family records; we may in fact point out not a few statements, which cannot have had any other source but family vanity, which went so far as to forge consulships and triumphs, as Livy himself says.

Other forgeries again arose from national vanity, and these occur everywhere in those parts of the history which relate to any great calamity suffered by the Romans, especially the great calamities of the early times, such as the war with Porsenna, the sacking of Rome by the Gauls, and the defeat of Caudium, the whole narratives of which are falsified. Others arose from party spirit, which in primitive periods led to perpetual strife; one party raised false accusations against the other, and these were introduced into history; at other times attempts were made to palliate and conceal moral and political crimes. The people are described as being the cause of the worst misfortunes though they were innocent and their opponents were the guilty party; it was not the people but the *curiae* that condemned Manlius to death, and it was the *curiae* that pronounced the inglorious decision between the Ardeatans and Aricinians; nay we may be convinced that it was the *curiae* too who compelled Camillus[9] to go into exile.

Such falsifications accumulate, become interwoven with one another, and in the end produce a strange confusion. We may collect the rich materials though they are widely scattered, because party spirit prevented their being united, and by the process of criticism we may discover the constitution and character of the Roman nation, and in general outlines give their history down to the time at which we have the contemporary records of the Greeks, that is to the war with Pyrrhus and the first Punic war. Much will indeed remain obscure in our investigations, but we can accurately distinguish where this must be so and where not.

Roman History goes back to Latium and through Latium to Troy. Since the question was raised by Dion Chrysostomus whether Troy ever really existed, an immense deal has been written upon it, and also on the question whether Aeneas ever came to Italy. The treatise by Theodore Ryckius[10] upon this subject is very well known; he regards the arrival of Aeneas as an historical fact in opposition to Bochart, who was one of the last ingenious philologers of France[11], and whose intellect was at all events superior to that of Ryckius. Bochart's hypothesis concerning the influence of the Phoenicians is certainly carried too far. Now, however, the question would be put in a totally different manner, we should ask, Has the legend of the arrival of the Trojans on this coast any historical ground? Further, Did the legend originate with the Greeks and come over to Italy, or is it of native Italian growth, that is to say, is it one which we at least cannot trace to any Greek sources? If the latter be the case, there must be some truth at the bottom of it, and the less we take these ancient traditions literally, the more probability we find in them.

There existed unquestionably in the earliest times of Greece,

[9] Livy, iii. 71, 72.

[10] Theod. Ryckii *Diss. de Primis Italiae Colonis et Aenea* in Luc. Holstenii *Notae et Castigationes in Steph. Byzantium.* Lugd. Bat. 1684, fol.

[11] Salmasius was far less clear-headed than he.—N.

two nations who were very nearly akin to each other and yet were so different that the one did not even understand the language of the other, as Herodotus distinctly says: the language of the one when compared with that of the other was regarded as barbarous, and yet from another point of view they may be looked upon as very kindred languages. Several living languages, even now, stand in a similar relation to one another, such as the Polish and Bohemian, the Italian and Spanish, and if we do not look at the relationship quite so closely, the Polish and Lithuanian. The last two languages differ from each other immensely, but yet have a characteristic resemblance; the grammar of both is based upon the same principles: they have the same peculiarities, their numerals are almost the same and a great number of words are common to both. These languages therefore are sister languages and yet a Pole does not understand a Lithuanian. Now this is the manner in which we solve the question so often raised respecting the difference or identity of the Greeks and Pelasgians. When Herodotus tells us that they were different, we must indeed believe him, but on the other hand he joins the Hellenes and Pelasgians together, consequently there can have been no radical difference between the two nations.

In the earliest times, when the history of Greece is yet wrapt up for us in impenetrable mystery, the greater part of Italy, perhaps the whole of the eastern coast of the Adriatic, Epirus, Macedonia[12], the southern coast of Thrace with the peninsulas of Macedonia, the islands of the Aegean as well as the coasts of Asia Minor as far as the Bosporus were inhabited by Pelasgians.[13] The Trojans also must be regarded as Pelasgians; that they were not barbarians is confirmed by the unanimous opinion of all the Greeks and may be seen from Homer; they inhabit a Pelasgian country but their names are Greek. They are sometimes spoken of as more closely connected with the Arcadians, who were another essentially Pelasgic race, sometimes with the Epirots and sometimes with the Thessalians; Aeneas in one tradition migrates to Arcadia and there dies, and in another he goes to Epirus where Hellenus is settled. Thus, in Pindar's poem on Cyrene, we find

[12] The original inhabitants of Macedonia were neither Illyrians nor Thracians, but Pelasgians. Comp. C. O. Müller's Treatise on Macedonia, appended to Vol. I. of the Hist. and Ant. of the Doric Race, p. 467, etc.

[13] Even Aeschylus peoples all Greece with Pelasgians.—N.

Aristaeus, a Pelasgian hero from Arcadia, along with the Antenoridae. The connection between the Pelasgians and Trojans goes very far back, for Samothrace especially is the metropolis of Ilium; Dardanus comes from Arcadia, but passes through Samothrace, and, being married to Chryse, he proceeds thence to Troas. The Samothracians, according to one grammarian, were a Roman people, that is, they were recognised as the brothers of the Romans, namely of the Troico-Tyrrhenian Pelasgians. This connection has no other foundation than the kindred nature of the Tyrrhenians, Trojans, and Samothracians. Some accounts state that Dardanus went from Tyrrhenia to Troas, others that the Trojans went to Tyrrhenia. The temple and mysteries of Samothrace formed a point of union for many men from all countries[14]: for a great portion of the world at that time, the temple of Samothrace was like the Caaba of Mecca, the tomb of the prophet at Medina, or the holy sepulchre at Jerusalem. Samothrace and Dodona were to the Pelasgian nations what perhaps Delphi and Delos were to the Hellenic world. The distance of a great number of kindred tribes from those central points, was in this instance of no greater consequence than in the case of the Mahommedans, who are not prevented by distance from going as pilgrims to the sacred spot.

This race of the Pelasgians, which we can trace as far as Liguria, and which also inhabited at least the coasts of Corsica and Sardinia, disappears in the historical times as a body of nations: it consisted originally of a number of tribes with different names, of which afterwards we find only remnants and isolated tribes. A very extensive name for that part of the race which inhabited Epirus and the southern part of modern Italy, at least as far as Latium and the coast of the Adriatic, was Siculi, also Vituli, Vitelli, Vitali Itali; from these Italy derives its name.[15] Notwithstanding the wide extent of this Siculian or Italian name, it seems that in the earliest times Italy did not, as now, denote the country as far as the Alps; it is indeed possible that the changes which took

[14] We may certainly look upon this as an established fact, although the investigations concerning the mysteries themselves will never yield any positive results.—N.

[15] As K (or C) and T are identical, and only dialectically different, so the S is changed into the digamma or V, which, again, is often lost, especially at the beginning of words.—N.

place in consequence of the migration of the northern tribes separated the maritime countries of Etruria from Italy and confined
the name of Italy to the country south of the Tiber or even south of
Latium. This, however, is only a conjecture; but it is certain
that at one time Italy was bounded in the north by a line from the
Garganus in the east to Terracina in the west, and that the name,
after having been more limited, was again, after the time of Alexander the Great and previously to the extension of the dominion
of Rome, used in its former and wider extent. It seems to be this
earlier Italy that Pliny means, when he says it is *querno folio
similis*.[16] This statement he undoubtedly took from Timaeus, with
whom also originated the comparison of Sardinia to a sandal or a
foot-mark. It quite escaped Pliny's attention that Italy in his
time could not be described in any such way; and this is a
very characteristic instance of the hasty and thoughtless
manner in which he wrote.

In the south of Italy the earliest inhabitants were also
called Oenotri and Peucetii, in the north undoubtedly Liburnians and on the coast of Latium Tyrrhenians.

Whether the settlements on the coast north of the Tiber
were remnants of a people who had been driven back, or
whether they were only colonies, it is no longer possible for us
to decide. But there appear in central Italy besides these
tribes, which were analogous to the Greeks, nations of a different
kind which overwhelmed the former. These migrations seem
to have been similar to those met with in modern history,
where one nation has pushed forward another. The people
who threw themselves at the same time upon the Siculi in
Latium and upon the Itali in the south of Italy, and, having
partly expelled and partly subdued them, became assimilated to
them, are the Opici, a transition people, who in reality existed as
Opici in a few places only, but, being again amalgamated with
other subdued people, they produced new forms. They appear
under various names, which, however, have the same radical
syllable. Thus we find them under the name of Apuli, the termina-
tions -*icus* and -*ulus* being equivalent: hence the Italian population

[16] This is a remarkable example of the manner in which Pliny wrote; he
sometimes speak in his own name and sometimes gives extracts, but unfortunately his historical extracts are made with as little thought as those relating to
natural history, which are full of misapprehensions of Aristotle and Theophrastus.—N.

ceases in Apulia, extending apparently as far as Messapia, where a portion of the Itali maintained themselves in an isolated position. They further existed in the countries afterwards called Samnium, Campania, and, under the name of Volscians and Aequians, on the borders of Latium.

The Opicans again were pressed forward by the Sabines (Sabellians) who called themselves autochthons, and who traced their origin to the highest mountains of the Abruzzo, near Majella and Gran Sasso d'Italia. Cato somewhat strangely supposes these to have come from the small district of Amiternum. Now whether the Sabellians and Opicans differed from each other, as, for example, the Gauls and Ligurians did, or even in a less degree, as the Gauls and Cymri; or whether they belonged to the same stock and were separated from each other only politically, are questions which we cannot solve. The ancients did not know this, nor did they pay much attention to it. If we obstinately determine to see where no historical light is to be obtained, the intellectual eye is injured as is the physical, when it violently exerts itself in the dark. Varro indeed distinguishes between the Sabine and Oscan languages, but he knew so little of the ancient languages, in the sense in which W. v. Humboldt knows them, that little reliance can be placed on his statements respecting the affinity of languages. According to general analogy, I believe that there was a migration of nations in different directions, by the first impulse of which the Sabines may have been driven from their northern habitations; but this is a mere conjecture.

The Umbrians may possibly have belonged to the same stock as the Opicans. I should not like to attribute too much importance to the resemblance of their names, for nations that are nearest akin to one another often have very different names, and widely different nations frequently have similar ones. Thus the Getae and the Goths were for a long time erroneously looked upon as the same people; and fifty years ago it was the general opinion in Ireland and Scotland that the Fir-Bolgs[17] spoken of in the poems of Ossian were the ancient Belgians. But this is not correct; they were, as a very well informed Englishman wrote to me, a Danish colony. We must

---

[17] The Fir-Bolgs belong to the bardic history of Ireland, which describes them as the third immigration into Ireland; the Scots found them in Ireland governed by kings; to them is ascribed the building of the Cyclopian walls in Ireland.—ED.

be greatly on our guard against the miserable desire to construe
the history of nations from their names, a desire which has
given rise to so many hypotheses and fancies.   Much may be
learnt from the study of names indeed, but what in some cases
is correct ceases to be true in others, and becomes a source of
error and fanciful theories which we must shun as vermin and
serpents.   If I had not other evidence than the mere names, I
should hesitate to declare the Opicans and Umbrians identical.
But Philistus called the people who conquered the Siculians in
Latium Ombricans, and moreover the affinity of their languages
may be distinctly perceived from the remnants which have
come down to us.

These changes of nations, in which the earliest inhabitants
were driven out by one tribe and this again by another, are
the causes which render the history of the early Italian nations
so indescribably obscure and difficult for us, that, even where
we ourselves have a clear view, the misconceptions in our
authorities still maintain their ground, and ever and anon cause
fresh discussions.   A solution of these difficulties, free from all
objections, is utterly impossible.   He who is engaged in such
investigations must often be satisfied with evidence, which has
the appearance of truth, but he ought to be able to shew how
the misconceptions arose.

LECTURE II.

AT a period which we cannot chronologically define, there
existed a population of Siculians in the country afterwards
called Latium, which may however have borne this name from
the earliest times.   The remembrance of this population was
preserved at Tibur, part of which town was, according to Cato,
called Siculio.[1]   Elsewhere also in ancient authors, we find an
immense number of statements which place the existence of
this people beyond all doubt.   It is found under the same name

[1] In the printed collections of the fragments of Cato, I do not find this statement ; whence I suppose that Cato is here confounded with Dionysius who (i.16)
has the statement in question.—ED.

in southern Italy, and also in the island which to this day is named after them. According to one tradition, Sicelus went from Latium to the Oenotrians; according to another, the Siculians under different names were driven from their ancient habitations by the Opicans or Umbrians, and migrated to the island of Sicily. This migration only shews the combinations of those who wish to prove the contemporaneous existence of the same people in Latium and in Sicily. The migration is possible indeed, but it is also possible that it took place in quite a different direction. It is certain that the Siculians existed in the south of Italy in Homer's time, of which we find evidence in a passage from Mnaseas, a pupil of Aristarchus, a learned grammarian and historian quoted by the Scholiast on the Odyssey. He says also, that Echetus was prince of the Siceli in Epirus, so that he recognises this name even in those parts; we see from his explanation, that when the poet of the Odyssey speaks of the Siceli, he does not mean the inhabitants of Sicily, an island scarcely known to him, but the inhabitants of the south of Italy or the Pelasgians of Epirus.

The Siculi are the same as those whom Cato calls Aborigines. This name is explained by γενάρχαι, that is *ancestors;* or by *Aberrigines,* that is, *wandering people;* but it more probably signifies the people that have been from the beginning (*ab origine*). The nominative singular according to the Latin idiom must have been *Aboriginus.* There was a tradition that Latium was originally inhabited by autochthons, but Cato and C. Sempronius[2] said, that the Aborigines had come from Achaia, that is from the Peloponnesus, the whole of which was then called Achaia by the Romans. Others apply the epithet Argive to the particular places which were otherwise called Siculian, and Cato had done so even in the case of Tibur. Argos and Larissa are Pelasgian names occurring wherever Pelasgians are found, Argos probably signifying a *town,* and Larissa a *citadel* or *arx.* So long as the Peloponnesus was Pelasgian it was called Argos, just as Thessaly and, in this sense, the Argives are Pelasgians; the Ἀργεῖοι Πελασγοὶ in ancient tragedy are always mentioned together, the one being probably the wider and the other the more limited name.

Hesiod says of Latinus, πᾶσι Τυῤῥηνοῖσιν ἀγακλειτοῖσιν

---

[2] Probably C. Sempronius Tuditanus, the same whom Dionysius, i. 11, calls λογιώτατον τῶν Ῥωμαίων συγγραφέων.—ED.

ἀνάσσει. All we know about the Latins is the fact that they possessed a number of towns from Tibur to the river Tiber: how far they extended in the earliest times towards the Liris is uncertain. Cato, quoted by Priscian, states that the plain of the Volscians formerly belonged to the Aborigines; and it is certain that all the towns along the coast, such as Antium, Circeii and others, were at an early period Tyrrhenian. At that time, accordingly, the name Latium was of very wide extent, and even immediately after the time of the Roman kings it extended as far as Campania, but was afterwards restricted by the great migrations which took place after the expulsion of the kings. Hesiod of course refers to an earlier period. In the treaty of Rome with Carthage the names Latium and Latins extend along the coast beyond Terracina, and probably as far as Cumae.

The Pelasgian inhabitants of the whole of the western coast of Italy were called by the Greeks Tyrrhenians, and by the Latins *Turini, Tusci*, that is, *Tusici* from *Tusus* or *Turus;* for *s* is used in the early language instead of *r*, as in *Fusius* for *Furius*.

We must keep in mind that the Pelasgians and Aborigines were one and the same people. If we examine the traditions of nations we frequently find that the same events are related in various and entirely opposite ways. The story of a Jew taking merciless vengeance on a Christian, such as we read of in " The Merchant of Venice ", is found completely reversed in a Roman tale written shortly before Shakespeare's time; in this the Christian is represented as wishing to cut a piece of flesh out of the Jew's body. The migrations of the Goths proceed, according to some, from Scandinavia to the south, and according to others from the south to Scandinavia. Wittekind states that the Saxons came from Britain to Germany, while the common tradition describes them as having been invited from Germany to Britain. The Pelasgians about Mount Hymettus near Athens are said to have migrated from Tyrrhenia to Athens, and thence to Lemnos, while in another tradition the Tyrrhenians proceed from the Maeonian coast to Italy. In like manner, Cyrene, according to one tradition, received a colony from Thera; but according to another, Thera arose out of a clod of earth from Libya. In the earlier traditions, the Planetae are at the entrance of the Euxine, and the ship Argo on its voyage to Colchis sailed between them: in the later traditions, they appear in the Western sea and are an obstacle to the Argo on her return. The same contradiction appears in the case of the Aborigines. Dionysius in defiance of etymology applies this name to the people, who coming from the interior overpowered the ancient inhabitants. Varro did just the same: he is even worse than Pliny; he knows that the Latins are a combination of two nations, but he confounds every thing, representing the Aborigines as the conquering and the Siculians as the conquered people.[3] Following the example of Hellanicus he proceeds to trace the Aborigines to Thessaly, but then makes them migrate from the Upper Anio as far as the Upper Abruzzo, whither they are pushed by the Sabines. This tradition has a local and probable character, for in that district there existed a number of small townships; large towns on the other hand, such as we find in Etruria, are always a proof of immigration, the immigrating people usually settling together in considerable numbers. Dionysius must be excused for his error, since he trusted to the authority of Varro, who alone is responsible for the blunder of confounding the conquering with the conquered people.

One of the conquering tribes probably bore the name of Casci. Whether this was one of the names borne by the Tyrrhenians, Latins or Siculians, or whether the Casci were foreign immigrants, cannot be determined with certainty, though the latter is more probable. The name Casci has been preserved by Servius from Saufeius, a grammarian who seems to belong to the first century of the Christian era. They also occur under the name of Sacrani, from which Varro and Dionysius infer that they were a ἱερὰ νεότης. A tribe of the people who, under the names of Opicans, Oscans and Umbrians, inhabited the interior of Italy, or, more probably, had been pushed forward from the north and was pressed between the ancient Pelasgian places, settled in the Apennines about lake Fucinus (now Celano) towards Reate.

Their capital was called Lista, and they extended to the

---

[3] Varro had read immensely, but he ought not to be called a learned man, on account of his confusion. When I, as a young man, began these investigations, I could not see my way clearly in these matters though in the main points I saw correctly; I trusted too much to Varro's authority, and owing to his confusion of names I did not gain a clear insight till when I prepared a new edition of my work.—N.

boundaries of the Siculians who dwelt above Tibur towards the inland districts. There was a tradition that in their war with the Sabines, who had already taken Reate from them, and continued to push them onward, they had vowed a *ver sacrum*. This custom, observed by the Italian nations in times of misfortune, was preserved among the Romans also: a vow was made to dedicate to the gods all the cattle and in general every thing which the next spring might produce, and to send out as colonists the male children who were born in that season; the vegetable produce was either offered as a sacrifice or its value in money. Having made this vow, the *Sacrani* marched towards Latium and subdued the Siculians. In Latium they settled among the ancient inhabitants, and became united with them into one people bearing the name *Prisci Latini*, for the Casci must also have been called *Prisci*.[4] *Prisci Latini* is the same as *Prisci et Latini*, for the Latin language always expresses two ideas which are inseparably connected by the simple juxtaposition of the two words, mortar not being used by the ancient Romans in their language any more than in their architectural works. This has been clearly demonstrated by Brissonius who has also established the formula *populus Romanus Quirites;* but he goes too far in asserting that the Romans never said *populus Romanus Quiritium*, a position which has been justly controverted by J. Fr. Gronovius. In like manner we must explain *patres conscripti* as *qui patres quique conscripti sunt*, and also the legal formulae, *locati conducti, emti venditi*, and others. *Priscus* and *Cascus* afterwards signified *very ancient, old fashioned;* whence the phrases, *casce loqui, vocabula casca*. These conquerors spoke Oscan, and from the combination of their language with that of the Pelasgo-Siculians there arose that curious mixture which we call Latin, of which the grammar, and still more the etymology, contains so important a Greek element, which C. O. Müller has at my suggestion so admirably investigated in the first volume of his Etruscans. The primitive Oscan language is still preserved in a few ancient monuments; a few inscriptions in it were found at Pompeii and Hercu-

---

[4] It would be absurd to take *Prisci Latini* in Livy to mean ancient Latins; he took the formula of the declaration of war by the Fetiales, in which the expression first occurs, from the ritual books; it refers to the time of Ancus Martius; and before the time of Tarquinius Superbus there were no Latin colonies at all as distinguished from the rest of the Latins.—N.

lanum; the table of Bantia (Oppido) is perfectly intelligible.
Of the two elements of the Latin language, the Greek and the
not-Greek, the latter answers to the Oscan language. All
words relating to agriculture, domestic animals, produce of the
field, and the like, are Greek or akin to Greek. We see then
a conquered agricultural people, and a conquering one coming
from the mountains, which did not pursue agriculture.

Henceforth we lose all traces of the original tradition which
is supplanted by the story of the Trojan immigration. I shall
not here enter into any detail, but refer you to the minute
investigations contained in my history of Rome; the result of
which is that this last-named story has no authenticity whatever, but is only a later embellishment to express the relation
existing between the Trojans as Pelasgians, and the nations of
Italy which belonged to the same stock. The tradition of a
Trojan colony occurs in many parts of Italy, and the fact of
its having become more firmly established in regard to Latium
is purely accidental; it was kept up and nourished by the
diffusion of Greek poems which was far more extensive than
we commonly imagine.

The story of the Trojan settlement is comparatively ancient
among the Romans; even Naevius, in his poem on the Punic
war, gave a very minute account of it; the Ilians established
their claims among the Romans during the wars against Seleucus Callinicus. We could not take as our guide a person
who would treat seriously the accounts of the foundation of
Rome by Aeneas; some particular points in them are of a
really national character, but the period of time between the
events and their recorders is too great. Naevius wrote about
950 or 980 years after the time commonly assigned to the
destruction of Troy. It is little known how much Virgil altered
the ancient tradition of the settlement of Aeneas in Latium —
as a poet he had a perfect right to do so — for its ancient form
was rough and harsh, as Latinus was said to have fallen in the
war against Aeneas, and Lavinia who was first betrothed to
Aeneas and afterwards refused him, became a prisoner of war.
The earliest tradition, moreover, represented the settlement as
very small, for, according to Naevius, Aeneas arrived with only
one ship, and the territory assigned to him consisted, as Cato
stated, of no more than 700 *jugera*. Supposing this to be true,
how is it possible that a recollection of it should have been preserved for upwards of 900 years?

The original tradition is, that Aeneas at first for three years dwelt in a small town of the name of Troy; he is then said to have gone further inland and to have founded Lavinium; thirty years after this, Alba was founded, and 300 years after Alba the foundation of Rome was laid. This regular progression of numbers shews that the field is not historical, and there seems to be no doubt that the duration of Rome was fixed at 3000 years. There are in these traditions two different numerical systems, the Etruscan, with a *saeculum* of 110 years, and the Greek or Tyrrhenian in which the *saeculum* consisted of thirty years. This number thirty was at all times of great importance, because the period of the revolution of Saturn was then, as Servius remarks, believed to be completed in thirty years. Thirty ordinary years formed with the Greeks one Saturnian, and 100 Saturnian years constituted one great year. With this are connected the progressive numbers from the foundation of Lavinium to the building of Rome. The earliest history of Alba is worth nothing, as has been shewn by the acute Dodwell[5]; who elsewhere too often spoiled by his subtleties that which he had well begun. The chronology of the Alban kings, for example, in Dionysius is nothing but folly and falsehood, and their names are huddled together in every possible manner. This forgery, as we learn from Servius, was made at a late period by a freedman of Sulla, L. Cornelius Alexander of Miletus, who quickly became popular at a time when people delighted in having the history of a period of which nothing could be known.

Alba on the Alban lake is, in my opinion, the capital of the ruling conquerors; it is not owing to mere chance that it bears the same name as the town on lake Fucinus whence the *Sacrani* had come. When they were obliged to give up their country to the Sabines, they founded a new Alba on a lake, just as the Carthaginians built a new Carthage, the Milesians a new Miletus on the Black Sea, and as the English have so often done in the new world. This Alba Longa then was the seat of the Casci or Sacrani, and the earlier Latin towns within its territory probably experienced a twofold fate; some may have received a part of their population from the immigrants, and others may have been reduced to a state of dependence without receiving colonists. We have a tradition that these Latin towns were thirty in number and that all were colonies of

[5] De Cyclis, diss. x.

Alba, but this is opposed to another statement which declares all of them to have been originally Argive towns. Both may perhaps be maintained, if we suppose that an ἀποδασμός of the ruling people settled in each of the towns. This tradition as it stands is founded upon a misunderstanding: Alba had thirty *demi*, which as *perioeci* belonged to it, and they are the *populi Albenses* which I have discovered in Pliny. By this discovery their relation has become clear to me, and I have no doubt that the relation in which Alba stood to these Albensian towns was the same as that in which the *populus* of Rome stood to the *plebs*, and afterwards Rome to Latium. Previously to its destruction, Alba had no doubt the sovereignty of Latium, as Rome had afterwards. Alba therefore was surrounded by thirty *populi Albenses*, part of which were probably Alban colonies, and all of which constituted the state of Alba; and besides them there was a number of towns of the *Prisci Latini*, which were dependent upon Alba, whatever their condition may have been in the earliest times.

LECTURE III.

I BELIEVE that few persons, when Alba is mentioned, can get rid of the idea, to which I too adhered for a long time, that the history of Alba is lost to such an extent, that we can speak of it only in reference to the Trojan time and the preceding period, as if all the statements made concerning it by the Romans were based upon fancy and error; and that accordingly it must be effaced from the pages of history altogether. It is true that what we read concerning the foundation of Alba by Ascanius, and the wonderful signs accompanying it, as well as the whole series of the Alban kings with the years of their reigns, the story of Numitor and Amulius and the story of the destruction of the city, do not belong to history; but the historical existence of Alba is not at all doubtful on that account, nor have the ancients ever doubted it. The *Sacra Albana* and the *Albani tumuli atque luci*, which existed as late as the time of Cicero, are proofs of its early existence; ruins indeed no

longer exist, but the situation of the city in the valley of
Grotta Ferrata may still be recognised. Between the lake and
the long chain of hills near the monastery of Palazzuolo one
still sees the rock cut steep down towards the lake, evidently
the work of man, which rendered it impossible to attack the
city on that side; the summit on the other side formed the arx.
That the Albans were in possession of the sovereignty of Latium
is a tradition which we may believe to be founded on good
authority, as it is traced to Cincius.[1] Afterwards the Latins
became the masters of the district and temple of Jupiter.
Further, the statement that Alba shared the flesh of the victim
on the Alban mount with the thirty towns, and that after the
fall of Alba the Latins chose their own magistrates, are glimpses
of real history. The ancient tunnel made for discharging the
water of the Alban lake still exists, and through its vault a
canal was made called Fossa Cluilia: this vault which is still
visible is a work of earlier construction than any Roman one.
But all that can be said of Alba and the Latins at that time is,
that Alba was the capital, exercising the sovereignty over
Latium; that its temple of Jupiter was the rallying point of
the people who were governed by it; and that the gens Silvia
was the ruling clan.

It cannot be doubted that the number of Latin towns was
actually thirty, just that of the Albensian demi; this number
afterwards occurs again in the later thirty Latin towns and in
the thirty Roman tribes, and it is moreover indicated by the
story of the foundation of Lavinium by thirty families, in
which we may recognise the union of the two tribes.[2] The
statement that Lavinium was a Trojan colony and was afterwards abandoned but restored by Alba, and further that the
sanctuary could not be transferred from it to Alba, is only an
accommodation to the Trojan and native tradition, however
much it may bear the appearance of antiquity. For Lavinium
is nothing else than a general name for Latium just as Panionium
is for Ionia, *Latinus*, *Lavinus*, and *Lavicus* being one and the
same name, as is recognised even by Servius. Lavinium was
the central point of the Prisci Latini, and there is no doubt
that in the early period before Alba ruled over Lavinium,
worship was offered mutually at Alba and at Lavinium, as was

---

[1] *Albanos rerum potitos usque ad Tullum.* Festus, s. v. *prætor.*
[2] *Rom. Hist.* i. p. 201, fol.

afterwards the case at Rome in the temple of Diana on the
Aventine, and at the festivals of the Romans and Latins on
the Alban mount.

The personages of the Trojan legend therefore present themselves to us in the following light. Turnus is nothing else
but Turinus, in Dionysius Τυῤῥηνός; Lavinia, the fair maiden,
is the name of the Latin people, which may perhaps be so distinguished that the inhabitants of the coast were called Tyrrhenians, and those further inland Latins. Since, after the
battle of lake Regillus, the Latins are mentioned in the treaty
with Rome as forming thirty towns, there can be no doubt
that the towns, over which Alba had the supremacy in the
earliest times, were likewise thirty in number; but the confederacy did not at all times contain the same towns, as some may
afterwards have perished and others may have been added. In
such political developments, there is at work an instinctive
tendency to fill up that which has become vacant; and this
instinct acts as long as people proceed unconsciously according
to the ancient forms and not in accordance with actual
wants. Such also was the case in the twelve Achæan towns
and in the seven Frisian maritime communities; for as
soon as one disappeared, another dividing itself into two,
supplied its place. Wherever there is a fixed number,
it is kept up, even when one part dies away, and it ever continues to be renewed. We may add that the state of the
Latins lost in the West, but gained in the East. We must
therefore, I repeat it, conceive on the one hand Alba with
its thirty demi, and on the other the thirty Latin towns, the
latter at first forming a state allied with Alba, and at a later
time under its supremacy.

According to an important statement of Cato preserved in
Dionysius, the ancient towns of the Aborigines were small
places scattered over the mountains. One town of this kind
was situated on the Palatine hill, and bore the name of Roma,
which is most certainly Greek. Not far from it there occur
several other places with Greek names, such as Pyrgi and
Alsium; for the people inhabiting those districts were closely
akin to the Greeks; and it is by no means an erroneous conjecture, that Terracina was formerly called Τραχεινή, or the
"rough place on a rock;" Formiae must be connected with
ὅρμος, "a road-stead" or "place for casting anchor." As

certain as Pyrgi signifies "towers," so certainly does *Roma* signify
" strength³," and I believe that those are quite right who consider that the name Roma in this sense is not accidental.
This Roma is described as a Pelasgian place in which Evander,
the introducer of scientific culture resided.   According to tradition, the first foundation of civilisation was laid by Saturn,
in the golden age of mankind.   The tradition in Virgil, who
was extremely learned in matters of antiquity, that the first
men were created out of trees must be taken quite literally⁴;
for as in Greece the μύρμηκες were metamorphosed into the
Myrmidons, and the stones thrown by Deucalion and Pyrrha
into men and women, so in Italy trees, by some divine power,
were changed into human beings.   These beings, at first only
half human, gradually acquired a civilisation which they owed
to Saturn; but the real intellectual culture was traced to
Evander, who must not be regarded as a person who had come
from Arcadia, but as *the good man,* as the teacher of the alphabet and of mental culture, which man gradually works out for
himself.

The Romans clung to the conviction that Romulus, the
founder of Rome, was the son of a virgin by a god, that his
life was marvellously preserved, that he was saved from the
floods of the river and was reared by a she-wolf.   That this
poetry is very ancient, cannot be doubted; but did the legend
at all times describe Romulus as the son of Rea Silvia or Ilia?
Perizonius was the first who remarked against Ryckius, that
Rea Ilia never occurs together, and that Rea Silvia was a
daughter of Numitor, while Ilia is called a daughter of Aeneas.
He is perfectly right: Naevius and Ennius called Romulus a
son of Ilia, the daughter of Aeneas, as is attested by Servius
on Virgil and Porphyrio on Horace⁵; but it cannot be hence

---

³ It is well known that there is in Stobaeus (vii. 13) a poem upon Rome,
which is ascribed to Erinna. But as Erinna composed her poems at a time
when Rome cannot be supposed to have been renowned in Aeolia, commentators
have imagined the poem to be a hymn on Strength. But Strength cannot be
called a daughter of Ares; Strength might rather be said to be his mother. The
poem belongs to a much later date, and proceeding on this supposition it may
perhaps be possible for some one to discover the real name of the author. It
certainly belongs to the period subsequent to the Hannibalian war, and was
perhaps not written till the time of the emperors; but to me it seems most probable that the author was a contemporary of Sulla.—N.

⁴ *Gensque virum truncis et duro robore nata.*   Virgil, *Aen.* viii. 315.

⁵ *Carm.* i. 2.

inferred, that this was the national opinion of the Romans themselves, for the poets who were familiar with the Greeks, might accommodate their stories to Greek poems. The ancient Romans, on the other hand, could not possibly look upon the mother of the founder of their city as a daughter of Aeneas, who was believed to have lived 333 or 360 years earlier. Dionysius says that his account, which is that of Fabius, occurred in the sacred songs, and it is in itself perfectly consistent. Fabius cannot have taken it, as Plutarch asserts, from Diocles, a miserable unknown Greek author; the statue of the she-wolf was erected in the year A. U. 457, long before Diocles wrote, and at least a hundred years before Fabius. This tradition therefore is certainly the more ancient Roman one; and it puts Rome in connection with Alba. A monument has lately been discovered at Bovillae: it is an altar which the *Gentiles Julii* erected *lege Albana*, and therefore expresses a religious relation of a Roman gens to Alba. The connetion of the two towns continues down to the founder of Rome; and the well known tradition, with its ancient poetical details, many of which Livy and Dionysius omitted from their histories lest they should seem to deal too much in the marvellous, runs as follows.

Numitor and Amulius were contending for the throne of Alba.[6] Amulius took possession of the throne, and made Rea Silvia, the daughter of Numitor, a vestal virgin, in order that the Silvian house might become extinct. This part of the story was composed without any insight into political laws, for a daughter could not have transmitted any gentilician rights. The name Rea Silvia is ancient, but Rea is only a surname: *rea femmina* often occurs in Boccaccio, and is used to this day in Tuscany to designate a woman whose reputation is blighted: a priestess Rea is described by Virgil as having been overpowered by Hercules. While Rea was fetching water in a grove for a sacrifice the sun became eclipsed, and she took refuge from a wolf in a cave where she was overpowered by Mars. When she was delivered, the sun was again eclipsed and the statue of Vesta covered its eyes. Livy has here abandoned the marvellous. The tyrant threw Rea with her

---

[6] Numitor is a praenomen, but the name Amulius does not shew that he belonged to the gens Silvia: I therefore doubt whether the ancient tradition represented them as brothers.—N.

infants into the river Anio: she lost her life in the waves, but the god of the river took her soul and changed it into an immortal goddess whom he married. This story has been softened down into the tale of her imprisonment, which is un-poetical enough to be a later invention. The river Anio carried the cradle like a boat into the Tiber, and the latter conveyed it to the foot of the Palatine, the water having overflowed the country, and the cradle was upset at the root of a fig-tree. A she-wolf carried the babes away and suckled them[7]; Mars sent a woodpecker which provided the children with food, and the bird *parra*[8] which protected them from insects. These statements are gathered from various quarters; for the historians got rid of the marvellous as much as possible. Faustulus, the legend continues, found the boys feeding on the milk of the huge wild-beast, he brought them up with his twelve sons, and they became the staunchest of all. Being at the head of the shepherds on Mount Palatine, they became involved in a quarrel with the shepherds of Numitor on the Aventine—the Palatine and the Aventine are always hostile to each other—Remus being taken prisoner was led to Alba, but Romulus rescued him, and their descent from Numitor being discovered, the latter was restored to the throne, and the two young men obtained permission to form a settlement at the foot of Mount Palatine where they had been saved.

Out of this beautiful poem, the falsifiers endeavoured to make some credible story: even the unprejudiced and poetical Livy tried to avoid the most marvellous points as much as he could, but the falsifiers went a step farther. In the days when men had altogether ceased to believe in the ancient gods, attempts were made to find something intelligible in the old legends, and thus a history was made up, which Plutarch fondly embraced and Dionysius did not reject, though he also relates the ancient tradition in a mutilated form. He says that many people believed in daemons, and that such a daemon might have been the father of Romulus; but he himself is very far from believing it, and rather thinks that Amulius himself, in disguise, violated Rea Silvia amid thunder and lightning produced by artifice. This he is said to have done in order to have a pretext for getting rid of her, but being entreated by

---

[7] In Eastern legends, children are nourished with the marrow of lions.—N.
[8] Serv. on Virg. *Aen.* i. 274.

his daughter not to drown her, he imprisoned her for life. The children were saved by the shepherd, who was commissioned to expose them, at the request of Numitor, and two other boys were put in their place. Numitor's grandsons were taken to a friend at Gabii, who caused them to be educated according to their rank and to be instructed in Greek literature. Attempts have actually been made to introduce this stupid forgery into history, and some portions of it have been adopted in the narrative of our historians; for example, that the ancient Alban nobility migrated with the two brothers to Rome; but if this had been the case there would have been no need of opening an asylum, nor would it have been necessary to obtain by force the *connubium* with other nations.

But of more historical importance is the difference of opinion between the two brothers, respecting the building of the city and its site. According to the ancient tradition, both were kings and the equal heads of the colony; Romulus is universally said to have wished to build on the Palatine, while Remus, according to some, preferred the Aventine; according to others, the hill Remuria. Plutarch states that the latter is a hill three miles south of Rome, and cannot have been any other than the hill nearly opposite St. Paul, which is the more credible, since this hill, though situated in an otherwise unhealthy district, has an extremely fine air: a very important point in investigations respecting the ancient Latin towns, for it may be taken for certain, that where the air is now healthy it was so in those times also, and that where it is now decidedly unhealthy, it was anciently no better. The legend now goes on to say, that a dispute arose between Romulus and Remus as to which of them should give the name to the town, and also as to where it was to be built. A town Remuria therefore undoubtedly existed on that hill, though subsequently we find the name transferred to the Aventine, as is the case so frequently. According to the common tradition augurs were to decide between the brothers; Romulus took his stand on the Palatine, Remus on the Aventine. The latter observed the whole night but saw nothing until about sunrise, when he saw six vultures flying from north to south and sent word of it to Romulus, but at that very time the latter, annoyed at not having seen any sign, fraudulently sent a messenger to say that he had seen twelve vultures, and at the very moment the messenger arrived, there did appear twelve vultures, to which Romulus appealed. This account is impossible; for the Palatine and Aventine are so near each other that, as every Roman well knew, whatever a person on one of the two hills saw high in the air, could not escape the observation of any one who was watching on the other. This part of the story therefore cannot be ancient, and can be saved only by substituting the Remuria for the Aventine. As the Palatine was the seat of the noblest patrician tribe, and the Aventine the special town of the plebeians, there existed between the two a perpetual feud, and thus it came to pass that in after times the story relating to the Remuria, which was far away from the city, was transferred to the Aventine. According to Ennius, Romulus made his observations on the Aventine; in this case Remus must certainly have been on the Remuria, and it is said that when Romulus obtained the augury he threw his spear towards the Palatine. This is the ancient legend which was neglected by the later writers. Romulus took possession of the Palatine. The spear taking root and becoming a tree, which existed down to the time of Nero, is a symbol of the eternity of the new city, and of the protection of the gods. The statement that Romulus tried to deceive his brother is a later addition; and the beautiful poem of Ennius quoted by Cicero[9] knows nothing of this circumstance. The conclusion which must be drawn from all this is, that in the earliest times there were two towns, Roma and Remuria, the latter being far distant from the city and from the Palatine.

Romulus now fixed the boundary of his town, but Remus scornfully leapt across the ditch, for which he was slain by Celer, a hint that no one should cross the fortifications of Rome with impunity. But Romulus fell into a state of melancholy occasioned by the death of Remus; he instituted festivals to honor him and ordered an empty throne to be put up by the side of his own. Thus we have a double kingdom which ends with the defeat of Remuria.

The question now is what were these two towns of Roma and Remuria? They were evidently Pelasgian places; the ancient tradition states that Sicelus migrated from Rome southward to the Pelasgians, that is, the Tyrrhenian Pelasgians were pushed forward to the Morgetes, a kindred nation in Lucania and in Sicily. Among the Greeks it was, as Dionysius states,

<hr/>

[9] *De Divinat.* i. 48.

a general opinion, that Rome was a Pelasgian, that is a Tyrrhenian city, but the authorities from whom he learnt this are no longer extant. There is, however, a fragment in which it is stated that Rome was a sister city of Antium and Ardea. Here too we must apply the statement from the chronicle of Cumae, that Evander, who, as an Arcadian, was likewise a Pelasgian, had his *palatium* on the Palatine. To us he appears of less importance than in the legend, for in the latter he is one of the benefactors of nations, and introduced among the Pelasgians in Italy the use of the alphabet and other arts, just as Damaratus did among the Tyrrhenians in Etruria. In this sense, therefore, Rome was certainly a Latin town, and had not a mixed but a purely Tyrrheno-Pelasgian population. The subsequent vicissitudes of this settlement may be gathered from the allegories.

Romulus now found the number of his fellow-settlers too small; the number of 3000 foot and 300 horse, which Livy gives from the commentaries of the pontiffs, is worth nothing; for it is only an outline of the later military arrangement transferred to the earliest times. According to the ancient tradition, Romulus's band was too small, and he opened an asylum on the Capitoline hill. This asylum, the old description states, contained only a very small space, a proof how little these things were understood historically. All manner of people, thieves, murderers, and vagabonds of every kind flocked thither. This is the simple view taken of the origin of the clients. In the bitterness with which the estates subsequently looked upon one another, it was made a matter of reproach to the Patricians, that their earliest ancestors had been vagabonds; though it was a common opinion, that the patricians were descended from the free companions of Romulus, and that those who took refuge in the asylum placed themselves as clients under the protection of the real free citizens. But now they wanted women, and attempts were made to obtain the *connubium* with neighbouring towns, especially perhaps with Antemnae, which was only four miles distant from Rome, with the Sabines and others. This being refused, Romulus had recourse to a stratagem, proclaiming that he had discovered the altar of Consus, the god of counsels, an allegory of his cunning in general. In the midst of the solemnities, the Sabine maidens, thirty in number, were carried off, from whom the curiae received their

names: this is the genuine ancient legend, and it proves how
small ancient Rome was conceived to have been.   In later
times the number was thought too small, it was supposed that
these thirty had been chosen by lot for the purpose of naming
the curiae after them; and Valerius Antias fixed the number of
the women who had been carried off at five hundred and twenty-
seven.   The rape is placed in the fourth month of the city,
because the consualia fall in August, and the festival comme-
morating the foundation of the city in April; later writers, as
Cn. Gellius, extended this period to four years, and Dionysius
found this of course far more credible.   From this rape there
arose wars, first with the neighbouring towns which were defeated one after another, and at last with the Sabines.   The
ancient legend contains not a trace of this war having been of
long continuance; but in later times it was necessarily supposed
to have lasted for a considerable time, since matters were then
measured by a different standard.   Lucumo and Caelius came
to the assistance of Romulus, an allusion to the expedition of
Caeles Vibenna, which however belongs to a much later period.
The Sabine king, Tatius, was induced by treachery to settle
on the hill which is called the Tarpeian arx.   Between the
Palatine and the Tarpeian rock a battle was fought, in which
neither party gained a decisive victory, until the Sabine women
threw themselves between the combatants, who agreed that
henceforth the sovereignty should be divided between the Romans and Sabines.   According to the annals, this happened in
the fourth year of Rome.

But this arrangement lasted only a short time; Tatius was
slain during a sacrifice at Lavinium, and his vacant throne was
not filled up.   During their common reign, each king had a
senate of one hundred members, and the two senates, after consulting separately, used to meet, and this was called *comitium*.
Romulus during the remainder of his life ruled alone; the
ancient legend knows nothing of his having been a tyrant:
according to Ennius he continued, on the contrary, to be a
mild and benevolent king, while Tatius was a tyrant.   The
ancient tradition contained nothing beyond the beginning and
the end of the reign of Romulus; all that lies between these
points, the war with the Veientines, Fidenates, and so on, is a
foolish invention of later annalists. The poem itself is beautiful,
but this inserted narrative is highly absurd, as for example the

statement that Romulus slew 10,000 Veientines with his own hand. The ancient poem passed on at once to the time when Romulus had completed his earthly career, and Jupiter fulfilled his promise to Mars, that Romulus was the only man whom he would introduce among the gods. According to this ancient legend, the king was reviewing his army near the marsh of Caprae, when, as at the moment of his conception, there occurred an eclipse of the sun and at the same time a hurricane, during which Mars descended in a fiery chariot and took his son up to heaven. Out of this beautiful poem the most wretched stories have been manufactured; Romulus, it is said, while in the midst of his senators was knocked down, cut into pieces, and thus carried away by them under their togas. This stupid story was generally adopted, and that a cause for so horrible a deed might not be wanting, it was related that in his latter years Romulus had become a tyrant, and that the senators took revenge by murdering him.

After the death of Romulus, the Romans and the people of Tatius quarrelled for a long time with each other, the Sabines wishing that one of their nation should be raised to the throne, while the Romans claimed that the new king should be chosen from among them. At length they agreed, it is said, that the one nation should choose a king from the other.

We have now reached the point at which it is necessary to speak of the relation between the two nations, such as it actually existed.

All the nations of antiquity lived in fixed forms, and their civil relations were always marked by various divisions and sub-divisions. When cities raise themselves to the rank of nations, we always find a division at first into tribes; Herodotus mentions such tribes in the colonisation of Cyrene, and the same was afterwards the case at the foundation of Thurii; but when a place existed anywhere as a distinct township, its nature was characterised by the fact of its citizens being at a certain time divided into *gentes* (γένη) each of which had a common chapel and a common hero. These *gentes* were united in definite numerical proportions into *curiae* (φράτραι). The *gentes* are not families but free corporations, sometimes close and sometimes open; in certain cases, the whole body of the state might assign to them new associates; the great council at Venice was a close body, and no one could be admitted whose ancestors had not been in it, and such also was the case in many oligarchical states of antiquity.

All civil communities had a council and an assembly of burghers, that is a small and a great council; the burghers consisted of the guilds or *gentes*, and these again were united, as it were, in parishes; all the Latin towns had a council of 100 members, who were divided into ten *curiae ;* this division gave rise to the name of *decuriones*, which remained in use as a title of civic magistrates down to the latest times, and through the *lex Julia* was transferred to the constitution of the Italian *municipia*.   That this council consisted of one hundred persons has been proved by Savigny, in the first volume of his history of the Roman law.   This constitution continued to exist till a late period of the middle ages, but perished when the institution of guilds took the place of municipal constitutions. Giovanni Villani says, that previously to the revolution in the twelfth century there were at Florence 100 *buoni uomini*, who had the administration of the city.   There is nothing in our German cities which answers to this constitution.   We must not conceive those hundred to have been nobles; they were an assembly of burghers and country people, as was the case in our small imperial cities, or as in the small cantons of Switzerland.   Each of them represented a gens; and they are those whom Propertius calls *patres pelliti*.   The *curia* of Rome, a cottage covered with straw[10], was a faithful memorial of the times when Rome stood buried in the night of history, as a small country town surrounded by its little domain.

The most ancient occurrence which we can discover from the form of the allegory, by a comparison of what happened in other parts of Italy, is a result of the great and continued commotion among the nations of Italy.   It did not terminate when the Oscans had been pressed forward from lake Fucinus to the lake of Alba, but continued much longer.   The Sabines may have rested for a time, but they advanced far beyond the districts about which we have any traditions.   These Sabines began as a very small tribe, but afterwards became one of the greatest nations of Italy, for the Marrucinians, Caudines, Vestinians, Marsians, Pelignians, and in short all the Samnite tribes, the Lucanians, the Oscan part of the Bruttians, the Picentians and several others were all descended from the Sabine stock, and

---

[10] *Recens horrebat regia culmo.*   Virgil.

yet there are no traditions about their settlements except in a few cases. At the time to which we must refer the foundation of Rome, the Sabines were widely diffused. It is said that, guided by a bull, they penetrated into Opica, and thus occupied the country of the Samnites. It was perhaps at an earlier time that they migrated down the Tiber, whence we there find Sabine towns mixed with Latin ones; some of their places also existed on the Anio. The country afterwards inhabited by the Sabines was probably not occupied by them till a later period, for Falerii is a Tuscan town, and its population was certainly at one time thoroughly Tyrrhenian.

As the Sabines advanced, some Latin towns maintained their independence, others were subdued; Fidenae belonged to the former, but north of it all the country was Sabine. Now by the side of the ancient Roma we find a Sabine town on the Quirinal and Capitoline close to the Latin town; but its existence is all that we know about it. A tradition states, that there previously existed on the Capitoline a Siculian town of the name of Saturnia[11], which, in this case, must have been conquered by the Sabines. But whatever we may think of this, as well as of the existence of another ancient town on the Janiculum, it is certain that there were a number of small towns in that district. The two towns could exist perfectly well side by side, as there was a deep marsh between them.

The town on the Palatine may for a long time have been in a state of dependence on the Sabine conqueror whom tradition calls Titus Tatius; hence he was slain during the Laurentine sacrifice, and hence also his memory was hateful.[12] The existence of a Sabine town on the Quirinal is attested by the undoubted occurrence there of a number of Sabine chapels, which were known as late as the time of Varro, and from which he proved that the Sabine ritual was adopted by the Romans. This Sabine element in the worship of the Romans has almost always been overlooked[13], in consequence of the prevailing

[11] Varro, L.L. v. (iv.) 42.

[12] Ennius calls him a tyrant in the well-known verse: *O Tite, tute, Tati, tibi tanta tyranni tulisti.*—N.

[13] I have spent many days at Rome in searching after the ancient churches, which were pulled down at the time when the town was splendidly rebuilt; but I never was able to see my way, until I read the work of a priest of the seventeenth century, who pointed out the traces of them which still exist; and I conceive that it was in a similar manner that Varro pointed out the sites of the Sabine chapels and *sacella* on the Quirinal and Capitoline.— N.

desire to look upon every thing as Etruscan; but, I repeat, there is no doubt of the Sabine settlement, and that it was the result of a great commotion among the tribes of middle Italy.

LECTURE IV.

THE tradition that the Sabine women were carried off, because there existed no *connubium*, and that the rape was followed by a war, is undoubtedly a symbolical representation of the relation between the two towns, previous to the establishment of the right of intermarriage; the Sabines had the ascendancy and refused that right, but the Romans gained it by force of arms. There can be no doubt, that the Sabines were originally the ruling people, but, that in some insurrection of the Romans various Sabine places, such as Antemnae, Fidenae and others, were subdued, and thus these Sabines were separated from their kinsmen. The Romans therefore re-established their independence by a war, the result of which may have been such as we read it in the tradition—Romulus being, of course, set aside—namely that both places as two closely united towns formed a kind of confederacy, each with a senate of 100 members, a king, an offensive and defensive alliance, and on the understanding that in common deliberations the burghers of each should meet together in the space between the two towns which was afterwards called the *comitium*. In this manner they formed a united state in regard to foreign nations.

The idea of a double state was not unknown to the ancient writers themselves, although the indications of it are preserved only in scattered passages, especially in the scholiasts. The head of Janus, which in the earliest times was represented on the Roman *as*, is the symbol of it, as has been correctly observed by writers on Roman antiquities. The vacant throne by the side of the *curule* chair of Romulus points to the time when there was only one king, and represents the equal but quiescent right of the other people.[1]

That concord was not of long duration is an historical fact

------

[1] Comp. above, page 40.

likewise; nor can it be doubted that the Roman king assumed the supremacy over the Sabines, and that in consequence the two councils were united so as to form one senate under one king, it being agreed that the king should be alternately a Roman and a Sabine, and that each time he should be chosen by the other people: the king, however, if displeasing to the non-electing people, was not to be forced upon them, but was to be invested with the *imperium* only on condition of the auguries being favourable to him, and of his being sanctioned by the whole nation. The non-electing tribe accordingly had the right of either sanctioning or rejecting his election. In the case of Numa this is related as a fact, but it is only a disguise-ment of the right derived from the ritual books. In this manner the strange double election, which is otherwise so mysterious and was formerly completely misunderstood, be-comes quite intelligible. One portion of the nation elected and the other sanctioned; it being intended that, for example, the Romans should not elect from among the Sabines a king devoted exclusively to their own interests, but one who was at the same time acceptable to the Sabines.

When, perhaps after several generations of a separate existence, the two states became united, the towns ceased to be towns, and the collective body of the burghers of each became tribes, so that the nation consisted of two tribes. The form of addressing the Roman people was from the earliest times *Populus Romanus Quirites*, which, when its origin was forgotten, was changed into *Populus Romanus Quiritium*, just as *lis vin-diciae* was afterwards changed into *lis vindiciarum*. This change is more ancient than Livy; the correct expression still continued to be used, but was to a great extent supplanted by the false one. The ancient tradition relates that after the union of the two tribes the name *Quirites* was adopted as the common designation for the whole people; but this is erroneous, for the name was not used in this sense till a very late period. This designation remained in use and was transferred to the plebeians at a time when the distinction between Romans and Sabines, between these two and the Luceres, nay, when even that between patricians and plebeians had almost ceased to be noticed.[2] Thus the two towns stood side by side as tribes

[2] This is not my discovery: it belongs to the great president of the French Parliament, Barnabas Brissonius, from whom we may still learn much, although

forming one state, and it is merely a recognition of the ancient tradition when we call the Latins Ramnes, and the Sabines Tities: that the derivation of these appellations from Romulus and T. Tatius is incorrect is no argument against the view here taken.

Dionysius, who had good materials and made use of a great many, must, as far as the consular period is concerned, have had more than he gives; there is in particular one important change in the constitution, concerning which he has only a few words, either because he did not see clearly or because he was careless.[3]   But as regards the kingly period, he was well acquainted with his subject; he says that there was a dispute between the two tribes respecting the senates, and that Numa settled it, by not depriving the Ramnes, as the first tribe, of any thing, and by conferring honours on the Tities.   This is perfectly clear.   The senate, which had at first consisted of 100 and now of 200 members, was divided into ten *decuries*, each being headed by one, who was its leader; these are the *decem primi*, and they were taken from the Ramnes.   They formed the college, which, when there was no king, undertook the government one after another, each for five days, but in such a manner, that they always succeeded one another in the same order, as we must believe with Livy, for Dionysius here introduces his Greek notions of the Attic *prytanes*, and Plutarch misunderstands the matter altogether.

After the example of the senate the number of the augurs and pontiffs also was doubled, so that each college consisted of four members, two being taken from the Ramnes and two from the Tities.   Although it is not possible to fix these changes chronologically, as Dionysius and Cicero do, yet they are as historically certain as if we actually knew the kings who introduced them.

Such was Rome in the second stage of its development.

---

we may correct a great many trifling errors of detail into which he fell; but where should we now be, had there not been such men as Brissonius, Scaliger, and Cujacius.   Brissonius however on the point here in question goes too far; for he wishes to emend every where: all exaggeration injures truth, and the consequence was, that many persons altogether refused to follow him because he often erred.   The ingenious J. F. Gronovius opposed him, and referred to passages in Livy which were against him; but, as was remarked above, the erroneous expression was established previously to the time of Livy.—N.

[3] See Hist. Rom. vol. ii. p. 179, 220, etc.

This period of equalisation is one of peace, and is described as the reign of Numa about whom the traditions are simple and brief. It is the picture of a peaceful condition with a holy man at the head of affairs, like Nicolas von der Flue in Switzerland. Numa was supposed to have been inspired by the goddess Egeria, to whom he was married in the grove of the Camenae, and who introduced him into the choir of her sisters; she melted away in tears at his death, and thus gave her name to the spring which arose out of her tears. Such a peace of forty years, during which no nation rose against Rome because Numa's piety was communicated to the surrounding nations, is a beautiful idea, but historically impossible in those times, and manifestly a poetical fiction.

The death of Numa forms the conclusion of the first *saeculum*, and an entirely new period follows, just as in the Theogony of Hesiod the age of heroes is followed by the iron age; there is evidently a change, and an entirely new order of things is conceived to have arisen. Up to this point we have had nothing except poetry, but with Tullus Hostilius a kind of history begins, that is, events are related which must be taken in general as historical, though in the light in which they are presented to us they are not historical. Thus, for example, the destruction of Alba is historical, and so in all probability is the reception of the Albans at Rome. The conquests of Ancus Martius are quite credible; and they appear like an oasis of real history in the midst of fables. A similar case occurs once in the chronicle of Cologne. In the Abyssinian annals, we find in the thirteenth century a very minute account of one particular event, in which we recognise a piece of contemporaneous history, though we meet with nothing historical either before or after.

The history which then follows is like a picture viewed from the wrong side, like phantasmata; the names of the kings are perfectly fictitious; no man can tell how long the Roman kings reigned, as we do not know how many there were, since it is only for the sake of the number, that seven were supposed to have ruled, seven being a number which appears in many relations, especially in important astronomical ones. Hence the chronological statements are utterly worthless. We must conceive as a succession of centuries, the period from the origin of Rome down to the times wherein were constructed the

enormous works, such as the great drains, the wall of Servius
and others, which were actually executed under the kings, and
rival the great architectural works of the Egyptians. Romulus and Numa must be entirely set aside; but a long period
follows, in which the nations gradually unite and develop
themselves until the kingly government disappears and makes
way for republican institutions.

But it is nevertheless necessary to relate the history, such as
it has been handed down, because much depends upon it.
There was not the slightest connection between Rome and
Alba, nor is it even mentioned by the historians, though they
suppose that Rome received its first inhabitants from Alba; but
in the reign of Tullus Hostilius the two cities on a sudden appear as enemies: each of the two nations seeks war, and tries
to allure fortune by representing itself as the injured party,
each wishing to declare war. Both sent ambassadors to demand
reparation for robberies which had been committed. The form
of procedure was this: the ambassadors, that is the Fetiales,
related the grievances of their city to every person they met,
they then proclaimed them in the market place of the other
city, and if, after the expiration of thrice ten days no reparation was made, they said: " We have done enough and now
return," whereupon the elders at home held counsel as to how
they should obtain redress. In this formula accordingly the
res, that is the surrender of the guilty and the restoration of
the stolen property must have been demanded. Now it is
related that the two nations sent such ambassadors quite simultaneously, but that Tullus Hostilius retained the Alban ambassadors, until he was certain that the Romans at Alba had
not obtained the justice due to them, and had therefore declared war. After this he admitted the ambassadors into the
senate, and the reply made to their complaint was, that they
themselves had not satisfied the demands of the Romans. Livy
then continues: *bellum in trigesimum diem dixerant*. But the
real formula is, *post trigesimum diem*, and we may ask, Why
did Livy or the annalist whom he followed make this alteration?
For an obvious reason: a person may ride from Rome to Alba
in a couple of hours, so that the detention of the Alban ambassadors at Rome for thirty days, without their hearing what
was going on in the mean time at Alba, was a matter of impossibility: Livy saw this, and therefore altered the formula.

But the ancient poet was not concerned about such things, and without hesitation increased the distance in his imagination, and represented Rome and Alba as great states.

The whole description of the circumstances under which the fate of Alba was decided is just as manifestly poetical, but we shall dwell upon it for a while in order to show how a semblance of history may arise. Between Rome and Alba there was a ditch, Fossa Cluilia or Cloelia, and there must have been a tradition that the Albans had been encamped there; Livy and Dionysius mention that Cluilius, a general of the Albans, had given the ditch its name, having perished there. It was necessary to mention the latter circumstance, in order to explain the fact that afterwards their general was a different person, Mettius Fuffetius, and yet to be able to connect the name of that ditch with the Albans. The two states committed the decision of their dispute to champions, and Dionysius says, that tradition did not agree as to whether the name of the Roman champions was Horatii or Curiatii, although he himself, as well as Livy, assumes that it was Horatii, probably because it was thus stated by the majority of the annalists. Who would suspect any uncertainty here if it were not for this passage of Dionysius? The contest of the three brothers on each side is a symbolical indication that each of the two states was then divided into three tribes. Attempts have indeed been made to deny that the three men were brothers of the same birth, and thus to remove the improbability; but the legend went even further, representing the three brothers on each side as the sons of two sisters, and as born on the same day. This contains the suggestion of a perfect equality between Rome and Alba. The contest ended in the complete submission of Alba; it did not remain faithful, however, and in the ensuing struggle with the Etruscans, Mettius Fuffetius acted the part of a traitor towards Rome, but not being able to carry his design into effect, he afterwards fell upon the fugitive Etruscans. Tullus ordered him to be torn to pieces and Alba to be razed to the ground, the noblest Alban families being transplanted to Rome. The death of Tullus is no less poetical. Like Numa he undertook to call down lightning from heaven, but he thereby destroyed himself and his house.

If we endeavour to discover the historical substance of these legends, we at once find ourselves in a period when Rome no longer stood alone, but had colonies with Roman settlers, possessing a third of the territory and exercising sovereign power over the original inhabitants. This was the case in a small number of towns for the most part of ancient Siculian origin. It is an undoubted fact that Alba was destroyed, and that after this event the towns of the *Prisci Latini* formed an independent and compact confederacy; but whether Alba fell in the manner described, whether it was ever compelled to recognise the supremacy of Rome, and whether it was destroyed by the Romans and Latins conjointly, or by the Romans or Latins alone, are questions which no human ingenuity can solve. It is however most probable, that the destruction of Alba was the work of the Latins, who rose against her supremacy: whether in this case the Romans received the Albans among themselves, and thus became their benefactors instead of destroyers, must ever remain a matter of uncertainty. That Alban families were transplanted to Rome cannot be doubted, any more than that the *Prisci Latini* from that time constituted a compact state; if we consider that Alba was situated in the midst of the Latin districts, that the Alban mount was their common sanctuary, and that the grove of Ferentina was the place of assembly for all the Latins, it must appear more probable that Rome did not destroy Alba, but that it perished in an insurrection of the Latin towns, and that the Romans strengthened themselves by receiving the Albans into their city.

Whether the Albans were the first that settled on the Caelian hill, or whether it was previously occupied cannot be decided. The account which places the foundation of the town on the Caelius in the reign of Romulus suggests that a town existed there before the reception of the Albans; but what is the authenticity of this account? A third tradition represents it as an Etruscan settlement of Caeles Vibenna. Thus much is certain that the destruction of Alba greatly contributed to increase the power of Rome. There can be no doubt that a third town which seems to have been very populous, now existed on the Caelius and on a portion of the Esquiliae: such a settlement close to other towns was made for the sake of mutual protection. Between the two more ancient towns there continued to be a marsh or swamp, and Rome was protected on the south by stagnant water; but between Rome and the third town there was a dry plain. Rome also had a considerable suburb towards the Aventine protected by a wall and a ditch, as is implied in the story of Remus. He is a personification of the plebs, leaping across the ditch from the side of the Aventine, though we ought to be very cautious in regard to allegory.

The most ancient town on the Palatine was Rome; the Sabine town also must have had a name, and I have no doubt that, according to common analogy, it was Quirium, the name of its citizens being Quirites. This I look upon as certain. I have almost as little doubt that the town on the Caelian was called Lucerum, because when it was united with Rome, its citizens were called Lucertes (Luceres). The ancients derive this name from Lucumo, king of the Tuscans, or from Lucerus, king of Ardea; the latter derivation probably meaning, that the race was Tyrrheno-Latin, because Ardea was the capital of that race. Rome was thus enlarged by a third element, which, however, did not stand on a footing of equality with the two others, but was in a state of dependance similar to that of Ireland relatively to Great Britain down to the year 1782. But although the Luceres were obliged to recognise the supremacy of the two elder tribes, they were considered as an integral part of the whole state, that is, as a third tribe with an administration of its own, but inferior rights. What throws light upon our way here, is a passage of Festus who is a great authority on matters of Roman antiquity, because he made his excerpts from Verrius Flaccus; it is only in a few points that, in my opinion, either of them was mistaken; all the rest of the mistakes in Festus may be accounted for by the imperfection of the abridgment, Festus not always understanding Verrius Flaccus. The statement of Festus to which I here allude, is, that Tarquinius Superbus increased the number of the Vestals, in order that each tribe might have two. With this we must connect a passage from the tenth book of Livy, where he says that the augurs were to represent the three tribes. The numbers in the Roman colleges of priests were always multiples either of two or of three; the latter was the case with the Vestal Virgins and the great Flamines, and the former with the Augurs, Pontiffs and Fetiales, who represented only the first two tribes. Previously to the passing of the Ogulnian law the number of augurs was four, and when subsequently five plebeians were added, the basis of this increase was different, it is true[4], but the ancient rule of the number being a multiple of three was preserved.   The number of pontiffs which was then four, was increased only by four: this might seem to contradict what has just been stated, but it has been overlooked that Cicero speaks of *five* new ones having been added, for he included the Pontifex Maximus, which Livy does not.   In like manner there were twenty Fetiales, ten for each tribe.   To the Salii on the Palatine, Numa added another brotherhood on the Quirinal; thus we everywhere see a manifest distinction between the first two tribes and the third, the latter being treated as inferior.

The third tribe, then, consisted of free citizens, but they had not the same rights as the members of the first two; yet its members considered themselves superior to all other people; and their relation to the other two tribes was the same as that existing between the Venetian citizens of the main land and the *nobili*.   A Venetian nobleman treated those citizens with far more condescension than he displayed towards others, provided they did not presume to exercise any authority in political matters.   Whoever belonged to the Luceres, called himself a Roman, and if the very dictator of Tusculum had come to Rome, a man of the third tribe there would have looked upon him as an inferior person, though he himself had no influence whatever.

Tullus was succeeded by Ancus.   Tullus appears as one of the Ramnes, and as descended from Hostus Hostilius, one of the companions of Romulus; but Ancus was a Sabine, a grandson of Numa.   The accounts about him are to some extent historical, and there is no trace of poetry in them.   In his reign, the development of the state again made a step in advance.   According to the ancient tradition, Rome was at war with the Latin towns, and carried it on successfully. How many of the particular events which are recorded may be historical, I am unable to say; but that there was a war is credible enough. Ancus, it is said, carried away after this war many thousands of Latins, and gave them settlements on the Aventine.   The ancients express various opinions about him; sometimes he is described as a *captator aurae popularis ;* sometimes he is called *bonus Ancus.*   Like the first three kings, he is said to have been a legislator, a fact which is not mentioned in reference to

[4] Namely 4 + 5, five being the plebeian number.

the later kings. He is moreover stated to have established the colony of Ostia, and thus his kingdom must have extended as far as the mouth of the Tiber.

Ancus and Tullus seem to me to be historical personages; but we can scarcely suppose that the latter was succeeded by the former, and that the events assigned to their reigns actually occurred in them. These events must be conceived in the following manner. Towards the end of the fourth reign, when, after a feud which lasted many years, the Romans came to an understanding with the Latins about the renewal of the long neglected alliance, Rome gave up its claims to the supremacy which it could not maintain, and indemnified itself by extending its dominion in another and safer direction. The eastern colonies joined the Latin towns which still existed: this is evident, though it is nowhere expressly mentioned; and a portion of the Latin country was ceded to Rome; with which the rest of the Latins formed a connection of friendship, perhaps of isopolity. Rome here acted as wisely as England did when she recognised the independence of North America.

In this manner Rome obtained a territory. The many thousand settlers whom Ancus is said to have led to the Aventine, were the population of the Latin towns which became subject to Rome, and they were far more numerous than the two ancient tribes, even after the latter had been increased by their union with the third tribe. In these country districts lay the power of Rome, and from them she raised the armies with which she carried on her wars. It would have been natural to admit this population as a fourth tribe, but such a measure was not agreeable to the Romans: the constitution of the state was completed and was looked upon as a sacred trust, in which no change ought to be introduced. It was with the Greeks and Romans as it was with our own ancestors, whose separate tribes clung to their hereditary laws and differed from one another in this respect as much as they did from the Gauls in the colour of their eyes and hair. They knew well enough that it was in their power to alter the laws, but they considered them as something which ought not to be altered. Thus when the emperor Otho was doubtful on a point of the law of inheritance, he caused the case to be decided by an ordeal or judgment of God. In Sicily one city had Chalcidian, another Doric laws, although their populations, as well as their dialects, were greatly mixed; but the leaders of those colonies had been Chalcidians in the one case, and Dorians in the others. The Chalcidians moreover were divided into four, the Dorians into three tribes, and their differences in these respects were manifested even in their weights and measures.[5] The division into three tribes was a genuine Latin institution; and there are reasons which render it probable that the Sabines had a division of their states into four tribes. The transportation of the Latins to Rome must be regarded as the origin of the plebs.

LECTURE V.

ALTHOUGH the statement that Ancus carried the Latins away from their habitations and transplanted them to Rome, as if he had destroyed their towns, cannot be believed because it is impossible, since the settlers would have been removed many miles from their possessions and would have left an empty country, yet it cannot be doubted that Ancus Martius is justly called the founder of the town on the Aventine. There arose on that spot a town which even to the latest times remained politically separated: it existed by the side of Rome but was distinct from it, not being included within the *pomoerium* so long as any value was attached to that line of demarcation.

In following the narrative as it has been transmitted to us, we now come to a period, which was probably separated by a great chasm from the preceding one. In the reign of Tarquinius Priscus, Rome appears in so different a light, that it is impossible to conceive him as the successor of Ancus, whose conquests were confined to a small space, and under whom Rome formed its first connection with the sea through the foundation of Ostia; whereas under Tarquinius, things are mentioned of which traces are visible to this day. Tarquinius is described as half an Etruscan, the son of Damaratus by an Etruscan woman. His father is said to have been a Bacchiad, who in

[5] When the Achaeans spread over the Peloponnesus, Sicyon first adopted their νόμιμα, and its example was gradually followed by the other towns, and thus the Doric laws almost disappeared. Attempts were made to compel Sparta also to abandon its old laws, but without success.—ED.

the revolution of Cypselus quitted Corinth with his immense wealth, and went to Tarquinii. His property descended to his son L. Tarquinius, as his elder son Aruns had died previously, leaving a wife in a state of pregnancy, a circumstance of which the elder Tarquinius was not aware. This account is commonly believed to be of considerable authority, because Polybius, though a Greek, mentions Tarquinius as a son of Damaratus, and because chronology is supposed not to be against it. But this is only an illusion, because the time depends upon the correctness of the chronological statements respecting the Roman kings, according to which Tarquinius Priscus is said to have ascended the throne in the year 132 after the building of the city; but if we find ourselves compelled to place him at a later period, the story of Damaratus and Cypselus, which may with tolerable certainty be referred to the thirtieth Olympiad, must fall to the ground. I have already remarked elsewhere, that the ancient annalists, with the sole exception of Piso, never doubted that Tarquinius Superbus was a son of Tarquinius Priscus, whence the time assigned to the latter must be utterly wrong; his relationship to Damaratus is therefore impossible.

The story of Damaratus belongs to the ancient tradition respecting the connection between Greece and Etruria, and the civilisation introduced from the former into the latter country. What Evander was to the Latins, that Damaratus was to the Etruscans or Tyrrhenians, as he is said to have made them acquainted with the Cadmean alphabet; and according to the most ancient Greek tradition he belongs to a period as remote as that of Evander. What caused him to be connected with Tarquinius Priscus was the fact of the ancient legend mentioning Tarquinii as the place where Damaratus settled, though it undoubtedly knew nothing of his belonging to the family of the Bacchiadae, which must be an addition made by later narrators, who every where endeavoured to connect the history of one country with that of another. The reason for making Damaratus proceed to Tarquinii may have been the fact that Tarquinii was an important city; but at the same time there is no doubt that a connection existed between Tarquinii and Corinth. It was formerly believed that the vases and other vessels found in Tuscany were of Etruscan origin; this idea was afterwards justly given up, but then a belief arose

that such vases never existed in ancient Etruria.   In our days
vessels are dug out of the ground at Corneto, which perfectly
resemble the most ancient Greek ones; I do not mean those
which were formerly called Etruscan, but those actually found
in Greece and belonging to the earliest times, especially the
Corinthian ones, of which representations are given in Dodwell.[1]   Pieces of such vases are found only in the neighbourhood of ancient Tarquinii; in all the rest of Tuscany scarcely
one or two of them have been discovered; in the north-
eastern part of the country, about Arezzo and Fiesole, the
Arretinian vases of red clay with raised figures are of quite a
peculiar form and very numerous, but do not occur any where
on the coast.   This artistic connection between Tarquinii and
Greece, especially Corinth, is accounted for in the tradition by
the statement that the artists Eucheir and Eugrammus accompanied Damaratus from Corinth.

Now when it was observed that Tarquinius Priscus was
referred to Tarquinii, and a comparison of this statement was
made with the tradition that the solemn Greek worship had
first been introduced by him into Rome, people at once said:
This must be the work of an ancient Greek; they compared
the Roman chronology, as it was laid down in the work of the
pontiffs, with the chronology of Greece, a comparison which
might be made after the time when Timaeus wrote his history.
They soon found that the combination became possible, if
Damaratus was represented as the father of Tarquinius.   This
Tarquinius Priscus or Lucumo is said to have gone to Rome
with his wife Tanaquil, an Etruscan prophetess, because at
Tarquinii he did not enjoy the full rights of a citizen.   On
his journey thither a marvellous occurrence announced to him
that heaven had destined him for great things; many glorious
exploits are ascribed to his reign; but our narratives here
diverge: that of Livy is very modest, but another represents
him as the conqueror of all the Etruscan towns.   All this
may be read in detail in Dionysius, and the accounts of it
belong to the ancient Roman annals, so that Augustus caused
these victories to be registered even in the triumphal *fasti* as
three distinct triumphs and with certain dates, as we see from
the fragments.[2]   The Romans had the more reason to believe

[1] Classical Tour, ii. p. 195.—ED.

[2] The destruction of this monument is the fault of those who made it; they
ought to have chosen a better material.—N.

these statements, because Tarquinius Priscus was mentioned as the king who united the town of the Sabines to that of the Romans and executed the gigantic works by which the valleys also were filled up.

The same tradition invariably calls Tarquinius Priscus, Lucumo; now this never was a proper name, but was the Etruscan title of a prince. Whenever the Romans wished to invent a story about the Etruscans, they called the men Lucumo, Aruns, or Lars. The last probably signifies "king." Aruns was an ordinary name, as we know from the inscriptions on Etruscan tombs, in which we can distinguish the names though we do not understand a single word. I have examined all the Etruscan inscriptions; and have come to the conclusion that their language is totally different from Latin, and that only a few things can be made out by conjecture, as for example, that *ril avil* means *vixit annos*. Lucumo does not occur in these inscriptions, and the ancient philologers, such as Verrius Flaccus, knew that it was not a name. The Romans had several traditions about a Lucumo, who is connected with the history of Rome; one, for example, was a companion of Romulus. All these Lucumos are no other than Lucius Tarquinius Priscus himself, that is, tradition has referred to him all that was related of the others. Livy says that at Rome he assumed the name Lucius Tarquinius Priscus, a statement for which scholars have charged Livy with rashness: it is rashness, however, only on the supposition that he took *Priscus* in the sense of "ancient." But it may often have happened to Livy when writing his first book, that he composed his narrative with the conviction that it was not all literally true, and that something else might be understood by it. Priscus was a common name among the Romans; it occurs in the family of the Servilii and many others; Cato was called Priscus before he obtained the name Cato, that is, *Catus*, the prudent. I am satisfied that Tarquinius was connected with the town of Tarquinii only on account of his name, and that he was in reality a Latin. This opinion is supported by the mention of Tarquinii, who after the expulsion of the kings dwelt at Laurentum, and by the statement, that Collatinus retired to Lavinium which was a Latin town. Moreover, the whole story of the descent of Tarquinius Priscus from Damaratus is overturned by the fact that Cicero, Varro, and even Livy, acknowledged the existence of a *gens Tarquinia :* and how totally different is a gens from a family consisting of only two branches, that of the kings and that of Collatinus? Varro expressly says: *Omnes Tarquinios ejecerunt ne quam reditionis per gentilitatem spem haberet.*

The desire also of accounting for an Etruscan influence upon Rome, contributed, independently of his name, towards connecting Tarquinius with Etruria. The Romans described Servius Tullius, who was an Etruscan, as a Latin of Corniculum, and made Lucius Tarquinius Priscus, who was a Latin, an Etruscan. Thus the whole account of his descent is a fable, and Tanaquil too is a perfect fiction, for the Romans gave this name to any woman whom they wished to characterise as Etruscan, it being a common name in Etruria, as we see in the inscriptions. In the ancient native tradition, Tarquinius was married to a Latin woman, Caja Caecilia, a name which must be traced to Caeculus, the founder of Praeneste. Her image was set up in the temple of Semo Sancus, for she was worshipped as a goddess presiding over female domesticity. This has a genuine national character; so much so that in the ancient legend the people are said to have rubbed off particles from the girdle of her brass statue, to be used as a medicine.

It is therefore historically certain that there was a Latin of the name of Tarquinius Priscus; but he most probably belonged to the Luceres, for whom he procured seats in the senate, one hundred being added, as *gentes minores,* to the two hundred senators who were *called up* by the king before the *gentes minores ?* In the insurrection of Tarquinius against Servius Tullius, these additional senators were his faction. The reign of Tarquinius, as I have already remarked, is probably separated by a great chasm ˚from the preceding period, for under him Rome presents quite a different appearance from what it had been before. The conquests ascribed to Ancus Marcius are confined to a very small extent of country: he made himself master of the mouth of the Tiber and fortified Ostia. But after him a state of things is described by the historians, of which traces are still visible. Even at the present day there stands unchanged the great sewer, the *cloaca maxima,* the object of which, it may be observed, was not merely to carry away the refuse of the city, but chiefly to drain the large˚lake, which was formed by the Tiber between the Capitoline,

Aventine and Palatine, then extended between the Palatine and Capitoline, and reached as a swamp as far as the district between the Quirinal and Viminal. This work, consisting of three semicircles of immense square blocks, which, though without mortar, have not to this day moved a knife's breadth from one another, drew the water from the surface, conducted it into the Tiber, and thus changed the lake into solid ground; but as the Tiber itself had a marshy bank, a large wall was built as an embankment, the greater part of which still exists. This structure, equalling the pyramids in extent and massiveness, far surpasses them in the difficulty of its execution. It is so gigantic, that the more one examines it the more inconceivable it becomes how even a large and powerful state could have executed it. In comparison with it, the aqueducts of the emperors cannot be considered grand, for they were built of bricks with cement in the inner parts, but in the more ancient work everything is made of square blocks of hewn Alban stone, and the foundations are immensely deep.

Now whether the *cloaca maxima* was actually executed by Tarquinius Priscus or by his son Superbus, is a question about which the ancients themselves are not agreed, and respecting which true historical criticism cannot presume to decide. But thus much may be said, that the structure must have been completed before the city encompassed the space of the seven hills, and formed a compact whole. This, however, was effected by the last king, and accordingly if we wish to make use of a personification, we may say that the great sewer was built in the time of Tarquinius Priscus. But such a work cannot possibly have been executed by the powers of a state such as Rome is said to have been in those times; for its territory extended from the river not more than about ten miles in breadth, and, at the utmost, from thirty to forty in length, which is not as large as the territory of Nürnberg: and this objection is the more weighty when we take into consideration all the difficulties of an age in which commerce and wealth had no existence. A period must therefore have been passed over in our histories, and we now all at once see Rome as a kingdom ruling far and wide, and quite different from what it had been before. Of this extensive dominion no mention is made by Livy, though he expresses his wonder at these architectural structures; he conceives that time still as the state of the city's infancy, and is therefore under the same erroneous belief as Cicero and all the later writers, namely, that the kingly period must be regarded as an age in which Rome was extremely weak. The statement of Dionysius, that the Etruscan towns, the Latins, and the Sabines paid homage to Tarquinius, might therefore seem to be more deserving of credit, but all the accounts of the manner in which this state of things was brought about, are so fabulous and fictitious, that it is evident they must have been manufactured by those who attempted to solve the mysterious problem; and we have no historical ground to stand upon. But in whatever way Tarquinius Priscus may have been connected with the Tuscan traditions about the conquests of Tarchon, we can with certainty say, that at that time Rome was either herself the mistress of a large empire, or was the seat of a foreign ruler; at any rate, Rome at one period was the centre of a great empire.

Another no less mysterious undertaking is ascribed to the reign of the same Tarquinius Priscus: he wanted, it is said, to double the Romulian tribes, that is, to add three new tribes with names derived from his own and those of some of his friends. This plan was opposed by the augur Attius Navius, because the three tribes were inseparably connected with the auspices. The tradition probably did not run as Livy relates it, but as we read it in Dionysius, that Tarquinius himself cut through the wet stone, and in doing so injured his hand. The king now is said, not indeed to have formed three new tribes, but to have added new centuries to the ancient ones.[3] In this tradi-

[3] No ancient nation could change its division without altering its whole character. This is not the case in modern states, for when at Florence the small guilds were added to the seven great ones, it produced little change, and even if the number had been changed to twelve, it would have been of no consequence. But if in antiquity an Ionic nation, for example, which had four tribes, had assumed a different division, it would have been equivalent to a revolution, and could have been done only by entirely changing the character of the people. When the number of tribes at Rome had been reduced to twenty, and was afterwards raised to upwards of thirty, this was done because the inviolability of form had been given up in consequence of other circumstances. Cleisthenes is said to have increased the four Attic tribes to ten; but I believe that he never divided the *demos* into ten tribes, and that the throwing together of the *demos* and the *politae*, which caused the four ancient tribes to disappear, took place at a later time. It is a singular fact, that we can describe the ancient Roman constitution with much more certainty than that of Athens at the same period, although the extant Attic historians lived scarcely a century after the great changes.—N.

tion, therefore, mention is made of the unalterableness of the tribes, and of the ruler's intention to double the population by the admission of new citizens, an intention which the ancient citizens opposed by an appeal to the sacred rites of religion. But we here see a ruler who is not a mere magistrate, but one who has it in his power to give weight to his authority: as far as the form was concerned he yielded, but he virtually introduced the change by forming second centuries. Centuries and tribes were originally identical, each tribe containing one hundred *gentes;* but what these second centuries were, is quite uncertain. One supposition is, that, as many of the old gentes had become extinct, Tarquinius formed new ones; supposing, for example, that those of the Ramnes had thus been reduced to fifty, the king would have added fifty new gentes as *secundi Ramnes*, to complete the number one hundred. We have an example in the Potitii, who became extinct in the time of Appius Claudius, when, it is said, they still consisted of twelve families. The history of exclusive families shows how rapidly they become extinct: in Styria there were formerly 2,000 noble families; at present there scarcely exist a dozen: in the duchy of Bremen the nobles entitled to take part in the diet were within fifty years reduced to one half of their original number, only because they tolerated no marriages except among themselves. In Lüneburg the government was formerly in the hands of the houses (*gentes*), of whom at present only one remains. It is not impossible that Tarquinius may have united the remnants of the ancient curiae, and then supplied the number of the wanting gentes. What recommends this conjecture, is the fact that there continued to be some difference between the old and the new gentes; the new centuries certainly had not so much influence as they would have had, if they had been constituted as separate tribes.

It is a very dangerous thing to seek for allegories in historical statements, and then to presume to derive from them historical facts. Thus as Ancus Marcius was the creator of the plebs, and as Tarquinius is said to have been murdered by the Marcii, we might infer that Tarquinius, who belonged to the Luceres, and had introduced them into the senate, perished in an insurrection of the plebeians. But this is a most hazardous conjecture, and for this reason I have not printed it in my history. In mentioning it here I rely on that confidence which a man may claim who has devoted himself to these investigations for eighteen years almost uninterruptedly, and who even before that time had with fondness spent many a year upon them. Do not mistake possibilities for historical results.

The tradition which represents Tarquinius as the acknowledged head of the twelve Etruscan towns leads us to speak about the Etruscans. Of all the nations of antiquity they are perhaps the one concerning which the most different things have been said, though our materials are of the slenderest kind, and concerning which accordingly the greatest misconceptions have been formed. The impositions of such persons as Annius of Viterbo, Inghirami and others, are of the most impudent character, and yet have become the groundwork of many later productions: they misled Dempster, and through him Winckelmann was deceived. In the eighteenth century the Italians ceased indeed to forge documents, but with the greatest conceit they pretended to explain the inexplicable. Many Etruscan monuments with inscriptions exist, but few are large. Five years ago an altar was dug out which is covered on three sides with inscriptions; a cippus was found at Perugia, a coffin at Bolsena, etc. These monuments have been published either separately or in collections, particularly by Lanzi; some works of art also bear inscriptions; to interpret them has a great charm, because if we could read them, a new light would be thrown upon our investigations. This has given rise to the confident assertions that they can be explained, and the most arbitary interpretations have been put upon them. The Eastern languages and the Celtic have been resorted to for assistance, until at length Lanzi proceeded on the supposition that the Etruscan was a kind of Greek, and, contrary to all the rules of grammar, arbitrarily made out some bad Greek; with all our Etruscan monuments, we know nothing, and are as ignorant as we were of the hieroglyphics previously to the time of Champollion; nothing but large bilingual inscriptions can be of any assistance. We may say with certainty that the Etruscan has not the slightest resemblance to Latin or Greek, nay, not to any one of the languages known to us, as was justly remarked even by Dionysius. This passage of Dionysius has been intentionally overlooked, or its positive meaning has been distorted into a conditional one. The Umbrian on the Eugubinian tables resembles Latin.

Dionysius states that the Etruscans looked upon themselves as an original people descended from no other race, and which called itself Rasena[4] and knew nothing of the names Tyrrhenians and Etruscans; nor of the Grecian traditions respecting them. But the Greeks had two distinct traditions about the Tyrrhenians, which they referred to the Etruscans: the one recorded by Hellanicus stated that Pelasgians from Thessaly had settled at Spina at the mouth of the Po, whence they proceeded across the mountains into Etruria; according to the second related by Herodotus, the Lydians, in the time of Atys, are said to have been visited by a famine, whereby a part of the people was obliged under Tyrrhenus to emigrate to Italy. This latter statement is controverted by Dionysius with that sound criticism which we sometimes meet with in his work, that neither the language nor the religion of the Etruscans bore any resemblance to that of the Lydians, and that neither the Etruscans nor the Lydian historian Xanthus were acquainted with it.[5] Dionysius here saw correctly, because he was not confined to books, but could judge from personal observation. The other tradition he treats differently; he does not give it up, but refers it to the Aborigines and not to the Etruscans. The Italian antiquaries, on the other hand, have either clung to the Lydian tradition, or referred the emigration of the Pelasgians from Thessaly to the Etruscans, and they say that the inhabitants of Cortona (Croton) were not at all different from the neighbouring tribes, notwithstanding the protestation of Herodotus. I can here give only the results of my investigations about the Etruscans. In the new edition of the first volume of my Roman history, I have proved that the name Tyrrhenians was transferred by the Greeks to the Etruscans, just as we use the name Britons when we speak of the English, or Mexicans and Peruvians in speaking of the Spaniards, in America, because the Britons, Mexicans and Peruvians originally inhabited those countries, although a new immigrating nation has established an order of things so entirely new that we perceive no more traces of

---

[4] Rasena, probably not Rasenna; *Ras* is the root and *ena* the termination: as in Porsena, Caecina; the Etruscans, like the Semitic nations, did not double the consonants.—N.

[5] C. O. Müller has shewn that the work of Xanthus was undeservedly looked upon by the Greeks as spurious.—N.

an earlier condition than if it had not existed at all. The
Tyrrhenians were a people quite different from the Etruscans,
but inhabited the sea coast of Etruria, as well as the whole
southern coast, as far as Oenotria, that is Calabria and Basili-
cata. These Tyrrhenians were Pelasgians just as much as
those of Peloponnesus and Thessaly, and when we read in
Sophocles of Τυρρηνοί Πελασγοὶ in Argos, when according
to Aeschylus, Pelasgus, son of Palaechthon, ruled in Argos,
when according to Thucydides Tyrrhenians lived on mount
Athos and in Lemnos, and according to Herodotus at the foot
of Hymettus, we must recognise them everywhere as branches
of the same stock. In the history of Asia Minor there is a
gap beginning after the destruction of Troy, and we must
fill it up by supposing that the Lydians, Carians and Mysians
advanced from the interior towards the coast into the territory
of Troy, and that the Maeonians and other Pelasgian tribes
were partly subdued and partly expelled. The Maeonians,
who are always distinguished from the Lydians, were likewise
Tyrrhenians, and are so called by Ovid in the fable of Bacchus.
These were the Tyrrhenians that gave their name to the
western coast of Italy and to the Tyrrhenian sea, and whom
the Romans called Tusci. Both names were afterwards transferred to the Rasena who descended as conquerors from the
Alps. This view at once renders the account of Herodotus
perfectly clear, and is now generally adopted both in Germany
and England. The tradition in Herodotus is a genealogy
intended to explain how it happened that Lydians existed
in Italy as well as in Lydia.

There is one difficulty, which though it does not weaken
the evidence of my view, is nevertheless a surprising fact,
namely, that after the Etruscan conquest of the Tyrrhenian
country, the language of the Rasena is the only one that is
found on the many monuments, and that we do not find a
trace of inscriptions in a language akin to the Greek, such as
we must suppose the Tyrrhenian language to have been. But
in the first place, almost all the inscriptions have been discovered in the interior of the country, about Perugia, Volterra,
Arrezzo and other places, where the original population was
Umbrian and only a very few on the coast about Pisa, Popu-
lonia, Caere and Tarquinii; some more have lately been found
at Tarquinii, but have not yet been published. We might

also say, although no Tyrrhenian inscriptions *have* hitherto
been found, still they may yet be discovered; but such an eva-
sion is worth nothing.   Under the rule of a conquering nation
which imposes a heavy yoke on the conquered, the language
of the latter frequently becomes quite extinct: in Asia and
many other countries, it was the practice to forbid the use of
the vernacular tongue, in order to prevent treachery.   The
Moors were, in many respects, mild rulers in Spain, and the
country flourished under them; but in Andalusia one of their
kings forbade the Christians to use the Latin language, under
penalty of death, the consequence of which was that a hundred years later not a trace of it occurs.   The whole Christian
population of Cæsarea spoke Greek down to the eighteenth
century; when a pasha prohibited it, and after the lapse of
thirty or forty years, when my father visited the place, not one
of the inhabitants understood Greek.   When the Normans
conquered Sicily, the only languages spoken in the island were
Greek and Arabic, and the laws were written in Greek as late
as the time of the emperor Frederic II., but afterwards it disappears all at once.   The same thing happened in Terra di
Lecce and Terra di Otranto, where afterwards the names were
Italian, while the language of common life remained Greek,
until 200 years later, in the fifteenth century, it died away.
In Pomerania and Mecklenburg the Wendic language disappeared within a few generations, and that without an immigration of Germans, but merely because the princes were
partial to the German language; the conquerors of Branden-
burg forbade the use of Wendic under penalty of death, and
in a short time nothing was spoken but low German.   The
Etruscans had quite an aristocratic constitution, and lived in
the midst of a large subject country; under such circumstances
it must have been of great importance to them to make their
subjects adopt the Etruscan language.

The conquering Rasena must have come down from the
Alps, since according to Livy and Strabo the Raetians as well
as the other Alpine tribes, the Camuni, the Lepontii on the
lake of Como, and others, belonged to the race of the Etruscans.   No ancient writer has ever asserted that they withdrew
from the plains into the Alps in consequence of the conquests
of the Gauls, and it would be absurd to think that a people

which fled before the Gauls from the plain of Patavium, should have been capable of subduing Alpine tribes, or should have been tolerated among them, unless the Alpine districts had before been in the possession of their kinsmen. There is a tradition, probably derived from Cato, that the Etruscans conquered 300 Umbrian towns; these towns must be conceived to have been in the interior of Tuscany, a part of which bore the name of Umbria for a long time after; and a river Umbro also is mentioned. The Etruscans therefore are one of the northern tribes that were pushed southward by the pressure of those early migrations of nations which are as well established in history as the later ones, although we have no written records of them; they were migrations like that which had pressed forward the Illyrians, in consequence of which the Illyrian Enchelians about the fortieth Olymiad penetrated into Greece and plundered Delphi, as Herodotus relates. Such a migration must have driven the Etruscans from the north. They at one time inhabited Switzerland and the Tyrol; nay, there can be no doubt that the Etruscans in those countries experienced the same fate as the Celts in Spain, and that some tribes maintained themselves there longer than others. The *Heidenmauer* (the heathen-wall) near Ottilienberg in Alsace, which Schweighäuser has described as one of the most remarkable and inexplicable monuments, is evidently an Etruscan work; it has exactly the character of the Etruscan fortifications, such as we find them at Volterra, Cortona, and Fiesole. Some have called this kind of architecture Gallic, but without any foundation, as we see from Cæsar's description, as well as from other ruins and buildings in Gaul.

In central Italy there are two essentially different modes of fortification; the one consists of what are commonly called Cyclopean walls formed of polygonal stones which are put together intentionally without any regular order; such a wall is raised around a hill so as to render it almost perpendicular, but on the top of the hill there is no wall; a path (*clivus*) accessible on horseback leads to the top and there are gates both below and above. In this manner the Roman and Latin hills were fortified. The other kind of fortification is Etruscan: on the highest ridge of a hill difficult of access, a wall is built, not of polygons but of parallelopipeda of extraordinary dimensions and very rarely of square blocks; the wall runs along

the ridge of the hill in all directions; such is the case at
Volterra, and of the same kind is the above mentioned wall in
Alsace. I do not place the construction of the latter in a
very remote time, but conceive it to be the work of a tribe
akin to the Etruscans, which long maintained itself in that
country against the Celts; although I must add, that I should
not like to refer to the wall in question as an irrefragable
argument for the existence of such a tribe in that district.
Now the Etruscans first settled in twelve towns in Lombardy,
extending to about the present Austrian frontier towards Piedmont (Pavia was not Etruscan), in the south from Parma to
Bologna, and in the north from the Po to Verona; they then
spread farther, and in the country south of the Apennines they
either founded or enlarged twelve other towns, from which
they ruled over the country. The common opinion is, that
the Etruscans were a very ancient people in Italy, and I
myself entertained this view for a long time; but in Tuscany
they were not very ancient, and in the southern part of Tuscany, which now belongs to the papal dominion, they did not
establish themselves till a very late period. Herodotus relates,
that about the year of Rome 220 the unfortunate Phocaeans
were conquered in a sea fight by the Agyllaeans of Corsica
and the Carchedonians, and that those of them who were
taken prisoners were stoned to death. When Heaven punished the Agyllaeans for this cruelty, they sent to Delphi, and
Apollo ordered them to offer Greek sacrifices, and worship Greek
heroes. Now all writers are unanimous in stating that Agylla
bore this name as long as it was Pelasgian, and that afterwards
the Etruscans called it Caere. We may with great probability
look upon Mezentius, the tyrant of Caere in the legend which
Virgil with his great learning introduced into his poem as the
Etruscan conqueror of Caere; he afterwards appears as the
conqueror of Latium, and demands for himself the tenth of its
wine or even the whole produce of the vineyards. The Etruscan conquests belong to the period of the last kings of Rome,
and are connected with the expeditions of the Etruscans against
Cuma and into the country of the Volscians; they spread
into these districts about the time between the sixtieth and
seventieth Olympiads; according to Cato's statement, which is
certainly of great weight, they founded Capua in the year of
Rome 283. The shortness of the time in which that town is said

to have risen to greatness and declined again, which Velleius mentions as an objection, cannot render the fact improbable. Capua had after all existed for 250 years before it became great, and New York is a far more surprising instance of rapid growth. The flourishing period of this people therefore was the time when Hiero of Syracuse defeated them near Cuma, and they began to decline at the beginning of the fourth century of Rome; the Romans were then rising, and about the middle of that century the Gauls deprived the Etruscans of the northern part of their dominion, their possessions about the river Po.

When people began to perceive that the Alban origin of Rome could not be maintained, Rome was looked upon as an Etruscan colony, and I myself brought forward this opinion. It forms the ground-work of the first edition of my history, because I then considered the Albano-Latin origin to be erroneous; the Etruscan origin seemed to me to be confirmed by several circumstances, particularly by the statement of one Volnius in Varro, thatthe names of the earliest Roman tribes were Etruscan; and also by the observation that the secret theology of the Romans had come from Etruria, that the sons of the first ten in the Roman senate learned the religious laws in Etruria; and lastly, that the worship of Jupiter, Juno, and Minerva in the Capitol was probably of Etruscan origin. But an unbiassed examination afterwards convinced me that this theory was unfounded; and that the two original elements of the Roman state were Latin and Sabine (though I do not wish to dispute the later addition of an Etruscan element), that Rome is much older than the extension of the Etruscans in those districts, and consequently that either the statement of Volnius is groundless, or the names of the tribes are of a more recent date than the tribes themselves, and lastly, the great influence of the Etruscans about the time which is commonly designated as the reign of Tarquinius Priscus and Servius Tullius is perfectly sufficient to explain all the Etruscan institutions at Rome. No ancient writer ever speaks of an Etruscan colony at Rome. The only question now is, whether the Etruscans extended their dominion at so early a period, that even in the time of Tarquinius Priscus they were in possession of Tarquinii and the neighbouring places, or whether they did not begin to appear about and beyond the Tiber till the sixtieth Olympiad.

Before we proceed to describe the changes which took place in

those times, we must give the history of the Etruscans as far as it
is known, and add a sketch of the earliest constitution of Rome.

All we know of the history of Cuma is very obscure. Its
foundation is assigned to a period more remote than that of
any other Greek city in that district, which could not have
been done had not Cuma ceased at an early period to be a
Greek town and come into the hands of the Oscans, before
people in that country began to write Greek. All towns
undoubtedly had eras from their foundation, the fixed chronological data furnished by which were afterwards reduced to
Olympiads; for it was not till very late that the Greeks began
to reckon according to Olympiads. Timaeus (Olymp. 120—
130) was the first who did so; Theophrastus did not. Now
where a town like Cuma was lost to the Greeks, they had no
trace of the era of its foundation, nor anything to take as a
guide except the genealogies of its ctistae (κτίσται.) When
therefore, it was stated that this or that person had founded a
town, they ascended genealogically backward to Troy and the
heroes; and this is the reason why Cuma was thought to be
200 years older than the surrounding Greek towns: its era
had been lost very early, but it was certainly not older than
those of the other cities of similar origin. All that was known
about Cuma probably existed in Neapolitan chronicles, of
which Dionysius made use. His description indeed of the
war waged by the Etruscans against Cuma is mythical, for the
Volturnus is said to have flowed back towards its source and
the like; but this is a secondary matter; Herodotus too is
mythical, when he describes the destruction of the Carthaginian army which fought against Gelon, but the occurrence
of the war itself is not on that account to be doubted. About
the sixty-fourth Olympiad, the Cumans were in their highest
prosperity and in possession of Campania; if therefore the
Etruscans besieged Cuma at that time, they must then have
been a conquering nation, a fact which beautifully agrees with
Cato's statement, that Capua existed only 260 years after its
foundation, meaning that it then became an Etruscan colony.
We thus obtain the period from 250 to 280 years after the
building of Rome (according to our common chronology) as
the time during which the Etruscans must have crossed the
Tiber. Between A.U. 220 and A.U. 230, Herodotus represents
Agylla as a town which consulted the oracle of Delphi; but

that the Etruscans, who were so proud of their own religion, should have done so, is wholly inconceivable, more especially as there existed an inveterate hatred between Etruscans and Greeks; hence the Romans received from the *libri fatales* which were of Etruscan origin, the command to sacrifice a Greek man and woman and a Gallic man and woman.[6] This national hatred shews itself everywhere, as in Pindar and in the Bacchic fable, where things are said of the Tyrrhenians which must be referred to the Etruscans. The Etruscans accordingly appear on the Tiber much later than is commonly supposed; they gradually extended their sway, attained the height of their power, maintained it for two generations, and then declined with ever-increasing speed.

The early Etruscan history is scarcely known to us at all; in Tuscany we find twelve towns, perfectly independent of one another, yet at times united in common undertakings. Each of these towns was governed according to custom by a king, but there is no trace in any of the Italian nations of hereditary monarchies such as we see in Greece; these towns moreover formed no artificial confederacy, but a league sometimes arose spontaneously, when they were assembled for common deliberation near the temple of Voltumna; they had also one priest, who presided over the whole nation. It seems probable—as the Romans did not understand the Etruscan language, we must take their statements with great caution— that in general enterprizes one of the kings was chosen, whose sovereignty the other towns recognised, and to whom they gave up the ensigns of royalty; but this distinction does not appear to have always been the result of an election, the supremacy being often assumed by some one town; thus Clusium was the capital of Etruria in the war with Porsena. Our historians conceive Rome to have stood in the same relation to these Etruscan towns, which are said to have sent to Tarquinius Priscus, or, according to others, to Servius Tullius, the ivory throne and the kingly insignia. Neither story is historically true, but it is an indication that under her last kings Rome was at the head of a mighty empire, which was much larger than in the first 160 years of the republic: and of which Rome itself still preserves traces. It seems to have been recognised as the capital more particularly in

[6] Liv. xxii. 57. It was not from the Sibylline books, as Plutarch says.—N.

relation to Etruria, but this is only a transitory circumstance which may have been changed several times even under the kings.

The Etruscans bear all the marks of an immigrating people, and were probably not much more numerous than the Germans, who at the beginning of the middle ages settled in Italy. The towns possessed the sovereignty, and in the towns themselves, the burghers. The territories of the towns were large but had no influence; and it was this very oligarchical form of government, which rendered Etruria weak by the side of Rome, since arms could not be put into the hands of the people without danger.

Dionysius, who very carefully gives us the exact expressions of his authorities, says, that the magnates of the Etruscans assembled with their clients for war. Among the Romans to enlist the clients, was only a last resource when the plebeians refused to go out to fight. Other circumstances also suggest that Etruria was inhabited by clients under a territorial aristocracy. During the advance of the Gauls, when the people on the left bank of the Tiber deserted Rome, she attached to herself those on the right bank; Caere obtained the isopolity; and four new tribes were formed of those who during the war had deserted Veii and Falerii.[7] The history of the insurrection of Vulsinii also shows the people in the condition of subjects, as I have shewn in the first volume of my Roman history. The Vulsinians gave to their clients the constitution of a plebs in order to ward off the Romans; the plebs afterwards crushed their former masters, and the latter then threw themselves into the arms of the Romans, and allowed them to destroy their town. Such an oligarchy existed everywhere, whence we find so small a number of towns in Etruria, the whole country from the Apennines to Rome containing no more than twelve. The power of the nation therefore was only in the first stage of its development; there was no continuous and growing life, nor any elements of a national existence as among the Romans and Samnites, who evidently did not oppress the old Oscan population, but became one

[7] They were evidently not formed of *transfugae*, as Livy says, but of whole tribes which joined Rome in order to escape oppression; this is perfectly according to analogy, for only two tribes were formed out of the Volscians, and the same number also out of the Sabines.—N.

with it and even adopted their language. The Lucanians, on the other hand, who were a branch of the Sabines, stood in quite a different relation to the ancient Oenotrians, for otherwise the number of their citizens would have been very different from that mentioned by Polybius. Opposite kinds of policy in these cases bear opposite fruits. The insurrection of the Bruttians was nothing else than a revolt in which the Oenotrians, who had been clients even under the Greeks, broke their chains, when they came under new lords who treated them still more harshly. The Etruscans, notwithstanding their wealth and greatness, could not keep their ground against the Romans; their towns did not form a closely united state like that of the Latins, nay, not even like that of the Achaeans, and in the fifth century of Rome, most of them laid down their arms after one or two battles; the only exception was that very Vulsinii where the clients had been changed into a plebs and which defended itself for thirty years. The Samnites resisted Rome for seventy years, but the Lucanians for only a very short time.

The Etruscans have been treated with great favour by the moderns, but the ancients shewed them little respect. Among the Greeks, very unfavourable reports were current about their licentiousness and luxurious habits, although in regard to art, justice was done them to some extent; the perfection of all the mechanical parts of art and the old-fashioned forms had a great charm; the *signa Tuscanica* were as much sought after in Rome as old pictures are now among ourselves.

The Etruscans were esteemed especially as a priestly people, devoted to all the arts of prophecy, especially from meteorological and sidereal phenomena, and from the entrails of victims: the art of discovering the future by augury was the peculiar inheritance of the Sabellian people. All this must surely be regarded as a wretched system of imposture. I will not deny that the observations of lightning led the Etruscans to interesting discoveries: they were aware of the lightnings which flash forth from the earth, and which are now acknowledged by naturalists, but were denied as late as thirty years ago. I am now less than formerly inclined to believe that they were acquainted with conductors of lightning; such knowledge would not have been lost so easily; moreover it is not said that they attracted lightnings, but that they called them forth.

In history, the Etruscans show themselves in anything but a favourable light; they were unwarlike and prone to withdraw from an impending danger by acts of humiliation, as in modern times so many states have done between the years 1796 and 1813. The descriptions of their luxurious habits may be exaggerated, but they are not without foundation; for nearly two centuries they lived in the most profound peace under the dominion of Rome and exempt from military service, except in extraordinary emergencies, as in the Hannibalian war; and it must have been during that period that they possessed the immense wealth and revelled in the luxuries of which Posidonius spoke.

The Etruscans also had annals, of which the emperor Claudius made use; and some few statements may have been taken from them by Verrius Flaccus and Varro. Their most celebrated hero is Caeles Vibenna, who is the only historical point, properly speaking, which we know in the history of the Etruscans. Caeles Vibenna is said by some to have come to Rome and to have settled on the Caelian hill; but according to others, who followed the Etruscan traditions, he died in Etruria, and his general, Mastarna, led the remnant of his army to Rome, where he is said to have named the Caelian hill after his own commander. Caeles always appears, in our accounts, as a *condottiere*, as an independent general of a gathered host, unconnected with the towns, just like the Catalonian hosts at the beginning of the fourteenth century, and the East Indians in the eighteenth. His subsequent fortunes are not known; but the emperor Claudius states, from Etruscan books, that his faithful general, Mastarna, having gone to Rome and settled on Mount Caelius, was received into the Roman state under the name of Servius Tullius. This is possible enough, whereas the Roman tradition about Servius Tullius lies entirely within the sphere of the marvellous. The god of fire, it is said, appeared to Tanaquil in the ashes on the hearth, whereupon she ordered her maid to lock herself up there in bridal attire; the maid became pregnant and gave birth to Servius Tullius. As a sign of his descent from the god of fire, his head was surrounded by a fiery halo whenever, during his infancy, he was asleep; and in the conflagration of a temple his wooden statue which was within remained uninjured. Conceited expositors have cautiously attempted to give to this narrative also the appearance of history: many who think his descent from a servant maid inconsistent, make him the son of a noble of Corniculum, who is said to have died, leaving behind him his wife in a state of pregnancy, in which she was taken to the king's palace. Others say that his mother indeed was a servant, but his father a king; the fiery halo also is interpreted as a symbol of his precocious mind; *non latuit scintilla ingenii in puero*, as Cicero says. But the ancient poets were in earnest and did not mean any such thing. We have the choice; we may either leave the origin of Servius Tullius in obscurity, or believe that the Etruscan traditions are true. I am of opinion that Etruscan literature is so decidedly more ancient than that of the Romans, that I do not hesitate to give preference to the traditions of the former. As Tarquinius Priscus was represented to be an Etruscan, merely because it was clear that there existed an Etruscan element at Rome, which on account of his name was referred to Tarquinius, so people described Servius Tullius as belonging to another race, especially as Rome would not be indebted to an Etruscan for the important reforms ascribed to this king. But as they could not connect him with any distinct gens, they went back to mythology and represented him like Romulus as the son of a god, and like Numa as the husband of a goddess. The mother is of no consequence to the son of a god.[8] We cannot, however, draw any further inferences; for the statement that he was an Etruscan and led the remnant of Caeles Vibenna's army to Rome is of no historical value. Livy speaks of a war with Veii, but only in a hasty manner; from which it is evident he knew it to be a mere forgery in the Fasti.

In the tradition, Servius appears as a Latin who obtained possession of the throne not even by a regular election: to him are traced all the political laws, as all the religious laws are to Numa, a proof that neither of them appeared as an historical individual even to Livy. The gens Tullia, to which Servius must have belonged either by birth or by adoption, is expressly mentioned as one of the Alban gentes that settled on the

---

[8] The above passage respecting the Etruscan origin of Servius Tullius belongs to the lectures of the year 1826, but I was unwilling to suppress it, although further on (p. 99) we have a different view, taken from the lectures of the year 1828. The discussion here introduced may be compared with that in the *Rom. Hist.* vol. i. p. 385, etc., but the above is clearer and more definite.—ED.

Caelius, and accordingly belonged to the Luceres; thus we have here a king of the third tribe, or, since this tribe was closely connected with the commonalty, the throne is occupied by one of the commons who is said to have come from Corniculum. He obtained the sovereignty without an election, but was afterwards recognised by the *curiae.* Historical facts may be embodied in this tradition; but it is difficult to guess what legal relations were intended to be expressed by this story. Servius is important in three respects; he gave the city the legal extent which it retained down to the time of the emperors, though suburbs were added to it; he was the author of a constitution in which the plebs took its place as the second part of the nation; and he established an equal alliance with the Latins, who previously had been either in a state of war with, or of compulsory dependence on, Rome.

In these respects, Servius is so important that we cannot help dwelling upon him. For the sake of greater clearness, I shall here treat of Tarquinius Priscus and Servius Tullius as if they were historical personages, their names representing men who though not known to us, really existed, and in fact serving the same purpose as x, the symbol of an unknown magnitude in mathematics; we shall thus, as I have already remarked, start from the earliest appearance of Rome previously to the change ascribed to Servius.

In its primitive form Rome was a town on the Palatine surrounded by a wall and ditch, with a suburb and a Sabine town on the Quirinal and the Tarpeian Hill. Rome grew out of the union of the two towns whose united citizens were subsequently designated by the common name of Romans. Servius combined into one whole that which before was divided into parts, and inclosed the city on all sides with fortifications and walls no less than five miles in circumference. The accounts of this wall and moat are not fables; the wall was perfectly preserved as late as the time of Augustus and Pliny, so that there was no room for fiction. Dionysius, who generally derived his materials from books, cannot have been deceived here, for he must have often seen the wall, it being a common promenade for the Romans. Rome then, in the time of Servius, was a city as large as Athens after the Persian war, and in our days would be accounted a place of considerable importance.

All modern states, with the single exception of the canton of Schwyz, in their governments and divisions have reference to territorial circumstances. Each town is divided into districts and wards; and in constitutional governments the representation is based upon these divisions; whoever lives in a district elects and may be elected in it. But the ancients viewed the soil only as the *substratum* of the state, which they were of opinion existed in the individuals, so that certain associations gave a different character to the relation in which individuals stood to the state. Accordingly the state was divided into a number of associations, each of which again consisted of several families. Every one of these associations had its own assemblies, courts, religious rights, laws of inheritance and of other matters. Whoever belonged to one transmitted these peculiarities to his children and wherever he might live, whether within or without the state, he always belonged to that association. But those who did not belong to it by birth, could be admitted only by a deviation from the rule, if the association permitted it. A person might be admitted into the state with all the rights which the ancients limited to the citizens as such, the rights, for instance, of acquiring landed property and of appearing in the courts of justice; and yet if he did not belong to an association, he was only a pale-burgher, that is, he could not be invested with any office and was not allowed to vote. This was the principle of the earliest states of antiquity, the power of the state in this particular being limited to giving civil rights, or the rights of a pale-burgher, the state could not order an association to receive this or that individual as a member. In many states even the associations themselves had no power to admit a person, as, for example, where there existed close castes, among which there was no right of intermarriage. Such an association, consisting of a number of families, from which a person may withdraw, but into which he either cannot be admitted at all or only by being adopted by the whole association, is a *gens*.[9] It must not be confounded with our *family*, the members of which are descended from a common ancestor; for the patronymic names of the gentes are nothing but symbols, and are derived from heroes.[10] I assume

[9] The German word is *ein Geschlecht.* See p. 71.

[10] In what relates to the earliest times, antiquities and history cannot be entirely separated; the *commentarii pontificum* and also Livy and Dionysius set us the example in this respect.—N.

it is a fact which for the present requires no proof, that the Roman division of the nation into *gentes* answered to the γένη of the Greeks, and to the *Geschlechter* among our ancestors; of this postulate the sequel of my exposition will furnish sufficient historical evidence. Let us first consider the nation respecting which we have more satisfactory information, I mean the Greeks. Their γένη were associations which, notwithstanding their common name, are not to be regarded as families, descended from the same ancestors, but as the descendants of those persons who, at the foundation of the state, became united into such a corporation. This is expressly stated by Pollux (undoubtedly on the authority of Aristotle), who says that the *gennetae* were named after the γένη, and that they were not united by common origin (γένει μὲν οὐ προσήκοντες), but by common religious observances (ἱερά). We, further, have the testimony of Harpocration respecting the Homeridae in Chios; for he says that they formed a γένος which, according to the opinion of those learned in such matters, had no connection with Homer. These γένη moreover resemble the tribes of the Arabs: the Beni Tai are a body of 10,000 families, all of which cannot be descended from Edid Tai; in like manner, the clans of the Highlanders of Scotland were named after individuals, but regarded themselves as their relatives and descendants only in a poetical sense: there were no fewer than 5000 Campbells capable of bearing arms, who looked upon the Duke of Argyle as their cousin.

With regard to the Roman gentes we have no direct testimony like that of Pollux and Harpocration, that they were corporations without relationship; if we possessed Verrius Flaccus, we should undoubtedly learn something definite, but there is an important definition in Cicero's Topica: he there mentions the term *gentiles* as a difficult term to define, and it had become so, because time had wrought various changes in the original constitution of the *gentes;* in the time of Cicero they had lost much of their former importance, and courts of justice had pronounced decisions respecting them. Cicero says: *Gentiles sunt qui inter se eodem nomine sunt. Non satis est. Qui ab ingenuis oriundi sunt. Ne id quidem satis est. Quorum majorum nemo servitutem servivit. Abest etiam nunc. Qui capite non sunt deminuti. Hoc fortasse satis est.* According to this, then, the Scipios and Sullas were *gentiles*, for they were *eodem nomine*, etc.

Supposing a Cornelius had been assigned as a *nexus*, or been condemned to death on account of some crime, he would thereby have ceased to be a member of his gens, and have incurred what the English in feudal language termed a *corruption of blood*. If as an *addictus* he had children, they too were cut off, and did not belong to the gens. The addition *quorum majorum nemo servitutem servivit* excludes all *libertini* and their descendants, although they bore the gentile name of their *patronus ;* but all *peregrini* might of course by common consent be admitted. The latter point, however, is probably an addition which was foreign to the ancient gentile law; for in my opinion there was at first no difference at all in regard to freedmen, they as well as the patrons belonged to the gens; but this was controverted, as we learn from the interesting suit of the patrician and plebeian Claudii (the Marcelli) about the property of a deceased freedman.[11] On that occasion, it was a *res judicata* by the comitia of the centuries, that the patrician Claudii could not succeed to the property in dispute; whence was afterwards derived the doctrine that the *libertini* did not belong to the gens.

Now in this definition there is not a single word about a common origin, a point which could not have been over-looked; and hence it follows that the Roman gentes were of the same nature as the Greek γένη. *Genus* and *gens* are moreover quite the same word; similar variations often occur in the ancient language, as *cliens* and *clientus*[12], *Campans*[13] and *Campanus*, and so also *Romans* and *Romanus*. The genitives *Romanum* and *Romanom* are formed from the old contracted nominative.

It was a peculiarity of the institution of gentes, that the state was divided by legislation into a fixed number of associations, each forming in itself a small state, with many peculiar rights; it is possible that the expressions *jus gentium* and *jura gentium* originally signified something else, and something far more extensive than we understand by them. The number of the gentes is always found to bear so peculiar a relation to the state, that it can never have been the result of chance. In Attica there were 360, a number which the grammarians very

---

[11] It is mentioned in Cicero, *De Oratore.*

[12] I have not been able to discover the form *clientus,* but the feminine *clienta* justifies us in assuming the existence of a masculine in *us.*—Ed.

[13] Nonius, 486. 24; *Campas,* Plaut. *Trin.* ii. 4. 144 ed. Lind.—Ed.

correctly refer to the division of the year or of the circle
The same thing occurs in Germany: at Cologne there were
three orders, each containing fifteen gentes; at Florence their
number was thrice twenty-four, and in Dithmarsch thrice ten.
Now at Rome there were probably thrice one hundred gentes,
that is, three tribes each containing one hundred gentes,
whence Livy calls them *centuriae*, not *tribus*. Between the
division into tribes and that into gentes there usually existed
another, which was called in Greece φράτραι, and at Rome *curiae*,
answering to the *orders* at Cologne and to the *classes* in the
Lombard towns. These *curiae* were parts of a tribe, but comprised several gentes, probably always ten, for common religious
purposes. As each gens had its own *gentilician sacra*—for
sacra familiarum, which are sometimes mentioned by modern
writers, did not exist among the Romans,—the membership
of a *curia* implied special religious duties, and conferred the
right of voting in the assemblies of the people. The ancients
did not vote as individuals but as corporations, whence it was
customary at Athens from the earliest times, to levy armies
and to vote according to *phylae* (tribes) four of which might
be out-voted by six, although the number of individuals contained in the six might be much smaller than that of the four.
The Romans went even further, as they did not vote according
to tribes but according to *curiae*, the reason evidently being that
at first the Ramnes and Tities alone were the ruling citizens;
and to allow only these two to vote, would have given rise to
difficulties, since it might easily have happened, that one tribe
wished a thing which the other rejected, whereby collisions
would have been produced. But as each tribe was subdivided
into *curies*, and the votes were given according to this division,
that difficulty was removed, and one *curia* might decide a
question; this regulation therefore was necessary previously to
the admission of the third tribe to a share in the government.
At a later time, we find that the order in which the *curiae*
voted and the *praerogativa* were determined by lot, an arrangement which cannot have existed at first, since the Luceres as
well as the two others might thereby have been chosen to strike
the key-note. In this we have a glimpse of the innumerable
stages through which the Roman constitution passed in its
development; and it was this very gradual development which
secured so long a duration to Roman liberty. The secret of

great statesmen, who are met with as rarely as any other kind
of great men, is the gradual development and improvement of
the several parts of an actual constitution; they never attempt
to raise an institution at once to perfection.

Thus the *curiae* stepped into the place of the tribes. In the
reign of Tarquinius, the third tribe, composed of the *gentes
minores*, was admitted to the full franchise. The gentes are
so essential a part of the constitution, that the expressions were
gentes civium majores and *minores*, just as *gentes civium patriciae*
was the solemn expression for *patricii*. It is related that the
senate, which till then had consisted of two hundred members,
was increased by Tarquinius to three hundred by the admission
of the *gentes minores*. This can mean nothing else than that
he gave to the third tribe the full franchise, and admitted into
the senate a number of persons corresponding to that of the
gentes, for such is the natural course of things. At Cologne
too, the second and third orders obtained access to offices later
than the first. What Tarquinius did, was a great change in
the constitution, which was thus completed for the first *populus*.
The third tribe, however, was not at once placed on a footing
of perfect equality with the others, its senators being called
upon to vote when those of the two other tribes had already
done so; and there can be no doubt that their curies also were
not permitted to vote until after the others. As regards the
priestly offices, the members of the third tribe were admitted
only to the college of the vestals. Wherever we find *duumviri*,
they must be regarded as the representatives of the first two
tribes; *triumviri* do not occur till a later period, and wherever
they are patricians, they represent the three tribes. They are,
however, often plebeian, and in this case are connected with
the plebeian constitution, which I shall describe afterwards.

LECTURE VI.

It is one of the most widely spread peculiarities of the earlier
ages, and one of which traces have existed nearly down to our
own days, that a distinction was made between the ancient and
original citizens and those that were subsequently added

to them. This distinction was inconsistent with the notions entertained in the eighteenth century, and has nearly everywhere been abolished. In the United States of America the native population is extremely small; the office of president indeed can be filled only by a native, but in nearly every other respect it is perfectly indifferent how long a person has been in the country: and no distinction is made between the descendants of the first colonists and persons who have just settled there. In antiquity, on the other hand, admission to the franchise was every where more or less difficult, whether the stranger spoke a different language or belonged to the same nation or even to the same tribe of the nation. In nations divided into castes, the admission is quite impossible, though the law is occasionally modified to favour a wealthy or powerful individual, as in the case of a Rajah who became a Brahmin on condition of his causing a colossal golden cow to be made, large enough to allow him to creep in at one end and out at the other. In some parts of the world, even at this day, a stranger is prevented from performing civil acts, and from obtaining offices. The earliest constitution concerning which we have authentic information, though it is in part very obscure, is that of the Jews. They too had such a division; the nation consisted of ten tribes with unequal rights, corresponding to the tribes of the Romans; beside them stood those who had been admitted into the community of the Lord, that is the strangers. The Pentateuch expressly states that some nations were admissible, others not. The persons thus admitted into the community formed a multitude of people, who by religious consecration had become related to the Jews, but were neither contained in the tribes nor shared their rights. In later times, when the Jewish constitution becomes better known to us from contemporary records, the population is divided into Jews and Proselytes, and the latter again into Proselytes of righteousness and Proselytes of the gate.[1] The former had politico-civil rights but were excluded from civil honours; they might acquire land, make wills, marry Jewesses and the like. The Proselytes of the gate were obliged to conform to the Jewish rites and were

---

[1] These points connected with the second temple have been discussed by no one but the great Selden, without whom I should know nothing about them, since the Rabbinical language and literature are unknown to me. Selden's reputation has very much decreased, at least in Germany; but it ought not to be so.—N.

not allowed to act contrary to the ceremonial law, lest they might give offence to the Jews; but they did not participate in civil rights like the inhabitants of the country.

The same institutions, though obscurely described, existed in all the Greek constitutions: much that is untenable has been written about them, but if once rightly understood they furnish a key to all ancient constitutions. In Greece, there existed from the earliest times, by the side of the sovereign body of citizens, an assembly of native freemen who enjoyed civil rights, but had not everywhere the connubium with the ruling people; they were protected by the state and might appear in the courts of justice, but had no share in the government. The condition of foreigners, freedmen and slaves, who had no civil rights was quite different, they being protected against injustice and oppression by taking a citizen as their guardian or patron. It was a very general notion that on the one hand a person might be a native and yet exercise civil rights only to a certain degree, and, on the other, that a stranger had no civil rights at all.

The body of Roman citizens was now extended; it was originally an aristocracy, only inasmuch as the subject people who lived in the neighbourhood stood to those citizens in the relation of clients, for otherwise no aristocratic relation is perceptible. But when Sabine and Latin communities became united with Rome in such a manner as to obtain full civil rights and to be obliged to serve in the armies, there arose a class of persons who, in our German cities, were called *Pfahl-bürger* (Pale-burghers), an expression which no one has correctly and clearly understood[2]. In Germany the word *Pahl* or *Pfahl* (Engl. *pale*; in Ireland the counties about Dublin are said to be *within the English pale*) signified the district in the immediate vicinity of a city; the free people who inhabited it did not in reality possess the rights of burghers, which were peculiar to the gentes (*Geschlechter*), but merely civil rights. The word was then gradually extended and applied to those strangers also, who attached themselves to a country or city (the Greek Isopolites). The investigation of this subject, which is perfectly analogous to the origin of the Roman plebes, has given me much trouble, because in the sixteenth

---

[2] Schilter on Königshoven has some good remarks upon it.—N.

century those relations died away, and no accounts of them
are any where to be found. In the fifteenth century the word
Pfahlbürger still occurs; but in the sixteenth it is nearly obso-
lete.   J. v. Müller did not understand it, and used it without
attaching to it any definite idea.   When a country district, or
a town, or a knight, established such a connection with a city,
two consequences followed; first they mutually protected one
another in their feuds, and the strangers with their vassals
might remove to the city where their civil rights were perfectly free, and where they also had their own courts of justice;
but they did not form part of the ruling body; and in this
respect they were distinguished from the gentes or *Geschlechter*,
who exercised the sovereignty.   Many Transtiberine communities, both Latin and Sabine, entered into this relation with
Rome, and formed settlements, especially on the Aventine.   In
describing this, the Roman historians speak as if Ancus had
removed those people from their homes and given them settlements at Rome, a state of things which is inconceivable; for
all the country around Rome was previously occupied. so that
there they could not settle, and therefore they would have
been obliged to take up their abodes at a distance of many
miles from their fields.   It is very possible, however, that a
few of the highest rank were obliged to settle at Rome.

This pale-burghers' right was extended further and further:
the multitude which enjoyed it did not yet form a corporation,
but contained all the elements of one; they became so numerous at Rome and in the surrounding country, especially
through the alliance with Latium under Servius Tullius, that
the pale-burghers far surpassed the ancient population in
numbers, formed the main strength of Rome, and were especially employed in war.   With their increase, the decrease of
the burghers who married only among themselves kept pace.

In this manner arose the Roman plebes, in Greek δῆμος,
and, as we call it, the commonalty.   The demos comprised all
those who had the lower franchise, and therefore owed obligations to the state, but had no rights except their personal
freedom.   Thus the same relation is expressed by the words
δῆμος and πολῖται, as by *plebes* and *populus*, or *commonalty* and
burghers, or lastly *commune* and *cittadini*.[3]   I further believe

---

[3] These relations were so familiar to our ancestors, that in the old translation
of Livy published at Mayence, *populus* is throughout translated by *Geschlechter*,

that originally the city was not called πόλις but ἄστυ: πόλις like *populus* is a Tyrrhenian word, and both have the same meaning, *populus* being formed by reduplication from πόλις.   The commonalty was the principal part of the population in all states as far as numbers are concerned; but its development did not take place in antiquity in the same manner as in the middle ages.   In the latter, the commonalty lived within the walls of a city; and they often, as was the case at Geneva, settled around the city (*cité* or the nucleus of a town), in what was called *bourg, borgo* or suburbs, and were thence called *bourgeois*.   These suburbs in the course of time were fortified and obtained equal rights with the cities.   In Germany the case was the same, the name only being different, for *burghers* and *Geschlechter* are identical, and towns were formed, especially after the tenth century, when peace had been restored to the world.   Wherever in Gaul a *civitas* existed from the time of the Romans, it was called a *cité*; and where there was a royal villa, it often happened that a place sprung up in the vicinity under the protection of the king, and under the administration of the king's *major domus*.   This is the original meaning of *ville*, as contradistinguished from *cité*.   Hence in French towns a distinction is made between *la cité, la ville* and *le bourg*.   Where the commonalty sprang up within the walls, it had quite different elements.   Throughout the Germanic states, strangers were, on the whole, more kindly treated than in ancient times or in France.   The free settlers in the small Swiss cantons, as in Uri for example, were in reality oppressed commonalties; the inhabitants of St. Gervais were subjects of Geneva.   Among the Slavonic nations, as at Novogorod, such settlers were called *guests,* and their condition was in many respects easier than that of the natives.   In France, down to the time of the revolution, strangers were not able to make a will, and according to the *droit d'Aubaine,* the sovereign succeeded to their property if they were not naturalised. The same law also existed in England, where to this day

and *plebes* by *commonalty.*   There we meet with expressions such as this: " T. Quinctius was elected burgomaster from the *Geschlechter* and L. Genucius from the *commonalty,*" where Livy has *populus* and *plebes.*   This unsophisticated way of viewing things is the reason why the men of the sixteenth century, though without the learning which we require, yet comprehended many things quite correctly.   It is only a few weeks since I found this out.—N.

foreigners cannot acquire landed property. In all the towns of the middle ages in which commerce was the principal occupation, the commonalty soon formed itself into guilds, which obtained their own presidents, and masters of the guild, as well as their own laws and courts: penal jurisdiction could be granted by the kings alone, and wherever it was exercised the guilds took part in it. The masters of the guilds at first appeared in the council only for the purpose of taking care that their rights were not trespassed upon; but they soon became members of the council and finally obtained the upper hand. This is clearly seen in the Italian towns, as, for instance, in the seven ancient guilds at Florence. During the feuds of the Guelfs and Ghibellines, the burghers were still the masters; but soon after, about the time of Rudolph of Hapsburg, the guilds everywhere had the ascendancy, in Italy in the thirteenth, and in Germany about the middle of the fourteenth century, as at Zürich, Augsburg, Strasburg, Ulm, Heilbronn, and the imperial cities of Suabia. During the period of transition, the burghers shared the government with the guilds; wherever this was done, the union was brought about peaceably; but where the burghers refused, it was effected by a bloody contest, which mostly ended in the destruction of the burghers, though the case was sometimes reversed, as at Nürnberg, where the guilds were oppressed.

The union of the burghers and the commonalty or guilds was called in Greece πολιτεία, in Italy *popolo*, the meaning of which is somewhat different from the Roman *populus*.[4] The distinction between the burghers and the commonalty went so far, that at Florence, for example, in the *palazzo vecchio*, and also on books, one sees a lily as the armorial bearing of the city, by the side of a red cross on a silver ground as that of the commonalty (*il commune*). The expression *il commune* may very easily mislead; it does not denote the union between the two orders, but the commonalty, a fact to which Savigny has directed my attention; at Bologna there is a *palatium civium* and a *palatium communis*. The *Capitano del popolo* and the *Capitano di parte* at Florence are likewise difficult to understand. During the struggle between the Guelfs and Ghibellines, the *Capitano di parte*, that is, of the Guelfian

---

[4] The investigations into the history of the Italian towns which I have made, throw great light upon the whole development of the Roman constitution.—N.

party, drove the Ghibellines from the city: he was placed at
the head of affairs, and the franchise of the others was suspended. The only *Capitano* of the burghers was now nevertheless
called *di parte*.

Among the ancients, on the other hand, it was not the
guilds within the walls that formed the commonalty, but the
inhabitants of the country around the city, which consisted of
different elements and embraced both the noblest and the lowest. It is therefore a most preposterous notion, that the
plebes consisted of the poorer classes only. This error was
caused by the imperfection of the language, such as it appears
even in the writings of Plato and Aristotle, for the Greeks
had only one word δῆμος to designate the burghers, the commonalty, the union of both and, in short, the whole people as
well as the populace, in contradistinction to the rulers.
Dionysius knew the word δῆμος only as opposed to βουλή,
and ὄχλος is the proper term for the mass of poor people.
But even he is not free from misconception, which he transferred to Roman history, and as he is much more minute than
Livy, in describing these relations, he has led the restorers of
ancient history to adopt quite erroneous notions. Livy too
does not see clearly into the matter, but he has many passages,
from which it is evident that the annalists whom he followed
had taken the right view. A further cause of confusion
arose from the distress and debts which are often mentioned
as prevailing among the plebes, which, however, as we shall
hereafter see, must be referred to debts arising solely from
mortgages of landed proprietors. The plebes was distinct
from and opposed to the *populus;* the Romans in general
divided all the fundamental powers in nature, as well as in the
realm of spirits, into two parts, describing them as male and
female; for example Vulcan and Vesta are fire, Janus and
Jana the heavenly lights of sun and moon, Saturn and Ops
the creative power of the earth, Tellumo and Tellus the earth
as firm ground; and in like manner, the complete state consists of *populus* and *plebes*, which together constitute the whole.

Within the territory of the ancient city, which extended
about five miles on the road towards Alba, and the limits of
which can be very accurately fixed, there[5] lived under the

---

[5] I am sorry that I did not find this out while I was in Italy, for I had often
been where that limit must have existed, without noticing it. It was not till

protection of the *populus* a number of clients (*cluentes*, from *cluere*, to listen). It was owing to a great variety of circumstances, that these clients came to be connected with their patrons, in the same manner as vassals were with their feudal lords, so as to be obliged to ransom them from captivity, to provide dowries for their daughters, and to defend them in all cases of need and danger. Some of them may have been ancient native Siculians, who being subdued by the Cascans undertook those feudal obligations in order that their lives might be spared; strangers may have settled in the Roman territory as aliens and have chosen a Roman citizen as their guardian; some also may have been inhabitants of those places which were obliged to take refuge under the supremacy of Rome; slaves lastly who received their freedom stood to their former masters in the relation of clients. This class of persons must have been ever on the increase, so long as Rome was in a flourishing condition. The *asylum* in the ancient tradition must be referred to the *clientela*, for the clients had actually come together from all parts. But the free commonalties inhabiting the country districts were quite different: their origin was traced to the times of Ancus. Scaliger, by one of the most brilliant discoveries, found out that Catullus calls the Romans *gens Romulique Ancique*, where Romulus represents the burghers and Ancus the commonalty. The plebes now gradually increased, partly by the extension of the Roman dominion, and partly by the circumstance that, when a family of burghers became extinct and its former clients were without a feudal lord, they attached themselves to the commonalty; many also joined the plebes in consequence of the alliances of Rome with free towns. Such relations, however, are in their origin imperfect, but become more and more clearly developed in the course of time: at first they were entirely local, and es like Tellene, Ficana, and Politorum, were undoubtedly at first quite isolated and without any regularly organised power. There can be no doubt, that a *populus* and a *plebes* existed in all the towns of Italy and also in the Greek colonies of southern Italy and Sicily, the constitution of which bears a strong resemblance to that of the Italian states, and sometimes even adopted the same names.

last year that by a simple combination and with the assistance of Fabretti's map of the neighbourhood of Rome I made the discovery.—N.

LECTURE VII.

PREVIOUSLY to the time of Servius Tullius, the country about Rome was not united with the state, at least probably united only through the king, that is, the inhabitants were obliged to obey the government, but were otherwise treated as perfect strangers; they did not even possess the *commercium*, that is, no patrician could acquire landed property in the country districts any more than a plebeian could at Rome. The same regulation has existed in many countries down to recent times, so that the landed property of a peasant could never be acquired by a nobleman: a very wise and salutary regulation, which unfortunately has been abolished, in consequence of the erroneous belief that it was a foolish restriction. It is still less conceivable that the plebeians should have possessed the legal right of contracting marriages with the patricians; the children of such marriages in all cases followed the baser side. The Mensian law[1] did not invent this, but was merely a re-enactment, determining more minutely what was to be done in difficult cases. But there now appeared a legislator, who, on the one hand, gave to the commonalty a constitution which was complete in itself, and, on the other, devised forms by which this commonalty became united with the whole body of burghers. The former part of his legislation has been entirely overlooked, and the latter appeared quite mysterious to Livy and Dionysius; so great had been the change of affairs since the days of Fabius, who still had a correct view of these matters, though only two hundred years had elapsed from his time. Let him who thinks that this is impossible, look around himself: I believe that in this town [Bonn] there are not three, and at Cologne not ten persons, who can state precisely what the constitutions of these towns were two or three hundred years ago, nay, not even what they were previously to the year 1794. Of this fact I satisfied myself in 1808, in conversation with a Frieslander who had devoted himself to historical pursuits, but was unable to give me any account of the constitution of his country before the French revolution. The same is the case at Brussels. In countries where the

---

[1] Ulpian, *Fragm.* v. 8.—ED.

constitution has been as little changed as in England, it is easier to trace one's way back from the present to the past. It is scarcely credible how great a change two hundred years may bring about, and how distant the whole mode of thinking and living seems to be, when separated from us by some great event. Such was the case in Germany after the seven years' war: all German literature previous to that event presents to our minds a character of strangeness, whereas that of the period immediately succeeding seems to us as if it were more or less of yesterday. Such a crisis in literature and in the entire mode of thinking had taken place at Rome through the influence of Cicero; so that Livy, Virgil, and Horace, must have thought the authors of the preceding period as strange as we think those who wrote before Lessing and Goethe. The Julian law likewise had so completely changed many circumstances in the civil rights of the Latin allies, that the recollection of the preceding state of things was entirely obliterated. The new constitution was simple, and the ancient complicated institutions were no longer intelligible. Thus it becomes evident—and I beg of you to mark this well—that even ingenious and learned men like Livy and Dionysius did not comprehend the ancient institutions, and yet have preserved a number of expressions from their predecessors, from which we, with much labour and difficulty, may elicit the truth.

The statement of Dionysius, derived from Fabius, that Servius divided the city and the country, forming the territory of Rome into thirty tribes, is an instance of what I mean. The division of such a territory was topical: it was not a peculiarity of the Romans, but is also found in Greece, where Cleisthenes took the *ager Atticus* as the basis for the division of the Attic nation. The whole was divided into a fixed number of parts; and in order to effect this, the legislator did not count the large towns, but took a convenient number, such as one hundred, into which the country was to be divided, so that some large places were cut up into parts, while smaller ones were combined into one. These divisions according to a fixed number were so universal among the Romans, that when Augustus divided the city into fourteen regions he did not count the *vici*, but assigned a definite number of *vici* to each region. Now the legislator whom we call Servius Tullius divided the city of Rome in so far as it was inhabited by pale-burghers, into four, and the territory around it into twenty-six regions. This must be looked upon as true: but to prove that this statement of Fabius is correct would lead me too far. Here it must be observed, that the existence of a *populus* nearly always presupposes the existence of a *plebes* as its counterpart, and accordingly a plebes, though unimportant, must have existed even before the time of Ancus. Each of the three towns, *Roma*, *Quirium*, and *Lucerum*, had its own commonalty; these commonalties and the settlers on the Esquiliae under Ancus form the four city tribes; the first or *Palatina* corresponds to the Palatine, the second or *Collina* to the Quirinal, the third or *Suburana* to the Caelius, the Carinae and Subura, and the fourth or *Esquilina* to the Esquiline and Viminal. This arrangement must have been made before the building of the wall of Servius Tullius, as is clear from the existence of the Esquilina. The division was purely geographical, and not at all connected with certain families; the territory was the basis, so that the inhabitants of a certain district formed an association of peasants (*Bauernschaften*). It cannot surprise us to find such associations of peasants within the city, for at Antwerp some of the streets of the extended city are still called by a name (*Burschaften*) which indicates that originally they were inhabited by associations of peasants which formed themselves by the side of the ancient city. Such a division resembles our political divisions based on locality and domicile, but there is this difference, that ours are not permanent: so long as, e. g. I live at Bonn, I am a citizen of Bonn, but I should cease to be so if I were to remove to Cologne. When this division was made at Rome, every one received a name from the region in which he lived, but when he changed his abode he did not thereby cease to belong to the local tribe corresponding to the region in which he and his descendants were registered. I do not mean to say that a change was impossible, but all important changes belong to a time when the tribes had acquired quite a different and much greater importance than they had at first.[2] During the first generation, matters may have remained as they were established by the legislator, but in the course of time changes must have taken place, as people did not always continue to reside in the same district.

[2] In the canton Schwyz, likewise, the country people were divided into four quarters, in which they were enrolled and of which they remained members although they might take up their abode in another quarter.—N.

The names of the country tribes were originally derived not from the districts but from heroes, who were *eponymes* both for the tribes and the burghers; for it is evidently the object of this legislation to amalgamate the different elements of the people; and the recollection of former times, when those places had been independent, was to be effaced by the thought that they were Romans. They obtained common *sacra* like the tribes of the burghers, as is expressly mentioned by Dionysius, for in antiquity sacred rites were always a bond of union. The fact of the plebeian tribes having *sacra* is also established by the circumstance, that Tarquinius Superbus expressly forbade them. Every tribe or region in the city was subdivided into *vici* and those of the country into *pagi*, and each of these *vici* or *pagi* had its own magistrate, as every tribe had its *tribunus*. Regulations of the same kind were in force at Athens; when, for example, a person was enrolled at Acharne and removed to Sunium, he still remained an Acharnian. As these tribes in the earliest times all possessed equal privileges, there was no motive for wishing to be enrolled in another tribe; but afterwards when there arose a difference of political rank among the tribes, of which I shall speak hereafter, matters were changed; the city tribes became inferior to the country tribes, and to be removed from the latter to the former was a *nota ignominiae*, a practice which may be dated from the censorship of Fabius Maximus. The tribes contained only plebeians, the patricians being comprised in the *curies* which also included their clients. When a person became a Roman citizen without the suffrage, he was not received into a plebeian tribe, nor was it possible to be admitted by isopolity or by manumission, and consequently he could not be invested with any office, nor vote in the assembly. The qualification for voting in a plebeian tribe consisted in being a landed proprietor and agriculturist; whoever supported himself by any other occupation was excluded.

In this manner the legislator constituted the two corporations of the patricians and plebeians: he might have united them in two assemblies, as in modern states, but this was impracticable in those early times, as the two corporations regarded each other with hostile feelings. In order to effect an accommodation, Servius created the *centuries*, like the *concilio grande* at Venice, in which, as soon as they entered the hall, all were equal, poor or rich, every one being in simple attire. The object of the centuries was to unite the patricians and plebeians, as well as those who sprang up by the side of the latter and occupied their former position; and at the same time to exclude those who had no landed property, and could therefore give no guarantees to the state. The centuries accordingly contained the whole of the first estate; of the second, those who had the right of voting; of the third, those whose property was equal to that of the second; and lastly, persons engaged in certain honourable occupations. The statements of Livy and Dionysius have caused great confusion in this part of Roman history, as they conceived the tribes differed only in rank and property; they believed that the old citizens, that is the patricians, were divided into curies and were perfectly equal among themselves, but they imagine that this was an oppressive democracy which Servius Tullius abolished by the introduction of the centuries. It is the same error as that into which Sismondi has fallen, who fancies that the Italian towns, on their first appearance in history, were under a democratic government: a monstrous mistake! Had the Roman historians attentively studied the ancient law-books, these things certainly could not have remained obscure to them; but after all, we ourselves have not fared better, for it is now scarcely fifty years since Möser published his first works, stimulated by which we have at length begun to have a clear perception of the early institutions of our own country.

LECTURE VIII.

ACCORDING to the primitive institutions, the burghers[1] served not only on horseback, as was the case afterwards, but also on foot; the same was originally the case in the German cities. These burghers at first had nothing in common with a nobility. We may assume that each gens furnished one horseman and ten foot soldiers; hence the statement in Plutarch that the city

[1] The German word here is *ein Geschlechter*, which in early times, as in the Chronicle of Cologne, denotes a person belonging to a *Geschlecht.*—N.

at first consisted of about a thousand families. This looks very historical, but such additions, as *about* and the like, in Plutarch, Dionysius and other writers of later times, are meant as softeners of colours which appear to them too glaring; the statement is indeed very ancient, but is a symbolical representation of a legal relation rather than an historical fact. Rome in the earliest times contained one hundred gentes, and consequently one thousand foot soldiers, each of whom was considered to have been furnished by a family.[2] Along with these the country districts sent their contingents, which were probably levied according to the townships. The new legislation reformed the phalanx, exempted the burghers from the obligation to serve on foot, and made them serve on horseback with particular privileges. As the whole burthen of forming the infantry now devolved upon the commonalty or plebeians, corresponding privileges were granted to them, and thereby also the means of maintaining their freedom. Thus the population was divided into cavalry and infantry, the commonalty, however, not being excluded from the former. The infantry of all European nations in ancient times resembled the Greek phalanx. It was a mass which produced its effects by its irresistible onset: the men were armed with pikes, with which they advanced against the enemy in eight, ten, or twelve ranks. Barbarians did not fight in close masses, and the Asiatics were only archers. When, as at Rome, the soldiers were drawn up ten men deep, those in the rear were of course less exposed and did not require the same protection as those in front: when they properly closed their shields they needed no coat of mail, and the last rank not even greaves. Some also were light troops or slingers, who threw lead and stones. Every one in the infantry was obliged to equip himself at his own expense and in proportion to his property, the wealthier having to provide themselves with full armour, while those of small means were only required to serve as slingers. When a war was protracted, gaps arose, and after an unsuccessful battle, the first lines might be much thinned, so that a complement became necessary: in such circumstances those standing behind put on the armour of the slain, and stepped into their places. In all campaigns, however, there was also a reserve in case of need. These were the three elements of the Roman

[2] I have neglected to explain this in my history.—N.

army: the *legion* properly so called, the *light-armed*, and lastly the *reserve*, which took the place of those who had advanced from the hindmost lines to supply the place of those who had fallen in front.

Servius thus regarded the whole nation, populus and plebes, as an army, *exercitus vocatus;* but when this army marched against an enemy, it further required carpenters to build bridges, erect tents, and the like, and musicians; the former were constituted as one, and the latter as two centuries; and this addition really completed the army or *classis.*[3] These three centuries did not consist of plebeians, for no plebeian was allowed to engage in any other occupation than agriculture; if he did, he renounced his order, and the censors erased his name from his tribe (*capitis deminutio*), which, however, was not originally attended with any disgrace. There existed at Rome from the earliest time certain guilds, the institution of which was ascribed to Numa: their number was three times three, pipers, goldsmiths, carpenters, dyers, saddlers, tanners, coppersmiths, potters; and the ninth included all other kinds of artificers. The object of this undoubtedly was, to give to the city trades a corporative existence, as in the middle ages; but, as the persons contained in these centuries were usually freedmen and foreigners, the object of whose ambition was to quit these associations and become enrolled in a tribe, the guilds never attained any high degree of prosperity. At Corinth they were of greater importance. By this division into centuries, the plebeians were connected both with the patricians and the *aerarians;* carpenters and musicians, who were of so much consequence in war, had special centuries assigned to them, whereby they obtained the same rights as would have belonged to them if they had served in the army as plebeians. The carpenters, in consideration of their importance, were ranked with the first class, and the musicians with the fifth.

Lastly Servius also took notice of those free people who did not belong to the commonalty. Many of them undoubtedly entered the service either by compulsion or of their own accord;

---

[3] In the account of the battle of Fidenae, Livy is much puzzled by this word: the ancient annalist had the phrase *classibus certare*, which Livy mistook for *fleets,* and hence he expresses a doubt as to the possibility of an engagement between two fleets in the narrow river Tiber; but the phrase merely meant a battle between two armies in full armour.—N.

for I cannot believe that the *capite censi* and the *proletarii* did not perform any service at all; they did not fight against the enemy, but served only in the baggage train, as *lixae* and *calones*, who there is no reason for supposing were always slaves.

Servius thus had a perfectly organised army, which with the addition of the cavalry he made the representative of the nation. He composed the cavalry of the three ancient double tribes or six centuries of Tarquinius Priscus, and to them he added twelve other centuries of the plebes, consisting of the most distinguished persons of the commonalty. Those six centuries comprised the entire patrician order, which on the whole certainly had a small number of votes, but as we shall hereafter see, it had a preponderance in other respects: among them there was perfect equality, and no difference was made on account of age, each century having one vote. Within the plebeian order Servius Tullius separated the more noble and wealthy into two classes, the first consisting of those who had formerly belonged to the Latin nobility, and the second of those who had not. To the class of nobles he assigned the twelve remaining equestrian centuries, and this without any regard to their property, except that those who had become quite impoverished were probably omitted. This is a point which you must bear in mind; for, according to the prevalent opinion based upon an incorrect expression of Cicero (*censu maximo*), the members of these twelve centuries are said to have been the wealthiest among the plebeians. Had the *equites* been the wealthiest then as they were after the Hannibalian war, how senseless would the constitution have been! There would have been no division of property between 1,000,000 sesterces, the sum fixed for this class after the Hannibalian war, and 100,000; whereas, from the latter sum downwards, there appear a number of divisions. We have moreover the express testimony of Polybius, that the property qualification of the equites was something new and opposed to the ancient notions, according to which, descent was the determining point. Lastly, another proof is contained in the testimony that the censors could distinguish a plebeian by enrolling him among the equites, a fact which excludes classification according to property. Under Augustus, things certainly were different; for at that time the most distinguished men could not become equites without a certain amount of property.

Now what is to be understood by *census?* Among ourselves, every kind of property and all rights which can be estimated in money would be included in it. But among the Romans it was different; and it must be regarded as an undoubted fact, that the census affected only *res corporales*, that is substantial objects, and not *res incorporales*, such as debts. If, for example, I have a piece of land worth fifty thousand *asses*, and owe ten thousand to another person, my property in reality amounts to only forty thousand *asses ;* but such things were not taken into account in the census of the ancients, and debts were not noticed at all. This very important and decisive point has not been attended to by the earlier writers on Roman history, because they were not men of business. We must not regard the census as a property-tax, but as a land-tax or a complex of direct taxes: certain objects were estimated according to pre-scribed formulae, at a particular value; and a certain per-centage was paid on that estimate. In the Dutch part of Friesland, lands were valued in pounds, and upon these pounds a certain tax was levied; hence a piece of land was called *pon-demate.* The Roman census then comprised all property in land, and undoubtedly also all *res mancipi ;* but I am convinced that nothing was paid on outstanding debts, even though they might constitute the property of the richest man at Rome. The Attic census, on the other hand, was a real property-tax. The consequence was, that at Rome the whole mass of move-able property possessed very little influence; for the wealthiest capitalist might be entirely free from taxes, landed property having to bear all the burthens, but at the same time enjoying all the privileges: in this point the census accurately corre-sponds to our direct taxes, in imposing which likewise no notice is taken of any debts with which the property in land may be burthened.

All those Romans who were not contained in the equestrian centuries, were divided into such as possessed more than 12,500 *asses,* and those whose census did not come up to that sum. The former were subdivided into five classes; among them were no patricians, but all those plebeians whose census amount-ed to the specified sum, and the aerarians, that is, those who were not contained in the tribes, but whose property placed them on an equality with them; the aerarians were now what the plebeians had been before, and, if they acquired landed property, they were enrolled in a tribe. The first class comprised all those who possessed 100,000 *asses* or upwards, and their property might consist of land, metal, agricultural implements, slaves, cattle, horses and the like: it was divided into eighty centuries. All persons from the age of sixteen to forty-five were counted a *juniores*, those from forty-five to sixty as *seniores*. At Sparta a man was liable to serve in the army till his sixtieth year; but at Rome, the seniores had no other duty than to defend the walls of the city. The seniores undoubtedly did not form one half of the whole population; for under the favourable circumstances of a southern climate, thay could hardly have amounted to more than one third or more accurately to two sevenths; all persons alive above the age of forty-six may perhaps have been no more than one half the number of the juniores. There is every probability that at that time all civil rights and civil duties ceased with the sixtieth year. In Greece, a higher value was set upon the abilities of old age; among the Melians, the whole government was entrusted to the hands of the old men above sixty. Although the seniores at Rome were in number only about half as many as the juniores, yet they had an equal number of votes with them, and probably voted first.

The remaining four classes were valued at 75,000, 50,000, 25,000 and 12,500 *asses* respectively. The second, third, and fourth, had each twenty, and the fifth, thirty centuries. One hundred thousand *asses* were not a large property, being about the same value as 10,000 *drachmae* at Athens, one *as* being about $3\frac{1}{2}$ farthings English. In the army, each century served in a fixed proportion, so that a century which contained a smaller number of citizens performed a greater proportionate amount of military service than the more numerous ones. It was a combined levy from the tribes and the centuries. Within the thirty tribes, one man was always called up from each century of the juniores, so that each century furnished thirty men. Each succeeding class had to furnish a greater number of troops, in such a manner, that while the first furnished a single contingent, the second and third had each to furnish a double one, the fourth a single one, employed as dartsmen, and the fifth again served with a double contingent.

The object of the constitution, based as it was upon property, would have been completely lost, unless the first class had

had a preponderance of votes. The centuries in the lower classes became larger in the number of persons contained in them, in proportion as their property decreased, so that of thirty-five citizens possessing the right of voting six only belonged to the first class. Dionysius is here perplexed in the detail, but he 'had before him a distinct statement that the summing up was made according to property.

All those whose taxable property did not amount to 12,500 *asses* were again sub-divided into two sections: those who possessed more than 1500 *asses* still belonged to the *locupletes ;* those who had less were called *proletarii,* that is persons exempt from taxes: they formed one century. The *locupletes* embraced all the plebeians except the *proletarii,* and were so far quite equal among themselves; but between them and the *proletarii* there was a gulf; any *locuples,* for example, might in a court of justice be surety for another person, but not so a *proletarian :* it is clear that those only could be *vindices* with sums of money, who could prove from the registers of the censors that they possessed such money; there is moreover no doubt that only *locupletes* could be chosen by the praetor as *judices,* or come forward as witnesses, as is proved by the expression *locupletes testes.* The *proletarians* therefore belonged to quite a different category, but whether they were at that time allowed to vote in the plebeian tribes is uncertain.

Such was the constitution of the centuries of Servius, respecting which Livy differs from Dionysius, and both again from Cicero's statement in the second book *De Re Publica;* but this passage though very corrupt may be emended. The sum total is 195 centuries, of which 170 belonged to the five classes, two of the *locupletes* or *assidui* (the *accensi* and *velati*), two of the *proletarians* (the *proletarii* in a narrower sense, and the *capite censi*), the three centuries of the trades; and lastly the eighteen equestrian centuries, six consisting of patricians and twelve of plebeians. The passage of Cicero has given rise to several conjectures, all of which are erroneous, as, for example, that of the celebrated Hermann; but if a person is familiar with such investigations, all may be made clear by the Roman numerical combinations, which I have developed. the object of the whole institution was, that the minority should have a decisive influence[4], wealth and birth having all the

---

[4] The Abbé Sièyes, it is true, has said, *la minorité a toujours tort.*—N.

power; for the eighteen equestrian centuries and the eighty centuries of the first class were first called upon to vote; if they agreed on any question it was decided at once, as they formed the majority of centuries, though they contained by far the smaller number of citizens. Among persons of the same class again it was the minority which decided, because the forty centuries of the seniores contained far fewer voters than the juniores.

If this institution had had the meaning assigned to it by the historians, it would have been highly unjust towards the patricians, who surely still formed a considerable part of the nation. These historians did not see that the patricians did not belong to the classes at all — their presence in the centuries being only a representation, and consequently only of symbolical importance — but they merely said that the patricians probably voted with the wealthy, that is in the first class; now the patricians were by no means wealthy according to the census, since they possessed the floating capital only, not the allodia. But the alleged injustice did not exist, for the centuries stood to the *curies* in the same relation as the House of Commons stands to the House of Lords. No election nor law was valid, unless when sanctioned by the *curies*, which sanction is implied in the expression *ut patres auctores fierent;* the centuries moreover could not deliberate on any subject which had not been proposed by the senate, and no member of a century had the right to come forward and speak; which right was certainly possessed by the members of the *curies.* In the assemblies of the tribes, the discussion of subjects proposed by the tribunes seems indeed to have been permitted, until the votes were taken; but this permission was probably not often made use of. The power of the commonalty in the centuries was thus extremely limited; it was merely one step towards republican freedom. At that time the assembly of the tribes had nothing to do with the framing of laws; they could only elect their own officers and make arrangements concerning their local interests; three may have been among them regulations respecting the poor, for bread was distributed under the superintendence of their aediles at the temple of Ceres; but their most important power was conferred upon them by Servius Tullius, who granted to the plebeians the right of appeal to the assembly of the tribes against sentences of punishment pronounced by a magistrate upon disobedient individuals. The privilege of an appeal to he *curies* had long been possessed by the patricians.

The laws of Servius Tullius may have contained far more than we know, but Tarquinius Superbus is said to have completely abolished them, that is, they were not found in the *jus Papirianum*. It is stated that there were fifty laws. How far the equalisation of the two estates was carried is uncertain; but the exclusive right of the patricians to the domain land, and the pledging of a creditor's person are said to have been abolished. It is more certain that the legislator intended to lay down the kingly dignity and to introduce the consulship in its stead, so that the populus and plebes should each be represented by a consul, an idea which was not realised till one hundred and fifty years later by the Licinian law. Servius looked upon himself as a νομοθέτης like Lycurgus or Solon. This change in the form of government would have been easy, for the kings themselves were only magistrates elected for life, like the stadtholder in Holland, or the President in the United States, who is elected for four years; and such constitutions seem to have been very frequent among the early Italian nations. The election of two consuls appears to have been prescribed in the commentaries of Servius Tullius[5]; but it was not carried into effect, either because his life was taken away too early or because he himself deferred it. Tanaquil is said to have entreated him not to renounce the throne nor to forsake her and hers. What is ascribed to Servius Tullius was not entirely accomplished by this king, but occasioned the revolution of Tarquinius Superbus. Although Servius is stated to have reigned forty-four years, still Livy mentions only one war, that against Caere and Tarquinii, which was brought to a close in four weeks. Dionysius, too, relates no particulars that have even an appearance of truth. The time of his reign is much too long in our accounts, and it was probably very short.

The same legislator is said to have permanently settled the relations between Rome and the Latins. The report is, that he concluded an alliance with the latter and induced them to erect a common sanctuary on the Aventine, in which the tables of the league were set up, and in which Rome offered a sacrifice, a circumstance which, as Livy says, was a *confessio rem Romanam esse superiorem*. The investigation into the condition of the Latin people is one of the most difficult: at first every thing seemed to me to be a mass of confusion, and it

---

[5] Livy says: *duo consules creati sunt ex commentariis Servii Tullii.*—N.

was only step by step that I began to see clearly. It is a mistake of the ancients, which I shared with them till very recently, that Servius acquired the supremacy over the Latins; for this was not gained till the time of Tarquinius, and the very writers who ascribe it to Servius afterwards relate the same thing of Tarquinius. The foundation of the festival of the *Feriae Latinae* on the Alban mount was from very early times attributed to Tarquinius Priscus or Superbus, but a more correct view entertained also by some of the ancients is, that it originated with the Prisci Latini. If the head of the Latins offered up the sacrifice there, and the Romans merely participated in it, it was natural that in order to represent the equality of the two nations a counterpoise should have been formed on the other side, where Rome had the presidency and where the Latins were only guests. This was effected in the temple of Diana on the Aventine; the Latins subsequently, after recovering their independence, transferred this national property to a grove near Aricia. In former times, Alba had been a sovereign city; afterwards the Romans and Albans were united in friendship as two distinct peoples, and under Servius they joined each other in a federal union with a common sacrifice. This confederacy existed not only between the Romans and Latins, but also with the Sabines, and formed a great state, of which Rome was the centre, and there is no doubt that a portion of Etruria also was subject to it. This league we regard as the work of Servius, a view which recommends itself by its simplicity and removes the above-mentioned contradiction. At the time when the plebeians became citizens, the Latins approached the Romans more closely, and stepped into the position which the plebeians had just quitted: so long as there existed any life in the Roman people, we find a constant advance of those elements which had been added to it, and as soon as an old element decayed, the nearest succeeded to its place; those who were first allied were first admitted into the state and formed into plebeian tribes. In this manner the whole of the Roman constitution was in the perpetual enjoyment of a renewed vitality, never stopping in its development. The Roman people ever refreshed and renewed itself, and Rome is the only state, which down to the fifth century constantly returned to its own principles, so that its life was ever becoming more glorious and vigorous, a feature which Montesquieu regards as the only true movement in the life of states.

At a later period checks were employed to repress that which
was coming into existence, and then life began to withdraw and
symptoms of decay became visible.   Traces of this state of
things appeared even a hundred years before the time of
the Gracchi; in their age it broke out and continued to increase
for forty years, until it produced the war of the allies and
that between Sulla and Marius, from which the people came
forth as a disorderly multitude, which could no longer exist
in republican unity, but necessarily required the absolute
authority of a ruler.   It is not difficult to say how Rome
might have renewed and preserved herself for a few centuries
longer: the road to happiness lay open, but selfish and
foolish prejudices blinded the Romans, and when they were
willing to strike into the right path it was too late.

Respecting the gradual extension of the city, the most different opinions are current, which in the common works on
Roman topography, such as that of Nardini, form the greatest
chaos.   Order, however, may be introduced into it.   We must
take into consideration that the form of these statements is not
the same in all writers; for one account says that under this
or that king a particular hill was built upon, another that it
was included in the city, and a third again that the inhabitants
of the hill were admitted to the franchise.   The result of my
investigations is as follows: The ancient city of Rome was
situated on the Palatine; the *pomoerium* of Romulus mentioned
by Tacitus ran from the Forum Boarium across the Circus as
far as the Septizonium, S. Gregorio, the arch of Constantine,
the thermae of Titus, and thence back through the *via sacra*
past the temple of Venus and Roma; this whole circumference
formed the suburb around the ancient city, and was not
enclosed by a wall but by a mound and a ditch.   At that time
there existed on the Quirinal and the Tarpeian rock a Sabine
town, which likewise had its *pomoerium;* between the two
mounds and ditches ran the *via sacra*, in which stood the
Janus Quirini or *Bifrons*, a gateway on one side facing the
Roman and on the other the Sabine town; in times of peace
it was closed, because then intercourse between the two towns
was not desired; but in times of war it was opened, because
the cities were allied and obliged to assist each other.   An
instance perfectly analogous to this exists in the Gaetulian town
of Ghadames beyond Tripolis, which is inhabited by two hostile

tribes; it is divided by a wall into two parts, connected by a gate in the wall, which is closed during peace and opened during war.[6] The Caelian hill was included in the city according to some by Romulus, according to others by Tullius Hostilius, and according to others again by Ancus Marcius; but the fact is, that the hill, which had been inhabited before, was under Ancus united with the city by means of a ditch, the *fossa Quiritium*, running from the ancient ditch of the *pomoerium* as far as the *porta Capena;* this ditch, the first extension of Rome, was made partly for draining off the water, partly for the purpose of protection. The soil there contains too much water to favour excavations, otherwise the most beautiful antiquities would be found in the Circus: the obelisk was dug out thence in the sixteenth century. The *aqua Marrana* is not the *aqua damnata* of Agrippa: in the ancient Circus there was a canal which drew off the water. It is there that we have to seek the *septem viarum vicus*, where Ancus made the ditch, perhaps as far as the sewers (*cloacae*). On the Esquiline likewise there was a suburb. But the Roman and Sabine towns were as yet separated by the Forum, which was then a swamp. The whole district of the Velabrum was still part of the river or a lake, and until it was drained, a topical union of the two towns was impossible. The Janus was the only road, and probably formed a dike.

The works ascribed to Tarquinius Priscus, the immense sewers or *cloacae*, consisting of one main arm and several branches, were executed for the purpose of effecting this union of the two towns. The main arm (*cloaca maxima*), of very ancient architecture, is still to be seen, and still conveys the water into the river: its innermost vault is a semicircle, eighteen palms[7] in width, and is enclosed in two other stone vaults of *peperino* (a volcanic stone from the neighbourhood of Gabii and Alba), one above the other, in the form of semicircles. The hewn blocks are all $7\frac{1}{2}$ palms long and $4\frac{1}{6}$ high; they are fixed together without cement, and are kept in their places by the exactness with which they fit to one another in forming

---

[6] This fact is related by Lyon, *Narrative of Travels in Northern Africa*, London, 1821, 4to. p. 162. The two tribes inhabiting the town are the Beni Walid and Beni Wasid; but according to Lyon's account, the gate in the wall is closed in time of war.—ED.

[7] A Roman palm is about nine inches.—N.

the vault. In the course of 2000 years, the whole structure has not sustained the trace of a change, and earthquakes, which destroyed the city and upset obelisks, have left it unshaken; so that we may assert that it will last till the end of the world. This is the work which rendered it possible to give to Rome its subsequent and final limits: the whole quay is built of the same kind of stones, and shews the same architecture.

The other sewers begin between the Quirinal and Viminal, and run along under the Forum Augustum, the Forum Romanum, and the Forum Boarium to the Velabrum and *cloaca maxima*; they are equally well preserved, but lie deep below the surface of the earth. They were discovered in the time of pope Benedict XIV. They are executed in the same gigantic style, but of *travertino*, from which it is evident that they belong to a later period, though probably to the time of the republic, perhaps to the first half of the fifth century of Rome, shortly before the Hannibalian war. The whole district down to the river, and on the other side of the Capitoline hill, was now inhabitable; but greater designs for extending the city were soon formed. It was desirable to form a high and dry plain possessing the advantage of not being inundated, and to which in times of war the country people might take refuge, on the north side of the Esquiline: for this purpose Servius Tullius constructed his great mound from the *porta Collina* to the Esquiline gate, nearly a mile in length, and a ditch of one hundred feet in breadth and thirty in depth. The soil taken out of this ditch formed the mound, which was lined with a wall on the side of the ditch and was provided with towers. Scarcely anything is left of this enormous work, which amazed Pliny who saw it in a state of perfect preservation, but its direction is still perceptible. In the times of Augustus and Pliny, when it was still perfect, it served as a public walk for the Romans; and Dionysius must have seen and walked upon it often enough. Rome now encompassed all its seven hills, as by this mound the Viminal was first inclosed within the city, which thus acquired a circumference of more than five miles. Here then we have another proof of the absurdity of the opinion of Florus and others, who regarded the time of the kings as a period of infancy (*infans in cunis vagiens*); on the contrary, after the period of the kings, the greatness of Rome was for a long time on the decline.

LECTURE IX.

THE question now is, Who was Servius Tullius? I will not trouble you with the story in Livy; the miracles there related belong to poetry and to the lay of Tarquinius, but attention must be paid to the Etruscan tradition about Servius Tullius and to the fragment of the speech of Claudius on the tables of Lyons, containing the account of Caeles Vibenna and Mastarna, from ancient Etruscan historians.[1] Not the slightest notice has been taken of these tables since their discovery in 1560, and my attention was not drawn to them till I had published the first volume of my history, when I was censured by a celebrated reviewer for having overlooked those documents. I never was so much surprised by any literary discovery, for I then still believed in the Etruscan origin of Rome, and thought that this document might diffuse an entirely new light over the history of Rome. Caeles Vibenna must be an historical personage; he is too frequently and too distinctly mentioned to be fabulous, and his Etruscan name cannot have been invented by the Romans, as the Etruscan language was to them as foreign as Celtic is to us. Nor can it be doubted that he had a friend of the name of Mastarna. But when I examine the legislation ascribed to Servius Tullius,—allowing for whatever deductions must be made from historical certainty, especially in regard to chronology, though there is not the slightest doubt that Servius' reign preceded that of the last king, and that he was overthrown by Tarquinius Superbus who is thoroughly historical,—when, I say, I examine this legislation, I find it so peaceful and so liberal, that I cannot see how a *condottiere* of hired mercenaries (for such were his troops) could have drawn up such mild laws, and have wished to change the monarchy into a republic. The whole civil and political legislation of Servius Tullius has a completely Latin character, and his relation to the Latins also suggests that the lawgiver was of that nation. He may have been a native of Corniculum, and have ascended the throne contrary to established usage; he may have been the offspring of a marriage of disparagement

---

[1] Comp. above p. 67, etc.: it has there been observed that the following remarks belong to the year 1828, and must accordingly be regarded as the last results of Niebuhr's investigations into this subject.—ED.

and the son of one of the Luceres by a woman of Corniculum previously to the establishment of the connubium, and this may be the foundation of the story of his descent; but he surely was not a foreigner nor a commander of mercenaries. I have not the slightest doubt as to the honesty of the emperor Claudius, nor do I undervalue the importance of the Etruscan works (would that we had them! much that we do possess of ancient literature might be joyfully sacrificed for them), but we must not ascribe too high a value to them. What they really were, no one could know before A. Mai's discovery (in 1818) of the Veronensian Scholia on the Aeneid. We there find quotations from two Etruscan historians, Flaccus and Caecina, which immensely reduce the estimate of the value of Etruscan books for the early times, though they might perhaps be invaluable for the later history of that isolated nation. It appears that just as the Romans misunderstood the ancient Latin history and substituted the Tyrrhenian in its place, so the Etruscans adopted the traditions of the Tyrrhenians whom they subdued, and represented Tarchon, who acts a prominent part in Virgil, and may have occurred in the Roman tradition under the name of Tarquinius Priscus, as the founder of their empire from Tarquinii. If Claudius actually made use of the ancient rolls of the Etruscans, which were written backwards, and are mentioned by Lucretius, he was on slippery ground, and how much more so, if he followed Flaccus and Caecina, who wrote quite uncritically. Etruscan literature is mostly assigned to too early a period: from the Hannibalian war down to the time of Sulla, Etruria under the supremacy of Rome enjoyed profound peace, and it is to this period of somewhat more than a century, that most of the literary productions of the Etruscans must be referred. Previously to the social war, literature, as Cicero says, flourished in every part of Italy, but all knowledge of it is lost; there can be no doubt, however, that historical works were composed in other parts of Italy as well as at Rome. Now when a person read in Etruscan books of Caeles Vibenna and Mastarna, and made his combinations, he might with some vanity have asked himself; "What became of this Mastarna? he must surely have been Servius Tullius, whose birth is buried in obscurity." In this manner any one might hit upon this idea; and Claudius, owing to the dulness of his intellect, was the very person to believe such a thing. In like manner, he says of the *tribuni militares consulari potestate: qui seni saepe octoni crearentur*, though it is a fact that there were always six, half of them patricians and half plebeians, or promiscuously, or four patricians including the *praefectus urbi;* once only we hear of eight, in which case the two censors were included, as Onuphrius Panvinius has proved.[2] This may have happened in one or two other instances, but at all events Claudius committed a mistake. Our account of Mastarna therefore is apparently based upon a very slender authority; the Etruscan annals from which Claudius derived his information may have been ancient, but no one says that they actually were ancient. I have here dwelt so long upon this subject because there is an evident tendency, which will not cease very soon, to derive information on the history of Rome from that of Etruria. The discovery of the Etruscan language, and the consequent power of deciphering inscriptions in it, might be of some assistance; but it is hardly conceivable that inscriptions should furnish much light, for history was contained in books only.

The unity of the lay of the Tarquins from the arrival of Tarquinius Priscus down to the battle of lake Regillus cannot be mistaken: it is a splendid subject for an epic poet and would have been much more worthy of Virgil than that of the Æneid. It is credible enough, and seems to be derived from ancient traditions, that Servius Tullius was almost obliged to have recourse to force in order to carry his legislation, that he formed his centuries at his own discretion and on his own responsibility, and that they in return recognised him as king a second time, and confirmed his laws. In antiquity, all such changes were carried into effect in a similar manner. It is further stated, that the patricians were indignant at this legislation, although it took nothing from them, and only granted something to the second estate; that they made attempts to murder the king; and that for this reason he would not allow them to live on the Esquiline where his house stood, but compelled them to reside in the valley below: all this derives great probability as a tradition from its internal consistency. The real tragedy, however, is said to have originated in the king's own house. His two daughters, the one a pious and the other a wicked woman, were married to the two sons of Tarquinius

[2] Liv. v. 1. with the commentators.

Priscus: the pious one to the younger, L. Tarquinius, a gallant but ambitious youth, the wicked one to the elder, Aruns. The latter, seeing that her husband was inclined to renounce the throne, offered her hand to L. Tarquinius, and murdered her husband; he accepted the offer and carried out her designs. Tarquinius, then, it is said, formed a party among the patricians, and with them concerted the murder of Servius Tullius. When the king appeared in the curia, he was thrown down the steps, and afterwards murdered in the street by the emissaries of Tarquinius. Tullia, after having saluted her husband as king, on her return home drove over the corpse of her father, whence the street received the name of *vicus sceleratus*.

Although we are not under the sad necessity of considering this as an authentic account, still it may be regarded as an historical fact, that Servius lost his life in an insurrection of Tarquinius, and that the latter was supported by the whole body of burghers, but more especially by the Luceres, his own party (*factio regis, gentes minores*), who therefore derived the greater advantage from the revolution, while the first two tribes felt themselves oppressed. But I am as far from believing all the particulars that have been handed down about the daughters of the aged king, as I am from believing the story of Lady Macbeth. Our habits and manners differ so widely from those of southern nations, that we can form no idea of the possibility or impossibility of their crimes; but even admitting the *possibility* of these accounts, historical they certainly are not. It may be matter of history that the reign of Tarquinius Superbus was brilliant but extremely oppressive, and that he trampled the laws of Servius under foot; but the fearful massacres belong to the poem. Tarquinius has the misfortune to possess a fearful poetical celebrity, and probably to a much greater extent than he deserved. He cannot have entirely abrogated the Servian legislation: though it is possible that he stopped the assemblies of the plebeian tribes, abolished their festivals, and did not consult them on matters of legislation and in the election of magistrates. For the latter there cannot in fact have been much occasion, since the judges for capital cases were elected by the patricians. We read that Tarquinius executed enormous architectural works such as the magnificent Capitoline temple, after having prepared the area for it; and it is possible that he compelled the plebeians to perform such

heavy task work, that many made away with themselves, and
that in order to prevent this, he ordered their bodies to be
nailed on crosses; but we must here be cautious and scrupulous,
for the detail at any rate is uncertain, nor is every thing true
which cannot be asserted to be impossible. I am convinced
that Tarquinius did not abolish the Servian division into
classes, partly because it was an advantage to him to have the
improved military system, and partly because, from the connection he formed with Latium, we must infer the equality
of the constitutions of the two states, so that either Servius
Tullius gave a Latin constitution to Rome, or Tarquinius
Superbus a Roman one to the Latins.

LECTURE X.

ALTHOUGH there is not the slightest doubt of the historical
existence of Tarquinius Superbus, and although we may form
some conception of his revolution, still the account which we
have of the latter is more than doubtful. But a revolution
unquestionably did occur; and the constitution of Servius was
to some extent suspended for the advantage of the patricians,
especially those of the third tribe. It is surprising however
that, notwithstanding this, the third tribe appears after this
revolution to occupy a position inferior to that of the two
others. But the very fact that the interests of the first two
tribes did not harmonise with those of the third, prepared the
way for a popular revolution.

The statement that he entirely abolished the Servian constitution cannot be true, because in his reign the relation of
Rome to Latium continued as before. According to Livy and
Dionysius, the Latins, with the exception of Gabii, were induced to recognise the supremacy of Rome and of Tarquinius;
but Cicero in his work De Republica, says: *Universum Latium
bello subegit.* Of a war with the Latins, there is no trace any
where, and it must be left uncertain whether the other writers
omitted to mention it, or whether Cicero wrote that sentence
carelessly and thoughtlessly. It is probable, however, that

from the earliest times there existed irreconcileable differences between the poetical and historical tradition. The story of Turnus Herdonius has a very poetical colouring. Under Servius, the league with Latium had been one of reciprocity, but that country now entered into the condition in which we afterwards find the Italian allies, that is, the condition of an unequal alliance, by which they were bound *majestatem populi Romani comiter colere*. It would appear that on the accession of Tarquinius at Rome, the Latins refused to renew the alliance which they had concluded with his predecessor.

In the treaty between Rome and Carthage[1] we find Rome in possession of all the coast, not only of the Prisci Latini, but as far as Terracina, which then was probably still Tyrrhenian and not Volscian; its inhabitants in the Greek translation are called ὑπήκοοι. Rome concluded the treaty for them as well as for herself; and it was stipulated that if the Carthaginians should make conquests in Latium they should be obliged to give them up to Rome. This treaty is as genuine as any thing can be, and it is a strange fancy of a man otherwise very estimable[2], to look upon it as a forgery of Polybius. Here then we find Latium still dependent upon Rome, and this dependance is expressly attested by Livy: at the beginning of the republic the relation was one that had been recently established. Afterwards, when all the country as far as Antium rose against Rome, the power of the latter again appears to be on the decline. The *Feriae Latinae* were an assembly of all the Latin people (not merely of the Prisci Latini) on the Alban mount, where accordingly the Latin magistrates must necessarily have presided; but Dionysius relates that Tarquinius instituted the festival, and that a bull was sacrificed, of which the deputies of each town received a share (*carnem Latinis accipere*). The Milan scholiast on Cicero's speech for Plancius[3] says that there was a different tradition; for that some ascribed the festival to Tarquinius Priscus,—this is only an interpola-

---

[1] This document was preserved in the archives of the aediles; and Polybius, as he himself says, translated it not without great difficulty into Greek, since the Romans themselves were scarcely able to read and understand the ancient characters. Such a treaty had to be renewed from time to time, as was often the case in antiquity, and is still the custom in the states of North Africa.—N.

[2] U. Becker in Dahlmann's *Forschungen auf dem Gebiete der alten Geschichte*.—Ed.

[3] Orelli, tom. v. part ii. p.255.

tion for Tarquinius Superbus, caused by the hatred entertained against the latter, just as the foundation of the Capitoline temple was assigned to the former, — and others to the Prisci Latini, that is, to the earliest times. The latter statement is perfectly correct, for these festivals had existed long before Tarquinius, and were in fact as old as the Latin nation itself. But the other account also has some appearance of truth: it arose out of a misunderstanding which may easily be excused; for if Tarquinius Superbus acquired the supremacy over the Latins, it is natural to infer that he also became the president at their sacrifices, just as the Ætolians during their supremacy did at Delphi, whence the well-known expression in inscriptions ἱερομνημονούντων Αἰτωλῶν.

Now in order to be able to make the best use of Latium for his objects, since after all he did not quite trust the Latins, Tarquinius did not allow their troops to form legions by themselves or to serve under their own officers. He therefore combined the Roman and Latin legions, and then again divided them into two parts. The Latins had a division similar to that of the Romans; for both nations had centuries, those of the latter corresponding to the thirty tribes, those of the former to their thirty towns. Tarquinius united one Latin and one Roman century into one *maniple*, and the *primus centurio* was a Roman officer, just as in the East Indian possessions of the English the officers are always Europeans. Livy confounds the *primus centurio* with the *primipilus*. This is the origin of the *maniples*, and is the simple meaning of what Livy relates in a confused manner, though it is not difficult to discover his error.

If, however, we take the separate accounts, we feel not a little perplexed as to what we are to believe. Tarquinius is said to have founded colonies at Signia and Circeii, and to have conquered Gabii by a stratagem. Against the former I have nothing to say; but the latter is a forgery made up of two stories related by Herodotus about Zopyrus and Thrasybulus of Miletus. The treaty with Gabii however is authentic, and from it we must infer that Gabii was not contained in the confederacy of the thirty towns, the league with which had been settled before. The document of the treaty with Gabii existed in a temple as late as the time of Horace, and was one of the few documents that were preserved; Gabii accordingly must have concluded a regular treaty of *isopolity*.

It may easily be believed that Sextus Tarquinius committed the outrage on Lucretia; for similar things are still of every-day occurrence in Turkey, and were frequently perpetrated in the middle ages by Italian princes down to the time of Pietro Luigi Farnese (in the sixteenth century); in antiquity similar crimes are met with in oligarchies and tyrannies, as is well known from the history of Demetrius Poliorcetes at Athens. Cicero is quite right in saying that it was a misfortune that Sextus hit upon a woman belonging to one of the most power-ful families. I readily believe that the woman tried to avenge herself; but the whole of the subsequent events, by which the story acquired individuality, and its connection with the campaign against Ardea, are of no historical value. The king is said to have been encamped before Ardea, and to have con-cluded a truce for fifteen years; but Ardea was dependent upon Rome before that time, since it occurs among the towns on behalf of which Rome concluded the treaty with Carthage. All therefore that remains and bears the appearance of probability is, that Lucretia was outraged, and that her death kindled the spark which had long been smouldering under the ashes.

We are in the same perplexity in regard to the person of Brutus. He is said to have feigned stupidity, in order to deceive the king; and there were several traditions as to the manner in which he attempted to accomplish this object. His mission to Delphi along with the sons of Tarquinius, although the mission from Agylla at an earlier period cannot be doubted, seems to betray a later hand, and probably the same as introduced the stories from Herodotus into Roman history. It is further said that Tarquinius, in order to render the dignity of *tribunus celerum*, the highest after that of the king, powerless for mischief, gave the office to Brutus. But there is every reason for believing that the whole of Brutus' idiocy arose solely from his name. Brutus is undoubtedly an Oscan word connected with the same root as Bruttii; it signifies "a runaway slave," a name which the insolent faction of the king gave to the leader of the rebels because he was a plebeian. How is it conceivable that a great king, such as Tarquinius really was, should have raised an idiot whom he might have put to death to the dignity of *tribunus celerum*, for the purpose of rendering it contemptible? Tarquinius was not a tyrant of such a kind as to be under the necessity of weakening the state in order to govern it; he might have given it power and vigour and yet rule over it by his great personal qualities; nor did the Romans think differently of him, for his statue continued to be preserved in the Capitol with those of the other kings.

The following question formerly occupied much of my attention: how could Brutus who was a plebeian be *tribunus celerum*, since the *celeres* were the patrician *equites*? I think I have discovered the solution. Most writers speak of him as if he had been the only *tribunus celerum*, though it is certain that there were several, as is mentioned even by Dionysius, in his account of the priestly offices when relating the history of Numa. The *celeres* were the *equites*, but the plebeians too had their *equites* : now if each of the patrician tribes had its *tribunus*, is it not natural to suppose that, among the thirty tribunes of the plebeians, there was one who represented the plebeian *celeres* in opposition to the patricians, the plebeians thus appearing as a fourth tribe? The *magister equitem*, whose office is regarded as a continuation of that of the *tribunus celerum*, was not necessarily a patrician; for P. Licinius Crassus was elected to it. This magistrate was at the head of all the eighteen centuries of the *equites*, in which the plebeians preponderated. In the memorable peace between the two estates in the year of the city 388 the plebeians again appear in the light of a fourth tribe, since the three festal days, which were observed at Rome and corresponded with the three tribes, were increased by one, undoubtedly because the plebeians as a body were treated as equal to the patricians though in the eyes of the patricians not so perfectly equal as to entitle them likewise to have three days. My opinion therefore is, that Brutus was tribune of the *celeres* for the plebeians.

In order to give to the revolution its necessary sanction, it is said that Collatinus brought with him Brutus, and Sp. Lucretius brought Valerius. We may positively assert that Sp. Lucretius belonged to the Ramnes, Valerius to the Tities[4],

---

[4] The Fasti, such as we have them, mention four Valerii as sons of Volesus, viz. Publius Poplicola, Marcus, Manius, and Lucius; the last or his son Caius is mentioned only as quaestor. The ancient traditions, on the other hand, knew only two, Publius Poplicola and Marcus with the surname of Maximus. Wherever Volesus occurs, he is described as a Sabine; in the annals which Dionysius followed, he appears as one of the companions of Tatius; while others state that he went to Rome by the command of oracles, which is probably the more ancient tradi-

Collatinus to the Luceres; and Brutus, as we have above seen, may be regarded as a plebeian. It is universally acknowledged by the ancients, that Valerius belonged to the Tities; Cicero states that he was consul with Lucretius and resigned to him the fasces *quia minor natu erat;* but Cicero here confounds *gentes minores* with *minor natu,* the less favoured tribe being called *minor,* for we know from Dionysius that when the first two tribes were placed on an equality, the numbers of the third were called νεώτεροι (*minores*). Collatinus belonged to the gens of the Tarquinii, and was accordingly one of the Luceres. Brutus was a plebeian. Cicero's belief in the descent of the Junii Bruti from our L. Junius Brutus is undoubted, and is worth more than the denial of the writers after the battle of Philippi, when M. Brutus was to be regarded as a *homo insitivus,* that is as an outlaw. We learn even from Posidonius, that the question about the origin of the Bruti was a subject of discussion. Those who consider him to have been a patrician may mention various facts in support of their opinion: there is no doubt that many a patrician gens continued to exist only in some plebeian families, and a *transitio ab plebem* frequently occurred, especially in consequence of marriages of disparagement: the surname in such a case is usually plebeian, but the retaining of so illustrious a name as Brutus would not be surprising. However, so long as the consulship was not open to the plebeians, no Junius occurs among the consuls. In the first period of the republic we read of a tribune of the people called L. Brutus, who became conspicuous as the author of an important *plebiscitum* in the trial of Coriolanus (Dionysius also mentions him at the time of the *secessio,* but this is a forgery). This Brutus is a real personage; but, like the whole narrative of Coriolanus, he belongs to a different time.

Setting aside all the dramatic points in our narrative, we find that after the fall of Tarquinius four *tribuni celerum,* were in possession of the government; and thus formed a magistracy of four men, Sp. Lucretius being at the same time *princeps*

---

tion. To consider the four individuals as brothers, is one of the common genealogical errors; Dion Cassius calls Marcus only a *gentilis* of Publius; and the addition which all others give to the Valerii, *Volesi Filius* or *Nepos,* arose only from the ordinary desire to trace all the members of a *gens* to one common ancestral hero.—N.

senatus, and Valerius *praefectus urbi*. In Livy, every thing happens as on the stage; he mistakes the natural and necessary course of events; but in Dionysius we find some important traces of real history. These four men were in no way authorised to bring any resolution of their own before the assembled citizens, for the patricians could determine upon nothing unless it was preceded by a *senatus-consultum* ($\pi\rho o\beta o\acute{v}\lambda\epsilon v\mu a$), as in all the states of Greece—a fact which is repeatedly noticed by Dionysius. This was the case with the curies as well as with the centuries. The first branch of the legislature that acquired the initiative was the *comitia tributa;* and it is this circumstance which gives to the Publilian law its extraordinary importance. As long as the senate could do nothing without a proposal of the consuls, and the assembly of the people nothing without a resolution of the senate, so long the consuls had it in their power to repress almost every movement simply by obstinate silence. In the present instance, it would seem that the proposal for abolishing the kingly dignity was illegally brought before the curies by the *tribuni celerum;* but Livy suppressed the ancient account contained in the law-books for the sake of his own poetical narrative. The *tribuni celerum* assembled and resolved to propose the abolition of royalty; the proposal was brought before the senate by the *princeps senatus;* the senate and the curies sanctioned it, and this is the *lex curiata*. In order now to restore the constitution of Servius, the resolution of the curies was brought before the centuries also to obtain their sanction (the order is here a matter of indifference); and this is represented as if the army at Ardea had sanctioned the decree.

It is by no means certain that the consulship was instituted immediately after the expulsion of the kings: it is possible that at first Rome was governed by the four *tribuni celerum*, but it is also possible that the number of rulers was at once curtailed and reduced to two. This was certainly not an improvement; but it may have been prescribed in the Servian constitution with the distinct object of placing the commonalty on an equality with the patricians, that one consul should be a patrician and the other a plebeian; and thus it happened that of the first consuls Collatinus was a patrician and Brutus a plebeian; unless their consulship was preceded by that of Sp. Lucretius and Valerius Poplicola. The beginning of the consular Fasti is mutilated, the first part being wanting.

LECTURE XI.

THE consequences of the taking of Rome by the Gauls were not more serious for the city itself than for its history, the sources of which were thereby entirely destroyed. In all such cases, analogy and examples give us the best insight into the state of things, and the chronicles of many places furnish us with instances perfectly analogous in their beginnings. In my native country of Dithmarsch, they begin about 150 years before the conquest of the country, after the great change which formed the burghers and the peasantry into one organised whole, an event which is not touched upon but presupposed. In a similar manner, the Chronicle of Cologne begins its records long after the city was great and flourishing: there were indeed earlier records in all the towns of the middle ages, but they were little valued because they were too meagre, and had lost all their interest because living tradition was no longer connected with them. The chroniclers therefore began at a point which followed immediately after some memorable event. Such also was the case at Rome: there existed a history of the time of the republic but not from its commencement; it began somewhere about the *secessio*, and only a few incidents of the earlier period were recorded, such as the peace with the Sabines in the first consulship of Sp. Cassius, and the war with the Volscians. All the other events, as I have before shewn, were restored according to numerical schemes.

I have already observed, that when the consuls were chosen from the two estates, Brutus represented the plebeians as afterwards did Sextius Lateranus. It is very remarkable, that with regard to all these ancient institutions, the Licinian laws were really and essentially nothing else than a restoration and a re-enactment of those of Servius. The consuls were originally called *praetores* (στρατηγοί in Dionysius); and this was their designation until the time of the decemvirate, when their power was weakened, and the title of consul was substituted as denoting something inferior. Roman etymologists were much perplexed in the derivation of this word; we compare it with *praesul*, and *exsul; praesul* being one who is *before* another, *exsul*, one who is *out* of the state, and *consul* one who is *with* another, that is *collega*, whence *consulere*, to be together for the purpose of deliberating; it has nothing to do with *salire*. The ancients had no idea of etymology; and it is curious to observe how completely blind they were in this respect. The *being together* of a patrician with a plebeian, however, did not last long. It is stated that the expulsion of the Tarquins was at first by no means followed by bitter hostility against them, although an oath had been taken never again to allow a king to reign at Rome; so that it might almost appear doubtful whether the outrage said to have been committed on Lucretia had actually taken place. But the ancients were often inconceivably mild under such circumstances; and it is also possible that the influence of the royal family and of the third tribe was still so great, that it was necessary to grant to the Tarquins the right of election to the consulship instead of the hereditary royalty. In Greek history, too, the royal families become γένη ἀρχικά: the Codrids became archons; those who were elected for ten years, and, at first unquestionably, even those who were appointed for only one year were Codrids. But such an arrangement did not last long, for Collatinus was obliged to abdicate, and the whole gens Tarquinia was banished. It is not impossible that at that time there existed a Tarquinian tribe, the recollection of which was afterwards entirely lost. It is revolting to our feelings that Collatinus, the husband of Lucretia, should have been exiled, and if children of Lucretia were alive and were obliged with Collatinus to quit the country, their banishment would be a startling cruelty, but Lucretia's marriage with Collatinus belongs only to the poem, *neque affirmare neque refellere in animo est*. She was the daughter of Sp. Lucretius Tricipitinus; and this circumstance is much more emphatically mentioned than her marriage, the story of which was probably intended to palliate the fact that not all the Tarquins were exiled, it being necessary to explain why, after all that happened, a cousin of the king had been made consul; and this could not be done more easily than by referring to him the tradition of Lucretia.

The characteristic feature of the consulship is, that it was a limitation of the kingly power to one year, and was elective instead of hereditary; it was further stripped of all priestly functions, and received no τέμενος, which Cicero calls *agri lati uberesque regii*, large estates which were cultivated for the kings

by clients. These *agri* were now distributed among the commonalty in order that the restoration of royalty might become
impossible, and that the consuls might not have the same extensive powers as the kings. The strength of the kings consisted, as among the Franks, in their retainers. Clovis was not
allowed to appropriate to himself any portion of the booty, and
yet he ruled as a despot, and his successors still more so; but
for this power he was indebted to his *comitatus* alone. In the
middle ages and until the thirteenth century, the vassal of a
king was of less importance than a common freeman who carefully preserved his independence. The clients, who cultivated
the estates of princes, were their vassals.

The question now is, was the consulship of such a nature that
it was necessary to elect two patricians without any restriction,
or was it confined to the first two tribes, the Ramnes and Tities,
to the exclusion of the Luceres, or lastly was it a representation
of the patricians and plebeians? No one could offer himself
for the consulship, for at first the senate alone had the right of
proposing candidates. The first of the above hypotheses is
inconceivable; for if the first two tribes or the first two estates
had not been represented, it would have been much more natural to institute a triumvirate. But the idea of a triumvirate
does not occur in Roman history till a later time, a fact which
was entirely overlooked until I discovered the trace of it in
Joannes Lydus, an insignificant writer who had however the
use of excellent materials.

Of a plebeian consulship there is no trace down to the time
of Licinius. According to the treaty with Carthage which is
confirmed by a passage in Pliny, Horatius was elected in the
place of Collatinus, whereas in the common tradition Valerius
Poplicola is called the successor of Collatinus; thus we have
two irreconcilable statements side by side, and we are at liberty
to exercise our criticism here as in the kingly period. The
events assigned to the kingly period, occupying large spaces of
time, admitted of extension and contraction; and it is therefore
a natural illusion to consider as more authentic the subsequent
period, which is counted year by year, and in which only private persons appear on the stage. But the period of uncertainty extends very far down, for the poem which related these
occurrences came down to the battle of lake Regillus. The
story of Coriolanus formed the beginning of another separate

poem. The Fasti present the greatest differences. Three pairs of consuls are wanting in Livy, if compared with Dionysius, during the first thirty years; in regard to one pair, Livy seems to have found a gap in the Fasti, and those Fasti in which this gap did not exist were interpolated; in the two other pairs, Lartius and Herminius are only secondary personages who are mentioned along with the heroes. The necessity of extending the Fasti was felt, because they did not accord with the computation of years, and new consulships were thus forged, but the names were not taken at random, but from extinct families and heroes of secondary rank, and these names were inserted between the consulships of the Valerii in order to conceal their uninterrupted succession. We may therefore also form many conjectures upon other subjects. We know from Dionysius that the Horatii belonged to the *gentes minores*, so that the place of Collatinus was again filled by one of the Luceres; I therefore conjecture that it was perhaps intended that alternately two and two, first, one of the Ramnes and one of the Tities, and next, one of the Luceres and a plebeian should be at the head of the state. This conjecture however cannot be followed up any further. But if Valerius was not the colleague of Brutus, all that is related about him must fall to the ground. After the death of Brutus, Valerius Poplicola is said at first not to have elected a successor, and to have built a stone house on the Velia. The temple of the Penates, erroneously called the temple of Romulus, was situated at the foot of a steep hill, the Velia; the top of it, whereon stood the temple of Venus and Roma, and the arch of Titus, was the *summa Velia*, but the temple of Romulus was *infima Velia*. As the people, that is, the sovereign burghers, murmured at the building of a stone house, Valerius ordered it to be pulled down during the night, assembled the people, that is the concilium of the curies, appeared with his lictors without the axes, and ordered them to lower the *fasces* before the *concio*, whence he received the name of Poplicola. The *populus* here, too, is undoubtedly the patricians or the assembly of the burghers, from whom the consul derived his power, for such homage paid to the plebeian assembly would have been the act of a demagogue, and he would then have been called Plebicola. This beautiful narrative can have no historical value, because, according to the document, Valerius cannot have been consul alone, and tradition always mentions Sp. Lucretius as his first colleague. The reason of his not immediately filling up the vacant place in the consulship, is said to have been his fear of being opposed by one who had equal rights. Sp. Lucretius occurs in some Fasti as consul in the third year instead of Horatius, but then comes the unfortunate interpolation; and in order that the father of Lucretia might not be passed over, his consulship is transferred from the third to the first year.

The Valerian laws are beyond a doubt; and it is a fact that on the whole the Servian constitution was restored. The patricians, as Livy says, endeavoured to conciliate the plebeians; and Sallust too states, that after the revolution the government was at first carried on with just laws and with fairness, but that afterwards it became the very reverse. The election of the consuls by the centuries was preserved in the ritual books, and is therefore not quite certain. The statement, that the first law passed by the centuries was the Valerian law, by which the plebeians obtained the right of appeal to the commonalty, looks indeed very authentic, but is not so. It is quite possible that the first elections were made by the curies, as was afterwards unquestionably the case; but this is opposed to the express tradition that the condition of the plebes was at first far more favourable than afterwards.[1]

LECTURE XII.

ONE tradition about Tarquinius states that he went to Caere and thence to Tarquinii, others make him go to Veii to obtain the assistance of the Veientines. The emigration to Caere is nothing else than a disguise of the *jus Caeritum exulandi*, for this *jus exulandi* always existed between Rome and the *isopolites;* the *jus Caeritum* was especially mentioned in the ancient law-books, and the flight of Tarquinius was believed to have

---

[1] The remainder of this Lecture consists of an account of the artificial chronology of the early Roman history, and has been transferred from this place to page 3, etc. The following Lecture and a part of the next contained the account of the Etruscans, which has been inserted above, p. 55 etc., which seemed to be a more appropriate place.

occasioned it. The tradition of the books is that he went to Caere, and that of the poem that he went to Veii and led the Veientines against Rome. The annalists considered both as insufficient, and thought it most probable that he went to Tarquinii, where kinsmen of his might still have been living. Caere, whither the king's family is said to have gone, is not mentioned at all as having supported them during the war. Cicero, who saw the ancient history of Rome without its interpolations, knows nothing of a participation of the Tarquinians in the Veientine war; and in his Tusculanae, he merely says that neither the Veientines nor the Latins were able to restore Tarquinius. The battle near the forest of Arsia is purely mythical; Brutus and Aruns both fell fighting, and the god Silvanus loudly proclaimed the victory after 13,000 Etruscans and one Roman less had fallen on the field of battle. An account like this can be nothing else than poetry.

Lars or Lar[1] Porsena is an heroic name like Hercules among the Greeks, Rustam among the Persians, and Dietrich of Berne or Etzel in the German lays; the chief heroes of such heroic lays are frequently transferred into history and their names connected with historical events. The war of Porsena is one of those traditions which were most generally current among the Romans; and it is described as a second attempt of the Tarquins to recover the throne.

The Veientine war had had no effect, and there is no further account of it after the death of Brutus. Cicero undoubtedly looked upon this war of Porsena in no other light than as the expedition of an Etruscan conqueror; and it is certain that at that time the Romans were engaged in a highly destructive war with the Etruscans, in which they sank as low as a nation can sink. It was nothing but republican vanity that threw this immediate consequence of the revolution into the shade; and the same feeling gave rise to the dishonest concealment of the Gallic conquest. The tradition must have related a great deal about Porsena, as we may infer from the story respecting his monument at Clusium, which Pliny very credulously describes after Varro, who derived his account from Etruscan books: it is this account in particular, which shakes my faith

---

[1] *Lar* is an Etruscan praenomen which frequently occurs on monuments and probably signifies *king* or *god*. Martial's quantity *Porsĕna* is false: in *Vibenna*, *Caecina* and other words of the same termination, the penult is always long.—N.

in the authenticity of those books, which, to judge from this example, must have been of an oriental character. That monument is described as a wondrous structure, such as never has existed nor could exist, like a fairy palace in the Arabian Nights' Tales. Pyramids stood in a circle and their tops were connected by a brass ring, upon which at intervals rose other pyramids of immense bases, and so on through several stages; forming a pyramid of pyramids, a thing which could never have stood but must have fallen to pieces. It is inconceivable how Varro and still more a practical man like Pliny could have believed the existence of such a monstrosity, the impossibility of which must be manifest even to a boy. That it is an impossibility is confirmed by the fact, that neither Varro nor Pliny saw any traces of the work, whereas if it had really existed, its ruins would be visible at this day, like those of the temple of Belus at Babylon.[2]   There may have been an historical Porsena, who became mythical, like the German Siegfried, who has been transferred to a period quite different from the true one; or on the other hand there may have been a mythical Porsena, who has been introduced into history; but we must deny the historical character of every thing that is related about his war, which has an entirely poetical appearance. To what extent this is the case becomes evident, if we consider the account in its purity and stripped of all the additions made by the annalists. It is a peculiarity of all such poems that they are irreconcilable with other historical facts.

According to the common tradition, the Etruscans suddenly appeared on the Janiculum, and the Romans fled across the river; the poem did not even mention the conquest of the Janiculum, but the Etruscan army at once appears on the bank of the Tiber, ready to pass the Sublician bridge: there three Roman heroes oppose them, Horatius Cocles, Sp. Lartius and T. Herminius, probably a personification of the three tribes. While the Romans were breaking down the bridge, the three heroes resisted the enemy, then two of them, Lartius and Herminius, withdrew, and Cocles, who belonged to the tribe of the Ramnes, alone withstood the foe. After this, we have the account that the Etruscans crossed the river, and that the consuls drew them into an ambuscade on the Gabinian road: this

---

[2] Quatremère de Quincy once had the unfortunate idea of making an architectural restoration of this monument.—N.

is transferred entire from the Veientine war of A.U. 275, where the same thing occurs; the annalists made this interpolation, because it seemed strange to them that the poem should mention nothing further of the war than the defence of the bridge. Livy's account is ridiculously minute. We then find Porsena on the Janiculum. Now how is it possible that Rome could have suffered from such a famine as is presupposed in the story of Mucius Scaevola, if the Etruscans were encamped on that one hill only? for plunderers on the Roman side of the river were easily warded off. Livy states that Porsena carried on the war alone, whereas in Dionysius he appears allied with the Latins under Octavius Mamilius, an evident fabrication to render it intelligible how Rome was surrounded and suffering from famine. There is no mention of any hostility on the part of the Latins, until their great war. But, the fact is that the Etruscans were masters not of the Janiculum only: that the famine was raging furiously is acknowledged by the Romans themselves. In this distress Mucius Scaevola, according to the poem, undertook to kill the king, but by mistake he slew a scribe, who was clad in purple,—a mistake inconceivable in history, and pardonable only in a poem. Mucius then told the king that he was one of 300 patrician youths (one of each gens) who had resolved to murder him; whereupon Porsena concluded peace, reserving to himself the seven Veientine *pagi*, and keeping a garrison on the Janiculum.

If we go into detail and ask, whether such a person as Mucius Scaevola ever existed at all, we come to another question which has been well put by Beaufort[3]: how can Mucius be called by Livy and Dionysius a patrician or a *noble youth*, when the Scaevolae were plebeians? It is probable that the family of the Mucii Scaevolae appropriated this Mucius to themselves, and that in the ancient poems he had no other name but Caius; it is not till the seventh century that two names are mentioned, and afterwards Scaevola (left-handed) was added; whereas the family of the Scaevolae derived this name from quite a different circumstance, Scaevola signifying an amulet. It is impossible to determine how much truth there may be in the story of the ancient Scaevola; the account which has come down to us is evidently poetical.

[3] This war of Porsena and the period of Camillus are treated in an excellent manner by Beaufort, and that period seems to have been the centre round which the other parts of his work were grouped in subordination.—N.

Beaufort really threw great light upon this part of Roman history, by showing that the peace of Porsena was something very different from what the Romans represented it. Pliny expressly states, that by it the Romans were forbidden the use of iron for any other than agricultural purposes; and that hostages were given is acknowledged even in the common narrative: we thus see Rome in a state of perfect subjection: *arma ademta, obsides dati*, an expression which occurs so often respecting subdued nations. Pliny saw the treaty (*nominatim comprehensum invenimus*), but where, is uncertain; a tablet probably did not exist, but he may have found it in Etruscan books. Tacitus in speaking of the conflagration of the Capitol mentions in no less distinct terms the deepest humiliation of the Romans by Porsena, *sede Jovis optimi maximi quam non Porsena* DEDITA URBE, *neque Galli capta* TEMERARE *potuissent;* and what *deditionem |facere* means, is clear from the formula which Livy gives in describing the *deditio* of Collatia to Ancus Marcius, from which we see that it was a total surrender of a nation, comprising both the country and its inhabitants, and that it may be compared to the *mancipatio* or to the *in manum conventio* of women in the civil law. To this period of subjection we must also refer a statement in the *Quaestiones Romanae* of Plutarch, who though he was uncritical made use of good materials: he says that the Romans at one time paid a tithe to the Etruscans, and that they were delivered from it by Hercules. Now a tithe was paid when a person occupied a piece of land belonging to the state (*qui publici juris factus erat*), and the deliverance by Hercules denotes their liberation by their own strength; the payment of the tithe was the consequence of their having given up to the Etruscans themselves, and all that belonged to them (*feuda oblata*). A still stronger proof of the calamity of that time is the diminution of the Roman territory by one third, the thirty tribes established by Servius Tullius having been reduced to twenty, to which, in the year A.U. 259, the *tribus Crustumina* was added as the twenty-first.[4] It was quite a common custom with the Romans when a state was compelled to submit to them, to deprive it of a third part of its territory; it is therefore here also evident, since tribes correspond to regions, and since out of thirty tribes we find only

[4] That this number is correct—the manuscripts of Livy have thirty-one — has been shewn in the new edition of the first volume of my Roman history.—N.

twenty, that in consequence of its surrender to Porsena, Rome, about the year A.U. 260, had lost one third of its territory: of which fact other traces are contained in the *septem pagi agri Vejentium*, the surrender of which has already been mentioned· In the history, in order to conceal the capture of the city, Porsena was made the champion of the Tarquins, and thus it seemed as if the war had, after all, not turned out so unfortunately, since its main object, the restoration of the Tarquins, had not been obtained.

It is further related that after Porsena had returned home, he sent his son Aruns with a part of the army to Aricia, in order as Livy says (this is one of the passages in which he intentionally shuts his eyes to the truth), to shew that his expedition had not been quite in vain. But at Aricia, which was a very strong place, a stop seems actually to have been put to the progress of Porsena, through the assistance of Cuma, for Cumaean traditions also spoke of it: the Romans are said to have behaved with great generosity towards the fugitive Etruscans, whereby Porsena was induced to become their friend, to abandon the Tarquins, and to restore the seven Veientine *pagi;* after this Porsena is not again mentioned. Here we evidently have an awkwardly inserted piece of poetry. It continued to be a custom at Rome down to a late period, symbolically to sell the property of King Porsena previously to every auction; and Livy had good sense enough to see that this custom was not consistent with the statement that Porsena and Rome had parted as friends in arms (δορύξενοι). All becomes clear if we suppose that, after the defeat of the Etruscans at Aricia, the Romans rose and shook off their yoke, a supposition which gives to the story of Cloelia also a consistent meaning; otherwise her flight with the rest of the hostages must necessarily have been injurious. The great migration of the Etruscans is connected with the statement that Tyrrhenians from the Adriatic sea along with Opicans and other nations appeared before Cuma, though in the common chronology there is a mistake of from fifteen to twenty years at the least. These Tyrrhenians were not Etruscans, but the ancient inhabitants of the country, who were pressed forward by the advancing Etruscans and moved in the direction of Cuma.

The result of all this accordingly is, that the Romans carried on an unequal contest against the Etruscans and their king Porsena, to whom they submitted as their master; they lost a third of their territory, and of the rest they paid a tithe; the Etruscan power was broken at Aricia, whereupon the Romans took courage and rid themselves of their masters, but without recovering that part of their territory which lay beyond the Tiber, since even as late as the time of the Decemvirs the Tiber was their boundary, except that probably the Janiculum was Roman, as may be inferred from the law respecting the sale of debtors *trans Tiberim*. Whether the war of Porsena belongs to about the year to which it is assigned, whether it happened two or three years after the consecration of the Capitol, or at a later time, is an important question, in regard to which Livy and Dionysius contradict each other, and are both opposed to all the other authorities. It is easy to perceive that the poem about the war was inserted by the annalists, since the most ancient annals did not mention it at all. In like manner, the lay of the Nibelungen cannot be fixed chronologically; and Johannes Müller was obliged to use violence in order to obtain a fixed chronological point. Such poems know nothing of chronology. Valerius Poplicola appears in the battle of lake Regillus; and this determined what place should be assigned to the story. It is more probable, according to other accounts, that the war took place ten years later than is commonly supposed, that is, shortly before the beginning of the hostilities between the patricians and plebeians. I infer this from the statements respecting the census which I do not altogether reject, though I will not venture to assert that they are authentic in their present form: but they are certainly a sign of the rise and fall of the numbers of Roman citizens. The person with whom these statements originated, unless they were very ancient, had formed a view of Roman history according to which the number of citizens during the period in question rose from 110,000 to 150,000, and again sank to 110,000. If this rising or falling were in harmony with the annals, we might say that some speculator had represented his view in this numerical scheme; but such a person from vanity would never have mentioned a diminution of the population, for we find on the contrary that in times when the population is decreasing the annals mention victories and conquests. For this reason, I believe that some account, more ancient than the annals, intended to shew by a numerical scheme how Rome and Latium by unequal wars lost a part of their population. No one can answer for the correctness of the numbers, but the statement is independent of the annals. On this account I refer the statement—that, between the battle of lake Regillus and the insurrection of the plebes, Rome was for a long time deprived of one-third of its population—to the fact that the war of Porsena and the reduction of the Roman territory which was its consequence belonged to this very period; the reduced number of citizens nearly corresponds to the loss of one-third of the territory; and the circumstance that it does not perfectly correspond, arises perhaps from the fact that only the plebeians were counted, not the patricians, or that some of the inhabitants of the lost districts emigrated to Rome.

LECTURE XIII.

IN the history of Rome, as in that of most other nations, the same events are frequently repeated, just as after the Gallic conquest the Latins and their allies revolted from Rome, so they broke through the alliance which had been established under Tarquinius, as soon as Rome was humbled by the Etruscan conqueror. The confederacy between the two states which was formed under Servius Tullius, had become a union under Tarquinius, as notwithstanding the obscurity which hangs over all the detail, is clear from the combination of the Roman and Latin centuries into maniples. This combination is the more certain, as Livy mentions it in two passages, first in his account of the reign of Tarquinius, and secondly in the eighth book, where he describes the military system. The authorities from which he derived his information, contained testimonies quite independent of one another; and he quotes them without understanding them, but in such a manner that we are able to deduce from his statements the correct view of the annalists: when he wrote the second passage, he was certainly not thinking of the first. The relation between the two nations may have been arranged in such a way, that Rome alone had the *imperium*, but the Latins received their share of the booty; or

that the two nations had the *imperium* alternately. But in the
treaty with Carthage, we see that Rome had the supremacy
and that the Latins were in the condition of *perioeci*. The
result of the war, the only events of which are the conquest
of Crustumeria which is historical, and the battle of lake
Regillus which is poetical, was that the Latins from the condition of *perioeci* rose to that of equal allies, just as at Groningen
the surrounding districts were raised to an equality with the
city, and in all foreign transactions appeared only as one province with the city.

Tarquinius and his family are said to have been the first
cause of the war; and I readily believe that he was not unconnected with the movement, since his family connection with
Mamilius Octavius at Tusculum has an historical appearance,
but we cannot possibly class the battle of lake Regillus as it is
related, among the events of history. It never has occurred
to me to deny that the Romans endeavoured to restore
their dominion by war; but it is quite a different question,
whether a great battle was fought near lake Regillus under the
command of the dictator Postumius, in which the Latins
were conquered and thrown back into their former condition.
Nay, if we may infer the cause from its effects, which cannot
be done as surely in moral affairs as in physical ones, the Latins
were not by any means defeated, for they attained — after a
considerable time, it is true — their object, a perfectly free
alliance with Rome. The contrary might be inferred from the
circumstance that Postumius, who is said to have been dictator
or consul, was surnamed Regillensis; but the Claudii too were
called Regillani, and names derived from districts were quite
common among the patricians; the Sergii for instance were
called Fidenates; Regillensis may have been taken from the
town of Regillus, as some surnames were derived even from
parts of the city of Rome, as Esquilinus, Aventinus and others.
Gentes bearing such names stood to those places in the relation of patrons. Names derived from victories do not occur
till very late, and the greatest generals before Scipio Africanus,
did not derive surnames from the places of their victories,
as Livy himself remarks at the end of the thirtieth book.

The Romans imagined that they had gained a complete victory
in the battle, as is clear from the story about the Dioscuri: near
lake Regillus, where the whole district consists of a volcanic

tufo, the mark of a horse's hoof was shown in the stone (just as
on the Rosstrappe in the Harz mountain), which was believed
to have been made by a gigantic horse of the Dioscuri, a tradition which, down to the time of Cicero, lived in the mouths
of the people. After the battle, the Dioscuri, covered with
blood and dust, appeared in the comitium, announced the
victory to the people, gave their horses drink at a well, and
disappeared. Of this battle we have no accounts except those
in which there is an evident tendency to make it appear historical; but the poem nevertheless cannot be mistaken. The
descriptions of the battle in Livy and Dionysius have more
points of agreement with each other than is usual between the
two writers, though Dionysius's description more resembles
a bulletin, while that of Livy is fresh and animated, like the
Homeric description of a struggle between heroes, the masses
being entirely thrown into the background. The cessation of
the peace between the two states had been announced a year
before, in order that the many connections of friendship might
be dissolved as gently as possible, and that the women might
return to their respective homes. Tarquinius had gone to
Mamilius Octavius, his son-in-law, and all the Latins were
aroused. The dictator led the Romans against an army far
superior in numbers, and Tarquinius and his sons were in the
enemy's army. During the contest, the chiefs of the two armies
met: the Roman dictator fell in with Tarquinius, who being
severely wounded retreated, while the *magister equitum* fought
with Mamilius. T. Herminius and the legate M. Valerius as
well as P. Valerius fell, the last being slain while endeavouring
to rescue the body of M. Valerius. In the end, the Roman
equites gained the victory by dismounting from their horses
and fighting on foot. The consul had offered a reward to
those who should storm the hostile camp; and the object was
gained at the very first assault, in which the two gigantic
youths distinguished themselves.

Even the ancients were greatly perplexed about M. and
P. Valerius, for Marcus soon after re-appears as dictator, and
Publius had died even before the battle; both accordingly are
described as sons of Poplicola; but this is an unfortunate remedy,
since a P. Valerius as a son of Poplicola again occurs in the
Fasti afterwards. The poem however was not concerned about
Fasti and annals: we cannot regard the two Valerii as sons of

Poplicola, but as the ancient heroes Maximus and Poplicola themselves who here fought and fell.   The legend undoubtedly related that Tarquinius and his sons were likewise slain, and the statement that the king was only wounded arose from the record in the annals that he died at Cuma.   The introduction of the dictator Postumius was certainly a pure interpolation, and the poem undoubtedly mentioned Sp. Lartius, who could not be wanting here, any more than M. Valerius.   The reward offered by the dictator refers to the legend of the Dioscuri, as in the war against the Lucanians under Fabricius, when a youth carried the ladder to the wall, and afterwards, when the mural crown was awarded to him, was not anywhere to be found.

This battle forms the close of the lay of the Tarquins, as the lay of the Nibelungen ends with the death of all the heroes. I am as strongly convinced of this now as I was eighteen years ago.   The earliest period of Roman history is thus terminated, and a new era opens upon us.   There is no definite time to which the battle can be assigned; some suppose it to have taken place in A.U. 255, others in A.U. 258.   Some represent Postumius as consul, others as dictator, a sufficient proof that the account is not historical, for if it were, the Fasti would at any rate have accurately marked such an event.   It is not impossible that peace with the Latins was restored in A.U. 259; and if we were to take this statement literally, it would confirm the victory of lake Regillus.   It might be conceived that the Latins were defeated there, and submitted to the condition which Tarquinius had established for them; but that afterwards the senate, from other motives, restored to them the constitution of Servius Tullius; be this as it may, peace was renewed between the Romans and Latins before the secession of the plebes. For many years after the battle of lake Regillus, Livy records nothing about the Latins, whereas Dionysius relates a variety of events which however are arbitrary inventions: even down to the first resolution of the people that their prisoners should be restored to them, we know nothing of the history of this period, except that under Sp. Cassius, Rome concluded a treaty with the Latins, in which the right of isopolity or the *jus municipi* was conceded to them.   The idea of isopolity changed in the course of time, but its essential features in early times were these: between the Romans and Latins and between the

Romans and Caerites there existed this arrangement, that any citizen of the one state who wished to settle in the other, might forthwith be able to exercise there the rights of a citizen. This was called by the Greeks ἰσοπολιτεία, a word which does not occur till the time of Philip, when people began to feel the want of uniting in larger communities or states. Even before the war, a definite relation had existed between Rome and Latium, in which the *connubium* and *commercium* were recognised, the citizens of one state having the full right of acquiring quiritarian property in the other, of carrying on any trade and of conducting their law-suits in person and without a patron: they were in fact full citizens, with the exception of political rights. Such a relation may exist along with equality between the two states as well as with the supremacy of one; the change which now took place was that Rome recognised Latium as possessing equal rights with herself. Soon after the Hernicans also joined the league, so that then all the three states appeared in foreign matters as one state. This union ceased after the Gallic war. The treaty of Sp. Cassius in A.U. 261 is not to be regarded as a treaty of peace, but as the foundation of a legal relation; it is inconceivable how this treaty could have been mistaken, as was done even by the ancients, when they incidentally mention it. Dionysius quotes this treaty in words which display undoubted authenticity: he himself indeed can never have seen the tables in the *rostra*, for even Cicero in his speech for Balbus speaks of them in a manner which shews that he merely remembered having seen them; but many Roman authors, as Macer and others, must have known them, and Cincius, who lived two hundred years before was well acquainted with them. This, like the Swiss treaties may be called an eternal treaty, for it was to remain in force as long as heaven and earth endured. But thirty years afterwards it became antiquated through the influence of circumstances, and at a later period it was restored only for a short time. It established perfect equality between the Romans and Latins, which even went so far as to make them take the supreme command of the armies alternately. Either state when in distress was to be supported by the other with all its powers, and the booty was to be divided.

This treaty contains the key to the understanding of another event. It is about this time that we first meet with a dictator, which was properly speaking a Latin magistracy, and existed not only in particular towns, but might, as Cato states, rule over the whole Latin people. It is therefore probable that the Romans likewise now elected a dictator, who ruled alternately with a Latin one, whence the *imperium* was conferred for six months only. Among the Etruscans, the king of each town had one lictor, and the lictors of all the twelve towns, when they united for any common purpose, were at the disposal of the one common sovereign. In like manner, the twelve Latin and the twelve Roman lictors were given to the common dictator: the two consuls together had only twelve lictors, who attended upon each alternately. At that time we also find frequent mention of a *magister populi;* it is uncertain whether he was from the beginning the same person as the dictator, or whether he was elected from Rome alone, the dictatorship probably existing only in consequence of the connection with Latium. A consul might have been dictator without there necessarily being a *magister populi;* but whenever there was a *magister populi*, there must necessarily have been a dictator to represent Rome in transactions with foreign nations; for it is not natural that there should have been two names for the same office. It is probable that for a time there was a dictator every year, that office being sometimes given to one of the consuls, and sometimes to a person especially elected.

In the history of the period which now follows, we find ourselves upon real historical ground: we may henceforth speak with certainty of men and events, although now and then fables were still introduced into the Fasti. That errors did creep in is no more than the common lot of all human affairs, and we must from this point treat the history of Rome like every other history, and not make it the subject of shallow scepticism to which it has already been too much sacrificed. A new war broke out in which Cora and Pometia fell into the hands of the Auruncans: afterwards these towns are said to have been recovered by the Romans and Latins, a statement which is very problematical. At the beginning of this period we still meet with great discrepancies and absurdities; but of what consequence is it that Livy relates this war twice, or whether it happened in A.U. 251 or A.U. 258. We may safely assert that there was an Auruncan war, that Cora and Pometia were lost, but afterwards recovered. It is a singular thing that when a great loss was simply marked in the ancient annals of the Romans, the vanity of their descendants could not leave it as it stood, but attempted to compensate for the calamity by a bold lie. The deliverance of the city by Camillus is the most striking, though not the only instance in Roman history of this propensity; and Beaufort has well demonstrated its fictitious character; the account is in itself inconceivable, and is contradicted by Polybius, who states that the Gauls returned with the booty to their own country in consequence of an inroad of the Veneti; I do not mean to say that in this case the falsifier was not one of the ancient bards, for Camillus was as much a subject of poetry as the taking of Veii. In like manner every great defeat in the Samnite wars which cannot be concealed, is followed by a victory which is altogether unconnected with the course of events, and is intended to make up for the loss. The same thing occurs in the wars with the Volscians and Aequians. This is a common human weakness, which in disastrous times we ourselves may experience. The Italians of the fifteenth century insisted upon being the genuine descendants of the ancient Romans; and accordingly Flavius Blondus says that Charlemagne drove all the Lombards and other barbarians from Italy. When the news of the battle of Austerlitz arrived in the north of Germany, it was received with the greatest consternation; but a report soon spread and found its way even into the newspapers, that the French had gained a victory in the morning indeed, but that in the afternoon the Austrians and a part of the Russians rallied and most completely defeated the French. I witnessed similar absurdities in 1801 at Copenhagen. The history of Greece and of the middle ages is remarkably free of such fictions.

I therefore believe in the invasion of the Auruncans: when Rome was laid low by the Etruscans, she was forsaken not only by the thirty towns, whose common sanctuary was the temple of Ferentina, but also by the coast towns which had been Latin, and were recognised in the treaty with Carthage as being under the protection of Rome. There is little doubt that Antium and Terracina, like the Latin towns properly so called, shook off the Roman supremacy and expelled the colonists. Both these towns were afterwards unquestionably Volscian, but it is an erroneous opinion that they were so originally; they form no exception to the general Tyrrhenian population of the coast. In an ancient Greek ethnological work which was certainly not an invention of Xenagoras, but was derived from Italiot authorities, Antium is described as a town of the same stock as Rome and Ardea; and Romus, Antias and Ardeas are brothers. Terracina did not receive its Volscian name of Anxur till afterwards. These places became Volscian either by conquest or by voluntarily receiving Volscian *epoeci*, because they were in want of support, or lastly by being obliged after their revolt from Rome to throw themselves into the arms of the Volscians.

The Volscians were an Ausonian people, and identical with the Auruncans, so that the same war is sometimes called Volscian, sometimes Auruncan. They are said to have come from Campania, and the Auruncans in Campania are known to have been Ausonians, *Aurunici* and *Ausonici* being the same words. Cora and Pometia, two Latin colonies, are stated to have revolted to them; but we cannot determine whether they expelled the Latin colonists, or whether the taking of these places was a mere conquest. It is certain however that the Auruncans were in possession of Cora and Pometia, and penetrated even into Latium, where it is not impossible that they may have been defeated by the Romans.

LECTURE XIV.

SALLUST, who in the introduction of his lost history of the period subsequent to the death of Sulla gave, like Thucydides, a brief survey of the moral and political history of his nation, which is preserved in St. Augustin, says that Rome was ruled fairly and justly only so long as there was a fear of Tarquinius; but that as soon as this fear was removed, the *patres*[1] indulged in every kind of tyranny and arrogance, and kept the plebes in servile submission by the severity of the law of debt. In like manner, Livy states that the plebes, who down to the

----

[1] That is, the patricians; for all correct writers use the term *patres* only of the patricians and not of the senate.—N.

destruction of the Tarquins had been courted with the greatest care, were immediately afterwards oppressed; that until then the salt which belonged to the *publicum* had been sold at a low price, that tolls had been abolished, and that the king's domain had been distributed among the plebeians, in short the φιλάν-θρωπα δίκαια of Servius Tullius had been restored. Lastly, we must notice the ancient tradition, that Brutus completed the senate, *qui imminutus erat,* with plebeians: as he was *tribunus celerum* of the plebeians and afterwards plebeian consul, it is not at all unlikely that he admitted plebeians into the senate, though not such a large number as is stated. But this cannot have been of long duration; plebeian senators cannot have continued to exist down to the decemviral legislation; for Sallust, who in the speech of Macer displays an uncommon knowledge of the ancient constitution, says, and his statement is believed by St. Augustin, one of the greatest minds endowed with the keenest judgment, that the patricians *soli in imperiis habitabant;* whence it is probable that when things became quiet, they expelled the plebeians. Analogies are found in the histories of all countries, just because it is in accordance with human nature. There can be no doubt that a strong party of the exiled royal family had remained behind, as usually happens in all revolutions, or a new party may have formed and joined the exiles, as in the Italian towns of the middle ages. Whatever we may think of the battle of lake Regillus, and however little we may believe in the existence of a cohort of Roman emigrants in the army of the Latins, we may with confidence assume that the royal exiles were joined by a large number of Romans, who continued to keep up a connection with persons of the same party in the city, as did the φυγάδες in Greece; and as was the case in the great rebellion in Britain, when the Stuarts were abroad, and the Irish catholics and the Scotch presbyterians, who were subdued and partly expelled by Cromwell, joined the ancient nobles who were scattered about with the royal family; the same thing took place in the French revolution also. As long as Tarquinius, who was personally a great man, lived, the patricians hesitated to go to extremes in their innovations, though they insulted the plebeians and deprived them of the *imperia;* they may even have expelled them from the senate, and they certainly did not fill up with plebeians those places which became vacant by death.

The aristocratic cantons in Switzerland were always mild towards the commonalty when they were threatened by outward dangers, otherwise they were harsh and cruel; so also, immediately after the English revolution of 1688 the rights of the dissenters were far greater than twelve or fifteen years later. What particular rights the plebeians may have lost cannot be said; it is not improbable that the Valerian law respecting the appeal to the tribes was formally repealed; but that law had previously become a dead letter, because it could be maintained only by bringing a charge after the expiration of his office against the consul who had acted contrary to it; and this was a step which the plebeian magistrates no longer dared to take. But the real oppression did not begin till the fear of an enemy from without was removed.

Whether the law of debt had been altered by Servius Tullius, whether Tarquinius had abolished the Servian laws, and whether Valerius restored them, are questions in regard to which we cannot believe Dionysius unconditionally. Tarquinius is said to have completely destroyed the tables on which the Servian law was written, in order to efface the recollection of it. This sounds very suspicious; for if only a single person had taken a copy, the king's measure would have been of no avail; we may however infer from this statement that the law was not contained in the *jus Papirianum :* the plebes would surely have restored it after the secession, if they had been deprived of a right so expressly granted to them. It would therefore seem that we here have one of the plebeian forgeries.

The consequence of the law of debt was a revolution. Had the senate and the patricians known how to act with prudence, and had they divided the opposition party, a thing which is very easy in free states, the patricians would have been superior to the plebeians, not indeed in numbers but in many other respects; for the patricians were almost the only citizens that had clients, and there are many passages in Livy and Dionysius, from which it is evident that during the first centuries of Rome the number of clients was very great, that the patricians distributed the domain land in many small farms among them, and that they had them entirely in their power. These clients were not contained in the tribes, but through their patrons they were connected with the curies; they did not hold any hereditary property in land except by special permission of their patrons, so that they were altogether dependent on the patricians. The plebeians, on the other hand, consisted of quite different elements, Latin equites, wealthy persons, and a number of poor people; they were either landed proprietors or free labourers. These various elements might easily have been separated; those who occupied a high station, were ambitious to obtain offices and influence in the state, while the common people were unconcerned as to whether the first among them could obtain the consulship or not, but were anxious about very different things: the patricians with their want of patriotism and justice might thus easily have separated the mass from the noble plebeians; but their avarice was as great as their ambition, and thereby they oppressed the people doubly. The whole of the domain land was in their possession, and if they had given up to the poor small portions of it, they would have gained them over to their side and thus detached them from the rest of the plebeians: but as the patricians had exclusive possession of all the trade in money, they considered themselves sufficiently safe. The trade in money was undoubtedly of such a kind that all banking business was carried on by foreigners, or freedmen under the protection of a patrician, as at Athens by Pasion, who was a *metoecus*, and paid an Athenian citizen for allowing him the use of his name.[2] All money transactions at Athens were in the hands of the *trapezitae;* in Italy, during the middle ages, in those of the Lombards; and in our days in those of the Jews, none of whom have real homes: a poor plebeian may often have tried to borrow money of his neighbours, but was more frequently obliged to go to the city and procure the money at the bankers.

The expression *persona*, in legal phraseology, arose from the fact that a foreigner was not allowed to plead his own case in a court of justice; and as another was obliged to do it for him, he made use of a *mask* so to speak; the fact that in later times a *pereginus* could act for himself, and that a *praetor peregrinus* was appointed for this very purpose, did not arise from the multitude of business but from political causes. The patricians themselves cannot have possessed very large sums of money; but foreigners who went to Rome were obliged, like the clients, to place themselves under their protection; for which the

---

[2] Boeckh, *Publ. Econ. of Athens*, p. 480. second edit.

patricians of course received a compensation in money. It
may, however, have happened now and then that patricians did
business on their own account. According to this view, then,
their usury was, after all, not so sordid as is commonly
supposed.

The civil law for patricians was quite different from that for
plebeians, since they had come together from different states;
the twelve tables which laid the foundation of the political
principles by which Rome was to be governed, also first introduced one civil law for all. Among our own ancestors, too,
the law was not varied according to geographical position but
according to persons. The native population of Italy down to
the twelfth century had the Roman law, while the Germanic
population had the Lombardic and Salic laws; but when the
ancient municipalities were abolished and the different elements
united, it became customary to draw up regulations binding
upon the whole population; the people more and more forgot
their old peculiar institutions, and thus gradually arose the
statutes of each of the Italian towns. The law of debt for the
patricians was liberal, but that affecting the plebeians was
severe; it was in force among the plebeians themselves, but
became dangerous to them only in as far as it also existed
between them and the patricians. As soon as there is a possibility of becoming involved in debt, the number of small landed
proprietors decreases from century to century. A comparison
of the registers of Tivoli in the fifteenth century with those
of the present day, shews that the number of landed proprietors
was then fifty times greater than at present.

The general law of debt which is found in the East, among
the Greeks and the Northern nations, as well as among the
Romans, was, that the person who borrowed money pledged
himself and his family for the debt. Plutarch, in the life of
Solon, relates that at Athens there were nearly a thousand
bondmen for debt, who, unless they were able to pay, were
sold into slavery. Among the Romans this personal responsibility existed in the most rigorous form: a man might pay his
debt by personal labour, or sell his property for a certain time,
or, if the case was a very hard one, for life, or even sell his
own person, whereby his children who were yet in their father's
power, likewise, *per aes et libram*, came into the *mancipium* of
the purchaser, but on condition of their being permitted to

ransom themselves. In this state a person continued until he recovered himself *per aes et libram*. The personal imprisonment of insolvent debtors in our own times is a remnant of that ancient law, but has become meaningless, because a more humane feeling has abrogated the other part. The ancient Germans too might transfer their free allodia and their persons to another and become his clients.

In order to escape becoming an *addictus*, a man who borrowed money might sell his property for a time as security, but then he was bound in conscience to redeem it after a certain period. *Fides* obliged the creditor not to deprive the debtor of the opportunity of ransoming himself, his family, or his property; hence *Fides* was so important a goddess among the Romans, and without her, the severity of the law would have ruined every thing. If a person failed to pay his debt, his person was forfeited to his creditor, that is, he became *fiduciarius* in his *mancipium*; this, however, could not be done simply by *manum injicere*, but required the addiction by the praetor; the creditor claimed the debtor's person with these words: *Hunc ego hominem meum esse aio ex jure Quiritium,* at which declaration the five witnesses and the *libripens* before whom the contract had been concluded, had undoubtedly to be present. The praetor then fixed a time, and if after its expiration payment was not made, and the debtor was unable to prove the *liberatio per aes et libram*, he was addicted to his creditor. The ancient Attic law was just the same; but Solon abolished it and introduced in its stead the Attic law of security, from which the later Roman law was derived; for the equites in their important money transactions endeavoured to escape from the severity of the law of debt, by appointing foreigners as their agents, who were not subject to the Roman law. Hence arose the laws respecting the *chirographa* and *centesimae*, for at Rome small discount business was not done at all. The *addictus* was called *nexus* because he was *nexu vinctus: nexus* or *nexum* originally denoted every transaction that was made in the presence of witnesses by *traditio* and by weighing the money, which afterwards was customary only in cases of fictitious purchases, whereby a certain right of property was secured to the creditor in case of a neglect of payment.

A debtor might frequently pay his debt by labour, and an able-bodied man might employ his service very usefully at times when labour fetched high wages; supposing the son of an old man who had pledged himself was strong, the father would sell him to his creditor, and when the debt was paid by his labour he became free again. But the interest increased so enormously, that it was very difficult for a poor debtor to get rid of his burthen; if however he worked as a *nexus*, he at least paid the interest. During the period of such labour, his creditor exercised over him all the authority of a master over his slave. The numerous class of persons who paid the debts of others in labour is expressly mentioned by the ancients.

Bondage for debt, however, might also arise in another way. A person might become a debtor even without a contract; for example, by neglecting to pay a legacy, or the wages of a labourer engaged in his service; moreover, if a person committed a crime he was, according to the Roman law, obliged to pay to the injured party a certain compensation, *obligatio ex delicto*. All these circumstances constituted a second class of debtors; and in these cases there existed *addictio* without *nexus*, as was established by the twelve tables. The praetor condemned a thief to pay to the person robbed double the amount of the stolen property; and if this was not done within a fixed period, he assigned him to the injured party as a bondman. In like manner, if a person asserted that another had purchased a thing from him without paying for it, and if the latter could not deny the debt (*aes confessum*), the creditor might demand the debtor's *addiction* for a time (*vinculam fidei*), whereby the other was naturally frightened to such a degree that he made every effort to pay. It is only to such cases that the expression *vinculum fidei* referred, and not to the *nexum;* for in the former, a *vindicatio* might take place, and the keeping of a contract is out of the question. When a Roman stood *in nexu*, that is, when he had sold himself to another in case of his being insolvent, as the Merchant of Venice did to Shylock, he pledged his property in land, however much it might be burthened with debts, for the law of the twelve tables was *nexo solutoque idem jus esto;* the *addictus* was in quite a different condition, for he belonged to his creditor and had no power over his own person. In this manner, we may clear up the mystery which appears in our books, when we read that debtors who had sold themselves (that is *nexi*) nevertheless served in

the legions.[3]   Livy does not enter into the question, because
he does not see the difficulty; and Dionysius, who does see it,
gets into inextricable perplexities.

This law of debt was in a certain sense as necessary as our
strict laws relating to bills of exchange; but abuse is unavoidable, for the wealthy are not always merciful, but harsh, and
keep to the severity of the law.   The worship of Mammon
prevailed at Rome as much as in some modern countries, and
the severity of the actual law was very oppressive; a further
aggravation was its being only one-sided, for when a patrician
was in difficulty, his cousins or his clients were obliged to assist
him, whereas plebeians were in most cases obliged to borrow
money from the patricians.   A plebeian, when given over to
his creditor, might find himself variously circumstanced: he
might indeed have a mild master who allowed him to ransom
himself by his labour, but he might also have fallen into the
hands of a heartless tyrant, who locked him up in his *ergas-
tulum*, put him in chains, and by harsh treatment endeavoured
to induce his relatives to come forward to liberate him.

LECTURE XV.

SUCH was the condition of the law about the year A.U. 260,
when all at once a state of extraordinary general distress arose,
such as had never existed before, but such as we meet with
again about a hundred years later, after the Gallic calamity.
The cause of it must be sought for in the war of Porsena, whence
we may infer that the war belongs to a considerably later time
than that to which it is assigned by Livy.   The distress led to
disturbances, concerning the origin of which Livy's account
may be tolerably well founded.   An aged captain covered with
scars, had become the bondman of his creditor, because his house

[3] Among the commentators of Livy there are ingenious and learned men, who
have written on the condition of the *nexi*; but all their investigations have gone
in the wrong direction, if we except the explanation given by Doujat. But
those who wrote after him did not profit by his teaching, but returned to the old
errors, as, for instance, Drakenborch, though he quotes Doujat: a proof how
learned men without a knowledge of the world may err in such things.—N.

had been burnt down and his property carried away; he escaped from the dungeon in which he had been most cruelly
treated by his master, and appeared in the market-place
famished, covered with rags, and disfigured with bloody stripes.
The sight of the man produced a great commotion, and the
plebeians generally, both those who were similarly circumstanced and those who were not, refused to obey their tyrants
any longer. Livy's account of the manner in which the tumult
spread further and further, and how the senate at first provoked
the people and was afterwards frightened by them, is exqui-
sitely beautiful, and shews a profound knowledge of human
nature; but the detail cannot be regarded as an actual tradition,
but is only an historical novel. At the very time when the
senate and the consuls had come to the fearful conviction that
they could not rule over the commonalty unless it was willing
to obey, the Volscians, hearing of the discord at Rome, either
actually advanced, or a report was spread by the patricians
that they were on their march against Rome. But however
this may be, the senate resolved to levy an army. According
to the original constitution, the senate alone had not the power
to declare war, but a proposal had to be made to the curies
which had to sanction it: according to the Servian legislation,
the proposal had to be brought before the centuries also; but
these things were then no longer thought of, and the annalists
mention only the senate. The senate, then, resolved to levy
an army, and as the burden of the infantry fell upon the plebs
alone, their juniores were called up according to tribes (*nomina-
tim citabantur*); their answering was called *nomen dare*, and
their refusing *nomen abnuere*. Levies were on the whole made
in the same manner, down to the latest times of the republic.
But when the plebeians, either in consequence of oppression or
for other reasons, refused to serve, they did not answer (*non
respondebant*); and such a silence was the most awful thing
that could happen. As on this occasion, the plebeians did not
answer the call, the consuls knew not what to do; and the
plebeians loudly shouted that they would not be so foolish as
to shed their blood for their tyrants; the booty, they said, was
not shared by them, but was transferred to the *publicum* (the
chest of the patricians) and not into the *aerarium*, and that they
were becoming more and more impoverished, being obliged to
pledge themselves and their families to the patricians and serve

as bondsmen. The patricians were divided among themselves; and Livy relates that the *minores natu* among the *patres* were particularly vehement in their opposition, by which he probably means the *minores*, that is, the Luceres: young patricians cannot possibly be conceived as members of the senate at that time, for it was then a real γερουσία. The consuls (A.U. 259) belonged to different parties; Appius Claudius represented the interests of the wildest oligarchs, while Servilius was mild. As the danger was threatening, mildness alone could lead to a desirable result, and all attempts to levy the army by force were disgracefully defeated. Servilius then caused himself to be empowered by the senate to act as mediator. By an edict he summoned all whose persons were pledged, and promised them that they, as well as their children and relatives, should be safe as long as the war lasted, during which time no creditor should be allowed to enforce the law. Hereupon the plebeians flocked to the standards in large numbers. With the army thus formed, Servilius marched into the field and returned victorious. After the close of the war, he promised the army to exert all his influence with the senate to obtain the cancelling of the contracts of debt; but the senate granted nothing, the army was disbanded, Appius Claudius undertook the administration of justice, and without any regard to his colleague's promise, consigned all those who had been on the field of battle to their creditors or compelled them to enter into a *nexum*. The remainder of the year passed away in the greatest commotions. The succeeding consuls, A. Virginius and T. Vetusius (A.U. 260), were both moderate men, a proof that they were elected by the centuries; for the curies would have chosen the most infuriated oligarchs. The senate remained obdurate; the consuls could produce no effect upon it or upon the patricians. Another attempt was made to levy an army, but the same difficulties presented themselves; the consuls were accused of cowardice, but those who were presumptuous enough openly to attack the plebs, were in the end obliged to save their lives by flight. The real danger existed only on market days; for the plebs were the peasantry, and had so much to do that they could not come to the city except on market days, and when they were specially summoned. Agriculture in Italy requires extraordinary care, for a good harvest cannot be expected unless the fields are weeded several

times during the summer. The Romans plough their fields
five, six, or seven times, and continue the weeding until the
corn is about three inches high. It is almost incredible how
much labour agriculture requires in the south, though the
produce likewise is incredible. Hence the country people
were fully occupied the whole year round, and had no time to
attend to matters which were not absolutely necessary; the
only plebeians generally at Rome, were those residing in the
city. Hence the patricians felt safe: they had among themselves vigorous men, and were supported by large numbers of
clients, so that the plebeians contained in the four city tribes
unquestionably formed the minority, and thus it becomes intelligible how the patricians were enabled to control the plebeians
even without a standing or mercenary army. The burghers
in German towns likewise, as at Cologne, kept their ascendancy
over the commonalty, although the latter was far more numerous. Such a body of oligarchs maintains itself even by its
pride and by having many points of union. So long as the
nature of the plebs was unknown, it must have been inconceivable that the patricians were not in greater danger, since
if in any town the populace (for thus the plebeians are called
in some books) rises against the wealthy, the latter are easily
overpowered.

As the attempt to levy a second army failed, the question
was: What should be done? Some proposed that the promises
of Servilius should be kept and the contracts of debt cancelled;
but Appius declared that the spirit of the rebels must be broken,
and that a dictator ought to be appointed. The dictatorship
had been instituted for the purpose of having a magistracy not
subject to the restrictions of the consulship, and of avoiding
not only an appeal to the curies, but also that to the tribes
which had been introduced by Valerius. Appius wished that
the dictator should seize and put to death every one that
refused to serve; but this senseless advice would have been
followed by the most fearful rebellion. The foolish assembly
indeed adopted the plan, but the good genius of Rome led the
people to elect as dictator Marcus Valerius[1], a man distinguished
for his mildness and kind feelings towards the plebeians. Some

---

[1] This is the name given to him in all our authorities; and Dionysius alone
less correctly calls him Manius Valerius, which is a mere invention, because Marcus was said to have fallen in the battle of lake Regillus.—N.

call him a *gentilis*, and others a brother of P. Valerius Poplicola.
He renewed the edict of Servilius; and as the Volscians,
Aequians, and Sabines were in arms, he formed an army without any difficulty. The statement that it consisted of ten
legions is truly ridiculous. He gave to each of the consuls a
part of the army, reserving one for himself. The Romans
were again victorious, and on his return he demanded of the
senate that the promises made to the people should be fulfilled;
but the senate disregarded all promises, and declared that the
law must be complied with. Valerius might now have joined
the plebs or withdrawn: he did the latter, and resigned his
dictatorship. One consular army, or perhaps both, were still
under arms, and the patricians would not allow them to return,
because as long as an army was in the field, they could exercise control over it. Dionysius expressly states that by a
Valerian law the consuls had, by virtue of their *imperium*, unlimited power so long as they were at a distance of one mile
from Rome, and they could accordingly inflict military punishment upon any one who was obnoxious to them without a
court martial. It was for this reason that the senate would not
allow the army to return. This was a detestable policy; for
the army could not be kept in the field for ever, and the whole
safety of the senate depended on the conscientiousness of the
plebs, who it was expected would not violate their military
oath. The insurrection, however, did break out in the camp,
though with great moderation. It is said that the soldiers at
first intended to slay the consul, in order to be released from
the oath which they had taken to him personally; but they
only refused obedience, appointed L. Sicinius Bellutus their
leader, crossed the Anio in a body, and at a distance of three
or four miles from it encamped on a hill which was afterwards
consecrated, and hence called *Mons Sacer*. The whole plebeian
population of the city emigrated and encamped there, and
those who remained at Rome consisted of the patricians with
their slaves, and of the wives and children of the emigrants.

The patricians however did not take the latter as their
hostages; and the plebeians, on their part, abstained from all
devastations and only foraged in the neighbourhood to satisfy
their immediate wants. The patricians now acted a little more
like human beings: as long as their authority was not endangered, they indulged in every kind of effrontery and oppression,

as we find was invariably the case down to the passing of the
Hortensian law; but as soon as their power was set at defiance,
they became pusillanimous, and every new struggle ended in
disgrace.   They fancied the plebeians would have no courage,
and said to one another: " This time they are sure to lay down
their arms; we need only assume a threatening attitude." One
almost feels giddy at the contemplation of such madness, and
yet it will be repeated ever and anon as long as the world lasts.
The claims of justice cannot be suppressed by arms; and the
patricians forgot that they had to deal with a noble but infuriated animal.   When, therefore, the plebeians planted their
standards on the sacred mount, the eyes of the patricians were
all at once opened.   In the city the plebs possessed only two
quarters[2], the Aventine with the Vallis Murcia, and the Esquiline, both very well fortified, provided with gates and unquestionably occupied by armed garrisons.   The plebeians
therefore might have taken Rome without difficulty, as their
friends would have opened the gates to them; but it would
have been necessary to take by storm the other hills, all of
which were fortified, as well as the Forum.   If the plebeians
had done this their country would have perished, for the surrounding nations would not have remained quiet; the conduct
of the *patres* therefore appears perfectly mad, and it is inconceivable that the *plebs* once in arms did not proceed further.
An explanation seems to be contained in the fact that the
Latins were then at peace with Rome; and with their assistance the senate might have defied the plebeians.   It is a
remarkable phenomenon deserving great attention, that in
confederate republics the equality of their constitutions has no
influence whatever upon their furnishing mutual aid, for people
living under a democratic government frequently support the
aristocratic government of another nation.   In the great insurrection of Lucerne and Berne in the year 1657, the democratic
cantons supported the oligarchic governments against the peasants. Such phenomena explain how the senate could maintain
itself under the circumstances above described; allusions from
the annals to this source of strength for the patricians occur in
Dionysius, where Appius says, that the Latins would be very

---

[2] In the middle ages, the *popolanti* as far as the Corso were not genuine Romans,
but Slavonians and Albanese, who, under Innocent the VIII., had settled there,
and continued to speak their own language as late as the fifteenth century.—N.

willing to support the senate against the commonalty, if the
right of isopolity were granted to them.   Although the senate
and the *patres* made no use of the suggestions, yet it was
important for them to know that should matters come to
extremities they might have recourse to such an expedient.

LECTURE XVI.

ACCORDING to the statement of Dionysius, the secession lasted
four months, from August to December; but this is merely a
false combination based upon the fact, that the tribunes at all
times entered upon their office on the 10th of December.
There was also a tradition that the dictator drove in the *clavus*
on the ides of September, so that at that time there were no
consuls at Rome.   The disturbances, moreover, were said to
have broken out under the consuls Virginius and Vetusius;
Dionysius accordingly concluded that these consuls must have
laid down their office at the end of August, and that the insurrection lasted four months.   If the office of the tribunes had
never been interrupted, it would not be difficult to conceive
that the time of their appointment was regulated in the same
manner at first as afterwards; but Dionysius overlooked the
fact that during the decemvirate, the tribuneship was abolished,
and it is hardly conceivable that the tribunes should afterwards
have re-entered upon their office on the same day as before,—
they undoubtedly resumed their functions as soon as they were
again allowed to assemble.   The consuls entered upon their
office on the 1st of August; and it seems certain that the peace
between the two estates was concluded by the new consuls,
Vetusius and Virginius.   The secession cannot have lasted
more than about a fortnight, for the city could not have held
out much longer, and a famine would have occurred if the
legions had remained in possession of the fields.   The rapidity
of Livy's account also suggests only a short duration.

I believe it is now generally acknowledged that Roman history henceforth increases in authenticity; where absurdities and
impossibilities are mixed up with it, confidence in the whole

may indeed be shaken; but if we remove from history that
which is strange and incredible, and give a clear exposition of
the real relations of life, let no one say that thereby history is
injured or loses in dignity: such sentiments are unhealthy and
diseased.

The patricians perceived when too late that they had gone
too far, and were compelled to yield: in point of form they
were obliged to submit to a great humiliation by sending
ambassadors to the plebeians.   The list of the ten ambassadors
given by Dionysius is certainly authentic and taken from the
libri augurales : forgeries would indeed have been carried far
if such names were spurious.   The end of the secession can
only be understood by forming a clear notion of the state of
affairs: we must remember that the government in the city
could not only defend itself but could command also the allies,
who had taken their oath to the Roman state, that is to the
senate and populus, and looked upon the plebeians as rebels,
so that it was by no means the numerical superiority of either
of the two estates, which decided the question.   A formal
peace was negotiated by the feciales as between two free nations;
the patricians sent off ambassadors, and conducted the negotiations, notwithstanding their great humiliation, with a prudence
in form which deserves our admiration; their object was to
get out of the difficulties in which their mistakes had involved
them as cheaply as possible.   They could effect the reconciliation only by strengthening themselves externally by their
allies, or by dividing the plebeians.   To do the latter, two ways
were open to them: they might either gain over to their side
the plebeians of distinction, whereby, however, they would
have weakened their own power, or they might separate the
mass of the plebeians from their leaders.   The latter was the
surest means.   The debts of insolvents were cancelled, the
addicti were declared free, and the *nexum* where it existed was
dissolved, but the law of debt was not altered; an amnesty
likewise was of course stipulated for.   The cancelling of debts
was no great loss to the creditors, since the interest paid had
long ago exceeded the capital; fifty years later the rate of
interest was reduced to ten per cent, but at that time it may
have been fifty per cent.   Sully did similar things.

The only permanent result of the secession was the establishment of the office of the *tribuni plebis*, whom we are in the

habit of calling tribunes of the people. This was not in reality an innovation: on the restoration of the tribuneship after the second secession, the commonalty had twenty tribunes, that is one for each tribe, two of whom were invested with real power. The tribes consisted of two decuries, and each of them had its president, just as in the senate there were ten decuries, each of which had a *primus*, who together formed the college of the *decem primi*. Symmetrical arrangements occur everywhere in ancient constitutions, whence we may deduce from a given fact one which is not given. When therefore we read that the first tribunes were two in number who elected three more, we may safely infer that of the actual twenty or twenty-one tribunes, these two were the principal, and that under the new circumstances they only advanced to a higher sphere of official activity. The difference undoubtedly was that the earlier tribunes had been elected each by his own tribe, just as the phylarchs in the Greek states were chosen each by his own phyle, whereas the new tribunes were elected by the whole commonalty. The names of the first tribunes are C. Licinius and L. Albinius; and Sicinius, who was the commander of the plebes during their secession, is mentioned as one of the three that were subsequently added. The plebeians who could not recover the rights which the Servian constitution had granted to them were obliged to be content with a protection against oppression, and their new magistracy was therefore instituted *auxilii ferendi gratia;* the persons of the tribunes were by an oath declared inviolable (*corpora sacrosancta*), so that they could step in between the rulers and the oppressed and protect the latter. Considering the *esprit de corps* and the official power of the patricians, a tribune in former times would have had a difficult and useless task in bringing an accusation against a consul, since there existed another consul with equal powers, and both were backed by all the patricians; the consul would have ordered his lictors to seize and chastise a tribune who dared to make an appeal against him to the commonalty. But whoever henceforth laid hands on a tribune was outlawed, and if the consul did not give effect to the declaration of out-lawry, the tribune might summon the consul after the expiration of his office before the court of the curies, or perhaps even before that of the tribes. It was formerly customary in speaking of Roman institutions not to make any distinctions between the different periods; thus Justus Lipsius, an ingenious and very learned man, who as a philologer is infinitely above me, has by his authority done much mischief in Roman antiquities: whenever a magistracy or a military arrangement is mentioned, he and his followers speak of it as if it had always existed, and a tribune at the end of the third century is conceived as a magistrate with the same power as in the time of Cicero, as if he had at first possessed the same right of intercession and of making legislative proposals as afterwards.[1] The first tribunes can perhaps scarcely be called a magistracy of the commonalty, and certainly not of the state: they were in fact nothing else but persons in a position analogous to that of a modern ambassador, whose duty it is in a foreign state to protect the subjects of his own sovereign.

Hitherto the patricians had exercised their power without any control, and the plebeians had no share in the administration: hence arose the necessity for a magistracy which should be able to afford protection against magistrates, as well as private individuals, whenever members of the plebeian order should be injured or ill treated. The house of a tribune, therefore, was open day and night; he was not allowed to quit the city, but, like a physician, was obliged to be always ready to give his assistance. This idea is grand and peculiarly Roman, for nothing analogous occurs in the whole history of Greece. The tribunes moreover had the right to assemble the commonalty and to bring proposals before it; but at first we find scarcely any traces of this right having been exercised. The resolutions passed by the plebes on the proposal of a tribune were called *plebiscita*, while the resolutions passed by the patricians were termed *leges*. An allusion to this occurs in a passage of Livy, where the Etruscans say that the Romans now consisted of two nations, each with its own magistrates and its own laws, an expression the importance of which Livy did not perceive. It may be said in general that Livy did not alter the materials he found, but only omitted what he thought obscure or unnecessary. The *plebiscita* did not at first affect the whole of the state; and it was not till more than twenty years later that they acquired the character of resolutions,

---

[1] The same has been the case with Roman topography, for buildings which occur side by side on the Capitol have been regarded as works of the same period; but men of sense like Sarti act in a very different spirit. — N.

which might become law (A. U. 283). The only real magistrates of the plebeians were the *aediles*, a name which was also given to the local magistrates among the Latins; it is very probable that they acted as judges in disputes among the plebeians themselves, for the tribunes in the earliest times were not judges, though it may sometimes have happened that an appeal from the *aediles* was brought before them. In the civil law no change seems to have been made at that time.

The powers of the tribunes were thus very slender and modest: they were partly of a negative character, and partly administrative in a limited way, but not at all legislative, and I do not believe that the tribunes had the right to propose any change in the civil law even for their own order: however, their power was a seed from which a tree was destined to grow up that was one day to overshadow all others. It is a singular circumstance that the election of the tribunes was committed to the centuries, since it would have been far more natural to assign it to the tribes; but this is another proof how small were the advantages which the plebeians obtained by their first secession, for in the centuries the patricians exercised great influence through their clients, and thus about ten years later the patricians even succeeded in forming a party among the tribunes. The statement that they were elected by the curies is obviously false, but we may infer from it at any rate that they required the sanction of the curies, in order to prevent the election of obnoxious persons. The right of *veto* claimed by the English government on the election of Irish Catholic bishops is of the same kind. According to Livy, this original arrangement ceased even before the Publilian law, by which the election was committed to the tribes, and previously to which Piso supposes that there existed only two tribunes. I believe that the number five is indeed of later origin, but I do not think it likely that it did not exist before the Publilian law; for as this number answers to the five classes, how should it have been introduced at a time when the election no longer belonged to the classes, but to the tribes? It seems to me quite probable that the patricians, under the pretext of a fair settlement, contrived to gain some advantage for themselves also, and in this manner I account for the otherwise inexplicable circumstance, that ten years later we find the curies electing the consuls instead of the centuries; it was only a concession made to the plebeians that the election of one consul was given to the centuries, while the other, down to the restoration of the consulship after the time of the decemvirs, remained in the hands of the curies. It is not impossible that an assignment of lands was made; and it is very probable that a promise was given to restore the ancient legal relation of the *ager publicus*. The result of the secession was by no means as decided a victory of the plebeians over the patricians as our historians describe it: a firm basis had indeed been gained, and the plebeians subsequently made the best use of it, but the fruits could not be reaped without the greatest exertion.

The contract between the two orders was now solemnly concluded, like a peace, by a sacrifice, a *senatus consultum*, and a resolution of the curies on the one hand, and of the plebeians, who were yet in arms, on the other: a curse was pronounced on those who should ever attempt to break the treaty, but the patricians did all they could to shake off the yoke. The deputies of the plebes and the *decem primi* of the senate offered up the sacrifice in common: order returned and the state of affairs improved, but as that which ought to have been done was not done, the causes of new commotions and ferments for a long time to come were left in operation. I have called this treaty a *peace*, a word which is also used elsewhere on similar occasions: the Magna Charta of Liége, establishing the union between the burghers and commonalty, was called *la paix de Fexhe*.[2]

The Latins were now rewarded for the service they had done the senate, as is expressly mentioned by Dionysius on the authority of the excellent document which forms the groundwork of his account: they obtained the right of isopolity (*jus municipii*) in its original meaning, through the treaty of Sp. Cassius, which I have already mentioned.

These events which we see in a sufficiently clear light, are succeeded by the same darkness as hangs over the preceding period, and for a time we have nothing but the Fasti. Livy relates the history of Coriolanus soon after the peace between the two estates; but this cannot be its proper place. When a leaf of a book has been misplaced, it must be put right, if you do not wish its author to talk nonsense.

---

[2] The German expression for such a covenant is *Richtung.*—N.

The same is the case when an historical fact is assigned to a
wrong time.   I see no reason why I should not believe that
during a famine at Rome a Siceliot king sent a supply of corn
to the city; but tyrants do not appear in Sicily till some
Olympiads after the time in which the history of Coriolanus is
placed.   I believe that Coriolanus was first impeached by the
plebes, but no one would have dared to do this before the
Publilian law.   The Romans under Sp. Cassius could not have
disputed about the distribution of the *ager publicus*, if, as we
read, the Volscians had advanced as far as Lavinium. I further
believe that a L. Junius Brutus introduced the severe punishment for disturbing the tribunes while making their proposals,
but he who would assign the history of Coriolanus to the year
A.U. 262, could not possibly believe all these points. For this
reason, I maintain that the story of Coriolanus does not belong
to this period, but to some time after the Publilian law. Cn. or
C. Marcius may perhaps have maintained himself in the war
against the Antiatans, but he cannot have conquered Corioli,
for in the same year this town belonged to the league of the
Latin towns.   The whole history must either be rejected as a
fiction, or be assigned to quite a different time. But yet another
combination has been attempted. The temple of *Fortuna Mulie-*
bris on the Latin road between the fourth and fifth milestone
happened to stand on the spot where Coriolanus after his emigration was encamped and became reconciled.   Now the
entreaties of his mother and the matrons, which may indeed
be really historical, were connected with the name of *Fortuna*
Muliebris; and it was accordingly believed that that temple
though the time of its foundation was known, had been erected
in consequence of the event above referred to.   But Fortuna
Muliebris corresponds to Fortuna Virilis, who had her temple
at Rome, there being a male and a female divinity like Tellus
and Tellumo, just as the same contrast is expressed in *animus*
and *anima*.[3]

[3] See above p. 80.

LECTURE XVII.

LIVY says that he should not wonder, if his readers were wearied by his accounts of the wars with the Volscians and Aequians; and certainly every one must have had this feeling as soon as he became acquainted with Livy. The uniformity of these wars spoils the pleasure we have in reading the first decade. What rendered them tedious to Livy, was the fact that he did not divide them into periods, and as, with the exception of what we read in Dionysius, he is our only authority, it is difficult, and only to a certain degree possible, to obtain a clear view of the wars. The first period extends from A.U. 280 to A.U. 290: the beginning is involved in great obscurity, and the conquests of Tarquinius Superbus are very indefinite; afterwards the Volscians, under the name of Auruncans, invaded the Latin territory; then follow a number of little wars till about A.U. 290, and during the latter years the Volscians appear in possession of Antium, but lost it again. In the second period, things assumed a different aspect: the Aequians took a vigorous part in the Volscian war, Latium was completely crushed, and the war turned out very unfortunately for the Romans, Latins and Hernicans. This lasted till about A.U. 296, when the Romans concluded peace with the Volscians properly so called, and thus warded off the danger. The terms of the peace are very remarkable. In the third period, the Romans continued the war against the Aequians alone; it was not attended with very great danger and was carried on languidly by both parties. There then followed a fresh Volscian war against the Ecetrans, who were allied with the Aequians. This period, being the fourth, begins with the great victory of A. Postumius Tubertus (A.U. 324); henceforward the Romans made steady progress until the Gallic war; they took most of the Volscian towns and greatly weakened the Aequians. Then followed the Gallic calamity, in which the Aequians also may have suffered severely. Afterwards (this is the fifth period), the wars break out anew, but with quite a different character: the Aequians were then an insignificant enemy, the Volscians were in reality united with the Latins, and like the Latins themselves, fought for their independence. By dividing the wars into these five periods, they lose their intolerable sameness, and, at the same time, it becomes clear how the Volscians were enabled to maintain themselves.

I shall not dwell upon the details of these wars, for even the strongest memory cannot retain them; nor are the accounts of them authentic, because Livy, being tired of them, read his authorities carelessly, and has given only a hurried description. It must, however, be observed that after the treaty with the Latins, the enemy advanced in great force but made no important conquest until a later period; for Circeii continued to be a Latin town as late as the time of Sp. Cassius.

An event of great relative importance for Rome was the treaty with the Hernicans (A.U. 267). The right of isopolity must have existed between them even before, if it be true that in the reign of Tarquinius Superbus they took part in the festival of Jupiter Latiaris; a Roman tradition mentioned them as allies even of Tullus Hostilius. After the Etruscan calamity, they must have deserted Rome like the Latins and the Tyrrhenian coast towns, but the present treaty restored their old relations in a manner which was most advantageous for them. The Romans, Latins, and Hernicans were put on a footing of perfect equality, and the booty, as well as money and land, was to be divided among them in equal portions; when a colony was sent out, it received colonists from all the three people. Whether the annalists took a correct view of the matter (Livy and Dionysius differ very much from each other), or whether they merely supposed that as peace was concluded a war must have preceded, cannot be determined; but I am inclined to believe that the alliance was the result of a mutual want, since both nations were surrounded by the Volscians and Aequians, and the fortified towns of the Hernicans were of great importance to the Romans: a war between the Romans and Hernicans would at least have been very foolish. The Hernicans lived in five towns, Anagnia, Alatrum, Ferentina, Frusino and Verulae, which extended from east to west and are remarkable for their cyclopean fortifications. According to statements in Servius and the Veronensian Scholiast on Virgil, whom Mai has edited incorrectly, the Hernicans were descended from the Marsians and Sabines; their name is said to have been derived from *hernae* which in the Sabine language signified *rocks*.[1] It is strange that a nation in its own language should have designated itself by a mere surname, especially as the Marsians, Marrucinians and Pelignians lived on far higher mountains. The Sabine origin of the Hernicans is therefore somewhat suspicious, but still it might be true, even though the derivation of their name were a mere fancy. But another difficulty is this: if they proceeded from the Marsians they must have forced their way through the Aequians, which is quite improbable; and in after-times there appears no connection whatever between them and the Marsians. Julius Hyginus declares them to have been Pelasgians.

The Hernicans were a remarkable people: they resisted the Romans and were respected by them on account of their brilliant valour: the treaty with them is historically certain, and moreover that it was concluded not only with the Romans but also with the Latins; whence they received a third of the booty. But there were nevertheless Roman antiquaries—and Dionysius allowed himself to be deceived by them—who imagined that the Romans alone had the supremacy, and hence received two-thirds of the booty, and the Latins the remaining third; the Romans then, it is said, generously gave to the Hernicans one half of their share. But if the Romans and Latins together concluded an alliance with that brave people, it was no more than just that each of them should give up one-sixth of the booty; and Rome, according to Dionysius' own account, did not possess the supremacy over the Latins at all. The connection must afterwards have been dissolved by some arrangement, but the fact that the Hernicans insisted on retaining their privileges, subsequently led to their destruction.

Sp. Cassius is far the most distinguished man of those times, in the obscure accounts of which the principal memorable events are connected with his name; first the treaty with the Sabines (A.U. 254), undoubtedly with isopolity to judge from the census lists; and next this treaty with the Hernicans. In the latter the relation of Rome to the Hernicans was put upon a footing quite different from what it had been before, just as the relation of Athens to her allies became altered about Ol. 100 after the battle of Naxos. When Athens founded her second maritime power, the towns were far less dependent than before, and Demosthenes, in forming his great confederacy, acting with all the wisdom of an intelligent statesman, did not

---

[1] Arndt compares the German *Firn*.—N.

demand the supremacy for Athens, but merely that she should
be the soul of the league. Traitors like Æschines charged him
with degrading the dignity of Athens, because the Athenian
deputy was not to have more influence than one from a
Euboean town: they said that they wished to establish the
supremacy of Athens, but they were liars. If Demosthenes
had lived in the time of Pericles, I do not think that he would
have acted with this spirit of moderation; but his era was one,
in which every thing depended upon protecting the liberty
and independence of Greece against Philip; hence he willingly
concluded peace with any town that wished it, and only endeavoured to direct by his intelligence and energy the proceedings of the confederacy. Rome was placed in the same
position by Cassius; and from this alone we must see that he
was a great man, with a keen eye and a sound judgment. The
Etruscan war had destroyed the Roman dominions on the
right bank of the Tiber, the Volscians and Aequians were
advancing, the coast towns were lost, and Rome was obliged
to do not what she wished, but what she could. Later historians, guided by a blind love for their country, wanted to deny
such a state of things; and Livy and the writers whom Dionysius followed, were full of absurd admiration of the greatness
of their ancestors, and maintained that Rome had never been
weak. There may at that time have been fools or people like
Æschines, who declared Cassius a traitor because he regulated
his conduct by the circumstances of the case. In his third
consulship, after the treaty with the Hernicans, he wished to
be just towards the plebeians also, and this leads us to speak
of his important agrarian law.

The nations of antiquity, in carrying on war, generally
followed a principle of law different from that now in force.
We regard war as a single combat between the genii of two
states or between two imaginary states; the individual is not
affected by it in regard to his person, liberty and property, and
the law of war accordingly intends that he should be injured
as little as possible, and that he should never be the immediate
object of hostility; he is endangered only as far as it cannot be
avoided. Among the ancients, on the other hand, hostilities
affected every one belonging to the state; with us, the conquered state indeed loses its right to rule over the country,
while every individual continues to exist, as if no war had

taken place; but the ancients entertained quite different views. They took the whole property of the conquered and reduced them to a state of servitude; and this they did not only in wars of extermination; but even in ordinary wars the inhabitants of a conquered country lost their property: nay even when a place voluntarily surrendered, the inhabitants with their women and children came into the power of the conqueror, as we see from the formula of a *deditio*. In the latter case, the conqueror did not make the conquered his slaves, but they became his clients, and their landed property fell entirely into his hands. When such a place had suffered little and seemed to be worth preservation, the Romans sent to it 300 colonists, one from each gens, who were a *φρουρά* or *φυλακή*, and each of whom obtained two jugera of land for a garden; they further undoubtedly received the pasture land, either the whole or at least the greater part of it, and one third of the arable land, the remaining two thirds being left to the former inhabitants. Such was the nature of the original colonists. In other cases no colonists were sent out, it being thought unnecessary to keep a garrison in a place; and then the former inhabitants were sometimes driven out, but sometimes allowed to remain on condition of their paying a tax, usually a tithe. They then continued to live on their former property as tenants at will, who might be dispossessed at the pleasure of their masters. In those districts which had been laid waste in war or from which the inhabitants had been expelled, the Romans acted on a principle which is quite peculiar to themselves, and to which we find no parallel in the history of Greece.

This principle, or the *jus agrarium*, is to me the more interesting, as it was the first point that led me to a critical investigation of Roman history; for in my earlier years I had occupied myself more with the history of Greece. When, as a young man, I read Plutarch's biographies and Appian, the nature of the agrarian law was a perfect riddle to me. It had been believed that its intention was to interfere with property and to fix a certain limit to its extent, so that a person having above 500 *jugera* was deprived of the surplus, which went to increase the possessions of plebeians at the expense of patrician property. This crude notion of the law met with much favour, as for example, with Machiavelli, who lived in a revolutionary age, and with whom the means sanctified the end; and even

with Montesquieu, who however looked upon a repetition of
the past as an impossibility, since in his time every idea of
revolution was quite foreign to men's minds. His example
shows how bold speculative men become in matters which are
unknown to them and appear impossible: at that time revolutionary ideas were common in an apparently quite innocent
manner, even among men who during the revolution actually
embraced the very opposite side. There are persons who in times
of peace speak of their fondness for war, and revolutionary
ideas were similarly cherished during the profound peace of
the eighteenth century. Such ideas, however, were dangerous
for Europe, and when the revolution broke out, many persons
at first found everything smooth and natural whose hearts were
afterwards broken.

As Plutarch and Appian expressly state that the law affected
only the γῆ δημοσία, it was clear that something else must be
understood by it than ordinary property. The first who expressed an opinion that it referred to the *ager publicus* was
Heyne, in a program which he wrote at the time of the revolutionary confiscations; but the question, what is the *ager
publicus* remained unexamined, as in general Heyne often saw
what was right, but rarely carried it out. The historians who
after him wrote about the Gracchi, were quite in the dark
respecting the agrarian law. Once, when I did not yet see my
way in these difficulties, I asked the great Fr. A. Wolf about
it; but he, with all his extraordinary intellectual powers, had
the weakness to wish it to be believed that he knew everything,
and accordingly not knowing what answer to give me, he
assumed an air of not wishing to betray his secret, and said,
" I shall one day write about it." It was by a mere accident
that I was led to see the real nature of the *ager publicus*. It
was at the time when servitude was abolished in Holstein: the
peasants, both serfs and freemen, who had before transmitted
their estates as an inheritance from father to son, were deprived
of their possessions, and arbitrarily transferred to smaller and
inferior estates, while their former possessions were thrown
into large farms. These were revolting proceedings: in some
places the peasants opposed them, but were punished in consequence, and the same was done even with estates occupied
by freemen. My feelings were roused with the highest indignation, and the question naturally presented itself to my mind:

" What right have they to act in this manner?" This led me
to an investigation about leasehold property among different
nations, and thus I came to consider the *ager publicus* among
the Romans.

The general idea of the Italian nations was that the franchise
was inseparable from the soil, and that all property in land
proceeded from the state. The soil was only the *substratum*
on which the pre-conceived citizenship rested. This bears a
great resemblance to the feudal notions: for according to the
strict feudal law there was no land at all without its feudal lord,
all land proceeded from the sovereign as the supreme feudal lord,
and then came the under-tenures, though practically this idea
never existed in its full rigour. Another analogy occurs in
the East, especially in the East Indies, where the sovereign is
the real owner of the soil, and the peasant possesses it only on
precarious tenure. In the same manner, all landed property
among the Italian nations proceeded from the state.

LECTURE XVIII.

WHEN we read in Appian the statement that the *ager publicus*
was partly used for colonies and domain land, and partly let
to farm (the latter statement is found in Plutarch only), we
naturally ask, How is it possible that difficulties could arise?
The Roman republic had only to make the law that no one
should have more than a certain number of lots, and all evil
consequences were prevented. But the fact is, that Appian
and Plutarch misunderstood the ambiguous expression of their
predecessor.[1] I am not talking here about the letting of a
piece of land to farm, but of a tax which was imposed on the
estates; of corn the tenth (*decuma*), of fruit-bearing trees the
fifth (*quinta*), and of other things in proportion. Now if the
corn was delivered in kind, the state must have built large
store-houses; for the cattle grazing-money had to be paid, and

---

[1] One clearly sees that this is not an invention of Appian, but an extract
from the history of the Gracchi by Posidonius, who was not inferior to Polybius,
and whom Appian follows for that period, as, for the preceding one, he followed
Dionysius, Polybius, Fabius, and lastly, it would seem, Rutilius.—N.

this of course yielded a different return in different years. For these reasons a new system was adopted, and the produce of those taxes was let in farm to *publicani*. The forms of the Roman constitution have nearly always some analogy in the Greek states; and this is often the case in the civil law also, but in the agrarian law the Romans are quite peculiar. A Greek state conquered a country and founded colonies in it, but the *possessio agri publici* was not known among them, and there is only a single instance in which something similar occurs. From Xenophon's Anabasis we see that he consecrated an estate at Scillus to the Ephesian Artemis; the temple did not let this estate to farm, but received a tithe of its produce; and this tithe was farmed. It was not the whole produce of such an estate, but only a portion of it, that was given as an offering to the deity, just as a victim was never offered as a ὁλόκαυστον, but only a part of it was burnt in honour of the divinity. According to the Roman law, the state did not take from that which was *publicum* the highest possible amount of produce, but made known that every *Romanus Quiris*, who wished to cultivate a part of the conquered territory, might take it: this was the *occupatio agri publici;* the right belonged at first to the patricians only as the most ancient citizens, who might occupy a piece of land wherever they pleased. Such land was for the most part on the hostile frontier and in a state of devastation in consequence of war, whence the competition for it was not very great. There is no doubt that from the first the occupant was under the obligation of paying the *decuma* and *quinta*. It has always been overlooked that it was this rent which was let to farm by the government.

The expressions *agrum locare* and *agrum vendere* are synonymous, and have the same meaning as *fructus agri vendere* and *agrum fruendum locare*. A person in the possession of such an estate might in fact look upon it as his property as far as any third party was concerned, just like a leaseholder, from whom the owner may take the estate on certain conditions, but who is perfectly protected against any other party. This protection was afforded among the Romans by the possessorial interdicts, so that the possession became heritable also. The state, on the other hand, might step in at any time and say, " I want to establish a colony here or distribute the land *viritim*, and the occupant must make room;" to such a declaration by the state the occupant could make no opposition. It is, therefore, clear that the state could always dispose of the *ager publicus* and declare for example, that no more than a certain number of *jugera* should be in the hands of an individual, because others would thereby be excluded, and because the excessive influence of one person through the immense number of his clients, might become dangerous to the state.

This is the great difference between property and mere *possessio*. The *possessio* was given by the praetor through the edict by which a person was called upon to take it; and the praetorian *jus haereditatis* in its origin refers to this *possessio* alone: the praetor gave *possessionem bonorum secundum tabulas*. A person might by his will bequeath his property to whomsoever he pleased; but the *possessio* could be transferred to another only by sale in the presence of witnesses and by a fair contract; he who received it, proved his legal acceptance, and protected himself in his possession by the possessorial interdict; he had also witnesses that he had acquired the possession, *neque vi neque clam neque precario*. But what was to be done when the possessor died? By his will he might disinherit his children altogether, and leave his *property* to the most unworthy individual, without the praetor in early times having power to interfere; but in the case of *possessio*, of which he was the exclusive source, the praetor could interfere and give his decision according to a principle quite different from that applied to property, just as the Lord Chancellor of England decides according to equity. Even those who, like Livy and Dionysius, entertain an unfair opinion of the plebes and the tribunes, cannot deny that the patricians were usurpers of the public land; and yet, according to the letter of the law, they might claim it, and hence it may readily be conceived that they appeared to be perfectly just and honest men. It is an important advantage gained by the study of history, that we learn to judge fairly of men, and arrive at the conviction that honest men may belong to the most opposite parties, their worth being altogether irrespective of their party colours. This may be applied to the patricians; and when Livy and Dionysius, though both are anti-plebeian, say that the *ager publicus* was occupied *per injuriam* and ὑπὸ τῶν ἀναιδεστάτων πατρικίων, they are unjust in their expressions, as will be seen, if we go back to the original state of things.

According to the oldest law, none but the original Roman citizens of the three ancient tribes, that is the patricians could be admitted to the *possessio;* they received from the praetor as much land without any fixed limits as they thought they could cultivate; they paid nothing for it, and had only to employ their capital to render the land productive. But by the side of the populus, there now arose the plebs who constituted the real strength of Rome, formed the whole of the infantry, shed their blood in the wars, and made the conquests; the plebs, therefore, had an indisputable right to have their share in the conquests, which however the patricians continued to regard as their own exclusive property. There are distinct indications that even Servius Tullius had determined that no unlimited distributions should be made, but that one portion of the conquered territory should remain in the hands of the state, and the other be distributed among the plebeians as their real property. Squares were formed according to the rules of the science of the augurs, the lots were numbered and given to those who were to have shares; each lot consisted of a square (*centuria*). This is the origin of the division and assignment of land (*assignatio*), and of the law of Servius Tullius which was inseparably connected with the constitution of the plebes. Sallust's expressions would lead us to conjecture that after the banishment of the kings, the Servian regulation was renewed. But the patricians again deprived the plebeians of this advantage, and it was only the *ager regius* that was distributed; afterwards all conquered lands remained in the hands of the patricians, who even exempted themselves from paying the tithe. The tribunes were anything but mutineers, and being the natural representatives of their order, they only wished to enforce its rights. It is not impossible that the loss of a third of the Roman territory in the Etruscan war fell particularly hard upon the plebeians.

Sp. Cassius was the first who proposed an agrarian law, first to the senate, then to the curies, and at last to the centuries; or perhaps, first to the centuries and afterwards to the curies. This proposal was to re-enact the Servian law, to restore the *decuma* and *quinta*, to sell a portion of the conquered land, and to measure out and distribute the rest among the plebes. This is all we know about the Cassian law; the rest of Dionysius' statement shews, as, after mature deliberation, I can confidently assert, the distinct marks of a writer of the second half of the seventh century, and is compiled with great ignorance of the ancient times. The *senatusconsultum* of which he speaks is utterly without foundation. The law respecting the distribution of land is so closely connected with the whole fate of the plebeians, that it was probably talked of even in the negociations for the peace on the Sacred Mount; but under Cassius it became a reality. There is every appearance that it was passed, for down to the time of the decemvirs the agrarian law is mentioned as a right possessed by the plebes, though they were not allowed the enjoyment of it. Cassius thus appears as a very remarkable man; Cicero mentions him as a well-known person, and yet he is little spoken of.

It is an historical fact, that in the following year, Sp. Cassius was executed for high treason, and that out of his property (*ex Cassiana familia*) an offering was dedicated in the temple of Tellus in the Carinae. It seems probable that his execution by his own father was an invention made to soften down the glaring injustice of the deed. Even Dionysius is justly struck by the fact that Cassius who had then been thrice consul, should have been put to death by his father; the *leges annales*, it is true, did not exist at that time, but it is nevertheless incredible that a man who had been thrice consul, and had celebrated a triumph should still have been in his father's power. Another tradition followed by Dionysius and Cicero somewhat softens the account: the father of Sp. Cassius, it is said, declared in court that he considered his son guilty, and the latter was accordingly executed. The truth is that the *quaestores parricidii* summoned Cassius before the curies, and that the curies as his peers sentenced him to death. Thus the matter becomes intelligible: he had most deeply wounded the members of his own order who were delighted to take vengeance on him. Dionysius is puzzled by the account; but Livy avoids the difficulty by representing Cassius as having been condemned by the plebes, because the tribunes were envious of him,—as if at that time the tribunes had had the power to make such proposals! The question as to whether he was guilty or not was discussed by the ancients themselves: Dionysius considered him guilty, Dion Cassius thought him innocent, but God alone can know the truth. What he did was an act of the purest justice, but the same action may proceed from the best as well as from the worst motives, and it is just as possible that he may have wished to promote the good of the state, as that he may have aimed at the kingly dignity. To suppose that he entertained such a thought was by no means so absurd twenty-five years after the banishment of the kings, as it was seventy years later in the case of Sp. Maelius. Cassius was a very important man, otherwise he would not have been thrice consul, which for those times was something unheard of: with the exception of P. Valerius Poplicola no one had been so often invested with the consulship, and even in his case the Fasti are very uncertain. The manner in which Cassius concluded his treaties affords proof of a great soul; it is, therefore, very possible that he had the purest intentions of wisdom and justice; for considering the spreading of the Volscians, the situation of Rome was far from being without danger; and it was necessary to keep all its strength together. A great man unquestionably he was, whether he was guilty or not guilty, and the faction which condemned him was detestable. Dionysius has the strange statement that Cassius had children and that their execution also was talked of, but that they were spared, and that thenceforward the same mercy was shewn to the children of all criminals. This looks as if it were taken from the law books and resembles a new legal statute, but it may have been something quite different: we shall afterwards meet with a son of Sp. Cassius, and that in a place where we should least expect it. It is probable that the judge L. Cassius Longinus, A.U. 640, whose severity was almost cruelty, as well as the murderer of Julius Caesar, was descended from his gens: no wonder that this family attached itself to the plebes. The condemnation of Sp. Cassius by a Fabius, laid the foundation of the greatness of the Fabian family, a greatness to which there is no parallel in the Roman Fasti: for seven successive years (A.U. 269-275) one of the consuls was always a Fabius, just as a Valerius had been for five years at the beginning of the republic. The conclusion, therefore, naturally is that the Fabii were then in possession of supremacy, and that the tribe of the Tities was represented by them.

LECTURE XIX.

ONE of the disadvantages of a free government is the extraordinary difficulty of correcting any mistake that has been
committed; the efforts of the government to make amends are
rarely acknowledged by the people. An absolute prince may
do so without weakening his authority or incurring any
danger; but in a republic the case is different: if the people
were good-natured and conscientious enough to offer the hand
of reconciliation, things might go on well, but it is not so;
when a government wishes to make amends to those whom it
has offended, the first step the latter take is revenge. This
consideration, especially if Sp. Cassius did fall a quite innocent
victim, must serve to excuse the Roman rulers for committing
a fresh act of violence after his death, and altering the constitution to their own advantage; for the government could not
stop where it was, and least of all if it was conscious of a
crime; for if they had allowed the constitution to remain unchanged, it was reasonable to expect that in the free election of
the consuls by the centuries the plebeians would elect from
among the patricians none but men like Sp. Cassius. They
were obliged to do what Dionysius expresses so strangely in
saying that the plebes withdrew from the elections, and that
the noblest alone took part in them; as if by the Servian constitution, any one except the nobles could ever have decided a
question! The real state of the case is quite different; and I
shall relate it as it actually occurred, reserving my proofs for
another place.

In the year after the death of Cassius, or even in the very
same year, when consuls were to be elected, the election was
not made by the centuries, but the senate nominated the candidates, and the curies confirmed them But this gave rise to
the bitterest disputes between the plebes who were led by the
tribunes, and the consuls; for although the tribunes at that
time still required the sanction of the curies, yet the injustice
was so great, that not even the mildest could have borne it.
Hence the character of the tribuneships now became suddenly
changed: up to this time there is no trace of tribunitian commotions. But now the honor of their order was too much

insulted, for on the one hand the agrarian law was not carried into effect; and on the other, the government was in the hands of consuls who had been illegally elected. Accordingly the tribune Ti. Pontificius refused to allow a levy to be made, because the people were not bound to serve under an illegal government: the ancient annals would hardly have preserved his name if his opposition had not been the first that ever proceeded from a tribune. But an army was levied by force, the consuls either openly defying the tribunes and ordering the men who refused to answer to be seized and chastised, or causing the houses of those who lived in the country to be set on fire and their cattle to be taken away, or lastly transferring the place where the levy was to be made from the city to the country, whither the tribunician power did not extend. When in this manner an army had been raised, the despair of the plebeians went so far that they would rather allow themselves to be butchered by the enemy, than fight for their tyrants. This exasperation continued for two years, and in the end rose to such a pitch, that the senate, as though it were a concession, consented that one of the consuls, should, perhaps without a *senatusconsultum,* be elected by the centuries. The consequence was that the consul elected by the centuries met with no opposition on the part of the plebeians, while they resisted the other in every possible way. However, the times were so bad, and the surrounding nations acted with such boldness towards Rome, that the tribunes themselves saw, that it would be better to put up with injustice than to allow the republic to perish. The plebes accordingly in the following year, A.U. 272, conceded to the senate and curies the election of one consul. But at the same time they must have acquired the right to elect their tribunes without the sanction of the curies. Publilius could never have become tribune, if this change had not been made previously to his law. According to our traditions the number of tribunes must have been five, as early as that time.

During this period, the Volscian wars continued uninterruptedly, though they may not have been very important, so that the Latins and Hernicans alone were able to hold out against them. But one war weighed heavily upon Rome alone, — that against Veii. Veientine wars are mentioned under the kings, even from the time of Romulus, but they are quite apocryphal.

According to the most recent investigations, the town of Veii was about five miles in circumference, and was thus as large as Rome in the time of Servius Tullius. It is very remarkable, that two such large towns should have been situated so near each other, for the distance is not more than from twelve to fifteen miles; the fact shows, however, how strong was the contrast between the Etruscans and Latins in those times. Livy and Dionysius are very minute in relating the events of the war; and Livy believing all to be true, is very pleasing in his narrative. It may be regarded as authentic, that there was a long and difficult war against Veii. The detail in Livy contains nothing that is improbable; the account of the manner in which Cn. Manlius fell, and of the useless attempt to deceive fate especially, have an antique air. If we compare the accounts of this battle with those of the battle of lake Regillus, we shall find a considerable difference. The many stories about it were probably derived from the *laudationes* of the Fabian gens, which were continually repeated like the panegyric λόγοι ἐπιτάφιοι of the Greeks. I believe that the plebeians always refused obedience to the consul elected by the patricians; the Fabii on this occasion also doubted whether the plebeians would obey their commands; but as the latter were enthusiastic in the struggle, their co-operation decided the issue of the battle, and the Fabii became reconciled to them. Through this reconciliation, everything assumed a different aspect. One of the heads of the Fabii, who are called three brothers, but were probably gentiles, had fallen; two others saw that the oligarchs were throwing the republic into a desperate position. The Veientines were defeated, but the war continued; and although the Latins and Hernicans were in arms, yet the Volscians spread farther and farther, and concord was the thing most needful. The Fabii themselves accordingly declared that the agrarian law must be conceded to the plebeians; and the consequence was, that none of the Fabii was elected patrician consul, whereas the plebeians chose their former friend, Kaeso Fabius for their consul. A most formidable commotion now arose, and the Fabii were looked upon by their own order as traitors; their proposals being rejected, they quitted the city in a body 306 in number and formed a settlement on the Cremera, being joined by their whole gens and some thousands of plebeians. This must have been a settlement of a peculiar kind, for it was not a colony, having been formed *per secessionem*: it was a political emigration, because the Fabii had fallen out with their own order; and they founded a home for themselves independent of Rome.[1] It is said that only one of the Fabii survived, having been left behind at Rome as a child and in a state of ill health. Perizonius has sifted this account with great critical sagacity, and has shown how absurd it is to suppose that of 306 men in the prime of life all should have been without children, except one. The only surviving child moreover, appears a few years later as consul. The fact probably is, that the number 306, which is certainly symbolical, is not that of the warriors or even generals, as Livy says, but comprises the whole of the Fabian gens existing in the settlement, including women and children. If we were to suppose that they were 306 men capable of bearing arms, we should be obliged to estimate the number of all the patricians at an amount beyond all possibility. There can be no doubt that they had a large number of clients; and the fact of the latter's emigrating with them is a remarkable instance of the relationship existing between patrons and clients.[2]

The destruction of the Fabii on the Cremera is an historical fact, but the account of it is partly poetical, partly annalistic. The poetical story was, that the Fabii, trusting to the peace concluded with the Etruscans, went from the Cremera to Rome for the purpose of offering up a *sacrum gentilicium* in the city, —such a sacrifice indeed could be offered only at Rome, and

---

[1] It was probably an attempt to conquer the Veientines by the establishment of a fortified place in their territory, like the ἐπιτειχισμὸς of Decelea against Athens, for in those times a campaign lasted only a very short period, from a week to a fortnight; the garrison of a place either went out to meet the enemy, or shut themselves up within their own walls; and in order to prevent the inhabitants quietly returning to their fields after the departure of the enemy, the latter often founded a fortified place in the territory which they had invaded.—N.

[2] Livy says of the Fabii that they went out *infelici via porta Carmentali*; and Ovid, *Carmentis portae dextro via proximo Jano est: Ire per hanc noli, quisques es: omen habet.* This must be understood thus: all Roman gates had a double arch, through one of which people went out of, and through the other into, the city; the former was called *Janus dexter*, and the latter *Janus sinister*. The Carmental gate was situated between the Capitoline and Quirinal. Now as any one who wanted to go out was not allowed to pass through the left Janus, he was obliged to take a round-about way, if the place he wanted to go to was close to the Carmental gate: for the right Janus was ominous, as being that through which the Fabii had left the city.—N.

all the members of the gens were obliged to attend—and not suspecting that the Etruscans had any hostile intentions, they proceeded without arms. But the Veientines roused their kinsmen and occupied the road which the Fabii had to pass; the latter were surrounded by many thousands, who however did not venture to attack them in close combat, but killed them from a distance with slings and arrows. The *sacrum gentilicium* was undoubtedly the *statum sacrificium* of the Fabian gens on the Quirinal which is mentioned in the Gallic calamity.[3]

The other account is, that the Fabii, being drawn away farther and farther by flocks feeding in the neighbourhood, and after at length coming into a woody plain, were slain by a numerous Etruscan army. The clients are not again mentioned, but the fortress on the Cremera was taken by the Veientines. We might be tempted to suspect treachery here, and that the rulers of Rome perfidiously delivered the fortress up to the enemy: one of the Roman consuls, T. Menenius, is said to have been in the neighbourhood, and to have afterwards been criminally accused; but that suspicion seems hardly probable, and if the consul acted treacherously, it can have been only from personal hatred. The same consul was defeated and fled to Rome, and the fugitives threw themselves into the city, and did not even maintain the Janiculum, the garrison of which fled with them; the other consul appeared just in time to ward off the greatest danger, and it was with difficulty that the bridge was broken down. It is true there was a wall also running from the Capitol to the Aventine, which protected the city on this side of the river; but the breaking down of the bridge was necessary in order to isolate the suburb, which no doubt existed as early as that time. The Veientines were now masters of the whole plain; they pitched their camp on the Janiculum, crossed the river, and plundered all the Roman territory on the left bank of the Tiber. It was then about the middle of summer, and the new consuls entered upon their office on the first of August. The enemy had crossed the river unexpectedly on rafts, and thus it may have happened that the greater part of the harvest was destroyed, the farms burnt down, and that men and cattle fell into the hands of the enemy: the distress in the city rose to an extra-

[3] Livy, v. 46.

ordinary height. The Roman armies were encamped outside
the city, and hard pressed by the Veientines. But despair
gave them courage, and they resolved upon a daring enterprise,
which was to decide whether Rome should perish or be saved.
They crossed the river, defeated the Etruscans, and while one
part stormed the Janiculum, another made an attack from
above; they lost indeed an immense number of men, but they
drove off the enemy. I have already observed, that this account presents a striking resemblance to that of the war
with Porsena. One year later a truce was concluded with
the Veientines for forty years of ten months each, and was
honestly kept.

After these occurrences, the character of the tribuneship
shews itself in a peculiar manner: the tribunes summoned the
consuls of the preceding year before the people, not as our
authors represent it before the plebes, for they were yet much
too weak to sit in judgment on the sovereign magistrates, nay
not even before the centuries, which were for the most part
plebeian; but it was either not the tribunes at all but the
quaestors that summoned the consuls, or what is much more
probable, a great change had taken place by which the tribunes
were enabled to give effect to their right of accusing the
consuls before their own peers, that is, the *populus*, because the
magistrates who were bound to do so neglected their duty.
After the consuls were condemned to pay a considerable fine,
the tribunes proceeded to bring an accusation against their
successors. They were acquitted, but the exasperation rose
higher and higher. The tribunes had brought their accusation
before the burghers, and the case was one on which they had
the power to decide, for it was *majestas populi Romani imminuta
re male gesta*, and consequently a *crimen majestatis;* but the
tribunes now proceeded further. They summoned all the
consuls that had been in office since the time of Sp. Cassius,
before the plebeian commonalty, because they had not done
justice to the people in regard to the agrarian law; and this
step was taken according to an old Italian maxim, that when
two nations were united by a treaty any complaint respecting
a violation of the treaty should be brought before the injured
people. It is repugnant to our views that a person should be
the judge in his own case, but the practice existed among all
the ancient Italian nations, so that the Romans even followed

the principle of delivering up Roman citizens to an allied nation which had been offended by them; as examples, I may mention the surrender of Mancinus to the Numantines, of Postumius and his companions to the Samnites after the Caudine defeat, and of Fabius, who had offended the ambassadors of Apollonia. The surrender of those *qui in noxa sunt* was a general demand whenever there occurred a *rerum repetitio*. This principle is not found among the Greeks; it is based partly upon the noble idea that an oath before the actual trial is sufficiently binding, and partly upon a notion which is also found among the ancient Germans: with them any member of a family was obliged to come forward as a witness in a case affecting members of his own family, when he was called upon to do so (*consacramentales*); a custom which rested upon the noble idea of fidelity. It was a principle that no one could judge a member of his own order but only defend him; from which however frightful abuses arose. It is surprising how impartial courts of justice at Rome sometimes were; to be so, however, was less difficult on account of the circumstance, that the accused, up to the moment when the verdict was given, was at liberty to retire from Rome and betake himself to some one of the many allied towns. At Caere, for example, a Roman might demand to be received as a citizen. The origin of this right of withdrawing and claiming the right of citizenship elsewhere was traced in Roman books to the times of T. Tatius, who refused to deliver up his kinsmen to the inhabitants of Lavinium who had been injured by them: in consequence of this he was murdered, but afterwards the Romans surrendered the offenders to the Lavinians, and the latter the murderers of T. Tatius, that they might be tried.

It was upon this principle that the tribune Cn. Genucius, who belonged to a family which even at that time was great, summoned the patrician magistrates before the commonalty. He had promulgated his accusation against the consuls of the preceding year *in trinundinum*, and the plebeians themselves were to judge; their right to do so was by no means doubtful, according to the treaty solemnly sworn to upon the Sacred Mount; nor was the issue of the trial uncertain. But in the exasperation of parties, the patricians resolved upon the quickest expedient—they committed the monstrous crime of murdering Genucius; and with this murder the accusation dropped.

LECTURE XX.

DIONYSIUS justly observes that if the assassins of Genucius had been satisfied with their crime, the terror which they created might have been sufficient for their purpose. The tribunes were in the greatest alarm, for their sacred right was violated; as it was necessary for their houses to be open day and night, no precaution could protect them against a similar outrage, nor against the intrusion of disguised assassins; and even the boldest dreads such a danger. The murderers of Genucius were not discovered, and the general terror paralyzed everybody. The patricians exulted in their deed, and wanted to avail themselves of the first moment for making a levy, and for adding scorn and insult to their crime: their intention was to select the noblest of the plebeians, and in the field to put them to death or abandon them to the enemy. But they were too hasty in their insolence, and their exultation knew no patience: they summoned a distinguished plebeian, Volero Publilius, who had before been centurion, and wanted to enlist him as a common soldier. Distinguished and wealthy families existed among the plebeians as well as among the patricians; and to these the Publilii belonged. When Publilius refused to obey, the consuls sent their lictors to drag him *obtorto collo* before their tribunal, to strip him, and scourge him *servili modo*. The Roman toga was a very wide garment of one piece in the form of a semicircle; there was no seam in it, and a man might wrap himself entirely up in it: now if a person was to be led before a magistrate, the lictors threw the toga round his head and thus dragged him away, whereby they often nearly strangled him, the blood flowing from his mouth and nose. A person dragged in this manner endeavoured of course to defend himself by drawing the toga towards himself; the lictor then took a knife and cut a hole in the toga through which he put his hand and so forced his prisoner along. This is expressed by the phrase *vestem scindere*. But the lictors rarely made use of such violence, because the people did not easily tolerate it. Volero Publilius being resolute and strong, dashed away the lictor, ran among the plebeians and called upon the tribunes for assistance. The latter, however,

being themselves thoroughly terrified, remained silent, whereupon he addressed himself to the plebeians: the people rushed
in a body upon the pursuing lictors who were easily overpowered. The young patricians ran to the spot, and a struggle ensued, in which the tyrants were driven from the forum
in a very short time. On the following day, the consuls again
attempted a levy, but were equally unsuccessful, and they
then abstained from making any further trial in the course of
that year. The murder of Genucius had only rendered matters
far worse, and Volero Publilius was elected tribune for the
year following, a clear proof that the sanction of the curies was
no longer requisite.

An ordinary man would have summoned the consuls of the
preceding year before the court of the plebes; but this would
only have been a miserable piece of revenge. Publilius saw
that the great exasperation of the commonalty must be made
use of to gain permanent advantages for them; and for this
reason, contrary to the expectation of all, he took a step which
properly speaking he was not allowed to take, but it was the
beginning of a new order of things. He called upon the
plebes to declare that they had a right to discuss the affairs
of the state on the proposal of a tribune, and to pass valid resolutions; and further that the tribunes should no longer be
elected by the centuries, but by the tribes. These rogations,
which are much clearer in Dionysius and Dion Cassius (in the
abridgment of Zonaras) than in Livy, do not allude to one
circumstance, viz., that such resolutions of the tribes required
the sanction of the senate and curies in order to become law;
it is impossible that the Publilian law should have gone so far
as to make the same claims as the Hortensian, as is clear also
from the cases which occur. The development of the states of
antiquity shows no such abrupt transitions any more than
nature herself; and the demands made by the Hortensian law
would have been inconsistent and senseless in those times.

The manner in which business was now done was the following:—The tribunes made their legislative proposals on a
market day; for the people, the *populus* as well as the plebes,
could not transact business on all days, the curies and centuries
only on *dies comitiales*, and the tribes only on the nundines; it
was the Hortensian law that first empowered the centuries also
to assemble on the nundines. The accurate expressions are

populus jubet, *plebs scisit;* it was never said *plebs jubet* or *popu-liscitum*. The plebes at first met in the forum, but afterwards in the area Capitolina, the *populus* in the *comitium* or in a grove outside the *pomoerium*, called the *aesculetum* or *lucus Petelinus*. In the *concilium plebis* the votes were given by means of *tabellae*, and in the *concilium* of the curies, *viva voce*. There is no trace of its having been necessary to announce by a previous promulgation the subject of discussion in the *concilium populi*. The senate had no power to bring anything directly before the plebes; it could only commission the consuls to have a conference with the tribunes on any question; the curies on the other hand could not transact any busi-ness without a *senatusconsultum*, and in their assemblies nothing could be done without a curule magistrate or an *interrex*, who were not even allowed to show their faces at the meetings of the plebs.[1] Now when the tribunes wanted to bring a bill before the commonalty for deliberation, they exhibited it in the forum *in albo in trinundinum*, that is as a matter to be de-termined upon after fifteen days, the first nundines being included in the reckoning. A *concio advocata* might take place at any time, for the forum was always crowded, and the tribune might ascend the rostra and address the people, or give an opportunity of speaking to others, especially those who intended to speak against his proposal (*edocere plebem*). But such deliberations were only preliminary, not decisive; just as when the British parliament forms itself into a committee, in which mere resolutions are passed, or as when the French chambers have a preliminary deliberation upon a legislative proposal in the *bureaux;* the deliberation on the day when a question was to be put to the vote was quite different. It was necessary that every transaction of the *populus* as well as of the plebs should be completed before sunset, otherwise the day

---

[1] In our manuals of antiquities these distinctions are neglected. However valuable the earlier works on this subject are in reference to detail, they give us no assistance in comprehending the political state of Rome. The works of Si-gonius and Beaufort deserve to be recommended as containing ample materials arranged by ingenious men; in regard to later times we cannot be grateful enough to them, for the vast amount of information which they afford. The commentary of Manutius on Cicero's letters is quite indispensable for any one who wishes to understand that period, and his work *De Diebus* is excellent, but as to the earlier times, he too is in the dark even more than others. The work of Adam is in many respects invaluable, but the first part contains a great deal which is incorrect.—N.

was lost; the plebs had their auspices only in later times, but a flash of lightning or any similar phenomenon separated the *populus* (*dies diffissus*). When a tribune had promulgated his rogation *in albo* fifteen days previously, the decisive deliberation took place. We are too apt to represent to ourselves these proceedings as tumultuous; the people assembled early in the morning, the deliberation lasted the whole day, and one person rose after another speaking either for or against the proposal: the opposition endeavoured *eximere diem*, in order that it might be impossible to come to a conclusion before sunset: which was observed from the steps of the curia Hostilia[2], and then *suprema tempestas* was announced. In such cases, the tribune was again obliged to wait eight days and again to promulgate *in trinum nundinum*. This form must have been customary even in the earliest times in all the deliberations of the plebes, for there had been *plebiscita*[3] as long as the plebes existed.

If, on the other hand, the discussion was closed and the votes were to be taken, the tribune called upon the patricians and clients to withdraw, and as the *rostra* stood between the *comitium* and the forum, the *populus* withdrew to the former. Hereupon the forum was divided by ropes into a number of squares, into each of which a tribe entered, and each tribe then voted for itself under the management of its tribune. When it became known that the tribes had passed the resolution, the patricians had the right of rejecting it, just as in England the house of Lords and the king may reject a bill sent up by the house of Commons; but if the latter is determined to have the bill passed, it would be quite impossible to reject it; such a measure would be the signal for a dissolution of the government. The patricians would not allow matters to come to such a crisis, and therefore usually endeavoured to prevent the plebes from coming to an obnoxious resolution. We might ask, what advantage there was in preventing a resolution one day, since it might be carried the next? A great deal was gained; a respite of three weeks, in which perhaps a war might arise, which would put a stop to every thing; nay a

[2] The discovery of this place has been the key to all my investigations on Roman topography.—N.

[3] The orthography *plebisscita* is quite wrong; *plebi* is the ancient genitive of *plebes* just as *Hercules, Herculi; Caeles, Caeli; dies, dii.*—N.

matter might be dragged on through a whole year, but then the evil only increased and the exasperation of the people rose higher and higher. This is the folly which all oligarchs will be continually guilty of in some form or other as long as there are oligarchies. The patricians were blind enough not to see that if they could get up among the plebeians themselves a sufficiently strong party to oppose a proposal, the consequences would be the same as if a resolution were actually passed and afterwards rejected, but without any odium being attached to them. In the end the patricians never shewed sufficient courage to let matters come to a crisis: they always yielded but in a hateful manner, and reserved to themselves their ancient rights, no part of which they would give up except on compulsion.

LECTURE XXI.

THE great importance of the Publilian law is that the tribunes now obtained the initiative; until then it had been quite in the power of the senate and the patricians either to allow a legislative proposal to be discussed or to prevent it: the consul first made his proposal to the senate, and it was only after the latter had given its consent to the proposal, that it was brought before the curies or the curies and centuries. But as the tribunes were now at liberty to lay any proposal before the commonalty, they thereby acquired the power of introducing a discussion upon any subject which required it. There were points which urgently demanded a change, and among them many of the highest importance, which without the Publilian rogation would never have been discussed in a constitutional way. The Publilian laws therefore were beneficial, for had they not been passed, the indignation of the plebeians would have vented itself in another way, and the state would have been torn to pieces in wild exasperation; I cannot, however, blame the rulers of that time for not seeing the beneficial results of the laws. But the angry manner in which they opposed the tribunes was as blameable as it was injurious; the mode of their opposition threw the formal injustice upon the opposite side, for I cannot deny that the Publilian law was contrary to the existing order of things, and an irregularity. The senate might have disregarded such a *plebiscitum* altogether, or might have declared that the plebes were not qualified to pass it; but when the tribunes called upon the *populus* to withdraw from the forum, the patricians refused to go, and with their clients spread all over it, so that the plebeians were prevented from voting; they drove away the servants who carried the voting urns, threw out the tablets containing the votes, and the like. After this had been attempted once or twice more, the exasperation of the plebeians rose to the highest pitch and a fight ensued, in which the patricians and their consul Appius Claudius were driven from the forum. The consequence was a general panic among the patricians, because they saw that it was impossible to resist the infuriated multitude. But the plebeians did not stop here: they put themselves in possession of the Capitol but without abusing this victory, though the tribunes are generally censured. I do not mean to represent the plebeians as champions of virtue or their opponents as thorough knaves: such an opinion would be ridiculous, but the conduct of the plebeians contains a great lesson; those who in such times have the power in their hands, often abuse it, whereas the oppressed are moderate in their conduct, as we see especially in the case of religious parties. I believe the Jansenists at Utrecht would not have the excellent reputation which they fully deserve, if they were not the oppressed church: it is often a salutary thing for a man to belong to the persecuted party. The plebeians used their victory only to carry their resolution. Although Appius even now exerted all his influence to induce the senate to refuse its sanction, yet the senators were too much impressed with the greatness of the danger, and the law was sanctioned. Livy refers this law merely to the election of the tribunes, but Dionysius and Dion Cassius (in Zonaras) give the correct account. Livy did not clearly see the peculiar importance of these laws, but at the close of his narrative he mentions some points which presuppose what he has not stated.

Had the patricians been wise, they ought to have been pleased at the issue of the affair; no one at least could regard it as a misfortune. The repeal of such a law is impossible, but instead of seeing this, the patricians with their weakened powers continued attempting to undo what had been done, and were bent upon taking revenge. The plebeians still looked upon the consul whom they had not elected as illegal, and refused to obey him; in this predicament was Appius Claudius, who led an army against the Volscians, and on his march began to punish and torture the soldiers for the most trifling transgressions. Dionysius' account of these things is very credible, and seems to be founded upon ancient traditions. The plebeians opposed the consul with stubborn defiance, and would rather be punished than obey him. Immediately before the battle, they determined to take to flight, and accordingly ran back to the camp, although the Volscians were not on that account the less bent upon pursuing and cutting them to pieces; the Romans did not even remain in the camp, but continued their flight till they reached the Roman territory. There Appius did a thing which might seem to us incredible, were it not accounted for by the influence of the allies, the Hernicans and Latins who were under his command: he put to death every tenth man of the army, and led the survivors to Rome. The consequence was, that in the following year he was accused by the tribunes before the plebes; we may look upon Livy's masterly description of this as based upon the account of one who had a thorough knowledge of the events, though it is more detailed than he found it in the annals. Appius displayed the greatest defiance and haughtiness, and was resolved not to be softened down by entreaties; even the tribunes allowed themselves to be overawed by him. Both our historians agree in stating that a respite was granted to him by the tribunes, in order that he might make away with himself,—a fact which often occurs in the history of Rome, and more rarely in that of Greece. He availed himself of the concession even before the dawn of the ensuing day, and escaped further prosecution by suicide.

After this, the internal disputes ceased for a time, while the wars with foreign nations became more and more important. In the year A.U. 286, the Romans conquered Antium, or, according to a more probable account, Antium opened its gates to them. In our historians, the town appears as decidedly Volscian, and part of its inhabitants are said to have fled to the Volscians at Ecetra. I believe that the following is a correct view of the matter. Antium, like Agylla and the other coast towns, was originally Tyrrhenian, but there may have been a numerous party in the town which, feeling itself too weak to resist Rome and Latium, called in the assistance of the Volscians; and Ecetra, the south-eastern capital of this people, sent a colony to Antium. This colony was looked upon by a part of the citizens with hostile feelings, and when these citizens called upon the Romans for assistance, the Volscian colonists were expelled, and returned to Ecetra. The Volscians then attempted to recover what they had thus lost, and this gave rise to obstinate wars. After Antium had thrown itself into the arms of the Romans and their allies, it received a colony of Romans, Latins and Hernicans, a remarkable proof of the equal manner in which these three nations shared their conquests. Every one must see how Dionysius has distorted this event; Livy thinks that the Romans who were willing to join the colony, did not amount to a sufficient number. Antium now was akin to the three allied states, and the ancient Tyrrhenian Antiatans formed the commonalty of the town, while the colonists were the burghers; it is probable that each state sent 300 colonists, except the Hernicans, who sent 400, for among them, the division into four seems to have prevailed, whence the mention of the *cohortes quadringenariae*. The *Antiates mille milites*, who are met with in the later Volscian wars, seem to be these 1000 colonists. Such numerical calculations are anything but arbitrary, however much they may be opposed to our notions. But the success of the Romans in this war was only transitory; for as they were not the strongest in the field, and as the ancient inhabitants always fared ill under a colony, it is conceivable that ten years afterwards Antium was lost by the Romans, in the same manner as it had been gained. According to our division, the establishment of the colony at Antium concludes the first period of the Volscian war, which henceforth assumes quite a different character.

The Aequians, who at that time must have been a great people (Cicero, in fact, calls them *gens magna*), seem until then to have taken little part in the war; but the loss of Antium roused not only the Volscians of Ecetra to vigorous exertions, but also the Aequians. The subsequent misfortunes of the Romans are veiled over in our accounts; but the enemy seem to have advanced as far as the frontiers of the Roman territory, and all the Latin towns were conquered: the Volscians were

formerly found in the district of Velitrae, but henceforth they
appear every year on mount Algidus, and obtained possession
of the *arx* of Tusculum, which was reconquered from them
only with great difficulty.   Several Latin towns disappears
entirely.   Corioli was destroyed: Lavici became an Aequian
town; Gabii continued to be deserted within its walls as late
as the time of Dionysius; Praeneste is no longer mentioned,
and after a period of 100 years, when it reappears in history,
it was hostile towards Rome; it is probable that only the
nearest places, such as Tusculum and Lavinium, remained in
the hands of the Romans. The frontier of the Roman dominion
was on the other side of the hills of Tusculum; Circeii, Velitrae,
Norba and other towns farther East were lost.   It is certain,
therefore, that more than half of Latium was conquered by the
Aequians who penetrated into it from the Anio, and by the
Volscians who advanced from the sea coast.

Some allusions to these events are to be found in the account
of Coriolanus, for the Romans endeavoured to console themselves for these losses by ascribing them to one of their own
countrymen, a feeling which is quite natural.   In the time of
the French revolution, I have often seen emigrants rejoicing
at the victories of the French, although they knew that their
lives would be sacrificed should they fall into the hands of the
conquerors.   In like manner James the second when in exile
was delighted at the victories of the English.   The Romans
thus fancied that the Volscians lost all their power as soon as
Coriolanus was no longer with them.   But the whole story of
Coriolanus is neither more nor less than a poem, in which a
series of events belonging to various years is referred to one
man and to one period, which events moreover are placed many
years too early.   However hard the Romans may have been
pressed, it cannot be conceived that neither consuls nor armies
should have been sent against the enemy, while the latter in
their victorious career hastened from town to town.   It is only
in the enumeration of the places which were destroyed, that
we have had a hint as to those which became Volscian after
the destruction of Latium.

The Volscians penetrated so far, that it became necessary to
receive men and cattle within the walls of Rome, just as at
Athens in the Peloponnesian war; and this crowding together
of men and beasts produced a plague.   It is well known that

great depression always produces a susceptibility for epidemics. It was the despair of the Attic peasantry, who in the Peloponnesian war saw their farms burnt down and their olive plantations destroyed, that developed the germs of the epidemic. Physicians of Cadiz have pointed out to me a probable cause for the breaking out of the yellow fever which raged there in 1800: previously every thing was in a prosperous condition, but the despondency which arose from the influx of large numbers of poor unemployed people, increased and spread the disease with great rapidity. In most cases, the germs of an epidemic, though existing, do not come to an outbreak, for particular circumstances are required to develop them. Thus we may well believe the Romans, that the conflux of people, the want of water and cleanliness (it was in the month of August) greatly contributed to produce the epidemic; but it is probable that the great pestilence which thirty years later broke out in Greece and Carthage, began in Italy as early as that time. The rate of mortality was fearful: it was a real pestilence, and not a mere fever, which alone as persons were obliged to sleep in the open air, might, at that season of the year, have carried off thousands of people. Both consuls fell victims to the disease, two of the four augurs, the curio maximus, the fourth part of the senators, and an immense number of citizens of all classes, so that sufficient conveyances could not be found even to carry the dead to the river; the bodies were thrown into the *cloacae*, whereby the evil was increased. During this plague the Volscians and Aequians traversed the whole of Latium; the Latins offered resistance, but suffered a fearful defeat in the valley of Grotta Ferrata. In the following year we hear nothing of victories; the disease may have attacked the enemy also, and thus have saved Rome. After a few years the plague re-appeared as usual.

Much of the detail in our accounts of this war is not deserving of notice at all, a great part consists of later inventions for the purpose of giving to that dismal period some pleasing features. The scene of the wars is mount Algidus, which is not a mountain, but a cold interrupted table land several miles in circumference between Tusculum and Velitrae; it forms the watershed from which the streams flow partly towards the Liris and the Pontine marshes, and partly towards the Anio[1]. The

---

[1] Horace says: *Nigrae feraci frondis in Algido.* — N.

district is barren, and in antiquity, as is the case now, it was covered with ever-green stone-oaks; some years ago it was the constant haunt of robbers, in consequence of which I could not visit it, but I have collected accurate information about it. There the Aequians and Volscians always appeared and united their armies. The same district is the scene of the poetical story of Cincinnatus' victories over the Volscians. These victories, at least in the form in which they have come down to us, belong to a very beautiful poem, and are connected with the internal history of Rome, on which account I shall defer speaking of them, until I have related to you the commotions which occurred after the Publilian law.

LECTURE XXII.

THE Publilian law could not remain without consequences destructive of internal quiet, for it was the beginning of a great commotion that could not fail to be attended with violent shocks. The great subject of complaint with the plebeians was the unlimited power of the consuls: they had taken the place of the kings; their time of office was limited, but in power they were little inferior to the kings, and the consequences of their undefined power were manifested in the levies of troops. As the tribunes had now the right to make legislative proposals, C. Terentilius Harsa first brought forward a bill that five men should be appointed to draw up a law respecting the limits of the consular power. It was very difficult to execute this task, for the supreme power can never in reality be perfectly defined, and least of all in republics; it must ever be something uncertain so as to be able to act on extraordinary emergencies. This circumstance was recognised by the Roman republic in the formula *videant consules ne quid res publica detrimenti capiat;* in the earlier times this was quite common, and at such junctures it was hardly possible to determine between the legal use and the abuse of power. The task of these five men was of such a nature that we can well imagine men of the greatest honesty might say much for or

against the proposal. Some might demand a definition of the
consular power so as to prevent abuse, while others might
insist upon the government not being disarmed, in order that
it might not become powerless in times of danger; but there
ought to have been no venom in these differences of opinion.
It was perhaps intended from the very first that the measure
should be of a more extensive character, and it may even have
been intended to divide the consulship equally between the
two estates.

During the first year, the commotions were less violent than
in the next, for according to Dionysius, whose account is quite
correct, another tribune took up the *lex Terentilia* with this
extension, that decemvirs, five of the patres and five of the
plebeians, should be appointed to undertake a general revision
of the laws. The legislations of antiquity embraced not only
the civil and criminal law and the mode of procedure, but also
the political laws and regulations of a temporary nature. The
legislation of Solon, for example, was a complete reform of the
constitution, and at the same time regulated temporary matters,
such as the payment of debts. The notion of the period which
has just passed away, that general legislation ought to proceed
from a large assembly of lawyers was quite foreign to the
ideas of the ancients, who well knew that legislation must be
the work of a few, and the province of larger assemblies was
merely to adopt or reject it, the sanction resting with them.
This is the natural course of things, and hence the ancients
for the most part followed the maxim that legislation should
be quite independent of the magistracy: in all the republics
of antiquity, one man or a few were appointed to make the
laws, and the people said either Yes or No. Such also was
the case among the Romans: ten men were to be appointed
legibus scribendis, who however were to be invested with consular power. From the remains of the Roman laws, we see
that each was of great extent, which accounts for the fact, that
but few persons read the laws, and that most people were quite
ignorant of their contents: in this respect, the republican form
in such affairs is necessarily a mere shew. Dionysius very
happily expresses himself in saying that the Romans aimed at
ἰσονομία, and gained ἰσηγορία.[1] From an accidental expres-

---

[1] " Properly (in Herodotus and Thucydides ἰσονομία is that state of freedom
where no man is beyond or above the law; it is neither a τυραννίς nor a δυναστεία;

sion of Tacitus we know that the ancient laws were, for the most part, traced to the kings Romulus, Numa, Tullus and Ancus. This shews that each of the three ancient tribes and the plebes had their separate laws, which were ascribed to their respective archegetes. These tribes and the plebes, which had originally been distinct communities, continued to preserve their ancient statutes, even after their union into one state. I believe that more than a hundred different statutes existed in the papal dominions previously to the French revolution, and many an Italian village containing not more than one hundred houses has its own statute or customary law; the late Abbé Morelli had collected three hundred different statutes in Italy. The same was the case in the middle ages in many parts of Germany, though in some instances one and the same law was in force over a large extent of country. It is not even certain whether the whole of the plebes had the same law, or whether a different one was not established in places like Medullia and Politorium; this hypothesis, it is true, is opposed to the statement that Servius Tullius abolished all differences among the plebeians by dividing them into tribes; but on the other hand it is supported by the existence of places like Cameria and others, which were Roman colonies and formed separate commonalties. The ancients had a tradition that the clause in the twelve tables ordaining that the *Fortes* and *Senates* should have equal rights, referred to certain places such as Tibur.

The heads of the plebes might very well insist upon the establishment of equal laws for all, an object which was beneficial not only to them but to the state in general, for the disadvantages of such different statutes must have been great and keenly felt: the purpose of the reform, therefore, was the abolition of every thing which established painful and oppressive differences between the two orders; and the tribunes were justified in demanding it. There still was no connubium between patricians and plebeians, and the children of mixed marriages followed the baser side (*deteriorem partem sequi*). In the middle ages, Lombards, Franks, Romans and others lived together for centuries in the cities of Italy, each nation having its own peculiar laws; but the inconveniences arising from this

ἰσηγορία (in Demosthenes) is that state where every free citizen is of equal rank." See *Hist. of Rome*, ii. p. 281, note 640.

circumstance subsequently caused common statutes for all the inhabitants of a town to be drawn up.

The tribunes, however, went further, and as the legislation was also to comprise the political law, the legislators were at the same time to make a reform of the constitution. The Publilian laws had awakened in the nation a life which was not in harmony with the ruling power: a new state of things was necessarily springing up, which soon found itself in conflict with that which was established. Whether the patricians foresaw to what extent this law would operate, or whether it was, from the beginning, intended to be more comprehensive than we know, certain it is that they made the most vehement opposition to the law, and had recourse to acts of violence similar to those which they had practised before. Kaeso Quinctius, a son of Cincinnatus, made himself particularly notorious; he repeated all the intrigues of Appius Claudius, and heading the young men of his own age and rank and the clients, he by violence prevented the plebeians from voting. A law (*lex Junia*) against such violence was passed either then or the year before, which declared every one who disturbed the tribunes in their functions guilty of high treason towards the commonalty.[2] A person guilty of this crime was obliged to find sureties for a sum of money to be fixed by the tribunes (the usual number of sureties was ten, each for 3000 asses), and if he did not await his verdict, the money was forfeited to the commonalty. In virtue of this law, the tribunes of the year following brought an accusation against Kaeso Quinctius before the commonalty. On the trial he was charged with having, in conjunction with a band of young patricians, maltreated a plebeian so that he died. To us this seems incredible, but it was not so in antiquity: in like manner the pentalides in Mitylene ran about with clubs assaulting the plebeians of Mitylene. Nay, even in modern times similar things have been done: during the minority of Louis the Fourteenth such scenes occurred in the streets of Paris, where no one dared to walk without arms, there being constant danger of an attack. In the time of Queen Anne, there existed a band of young nobles in London called Mohocks, who roamed

---

[2] It seems almost inconceivable that Dionysius should place the passing of this law thirty years earlier (A.U. 262); his reason perhaps was that Coriolanus was said to have been condemned by it.—N.

through the streets in disguise and attacked the people; and in the reign of King William, Lord Bolingbroke, as we see from Swift's correspondence, belonged to such a band. Things of this kind could not now occur in any European city, thanks to police regulations, which, however much blamed by some people, are of incalculable benefit. The accusation excited so much exasperation against Kaeso Quinctius, that he did not dare to appear before the plebes, but quitted the city. It is related, that his father was reduced to poverty in consequence of the tribunes having exacted from him the sums for which sureties had been given. This is impossible; for the tribunes had claims on none but the sureties, and if the latter wanted to come upon the father, a *sponsio* must have preceded: even then, a man of so noble a family cannot possibly have been deprived of rights which belonged to the meanest of his order; he might surely have required his gentiles and clients to indemnify him. The whole account, like so many others, is an invention in which a foundation of truth is embellished and exaggerated; this making-up of the story might have been done with sufficient skill to deceive us, but fortunately it is managed so awkwardly that we cannot be misguided. Cincinnatus is one of those characters whose names stand very high in tradition, but concerning whom the records of history are extremely scanty and almost amount to nothing. He afterwards appears as consul without anything particular being related of him; it is only in the Aequian war that any striking fact is recorded of him. There is a halo of wealth and a halo of poverty; the latter shines more especially in rhetorical times when no one wishes to be poor, and when it appears inconceivable that a great man should be poor. We may pass over the old story of Cincinnatus ploughing his fields, etc. etc.; but the great enthusiasm which arose from it is a mere interpolation in history. Perizonius has observed that the same story is related of the dictator Atilius Serranus (*te sulco Serrane serentem*), and is therefore quite apocryphal: it was probably manufactured out of the name Serranus (from *serere*), which is surely more ancient than the dictator who bore it. The story of Cincinnatus was preserved in a poem on his dictatorship, of which the following is the substance.

A Roman army under the consul Minucius was surrounded by the Aequians on mount Algidus; the senate, it is said, sent an embassy to Cincinnatus, to offer him the dictatorship

The ambassadors found him on his small farm of four jugera, on the other side of the river, engaged in ploughing. Having heard the command of the senate, he complied with it, though his heart bled at the recollection of the fate of his son. He then chose a gallant but poor patrician, L. Tarquitius, for his *magister equitum*, and ordered all men capable of bearing arms to enlist, every one being required to bring with him twelve palisades and provisions for five days. The army broke up in the night, and, on its arrival the following morning, marched in a column around the Aequian camp; the consul sallied out from within, and the Aequians, who were themselves surrounded by a ditch and palisades were obliged to surrender.

The whole story is a dream as much as anything that occurs in the *Heldenbuch*. If the Roman army had been in the centre and surrounded by an Aequian army, and the latter again by a line of Romans, the Romans would have formed a circle of at least five miles in circumference, so that the Aequians might have broken through them without any difficulty. I do not mean, however, to assert that the dictatorship of Cincinnatus is altogether unhistorical, though it is strange that a similar event is afterwards related in the siege of Ardea, in which the same Cloelius Gracchus is mentioned as commander of the Aequians. Cincinnatus now made use of his power to get Volscius, who had borne witness against Kaeso Quinctius, sent into exile, probably by the curies, for the centuries do not seem to have then possessed judicial power. At that time, Kaeso Quinctius was no longer living, according to the express statement of Livy: he had probably fallen the year before in consequence of transactions which shew those times in their true colours. After he had gone into exile, the tribunes observed symptoms of a conspiracy among the young patricians, and there were reports that Kaeso was within the city. It is further related that during the night the city was surprised from the side of the Carmental gate, which was open, by a band of patrician clients, under the command of the Sabine, Appius Herdonius, who had come down the river in boats. It is manifest that it would have been impossible to collect a sufficient number of boats to convey an army of 4,000 men, without its being known at Rome, more especially as the Romans were at peace with the Sabines; and admitting that it was necessary to leave the gate open on account of a consecration, it must surely have been guarded by double sentinels; the enemy, moreover, could not possibly pass the field of Mars and occupy the Capitoline hill without being observed.   There must, therefore, have been treachery.   In the night, the people were roused from their sleep by a cry that the Capitol was in the hands of the enemy, who massacred every one that did not join them, and called upon the slaves to make common cause with them.   This naturally created not only the greatest consternation, but a general mistrust; the plebeians imagined that it was an artifice of the patricians who had stirred up their clients to take possession of the Capitol, in order thereby to intimidate the plebeians; they further believed that, as during a *tumultus*, the consuls would command them to take the military oath unconditionally, lead them to a place beyond the limits of the tribunitian power, and then require them to renounce their rights.   The tribunes accordingly declared that they could not allow the commonalty to take up arms before the laws were passed.   We may indeed believe that the government was innocent in this affair, but it seems certain that there was evidence of a conspiracy in which Kaeso Quinctius was an accomplice, and that a promise had been given to Appius Herdonius to make him king of Rome if the undertaking should succeed.   It is not impossible that this may rather have been a conspiracy of the *gentes minores*, for we can still perceive a great gulf between them and the *majores*.   When the real state of the case became known, the tribunes gave up their opposition and allowed the commonalty to take the oath; whereupon the Capitol was stormed under the command of the consul.   At this time there seems fortunately to have been a truce with the Aequians, but yet Rome was in a most dangerous condition, since no firm reliance could be placed upon the continuance of the truce.   The consul Valerius, the son of Poplicola, the same who is said to have fallen at lake Regillus, was killed; the Capitol was taken by storm, the slaves found there were nailed on crosses, and all the freemen were executed.   There seems to be no doubt that Kaeso Quinctius was among the latter; and this may have led his father in the following year to take revenge in a manner which is pardonable indeed, but ignoble, by exiling Volscius the accuser of his son.   The tribunes of the people are said to have prevented this accusation being made, a remarkable instance of the greatness of their power even at that time; but perhaps, they only afforded protection to the accused, and did not allow him to be violently dragged into court. The expression *patricios coire non passi sunt* is not applicable till later times. The disputes about the trial lasted for a couple of years, Cincinnatus either as consul or dictator (probably the latter), refusing to lay down his office until he should have obtained the condemnation of Volscius. The latter went into exile; his surname Fictor, probably from *fingere*, is one of the examples in which either the name arose from the story, or the story from the name: so that the statement, "the plebeian M. Volscius Fictor was condemned," gave rise to the story that he had given false evidence.

It is obvious, that Cincinnatus has undeservedly been deified by posterity: in the time of the decemvirs and tyrants, he did nothing; and twenty years after this occurrence, he acted completely in the interest of a faction, and shed the innocent blood of Maelius.

LECTURE XXIII.

AFTER the war of A.U. 296, the history of Rome takes a different turn. We have no express statements as to the circumstances which gave it this new direction; but the concurrence of several circumstances leaves no doubt that at that time the Romans concluded a peace and treaty of friendship with the Volscians of Ecetra, on condition of restoring Antium to the Volscians, so that this town assumed the character which it retained for 120 years, that is, till after the Latin war. Henceforth then, the Volscians no longer appeared every year on mount Algidus, and the Aequians alone continued to be enemies, but they were of no importance. From this time the Antiatans and Ecetrans took part in the festivals on the Alban mount, that is, in the Latin holidays; this is referred to the times of Tarquinius Superbus, but at that time Antium was not yet a Volscian town.

Previously to the year A.U. 290, the census amounted to 104,000, and after the plague, this number was diminished

only by one eighth, whereas one fourth of the senators had
been carried off; but the cause of this apparent discrepancy is,
that the Volscians had been admitted to the right of *municipium:*
citizens they were not, and consequently as the census lists
must have included them, they did not embrace Roman citizens only.   But it is more especially the story of Coriolanus
that furnishes a proof of this treaty.   He is said to have made
the Romans promise to restore the places which they had
taken from the Volscians, and to admit the Volscians as isopolites.   Both things were done: Antium was restored, and the
rights of isopolity were granted.   We must either suppose that
the events recorded of the great Volscian war were transferred
to this story, or that the episode about Coriolanus formed the
catastrophe of this war, which was followed by the peace; that
is, that Coriolanus really was the commander of the Volscians,
and mediated the peace between them and the Romans.

These wars, from A.U. 262 to A.U. 266 belong to the category of impossibilities, and that the history of Coriolanus is
inserted in a wrong place is perfectly clear.   The law against
the disturbers of the assembly of the people could not have
been passed previously to the Publilian rogations.   If the
Volscians had appeared at the gates of Rome as early as is
stated by our historians, no domain land would have been left
about the distribution of which the consul Sp. Cassius could
have proposed a law, and there would have been no subject of
dispute.   After the unfortunate Volscian wars, in fact, the
commotions about the agrarian law really did cease, because
the matter in dispute no longer existed.   Further, if the war
of Coriolanus in A.U. 262 had been carried on in the manner
in which it appears in our accounts, the Romans would have
had no place to restore to the Volscians: whereas after the
great Volscian war, Rome was in possession of several important places and was obliged to restore Antium.   Lastly, the
isopolity which was demanded was actually granted in the year
A.U. 296, as is proved by the numbers of the census.

As regards the giving up of Antium, the Roman historians
say that it revolted; which in the case of a colony is absurd.
The Roman colony was only withdrawn, and the ancient Tyrrhenian population was left to the Volscians.   Nay, the very
circumstance, in consequence of which the war of Coriolanus
is said to have broken out, namely the famine during which

a Greek king of Sicily is stated to have sent a present of corn
to Rome, points to a later period. After the destructive
Veientine war in the consulship of Virginius and Servilius,
the fields around Rome had been set on fire at harvest-time
and were laid waste also at the following seed-time. In A.U.
262, Gelo was not reigning at Syracuse, but at the utmost was
a prince of the insignificant town of Gela. Compared with the
old Roman annalists, who mentioned the tyrant Dionysius as
the king who had sent the present, Dionysius is very sensible,
for he proves that that monarch did not reign till eighty years
later; but Dionysius himself must be severely censured for
mentioning Gelo. After the Veientine war, indeed, according
to the more probable chronology, Gelo, or at least his brother
Hiero, was king of Syracuse, and owing to his hostility towards the Etruscans, he may actually have had good reasons
for supporting the Romans. All circumstances therefore point
to this as the real time. The story of Coriolanus is so generally
known that I need not give a long account of it. The cause of
its being transferred to a wrong place was the mention of the
temple of Fortuna Muliebris, as I have already remarked, but
this temple certainly belongs to an earlier period: a daughter
of Valerius Poplicola is said to have been the first priestess.
Now if it were connected with the history of Coriolanus, his
wife or mother would undoubtedly have been appointed the
first priestess, as a reward for their services in behalf of the
state.

The story runs as follows:—C. or as others name him, Cn.
Marcius Coriolanus, a very eminent young patrician, probably
of the lesser gentes (for these are more particularly opposed to
the plebes), greatly distinguished himself in the wars against
the Antiatans. He was an officer in the army which the consuls led against the Volscians: the year to which this campaign
belongs was, of course not mentioned in the poem. The army
besieged Corioli; the Volscians advancing from Antium wished
to relieve the place, but Coriolanus took it by storm while the
army of the consul was fighting against the Antiatans. From
this feat, he received his surname and acquired great celebrity.
But while in the war he appears as a young man, he is at the
same time a member of the senate and at the head of the oligarchic faction. A famine was raging in the city: in contradiction to the plebeian statement that the plebes during the

secession destroyed nothing, we are told that they had in fact laid waste the country; but the whole account is evidently of patrician origin, and has a strong party colouring. Various but useless attempts were made to procure corn; money was sent to Sicily to purchase it, but the Greek king sent back the money and gave the corn as a present: it was perhaps a gift from the Carthaginians. The senate, it is said, debated as to what was to be done with the corn, and Coriolanus demanded that it should neither be distributed nor sold, unless the commonalty would renounce the rights they had lately acquired— they were to give up their birth-right for a mess of pottage. Another proposal not much more praiseworthy, was that the corn should be sold to the commonalty as a corporation, from which individual members might afterwards purchase it; hence the plebeians were to pay the purchase-money twice: this plan was adopted, but it naturally produced great exasperation, and on this occasion it also became known that Coriolanus had insisted upon making use of the distress for the purpose of abolishing the privileges of the plebeians. Livy relates the course of events briefly; but Dionysius gives a very full account of them. According to the former, the tribunes brought a charge against Coriolanus as guilty of a violation of the peace; and in this they were fully justified by the sworn treaty of the sacred mount. The charge was, of course (though Dionysius does not see this) brought before the plebes, and Coriolanus being summoned before the court of the tribes, had the right to quit the country before the sentence was pronounced. A person could do this after he had given sureties, but it was not done in the way usually supposed. He who had to dread an unfavourable issue could not go into exile in the manner described in our manuals of antiquities, but he might wait till all the tribes had voted except one, as Polybius says. When the majority had decided against him he was condemned; but if he had taken up his abode as a citizen of a Latin town, for example, the decision was void, but the sureties, at least in later times, had to pay. Livy says that Coriolanus met the accusation with haughtiness, but that on the day of judgment he departed before the sentence was pronounced. Coriolanus was perhaps the first who was allowed to give sureties. The common tradition is, that he now went to the Volscians. This is true (and up to this point indeed I believe the whole story),

but his going to Attius Tullus at Antium is apocryphal, and a
mere copy of the story of Themistocles going to Admetus king
of the Molossians. He is said to have stirred up the Volscians,
who were quite desponding, to venture again upon the war:
this is a Roman exaggeration intended to disguise the distress
which had been caused at Rome by the Volscian arms. It is
further related that he conquered one place after another; first
Circeii, then the towns south of the Appian road, and next
those on the Latin road; and that at last he advanced even to
the gates of Rome. This is irreconcilable with what follows:
Coriolanus now appears at the Roman frontier on the Marrana,
the canal which conducts the water of the low country of
Grotta Ferrata into the Tiber, about five miles from Rome.
The Romans sent to him an embassy, first of ten senators to
whom he granted a respite of thirty days, and then of three
more, as the fetiales did when a war was not yet determined
on; thereupon priests were sent to him and at last the matrons,
who moved his heart and induced him to retire.

All this is very poetical, but is at once seen to be impossible when closely looked into. Livy makes a curious remark,
in saying that the fact of the consuls of this year having carried on a war against the Volscians would be altogether unknown,
if it were not clear from the treaty of Spurius Cassius with the
Latins, that one of them, Postumus Cominius, was absent, the
treaty being concluded by Cassius alone. But Livy thinks
that the glory of Coriolanus, which eclipsed every thing else,
was the cause of the omission—a valuable testimony! the ancient traditions then did not state that the consul had anything
to do with the falling of Corioli, but attributed it to Coriolanus
alone. Now, as we have before seen, it is not true that Coriolanus received his surname from the taking of Corioli, such
names derived from conquered places not occurring till the
time of Scipio Africanus: further, Corioli at that period was
not a Volscian but a Latin town; it became Volscian in the
great Volscian war, which we call the war of Coriolanus, and
was not destroyed till afterwards. The fact of its being a
Latin town is clear from the list of the thirty towns which
took part in the battle of lake Regillus, though I admit that
this list may not have been originally drawn up with reference
to that battle, but rather to the treaty of Sp. Cassius. The
name of Coriolanus thus signifies nothing more than the names

Regillensis, Vibulanus, Mugillanus and others, and was derived from Corioli, either because that town stood in the relation of *proxenia* or *clientela* to his family, or for some other reason.

Nothing therefore is historically known about Coriolanus, beyond the fact that he wanted to break the contract with the plebeians, and that he was condemned in consequence. His subsequent history is equally apocryphal. He was condemned as a man who had violated sworn rights (*leges sacratae*), and whoever was guilty of that crime, had accursed himself and his family; it is further said, that such persons were sold as slaves near the temple of Ceres. How then could his wife and children continue to live at Rome, if such a sentence had been pronounced upon them? It is impossible to think of mercy in those times. The places against which Coriolanus had made war were allied with the Romans, and as whoever made war against them was at war with Rome, the Romans ought to have marched out against him. Consequently, when he appeared before Rome he could no longer offer peace or war, but only a truce or terms of a truce; and the Romans, on the other hand, could not possibly conclude peace on their own responsibility, without consulting the Latins and Hernicans. The old tradition goes on to say, that the *interdictio aquae et ignis* which had been pronounced against Coriolanus was withdrawn, but that he did not accept the withdrawal, and made demands on behalf of the Volscians; but when the matrons had moved him, he departed and dropped all the stipulations he had made for them. From that moment we find no further trace of him, except the statement of Fabius, that up to an advanced age he lived among the Volscians, and that one day he said: " It is only in his old age that a man feels what it is to live in exile away from his country." Others, seeing that the Volscians could not have been satisfied with such a mode of acting, stated that they followed him on account of his personal influence, but that afterwards, being abandoned by him, they stoned him to death on the accusation of Attius Tullus. But this was not believed by Livy, because it was contrary to the account of Fabius.

We cannot say that the whole history of Coriolanus is a fiction, he is too prominent a person in Roman tradition to be altogether fabulous. But as regards the statement that he was a commander of the Volscian armies, it must be traced to the natural feeling that it is less painful to be conquered by one's own countrymen than by foreigners: with such national feelings, the Romans pictured to themselves the Volscian war, and thus consoled themselves and the Latins for the disgrace of the defeat, in consequence of which the Volscians made such extensive conquests. In the same spirit, they invented stories about the generosity of Coriolanus and about his death. I believe that Fabius was right in asserting that Coriolanus lived in exile among the Volscians to his old age. The statement that Rome was on the brink of destruction is probable, and it may be admitted that the description of the distress is not quite fictitious, but it cannot be denied that the three different embassies of senators, priests and matrons, are inventions made for the purpose of elevating the hero. The two estates mutually decry each other in their accounts; hence the plebeians appear from the first quite downcast and the patricians quite proud, as if they would hear of no reconciliation with Coriolanus.

I believe that the truth is very different. At that time there still existed a great many who had emigrated with the Tarquins, and they gathered together wherever they found a rallying point; now I believe that Coriolanus, after withdrawing to the Volscians, formed such a rallying point for them. As he thus found a small army of Roman emigrants who were joined by Volscians, he marched with them to the Roman frontier, not that he imagined he would be able to force his way through the gates or walls of Rome, but he encamped near it and declared war, just like the persons in Dithmarsch who had renounced their country. He first granted a term of thirty days, that the senate might consider whether his demands were to be complied with or not. As the senate did not come to a decision, he waited three days longer—a term which a state or general demanding reparation takes to consider whether he shall declare war, or in what manner he is to treat the proposals that may have been made to him. Coriolanus was undoubtedly joined by the partizans of Tarquinius, by many who had been sent into exile in consequence of crimes, and lastly by Volscians. The republic invited him to return; the entreaties of his mother, his wife and the other matrons, who implored him, can have no other meaning than that he should return alone and not bring with him that terrible band of men. He probably answered that he could not return alone

and forsake his companions. If he had returned, he could
have done nothing else than set himself up as a tyrant, as was
so often the case in Greece with the φυγάδες, whose return was
a real scourge to their country, they being almost under the
necessity of crushing the party by whom they had been expelled. We here see him act in a noble spirit, refusing to
return in this manner, and rather dismissing his own relatives
on whom he was obliged to make an impression by renouncing
his own country: a great man might indeed make such an
impression in those times.   Towards the Volscians he behaved
with perfect justice, and it is possible that he actually came
forward as mediator between them and Rome, and prevailed
upon the latter to give up Antium and grant the isopolity. He
thus discharged his duty towards those who had received him,
and Rome gained through him the immense advantage of a
reconciliation with her most dangerous enemy; the Volscians
had pressed Rome most severely, and there now remained only
the Aequians, whom it was easy to resist. The childish vanity
of the Romans has so completely disguised this Volscian peace
that until our own times, no one understood it; without it, the
whole history would be incoherent; it saved Rome and gave
her time to recover her strength; an opportunity which she
used with great wisdom.

LECTURE XXIV.

It is one of the distinguishing features of the history of
Rome, that many an event which had every appearance of
being ruinous was the very means of producing a favourable
crisis in her affairs.   After the plague and the unfortunate war
of the Volscians, we might have expected to see Rome reduced
to extremities: the peace with the Volscians was, in the eyes
of posterity, to some extent a humiliation, and for this reason
they concealed it; but how wise and advantageous it was for
Rome under the circumstances, we have already seen; we may
assert that through it Rome acquired a power which it would
never have obtained even by the most successful issue of the

war. The destruction of the Latin state virtually did away with the equality which was secured by the treaty of Sp. Cassius. The common opinion, as found in Dionysius, and also in Livy, is, that the Latins were subjects of the Romans, and that the war under Manlius and Decius in the year A.U. 410 (415), was a kind of insurrection. This is contradicted by the statement of Cincius in Festus, according to which the Latins, in his opinion, ever since the time of Tullus Hostilius formed a distinct republic, and had the supremacy alternately with Rome. The truth of the matter is this: from the time of Servius Tullius down to Tarquinius Superbus, the Latins stood in the relation of equality with Rome, but under Tarquinius they were subdued; this state of submission was interrupted by the insurrection of Latium after the expulsion of the kings, but was perhaps restored for a few years after the battle of lake Regillus, until at length equality was re-established by the treaty of Sp. Cassius. It actually existed for a period of thirty years; but when the Latin towns were partly occupied and partly destroyed by the Volscians, and when scarcely the fourth part of the Latin confederacy continued to exist; this remnant could of course no longer lay claim to the same equality with Rome as the entire confederacy had done before. It can be proved that at the beginning of the fourth century of Rome, the Latin towns had ceased to be united by any internal bond; they scarcely had a common court of justice, and some towns, such as Ardea, stood completely alone. The Latins now again came under the supremacy of Rome, as in the reign of Tarquinius Superbus. To distinguish what is true for different periods is the only thread that can guide us through the labyrinth of Roman history. Isolated statements must be examined with great attention, and not be absolutely rejected; even contradictions are of importance in their place. As regards the Hernicans, I cannot say with perfect certainty whether they were reduced to the same condition as the Latins, though it appears to me very probable. After the Gallic conflagration, the Latins again shook off the Roman dominion and renewed their claims to equality. This claim gave rise to a war which lasted thirty-two, or according to the more probable chronology, twenty-eight years, and ended in a peace by which the ancient treaty of Sp. Cassius was restored. Owing to the consequences of the Volscian war, Rome in the meantime enjoyed the advantage of standing alone and being unshackled.

In the city of Rome itself the ferment was still great, and according to Dion Cassius the assassination of distinguished plebeians was not an uncommon occurrence. Amid these commotions, the agrarian law and the bill for a revision of the legislature were constantly brought forward. It is impossible to say who induced the plebes to increase the number of their tribunes to ten, two for each class: their authority certainly could not be enlarged by this numerical augmentation. At the time of this increase, we meet with a strange occurrence, which however is very obscure. Valerius Maximus says that a tribune, P. Mucius, ordered his nine colleagues to be burnt alive as guilty of high treason, because, under the guidance of Sp. Cassius, they had opposed the completion of the election of magistrates. The times are here evidently in perfect confusion; for ten tribunes were first elected in the year A.U. 297, and the consulship of Sp. Cassius occurs twenty-eight years earlier. There are two ways in which we may account for this tradition: these tribunes had either acted as traitors towards the plebes, which is scarcely conceivable, as they were elected by the tribes: or P. Mucius was not a tribune of the people, or at least the sentence was not pronounced by him, but by the curies, who thus punished the tribunes for violating the peace. There must be some truth in the story since it is mentioned by Zonaras also (from Dion Cassius); it is not impossible that this occurrence is identical with the accusation of nine tribunes mentioned by Livy about the time of the Canuleian disputes.

I shall pass over the insignificant wars with the Aequians and Sabines, as well as some legislative enactments, though they are of great interest in Roman antiquities, and dwell at some length upon the Terentilian law; in which the tribunes demanded an equality of rights for the two estates. It would be highly interesting if we could know the detail of the disputes on the Terentilian law; but this is impossible, and we have only quite isolated statements to guide us. One of them is, that a trireme, with three ambassadors, was sent from Rome for the purpose of making a collection of the Greek laws, especially those of Athens. The credibility of this account has been the subject of much discussion, and I now retract the opinion which I expressed in the first edition of my Roman history; I had then, like my predecessors, not considered that the two questions whether the Roman law was derived from the Attic law, and whether Roman ambassadors did go to Athens are perfectly distinct. If a person asks: Are the Roman laws derived from those of the Athenians? the answer must be decidedly negative. There are only two Solonian laws, which are said to be found in the Pandects also, but these are quite insignificant and might with equal justice be derived from the laws of other nations; it would not be difficult to find some German laws which likewise agree with Roman ones. Moreover we cannot tell how far the national affinity between Greeks, Romans, and Pelasgians, might produce a resemblance in their laws. Nothing that is peculiar to the Roman law is found in the Attic law; the former is quite peculiar in the law of persons and in the law of things. The Greeks never had the law of paternal power as we find it at Rome; they never had a law by which a wife in marrying entered into the relation of a daughter to her husband; and in regard to property they never had any thing like the *jus mancipii;* the distinction between property acquired by purchase and absolute property, between property and hereditary possession does not exist in the Attic law; the Roman laws of inheritance, of debt and of contracts of loan, were perfectly foreign to the Athenians, and the Roman form of procedure again was quite different from that of the Athenians. These points are well known to every one acquainted with the Attic orators. The Attic law belongs to a much later time, when the ancient forms had already become greatly softened and polished; in them we behold a state of civil society which was wanting in the very thing which characterizes the Romans. All that we know of the laws of other Greek nations is equally foreign to those of Rome, and if perchance the laws of the states of Magna Graecia had any resemblance to the Roman, it certainly must have originated in their common Italian origin; thus the law of *ager limitatus* in the table of Heraclea seems to have been like the law established at Rome.

From these circumstances, many have concluded that the account of the embassy to Greece is not entitled to belief, but the case may be looked upon in a different light. There is, perhaps, none of us who has not at some time or other, after mature consideration, undertaken things which have never been accomplished: this may happen to a state as well as to individuals. The embassy falls exactly in the time of Pericles, between the Persian and the Peloponnesian wars, when Athens was at her highest prosperity, and when the fame of that most powerful and wise city had spread far and wide. The fact that at a much later period (the age of Cassander) when a bust was to be erected to the wisest among the Greeks, the Roman senate did not select Socrates, but Pythagoras, was quite in the spirit of an Italian nation; but their setting up a statue to Alcibiades as the bravest of the Greeks shews how familiar Athens was to the minds of the Romans; I may add that they did not judge incorrectly in regarding Alcibiades as the bravest. It may, therefore, after all, not have been quite in vain that the Romans sent an embassy to Greece; and they appear to have made the proper use of it in regard to their political constitution.

Another tradition respecting this legislation states, that Hermodorus, a wise Ephesian, who was staying at Rome, was consulted by the decemvirs. He is said to have been a friend of the great Heraclitus, and to have been exiled from Ephesus because he was too wise.[1] A *statua palliata*, which was believed to be of him, was shewn at Rome down to a late period: the tradition is ancient, and Hermodorus was not so celebrated as to induce the Romans without any motive to call him their instructor. He might act as adviser, as it was the avowed object of the legislation to abolish the differences between the two estates, to modify the constitution so as to make them as much as possible form one united whole, and lastly to effect a limitation of the consular *imperium*. But the civil code was not by any means derived from Greek sources; for there are provisions in Roman law which it is certain were expunged from the law of Athens even by Solon; the criminal code presents still greater differences.

It was from the beginning the intention to appoint a mixed commission of legislators. In Livy it seems as if the plebeians had entertained the unreasonable idea of choosing the legislators, five in number, from their own order exclusively; but Dionysius states the number at ten, the intention evidently being that five should be patricians and five plebeians. Now

---

[1] ἡμέων μηδεὶς ὀνήϊστος ἔστω.

there is another strange statement in Livy, namely, that the plebeians urgently entreated that if a revision of the laws was to be undertaken, and the patricians would not allow them to take a part in it, the patricians themselves might begin it alone, and confer with them concerning the principles only. The rational conclusion was therefore come to that the members of a mixed commission would be involved in perpetual quarrels, and that it would be better to elect them from only one estate, provided the fundamental principles were agreed upon. It is, nevertheless, a remarkable fact that all authors concur in stating that the obnoxious laws, those which were injurious to plebeian liberty, were contained in the last two tables, the work of the second decemvirs; the first ten are not blamed, they merely granted isonomy, respecting which the parties had already agreed, as Appius is made, by Livy, to say — *se omnia jura summis infimisque aequasse*. The laws, which had hitherto been different for patricians and plebeians, now became the same for both orders, so that personal imprisonment and personal security might take place in the case of a patrician also.

There can be no doubt that the first ten decemvirs were all patricians of ancient families, and according to the recently discovered consular Fasti their title was *decemviri consulari potestate legibus scribendis*. They were appointed in the place of the consuls, the *praefectus urbi*, and the *quaestors*. But are Livy and Dionysius right in saying that the tribuneship likewise was suspended? It is incredible: for it would have been madness in the plebeians thus to allow their hands to be tied, and to renounce the protection of their tribunes; it is not till the second decemvirate that we find the plebeians *appellationi invicem cedentes*, and then C. Julius brought a criminal case before the people. The tribunes must have said: we agree that there shall be ten patrician lawgivers, but the continuance of the *leges sacratae* is to us a guarantee of our rights;—and the *leges sacratae* referred to the tribuneship. The error is very conceivable, and undoubtedly arose from the fact that the tribuneship was suspended under the second decemvirate. If we bear in mind that under the first decemvirs the tribuneship was not suspended, and that the object of their labours was a common law for all, every thing becomes clear; all points in regard to which there might be a collision of the two estates, were reserved for subsequent deliberation.

But besides this task of establishing a general law, the commissioners had to settle the constitution on the principle that the two estates were to be put on a footing of equality. In the projected constitution, two points were agreed upon, namely that the tribuneship should be abolished, and that the highest power should be given to men of both orders. The last five names mentioned by Livy in the second decemvirate are plebeian and belong to families which do not occur in the Fasti previously to the Licinian law, and afterwards only as plebeian consuls; Dionysius expressly recognises three of them as plebeians, and the two others who, it is said, were chosen by Appius and the nobles from the lesser gentes, were likewise plebeians, as must be evident to every one acquainted with the Roman gentes; whence Livy places them at the end of his list: the mistake of Dionysius arose from a confusion of the two decemvirates.[2] The first decemvirate represented the *decem primi* of the senate, who were elected after a προβούλευμα of the senate by the centuries; but the second was a συναρχία similar to that of the Attic archons, perhaps occasioned by a knowledge of the Attic laws. The second election was quite different from the first, the noblest, like the lowest patricians, canvassed for the votes of the plebeians (canvassing here appears for the first time), so that the election was perfectly free. Of these decemvirs six were military tribunes, three patricians and three plebeians, and these six were in reality the commanders in war; of the remaining four, two must be regarded as invested with censorial power and with that of the *praefectus urbi* combined with the presidency of the senate; the other two who had the authority of quaestors, had likewise in certain cases to perform military functions. One in each of these two pairs, of course, was a patrician and the other a plebeian. Now when Dionysius read that there were three patrician and three plebeian military tribunes, he might easily overlook the fact that the remaining four were likewise equally divided between the two orders, especially as the ancient books were probably written in a language which was very unintel-

---

[2] As long as I see such an error, and cannot rationally explain it, except on the supposition that it was committed by the author in a thoughtless moment, I feel uneasy; I cannot rest until I discover the source of the error; and I beg of you to exercise your minds in the same manner. Most of the errors in Livy and Dionysius are not the result of ignorance but of false premises.—N.

ligible to him. The three decemvirs whom Dionysius recognises as plebeians are, Q. Poetelius, C. Duilius and Sp. Oppius.

This constitution was intended to remain for ever. We can distinctly see what was the task the decemvirs had to perform and how they endeavoured to do it. The distinction between the gentes majores and minores disappears from this time. The legislators considered the state from the point of view of the government, and they reasoned thus: " Since the Publilian law the state has been unfortunate; the tribunes have the power of discussing any subject whether agreeable or not; it is therefore a matter of importance to transfer this right of the tribunes to the decemvirs, as thereby the plebes too would obtain what they could fairly claim, for the *plebes* and *populus* must stand side by side and yet form one whole. The plebes therefore no longer want their tribunes, since they may appeal from the patrician decemvirs to the plebeian ones. It is, moreover, fair that patricians and plebeians should have an equal share in the senate, but the plebeians are to come in gradually until they shall have reached a certain number. The two estates must be carefully kept apart, yet be endowed with equal powers. The former right of the gentes to send their representatives into the senate, and the custom of a curia (or perhaps the consuls though their power was much more limited than that of the censors of later times) electing a new member in case of a gens becoming extinct, are to be supplanted by a new institution, and a new magistracy must be created to superintend and decide upon the civil condition of the citizens, for example, to enrol an *aerarius* among the plebeians, or to raise the plebeian nobles to the rank of patricians." These are the principles on which the second decemvirs acted in their legislation: the consequences of these laws, and how little they answered the expectations formed of them, we shall see hereafter.

LECTURE XXV.

SCARCELY any part of the civil law contained in the twelve tables has come down to us; one of the few portions with which we are acquainted is an enactment of one of the last two tables, that there should be no connubium between the patres and plebes. This enactment is so characteristic, that we may learn from it the spirit which pervaded the whole legislation; it is generally regarded as an innovation, for example, by Dionysius, and by Cicero in his work *De Re Publica;* but this opinion is based upon the erroneous supposition that all these laws were new, as if previously the Romans had either had no laws at all or quite different ones. But it never occurred to the mind of the ancients to frame an entirely new legislation; all they did was to improve that which had been handed down to them by their ancestors. As the intention of the decemviral legislation was to bring the estates into closer connection and to equalise the laws for both, such a separation of the two orders assuredly cannot have been an innovation. In the middle ages too there is scarcely a single trace of such perfectly arbitrary legislation; and as I have been told by Savigny, it is not found any where except in the laws of the Emperor Frederick II. The opinion of our authors is based on nothing but their own conception of a new legislation, and is therefore of no authority; on the contrary, it is in the highest degree improbable that a separation of this kind, with all its subsequent irritation should have been introduced at a moment when so strong a desire after equality had been evinced.

But there are some other points which I do consider as innovations of the greatest importance, such as the unlimited right of making a will, which was established by the twelve tables. This right was conceded to every *pater familias*, but the later jurists introduced most important changes for the purpose of limiting this dangerous liberty: it cannot have existed from the earliest times. The consequence was a double form of making a will, namely in presence of the curies and *in procinctu*, that is before the symbol of the centuries, because they represented the *exercitus vocatus:* before these the testator declared his will, and if it was previously to a battle, the soldier made this declaration in presence of the army itself; when a patrician wanted to dispose of his property, the chief pontiff assembled the curies, which had to sanction his will. The reason of this lay in the nature of the circumstances. If a person left children behind him it was probably not customary in ancient times to make a will; but if he died without issue

his relatives succeeded to his property; if there were no relatives the property went to the gentes, and if the whole gens
was extinct it went to the curia. Formerly when I read in
the Aulularia of Plautus[1]: *Nam noster nostrae qui est magister
curiae, Dividere argenti dixit nummos in viros*, I used to think
that it was a pure translation from the Greek, for Euclio represents an aerarian, and how does he get into a curia? But the
whole relation is purely Roman: property was left to the curia,
and this inheritance was divided *viritim*.[2] Here then we have
a good reason why the sanction of the curies was required. It
is to be regretted that the leaf in Gaius which contained this
law is illegible. In like manner the plebeians too seem to have
had their gentilician inheritances, which ultimately fell to the
tribe, and hence here also the *exercitus vocatus*, that is the centuries, had to give its consent, because a will could not be made
without the auspices, which the plebeian tribes did not possess.
Similar regulations concerning the succession to property exist
to this day in the island of Fehmern, as I learned last summer
during an excursion. The inhabitants consist of two clans or
gentes with the laws and manners of Dithmarsch; and if a
member of these gentes wants to make his will, he must give
to his cousins (*gentiles*) a small sum as a compensation for the
money which in reality belongs to them as his gentiles. In
Dithmarsch itself this law has disappeared, nor have I been
able to discover any trace of it in other parts of Germany, a
proof that very important and general laws may often disappear and leave but few and slender vestiges. The curies when
called upon to sanction a will, were of course at liberty to
refuse it, but as it was a law of the twelve tables: *Paterfamilias
uti legassit super pecunia tutelave suae rei ita jus esto*, it is evident that the sanction was only *dicis causa*. This regulation
had an incredible influence upon Roman manners; but it was
necessary, because the connubium between the two orders was
not permitted, for even the child of a plebeian by a patrician
woman could not by law succeed to the father's property; and
if the father wished to make a bequest to such a child, he
needed a special law to enable him to do so. When the connubium was afterwards established, the freedom of making a

---

[1] i. 2. 29; comp. ii. 2. 2.—ED.

[2] The nature of the curies had become essentially altered in the course of time.
See *Hist. of Rome*, ii. p. 319.—ED.

will nevertheless continued to exist, and in the corruption of later ages, led to the most disgraceful abuses; the *lex Furia testamentaria* which for good reasons I assign to the period about A.U. 450, is a proof that a tendency to abuse was manifested even at that early time.

The law of debt likewise must have been contained in one of the last two tables, since Cicero describes them as thoroughly unfair; for this was binding upon the plebeians only: the last two tables undoubtedly consisted of nothing but exceptions.

The most important part of the decemviral legislation is the *jus publicum*, a fact which was formerly quite overlooked by jurists, who saw in it a code of laws like that of Justinian, only very scanty and barbarous. But Cicero and Livy expressly call it *fons omnis publici privatique juris*, and Cicero[3] in his imitations of the laws of the twelve tables also speaks of the administration of the republic. All the institutions, however, which continued to exist unaltered, were surely not touched upon in the twelve tables, as, for example, the whole constitution of the centuries; but we have very few traces of the changes in the public law which were introduced by them. One of them is the enactment, that no more *privilegia* should be granted, i. e. no laws against individuals, or condemnations of individuals. Hence we must infer that previously there existed regulations against individuals similar to the ostracism at Athens. It is probable, moreover, that the mutual accusations of the two orders now ceased, and that the centuries were regarded as a general national court. There is indeed no express testimony, but, even though it is not possible to answer for the authenticity of all cases recorded, it is, generally speaking, a fact well established by the events of history itself, that until then the accusations made by the tribunes were brought before the plebes, and those preferred by the quaestors, before the curies, but afterwards we hear no more of such accusations. Accusations before the tribes as well as before the curies certainly continue to occur in particular cases, but no longer in consequence of an opposition between the two orders.

The change by which the clients became members of the tribes—a fact which afterwards becomes clear—was probably made at the same time, for the plebeian tribes, independently

[3] In his work *De Legibus.*—N.

of their import as such, were also to form a general national
division; but though there are some plausible reasons for this
supposition, it is possible also that the change may not have
been introdueed till 100 or 120 years later. If Camillus was
condemned by the tribes, we may perhaps account for it in
this manner; his *tribules* certainly are mentioned in the trial.
Among the wise laws of the twelve tables which Cicero incor-
porates with his laws, he mentions, with reference to his own
tumultuous condemnation by the tribes, that a judgment *de
capite civis* could be passed only by the *comitiatus maximus*. We
certainly cannot assert that previously to the decemviral legislation, the centuries were not authorized to act as a court of
justice: I have discovered a formula which must belong to an
earlier period, and probably refers to the centuries as a court
of justice, and the time will probably come when we shall
arrive at a positive conviction on this point. If it was so, we
must suppose that the constitution of the centuries as a court
of justice took place shortly before the decemviral legislation,
for till then the *judicia capitis* belonged to the curies and tribes.
The trials of Coriolanus and K. Quinctius did not take place
before the centuries. If in later times we find an instance of a
condemnation by the curies, it must be regarded as an illegal
act of violence. The tribunes accordingly henceforth brought
a *crimen capitis* before the centuries, and a mere *multa* before
the tribes; it often happens too that the person who is condemned goes into exile and loses his franchise. Here we must
bear in mind the principle mentioned by Cicero in his speech
for Caecina, that exile did not imply the loss of the franchise,
for exile was not a punishment: the loss of the franchise did
not take place until a person was admitted to the citizenship
of a foreign state. From this point of view, we must look at
the condemnation of Camillus, if indeed he was actually condemned by the tribes and not by the curies, for the latter is
far more probable.

In this manner, the sphere of the nation as a whole became
greatly extended, and instead of appeals to the two orders
separately, there occur scarcely any appeals except those to the
centuries. The existence of this law sufficiently proves the
mistake of those who believe that the decemvirs assumed all
jurisdiction to themselves; the error arose from the belief, that
as the ancient right of appeal to the two estates had been

abolished, an appeal was now made from one college to another. The cases of appeal from the consuls to the people afterwards occur very rarely, and even those few instances are extremely problematical; the appeal to the assembled court of the commonalty was probably abolished, and according to a natural development of the constitution, the tribunes, as the direct representatives of the plebes, stepped into its place, since a resolution of the whole commonalty was after all only an illusion.

Other laws likewise which are mentioned, must perhaps be regarded as innovations, as for example that a person who had pledged himself for debt, should have the same rights as a free man,

Ever since the battle of lake Regillus the accounts of Livy and Dionysius are, in many years, in perfect harmony with each other, important discrepancies occurring but rarely. The history of the decemviral legislation also furnishes an example of this agreement, but other accounts, small as they are in number, do not agree with them at all; hence their agreement cannot be quoted as evidence that their statements contain historical truth, but merely leads us to suppose that the two historians by chance made use of the same sources for this period. The narrative of Livy is particularly beautiful and elaborate. The statement that a second set of decemvirs was appointed because two tables were yet wanting, is foolish; I have already expressed an opinion that it was probably intended to institute the decemvirate as a permanent magistracy, to abolish the consulship and tribuneship, and that the decemvirs of the second year were elected not as law-givers, but as the highest magistrates, and with power to add two tables to the ten already drawn up. My conjecture, which I here state with tolerable confidence, is that these decemvirs were not elected for one year only, but for several, perhaps for five: we are told that on the ides of May they did not lay down their office, and this is described as a usurpation. Had this been so, it would have been a true δυναστεία in the genuine Greek sense of the word in which it is the opposite of τυραννίς, a distinction unknown in the Latin language, although not without example in ancient history.[4]

---

[4] The constitutional history of Elis presents a true counterpart of that of Rome. The highest magistrate there was at first appointed for life; even in

In electing the decemvirs it must have been intended, as was the case ever after, that whoever had been invested with this office should become a member of the senate; but ten new members every year would have caused too great an increase, and it seems more easy to suppose that our authors overlooked the intention that they should hold their office for more than one year, than that the decemvirs arbitrarily prolonged the period of their office, a thing which they could not have ventured to do.

In the second year, history shows us the decemvirs in the possession of all magisterial power; they are said to have kept a guard of one hundred and twenty lictors (ῥαβδοφόροι), twelve for each as was the custom of all Greek oligarchs; these lictors therefore were to serve a purpose different from that of the consular lictors: they were to be like the σωματοφύλακες of the Greek tyrants. The decemvirs are described by Livy and Dionysius as profligate tyrants; but this account must be received with the same caution as the stories of most tyrants in antiquity, for the greatest monsters in history did not commit their crimes from a mere love of crime, but generally for some purpose. Cicero, moreover, relates that although the decemvirs did not behave quite as became citizens, yet one of them, C. Julius respected the liberties of the people and summoned a popular court to judge one who was not *reus manifestus*. Appius Claudius and Sp. Oppius were the presidents of the senate: they administered justice in the city, and were probably invested with censorial power. Livy very graphically says that the forum and the curia grew silent, that the senate was seldom convened and that no comitia were held. This was quite natural, for as the tribuneship of the people had been abolished, there was no comitia of the tribes nor any one to address the people in the forum; there were no politics to be discussed, for the constitution was quite new, and in the civil law, too, nothing further was to be done. The senate was

---

the Peloponnesian war the gentes in Elis were alone sovereign, the surrounding territory was in a subject condition, and all power was in the hands of a council of ninety men who were elected for life. The people was divided into three phylae, and each phyle into thirty gentes. Afterwards the country population obtained the franchise. All Elis was divided into twelve regions, and the nation into twelve tribes, four of which were lost in war, so that there remained only eight.—N.

rarely convoked, because the college of the decemvirs could do most things by itself; the patricians, therefore, went into the country and attended to their estates, many plebeians did the same, and there suddenly arose in the city a condition of the most profound peace. But the people had been so much accustomed to excitement that they longed for new commotions; a feeling of unhappiness came over them, because every thing which had stirred up their minds had now disappeared all at once. Whoever like myself, witnessed the period of the French revolution knows that great mental excitement becomes in the end as habitual and indispensable to man as gambling, or any other gratification and excitement of the senses. There is no feeling more painful than a sudden and perfect peace after a great revolution, and such a transition often becomes very dangerous. This was the case in the year 1648, when the Dutch had concluded peace with the Spaniards at Münster; contemporary writers relate the state of things which followed was intolerably tedious, the people became discontented and gave themselves up to a dissolute life, disputes arose between King William III. and the city of Amsterdam: any question however trifling was eagerly taken up in order to have an opportunity for giving vent to the passions. A similar state of feeling existed in France immediately after the restoration. Wherever men's minds are in this condition, ill feeling is necessarily produced between the government and the people: such was the case at Rome, and the people were dissatisfied with their new constitution. Hence even if the decemvirs had not been bad, or if Appius Claudius had been the only bad one among them, they could not easily have maintained themselves, nor would things have remained quiet. The plebeians had been disappointed in those members of their order who had become decemvirs; at first the tribunician protection is said not to have been missed, but gradually the plebeian decemvirs began to think it proper to use their power for their own advantage, and to share the *esprit du corps* of the others. Thus we can understand how the plebeian Sp. Oppius became even more odious than the rest, for he, as well as Appius Claudius, reduced creditors to the state of *addicti ;* such deeds had hitherto been done only by patricians.

Under these circumstances, it must have happened very opportunely for the decemvirs that a war with the Aequians

and Sabines broke out, for they thereby acquired the means of
occupying the people. It is related that the patriots L. Valerius
Potitus and M. Horatius Barbatus came forward in the senate
and demanded that the decemvirs should lay down their power
before an army was enrolled, but that a majority of the senate
resolved upon a levy being made at once.   But I consider the
speeches in Livy said to have been delivered on that occasion
to be nothing but empty declamations, prompted by the idea
that the decemvirs had usurped their power.   If those speeches
had been actually delivered, the so called patriots would have
been traitors to their country, for the enemy had invaded and
were devastating the Roman territory; resistance was necessary,
there was no time for deliberations.   Nothing, moreover, would
have been easier than to levy an army, since tribunes no longer
existed.   The story of L. Siccius, whom the decemvirs are said
to have caused to be assassinated, has in my opinion little probability: it looks a great deal too poetical.   All we can do is
to keep to the fact that two Roman armies took the field, while
the main army was stationed on Mount Algidus against the
Aequians.   In the meantime a crime was committed in the
city, of a kind which was of quite common occurrence in the
Greek oligarchies.   Appius Claudius became enamoured of the
daughter of a centurion, L. Virginius.   All accounts agree in
saying that her death, like that of Lucretia, was the cause of
the overthrow of the decemvirs; the statement is very ancient
and in no way to be doubted: the rape of women and boys is
a crime which was very commonly committed by tyrants
against their subjects; Aristotle and Polybius also expressly
inform us that the overthrow of oligarchies was often the
result of such violation of female virtue.   Appius Claudius
suborned a false accuser, one of his own clients, who was
to declare that the real mother of Virginia had been his
slave, and that she had sold the infant to the wife of
Virginius, who, being herself sterile, wished to deceive her
husband: this assertion, the accuser wanted to establish by
false witnesses; and Appius was resolved to adjudge Virginia
as a slave to his client; but this was contrary to the laws
of the twelve tables, for if the freedom of a Roman citizen
was disputed, he could demand to be left in the enjoyment
of it till the question was decided; only he was obliged to
give security, as a person's value could be estimated in money.

This was called *vindiciae secundum libertatem*, but Appius
wanted to assign her *contra libertatem*. All the people in the
forum then crowded around him entreating him to defer judgment, at least till her father, who was serving in the army,
could return. When the lictor attempted to use force, the
number of plebeians in the forum became so great and formidable, that Appius had not courage to abide by his determination, but requested the accuser to be satisfied with the security
until the next court-day; but in order to crush the possibility
even of a conspiracy, a court was to be held on the very next
day. At the same time he sent messengers to the camp with
orders that the father should be kept in the army; but
Virginius, whom the betrothed of the maiden and other relatives had previously sent for, appeared on the next morning in
the forum. The appearance of justice was now lost: if Appius
allowed the matter to come to a formal investigation, the
father would have unmasked the lie; for this reason Appius
declared his conviction that the maiden was the slave of the
accuser, and ordered her to be led away. The general indignation at this procedure gave Virginius courage, and under
the pretext of taking leave of his daughter and consulting her
nurse, he took her aside into a porticus and plunged into her
breast a knife which he had snatched from one of the stalls
round the forum. The bloody knife in his hands, he quitted
the city without hindrance, and returned to the camp. The
soldiers on hearing what had happened, unanimously refused
obedience to the decemvirs, and both armies united. From
this point our accounts contradict one another; some state
that the soldiers took possession of the Sacred Mount, and, as
in the first secession, of the Aventine; but others reverse the
statement. It is to be observed, that the commonalty then
had twenty leaders, and consequently was again under the
protection of its tribunes (phylarchs), who appointed from
among themselves two men who were to act as presidents and
negotiate with the rulers who were abandoned by the people
in the city. The *tribuni sacrosancti* had been abolished by the
decemviral constitution, but the tribunes as heads of the tribes
had remained; and, headed by these, the plebeians were now
in a more decided state of insurrection against the senate and
the decemvirs than they had been forty years before; at that
time they had seceded for the purpose of obtaining certain

rights, whereas now they were fully armed as for a war. In this war the decemvirs would necessarily have been over-powered, especially as it is clear that many of the patricians also renounced their cause, though, as Livy justly remarks, most of them loved the decemviral constitution, because it had delivered them from the tribunician power: but still many of them, such as Valerius and Horatius, were anxious that the ancient constitution should be restored, as they were convinced that the tribuneship acted as a salutary check upon the consular power. It was accordingly resolved to negotiate with the plebes, and peace was concluded.

We still possess some remnants of different accounts respecting the fall of the decemvirs: that of Diodorus is quite different from the above; it might be said to be taken from Fabius if it did not contain one strange circumstance. According to this account, matters came to a decision much more quickly than according to Livy, for peace is said to have been concluded on the very next day after the occupation of the Aventine. According to Cicero, the disruption lasted for a long time, nor does he know anything of Livy's statement that Valerius and Horatius were the mediators; he mentions Valerius afterwards as consul and continually engaged in reconciling the parties. These are traces of discrepant traditions, although the character of this period is in general quite different from that of the preceding one, and truly historical. According to a statement of Cicero, the plebeians marched from the Sacred Mount to the Aventine, which is certainly wrong, for they were always in possession of the Aventine; it is moreover probable that the obscure Icilian law referred to the fact, that the Aventine should be excluded from the union with Rome, and, as the real seat of the plebeians, should have its own magistrates. We must therefore suppose the meaning of the account to be that the army first occupied the Sacred Mount, and then marched towards the city where they united with the members of their own order on the Aventine. The Capitol was surrendered to the armed troops, and this surrender shows most clearly the difference between the present plebeians and those who had seceded forty years before; the plebeians had gained a complete victory.

The decemvirs laid down their office, and the first election was that of ten tribunes which was forthwith held under the presidency of the *pontifex maximus*, which was the strongest recognition on the part of the patricians; the inviolability of the plebeian magistrates thus became secured by the ecclesiastical law. It is a highly remarkable anomaly that they held their *concilia* in the place afterwards called the Circus Flaminius, which was to the plebeians what the Circus Maximus was to the patricians. These things happened in December, and henceforth the tribunes regularly entered upon their office in that month. For the purpose of restoring order in the state, it was resolved that two patrician magistrates should again be elected, but no longer with the former title of praetors but with that of consuls, as we are informed by Zonaras.

LECTURE XXVI.

THE very fact of the title of praetor being changed into consul is a proof that the magistracy was looked upon as something different from what it had been before : its dignity had diminished, for praetors are those who go before or have the command, whereas the word *consuls* signifies colleagues merely, and is quite an abstract name like decemvirs. This new form of the consulship, however, was not by any means intended as a restoration of the old constitution, or to take the place of the decemvirate, but was only an extraordinary and transitory measure. As a proof of this I may mention that the law which declared any one who did violence to a tribune or aedile an outlaw, was now extended also to judices and decemvirs. This law has been the subject of much dispute, but the mention of the decemvirs in it is well authenticated. Even the great Antonius Augustus, bishop of Taragona, a man very distinguished for his knowledge of ancient monuments and public law, but who notwithstanding his great historical talent was unfortunately wanting in grammatical accuracy, saw that the judices here mentioned were the centumviri, or the judges who were appointed by the plebeians, three for each tribe, to decide in all questions about quiritarian property. He mentions this

merely in a passing remark; but I have fully proved it in the
new edition of my history.   Most people understood these
judices to be the consuls, and therefore concluded that the
consuls were inviolable; it was just as great a mistake to
imagine that the decemvirs mentioned in the law were the
decemviri stlitibus judicandis, who did not exist till the fifth
century of Rome: the decemvirs are undoubtedly the *decemviri
consulari potestate,* and especially the plebeian ones, the patricians being already sufficiently protected by their ancient laws.

When the tribuneship was restored, the patricians may have
said: "You were right, for the praetors, as they formerly
existed, had too excessive a power, and hence we shared the
decemvirate with you; but now as you have your tribunes
again, you would acquire an overwhelming power, and you
must therefore leave the decemvirate to us alone."   This the
plebeians refused to do; and this put an end to the discussions
about the restoration of the decemvirate; the consular power
was retained, but with an important change.   According to
very authentic accounts, the elective assembly down to the year
A. U. 269 was in possession of a truly free right of election;
but after this time a change was made, first by a usurpation of
the curies, and afterwards by a formal contract that one of the
consuls should be nominated by the senate and sanctioned by
the curies, and that the other should be elected by the centuries.
In this election, the centuries might act with perfect freedom,
as in all their other transactions, which was probably the consequence of the decemviral legislation; but the consul elected
by them still required the sanction of the curies.

The power of the tribunes too was changed in one point.
Before this time all things had been decided in their college by
the majority, but according to Diodorus it now became law
that the opposition of a single tribune could paralyze the whole
college: this opposition was equivalent to an appeal to the
tribes, and was an exemplification of the principle *vetantis
major potestas.*   According to Livy this law had existed before;
but it is probable that it was at least not recognized until now,
when the relation of the tribunes to the commonalty was changed:
they were no longer the deputies, but the representatives
of their order, which was in reality a change for the worse,
though its evil consequences were not felt till several generations later.   Here we again perceive the skill and prudence of

the government, since they might hope always to find one at least in the college, ready to support their interests. Cicero says, that the tribuneship saved Rome from a revolution; if the people had been refused their tribunes, it would have been necessary to retain the kings.

The centuries had now obtained jurisdiction; according to the religious law, the comitia of the centuries had their auspices, the gods being consulted as to whether that which was to be brought before the comitia was pleasing to them. Now as the tribunes had the right to bring accusations before the centuries, it follows that they must have been entitled to take the auspices (*de coelo observare*). This is expressed in the statement of Zonaras, that the tribunes received permission to consult the auspices. According to a remark in Diodorus, any person should be outlawed who caused the plebeians to be without their tribunes. At the close of the year we meet with the strange circumstance of two patricians being among the tribunes; they were either patricians who had gone over to the plebeians, or the patricians acted upon the principle, which was perfectly correct, that the tribunes, considering their power of interfering in the movements of the state, were no longer the magistrates of a part of the nation, but of the whole nation. It is expressly attested, that at that time many patricians went over to the plebeians, but the other explanation also has great probability. From this time forward patricians are often mentioned as tribules of the plebeians, and in the discussions about the separation of the plebes and their settling at Veii, we read that the senators went about *prensantes suos quisque tribules;* and about fifteen years after the time of the decemvirs, Mamercus Aemilius is said to have been struck out from the list of his tribe, and to have been placed among the *aerarii;* Camillus too is stated to have applied to his tribules, though here, it might be said, we must understand his patrician gentiles. That in the time of Cicero all the patricians belonged to the tribes, is well known, Caesar belonged to the tribus Fabia, and Sulpicius to the tribus Lemonia. After the Hannibalian war, C. Claudius is made to say by Livy, that to strike a person from all the thirty-five tribes was the same as to deprive him of the franchise; and M. Livius removed his colleague Claudius from his tribe. More examples of the same kind might easily be accumulated. In the early times, there were both patrician and plebeian tribes, but at a later period the three patrician tribes of the Ramnes, Tities and Luceres are no longer spoken of, and they appeared in the centuries only as the *sex suffragia*. The whole Roman nation therefore was now comprised in the tribes. The same was the case at Athens, when the ten phylae of the demos became the only ones, and the four ancient mixed phylae disappeared. I formerly believed that this was the work of the decemviral legislation; but if we consider the care with which the decemvirs kept the two orders apart in other respects, we cannot possibly suppose, that they introduced a fusion in this particular. We must place the change somewhat later, and the fittest opportunity seems to be the time of the second censors, so that the change was made soon after the decemviral legislation. We read in the fragments of Dion Cassius, that the patricians preferred the condition of the plebeians to their own, because they had greater power, and that for this reason they went over to them. The power indeed of the plebeians at that time was not greater, but they had greater strength, and it could easily be foreseen to what, in the course of time, they would attain; many therefore may have thought it a more agreeable position to stand in the ranks of those who were advancing, than among those who were stationary, and could act only on the defensive.

The decemvirs were accused; Appius Claudius and Sp. Oppius died in prison. The latter was a plebeian, a proof that the plebeians must not be regarded as persons possessed of peculiar virtues. Wherever a state is divided into factions and the ruling party abuses its power, our sympathies go with the weaker party. Sp. Oppius was perhaps one of those who had before been very loud in his denunciations against tyranny, but afterwards became a tyrant himself. L. Virginius, who had been appointed tribune to avenge the blood of his daughter, brought a capital charge against Appius[1], and by virtue of his tribunician power ordered him to be thrown into prison. Livy's account here leads us to a curious point. It is a very general opinion that every Roman citizen had the right to escape from a sentence of death by going into exile. If this had been the case, we might wonder why the punishment of

---

[1] A. Virginius in Livy is probably a mistake of a copyist who was thinking of the earlier tribune of this name.—N.

death was instituted at all, and yet the ancient Roman laws
were not sparing of it; but the fact is different: the views of
the ancients in regard to criminal law differ from ours almost
more than in regard to any other subject. According to our
notions a criminal must be tried, even if he has been caught
in the act; we consider it almost a duty on his part to deny
his crime, and he must be convicted by evidence; advocates
may defend him and attempt to misguide the court. Of such
a mode of proceeding the ancients had no idea: when a person
had committed a crime, the statement of witnesses was sufficient to cause him to be forthwith apprehended and dragged
before a magistrate: if the crime was not a *delictum manifestum*,
the offender, if a plebeian, might call for the assistance of a
tribune and give security; if after this he was set free, he
might sacrifice his sureties and go into exile. But if he had
been caught in a *delictum manifestum in flagranti*, and the *testes
locupletes* declared that they were present and bore witness to
his identity, no trial took place: the criminal was dragged
obtorto collo, the toga being drawn over his head, before the
magistrate, who forthwith pronounced sentence. If the day
on which the criminal was caught, was not a court-day, he was
taken to prison until the next court-day. If, on the other
hand, a person committed a capital offence of such a kind that
catching him *in flagranti* was impossible, nevertheless the
accuser had the means of obtaining the imprisonment of the
culprit.[2] Appius Claudius, for example, was guilty of a capital
offence: he had deprived a citizen of his liberty, and Virginius
accused him without allowing him to give security, in order
that he might not escape; in such a case the accuser might
offer to the defendant a *sponsio* a kind of wager, consisting of
a sum of money (*sacramentum*) on the part of the accuser
against the personal liberty of the defendant. The accuser
said: You have deprived a citizen of his liberty; the accused
denied the charge, and if the judex chosen for the case declared
for the accuser, no further trial was necessary; the criminal
was forthwith led before the magistrate, and executed; if
however the judex decided against the accuser, the latter lost
the *sacramentum*. If the accused declined to accept the *sponsio*,
he was thrown into prison. The question now is, whether in
such a case as this the accuser was obliged to drop his suit or

[2] On this subject comp. *Hist. of Rome.* vol. ii. p. 370, fol.—ED.

to accept the security. The passages which decide this question, occur in Livy and Cicero. The accused remained in prison only till the next court-day, and thus the smallness of the prison at Rome becomes intelligible; confinement in its darkness was of itself a forerunner of death, and he who was thrown into it was lost. Cicero says: *carcerem vindicem nefariorum ac manifestorum scelerum majores esse voluerunt;* the criminal either had his neck broken in the prison, or was led out to be executed. The Greek customs connected with imprisonment are much more like those of our own times. I may here add the remark, that when an accusation was brought against a *filius familias*, the father acted as judge; if against a client, the patron.

Another part of the Roman criminal law entirely different from our own, was that relating to offences against the state. For many of them no punishment was fixed, it being a distinct maxim with the ancients, that the state must preserve itself—*salus publica suprema lex esto.* They well knew that the individual crimes against the state admitted of the greatest variety of shades, that the same external act might arise either from error or from the most criminal intention, and that accordingly it was impossible to fix a special punishment for each particular case. Hence both Greeks and Romans in all *judicia publica* granted to the accused himself the extraordinary privilege of proposing any definite punishment such as he thought proportioned to the nature of his offence, and that even in cases for which there already existed a precedent. The same privilege seems to have been transferred even to *judicia privata*, in those cases for which no provision was made in the criminal code. In modern times the foolish notion has been established, that a punishment should be inflicted only according to a positive law; and this sad mistake is adopted every where. The ancients followed the directly opposite principle: a boy who tortured an animal, was sentenced to death by the Athenian popular assembly, although there was no law for the protection of animals; it was on the same principle that a person who was only guilty of an act repulsive to the common feeling of honour, was condemned to die.

Up to this time the patricians seem to have claimed for themselves the privilege which exempted them from being thrown into prison; for it is related that Appius called the *carcer* the domicile of the plebeians. Virginius showed himself generous in granting to Appius time to make away with himself. But Sp. Oppius was executed, because his crime was of a different kind and not one against an individual who might be lenient towards him; for the story that he ordered an old soldier who had served for twenty-seven years to be scourged, and that this man came forward as his accuser, is evidently a fiction. The period of a soldier's actual service lasted twenty-eight years, and the introduction in this story of one who was in the last year of his military service, is evidently a representation of tyranny in general. The other decemvirs went into voluntary exile, and their property was confiscated. One of them was Q. Fabius, the ancestor of the subsequent gens Fabia. After these events, the tribune M. Duilius pronounced an amnesty for all who had been guilty of any offence during the preceding unhappy period. This precedent is of great importance in the history of judicial proceedings among the Romans. I had distinctly expressed my opinion upon these proceedings long before the discovery of Gaius, when the most absurd notions were current about the Roman criminal law; but the fragments of Gaius and the labours of Savigny have made everything much clearer.

At first the patricians had been in great consternation, and sanctioned all the laws which were proposed. Among them was one which gave to *plebiscita* the power of laws binding upon all, *ut quod tributim plebes jussisset populum teneret.* This law is one of the greatest mysteries in Roman history, and there is no possibility of giving an absolute historical solution of the difficulty, though I have formed a hypothesis respecting it, of the truth of which I am convinced. The law as stated above is recorded by Livy, who afterwards, in his eighth book, says of the second Publilian law *ut plebiscita omnes Quirites tenerent;* and in the same terms Pliny and Laelius Felix (in Gellius) quote the law of Hortensius which falls 160 years later, and of which Gaius says: *ut plebiscita populum tenerent.* Now on considering these three laws (the Publilian is mentioned only by Livy), they seem to enact the same thing; but is this really the case? was the law twice renewed because it had fallen into oblivion? If we examine the character of these laws in reference to the various times to which they belong, it will be seen that their meaning was different, and that the force of *plebiscita* was not interpreted always in the same manner. The result of my investigations is, that Livy, in mentioning the lex Valeria Horatia, was not accurate, because he himself did not see clearly, and because he was thinking of the well-known Hortensian law. The law probably ran thus: *quae plebes tributim jusserit*, QUARUM RERUM PATRES AUCTORES FACTI SINT, *ut populum teneant*, for from this time forward the legislative proceedings are often described as follows: when the tribunes had got the commonalty to pass a resolution, they then brought it before the curies, which forthwith voted upon it; this was an abbreviation of the ordinary mode of proceeding, according to which legislative proposals, after being sanctioned by the senate, were first brought before the centuries and then before the curies; according to the new arrangement, the consultation of the senate and the passing through the centuries were abolished. The change was very important; for now the discussion of a matter might originate with the plebes themselves. It is clear, on the other hand, that without the sanction of the curies the *plebiscita* had not the power of laws, as we see more especially during the contest about the Licinian laws; resolutions of the plebes may at that time have been termed *leges*, merely because they became *leges* as soon as they obtained the consent of the curies. In cases when the plebes and the curies were not divided by party interests, every thing was sanctioned by the latter. It must further be observed that this law was carried not by a tribunician, but by a consular rogation. The Publilian law had been rendered superfluous by the decemviral legislation, which did not recognise any *comitia tributa*.

The later Publilian law of the dictator Q. Publilius Philo has quite a different meaning; for it dispensed with the assent of the curies to a resolution passed by the tribes, because it was too tedious a proceeding, and the senate after all had the right of proposal. His law *ut plebiscita omnem populum teneant*, should in all probability run *ut plebiscita* QUAE SENATU AUCTORE FACTA SINT *omnes* Quirites TENEANT, for from this time it is often mentioned in regard to matters affecting the administration, that the senate commissioned the consuls to negociate with the tribunes to bring proposals before the tribes; but this occurs only in matters connected with the administration (ψηφίσματα), for example, that a person should be invested with an extraordinary *imperium*, and not in legislative matters (νόμοι). This shortening of the proceedings was useful: for religious reasons, the curies and centuries could be assembled only on certain days, whereas the tribes might and did assemble every day, not being restricted by the *dies nefasti*. It became more and more evident, that general assemblies were a mere formality and depended too much upon accidental circumstances: the supposed personal opinion in voting is only imaginary; impulse and example do everything. It also became every day more evident that the more the state increased the greater became the want of a regular government; it was accordingly of importance to the Romans to devise forms for preventing arbitrary proceedings on the part of the government and for preserving publicity. In this respect the Romans differed especially from the Greeks, inasmuch as they committed themselves with confidence to the personal guidance of individuals, which never occurred at Athens.

Lastly, the Hortensian law has a meaning quite different from the preceding laws: it introduced a true democracy, by enacting that in the case of legislative measures (for in regard to administrative measures the second Publilian law remained in force) a preliminary resolution of the senate should be unnecessary, and that the plebes should have power to pass any resolution; the curies were at the same time deprived of their functions. This was a decisive victory of the democracy. Administrative measures were resolutions on particular emergencies; and nothing of this kind could be brought before the plebes, even down to the end of the sixth century (A.U. 570), which had not previously been determined on by the senate; but for real laws a resolution of the plebes was sufficient. The ancient burghers thereby lost their power of regeneration, the balance was destroyed, and the scale sank on the side of democracy. The curies had been compelled even by the Publilian law, in the year A.U. 417, previously to the meeting of the centuries, to declare by a certain formula that they sanctioned whatever should be determined upon. It was a misfortune for the state that the curies had no means of regeneration: so long indeed as resolutions had to pass the centuries, it was not of much consequence, but the Hortensian law, which conferred all power upon the tribes alone, destroyed the salutary relations which had hitherto existed, and all the equipoise in the state.

In the first stage, these *plebiscita* were mere resolutions not affecting the state, but relating to such subjects as, for instance, the burial of an important person, the poll-tax, and the like; in the second, the plebes by virtue of the first Publilian law declared themselves authorized to draw up resolutions on general subjects, which however had to be taken into consideration by the consul, to be laid before the senate, and then to pass through the centuries and curies; in the third stage, after the Valerian law, a *plebiscitum* had the force of law as much as a resolution of the centuries, and was immediately brought before the curies and sanctioned by them. In the fourth, the later Publilian law rendered a *plebiscitum* a sufficient sanction of a resolution passed by the senate, which in urgent circumstances, when it was impossible to wait for the next *dies comitialis*, was communicated by the consul to the tribunes. It was sufficient if the tribunes announced a *concilium;* the *dies nefasti* affected only curule magistrates and the *populus*. If for example, at the end of a year an army was in the field, the senate would have been obliged to send its resolution to the centuries and then to have it sanctioned by the curies; but the shorter way now adopted was that the consuls were commissioned, *ut cum tribunis plebis agerent quam primum fieri posset ad plebem ferrent*. This does not occur previously to the Publilian law. The Hortensian law lastly, in the fifth stage, authorised the plebes to act as an independent legislative assembly.

The consuls now took the field against the Aequians and Sabines, and returned after a brilliant victory, and having probably also established a lasting peace with the Sabines. In the meantime the patricians had acquired fresh courage, and those men of their own order, who during the confusion had honestly wished to do their best, now became the objects of their hatred, and accordingly the senate refused the triumph to the returning consuls. This is the first occasion on which we see the overwhelming power of the tribunes, for they interfered and granted the triumph on their own responsibility; their right to do so may be much doubted; but the consuls accepted the triumph, and if they had been disturbed, the tribunes would have assisted them. This occurrence shows how great the exasperation must have been even at that early period;

in the year following it rose to such a height, that, as Livy says, the heads of the patricians met and discussed the plan of getting rid of their opponents by a general massacre, but this senseless scheme, for which they would have had to pay dearly, was not carried into effect.

The events which now occurred are very obscure, for the piety of posterity has thrown a veil over them. The people had got out of the painful stillness which followed the time of the decemvirate, but the constitution was yet far from having found its level, and there were disputes as to who was to govern. The plebeians demanded that either the consulship should be divided between the two estates, or that the decemviral form of government should be restored. In the following year, the patricians shewed somewhat more willingness to make concessions: the *quaestores parricidii*, hitherto a patrician magistracy, were for the first time elected by the centuries; Valerius and Horatius, the consuls of the preceding year, were elected, which assuredly was not a mere accident. Many of the ancients, as Tacitus, Plutarch, and even Ulpian, are in error in regard to these quaestores, but Gaius is right. There were two kinds of quaestores, the *quaestores parricidii*, who brought accusations of offenders against the state before the curies, and the six *quaestores classici* who in books on Roman antiquities are invariably confounded with the former. Tacitus says of the latter what can apply only to the former: "The quaestors," says he, "were at first elected by the kings, and afterwards by the consuls, as is clear from a lex curiata of Brutus." But Tacitus cannot have seen this lex, for the *quaestores parricidii* are synonymous with the *decemviri perduellionis*, and the latter were always elected by the curies, or rather by the Ramnes and Tities which they represented. It is indeed impossible that Poplicola caused the *quaestores classici*, or paymasters, also to be elected; but the two who had been formerly elected by the curies, and who sixty-three years after the banishment of the kings (according to Tacitus), that is, in the second year after the overthrow of the decemvirs, were elected by the centuries, are the ancient *quaestores parricidii*, whose office continued until it was merged in that of the *curule aediles*. Nine tribunes hereupon made the proposal to leave the censorship and quaestorship to the patricians, and either to share the consulship, or to institute military tribunes with consular power: only one of their colleagues was of a different opinion. It is not impossible that the story of nine tribunes having once been sentenced by the populus to be burnt at the stake, and of one traitor, P. Mucius, having carried the sentence into execution, may refer to this time.[3] In this case the populus means the curiae, which again usurped the power of passing such a sentence. Among these nine tribunes there was probably a son or grandson of Sp. Cassius, who had renounced his own order, and perished in the attempt to avenge his father or grandfather.

It was generally wished that the consuls and tribunes should be re-elected, but the consuls refused; and Duilius, who had been chosen to represent his colleagues, likewise refused to accept any votes for the tribuneship. This had evil consequences, and a division arose: the tribunes who wished to remain in office, probably had sufficient influence with their friends and followers to cause them to abstain from voting, so that only five tribunes were elected, who had to add five to their number. It is said that they also chose two patricians, which is an argument in favour of our assertion, that not long after the decemviral legislation, the importance of the tribes was doubled, inasmuch as they became a general national division.

A remarkable change which belongs to this period, is the abolition of the law forbidding the connubium between the patricians and the plebeians. This, as we know, had been an established custom from the earliest times, and had been incorporated in the laws of the twelve tables. Such a practice is usually not repulsive until it is written down among the laws; and thus, in this instance too, was raised the storm which occasioned the *plebiscitum* of Canuleius. This is generally regarded as the great victory of the plebeians; for the patricians, it is said, at last gave way, but reserved to themselves other rights. Livy looks upon it as a degradation of the ruling order. I will not quarrel with him for saying so, but if we look at the matter in its true light, it is evident that the existence of such a law injured none more than the patricians themselves. Mixed marriages between persons of the two estates had undoubtedly been frequent at all times, and as far as conscience was concerned they were perfectly legitimate.

[3] See above, p. 193.

The son of such a marriage never had the *jus gentilicium*, but was numbered among the plebeians, the consequence of which was, that the patrician order became continually less and less numerous. It is an acknowledged fact, that wherever the nobles insist upon marrying none but members of their own order, they become in course of time quite powerless. M. Rehberg mentions, that within fifty years one-third of the baronial families of the duchy of Bremen became extinct, and any body who wished to be regarded as equal to the rest had to shew sixteen ancestors. If the plebeians had wished to outwit the patricians, they certainly ought to have insisted upon the *connubium* remaining forbidden; and but for the Canuleian law, the patricians would have lost their position in the state one hundred years earlier. The law was passed, but whether it was in favour of the patricians or of the plebeians we know not. About such things we cannot speak with any probability, for even what appears absurd has sometimes really happened.

Afterwards, we once find three military tribunes instead of the consuls; and Dionysius on that occasion says, that it was determined to satisfy the plebeians by appointing military tribunes, three of whom were to be patricians, and three plebeians. But there were only three, and one of them was a plebeian. Livy foolishly considers all three to have been patricians. He thinks that the plebeians only wanted to have the right, but that having gained this they considered themselves unworthy of the office, and elected patricians. He speaks of the plebeians as if they had been unspeakably stupid, thus displaying the confusion of a man, who with all his genius, is yet in reality only a rhetorician, and proving that he was as little acquainted with the political affairs of Rome, as with the regulation of her armies. The probability is, that an agreement was made to give up the name of consul altogether, since the two orders were no longer separate, and to leave the election entirely free between them; but that, nevertheless, all kinds of artifices were resorted to, that the elections might turn out in favour of the patricians. In the early time, the clients of the patricians were not contained in the tribes. They, like their patrons, used to be sent away from the forum when the plebeians proceeded to vote, and whoever was not a member of a tribe, was either not contained in the centuries at all, or voted in them only with the artisans and *capite censi*. But from this time forward there is no mention of anything in which the plebes and clients appear as opposed to each other, and this ought to convince us how authentic our accounts are, and how little they partake of the nature of fables. Is it possible that a late falsifier of history, who lived in the seventh century, should have been able so accurately to separate legal relations? Such a man is always deficient in learning, and even a learned man would have blundered here. The clients henceforth appear in the tribes, and consequently also in the centuries. This we know, partly from express testimony, and partly from the circumstances themselves. The discussions of the plebeians now assume quite a different character; they lose all their vehemence, and the contest between two opposed masses ceases all at once. The rejection of plebeians at elections, and the like, no longer arose from any external opposition, but from the internal dissensions of the plebeians themselves. Formerly the college of the tribunes was always unanimous, while henceforth it is frequently divided, some of its members being gained over to the interests of the senate, and motions which used to be brought forward by the whole college, are now made by single tribunes. These are proofs that the fusion of the two estates had been accomplished.

LECTURE XXVII.

THE military tribuneship had been regarded as a kind of compromise. Among the first three, Livy mentions L. Atilius Longus and T. Caecilius.[1] Instead of the latter, Dionysius, in the eleventh book, has Cloelius; but nothing can be decided, since the readings in the eleventh book are all of a very recent date. If Caecilius is the correct name, there were two plebeians among them; and this would account for the vehemence with which the patricians insisted upon abolishing the military tribuneships.

[1] In some modern editions of Livy, we read Cloelius instead of Caecilius, but this is an emendation: the MSS. of Dionysius have Κλύσιον. — ED.

I believe that the censorship was instituted in the same year, A.U. 311, as the military tribuneships; and both therefore must have arisen from a common cause, a fact which Livy overlooks; and the circumstance of the first censors not being found in the Fasti, nor in the *libri magistratuum*, but only in one of the *libri lintei*, and that as consuls, is accounted for by the fact, that the censors were already elected in accordance with the laws of the twelve tables; and that when the patricians carried their point by violent commotion, the censors, of whom we have only one trace, were neither consuls nor military tribunes, but performed consular functions, and therefore took part in concluding the treaty with the Ardeatans. Livy could not explain this, nor could Macer make anything of it. It is strange to read in Livy, that the military tribunes were obliged to abdicate, because the *tabernaculum* had been *vitio captum*, and that T. Quinctius, as interrex (more probably as dictator), elected the two consuls, L. Papirius Mugillanus and L. Sempronius Atratinus, who, however, were not to be found in the Fasti; and yet he relates the affair as quite certain. It is still more surprising, that the year after he says of these first censors, that they were elected censors for the purpose of indemnifying those *quorum de consulatu dubitabatur, ut eo magistratu parum solidum magistratum explerent*, as if in the year A.U. 312 there could have been any doubt as to what had happened in 311. Livy is here guilty of the same thoughtlessness as when, in the history of the second Punic war, he confounds one Heracleitus, a Macedonian ambassador, with the celebrated philosopher Heracleitus.

Now as regards the nature of the military tribunes, it must be avowed that this magistracy is very obscure to us.[2] Livy says of them *eos juribus et insignibus consularibus usos esse*, and they are also called *tribuni militares consulari potestate;* but Dion Cassius, that acute observer, who at one time himself occupied the curule chair, states that the military tribunes were inferior to the consuls, that none of them ever obtained a triumph, although many had done things deserving of one. This perfectly agrees with history; we further find that a consul was never appointed *magister equitum*, while military

---

[2] The repetitions which occur here and elsewhere arise from the fact, that the discussion was interrupted at the close of the hour, and was taken up again at the beginning of the next Lecture. — ED.

tribunes were sometimes invested with that office. This seems to show that the military tribunes were not curule magistrates, that is according to Gellius' explanation, not such magistrates as were allowed to ride in a chariot (as *Juno curulis*, whose image was carried on a chariot); the consuls rode in chariots to the curia; the full triumph was called *triumphus curulis*, according to the *monumentum Ancyranum*, where the number of the *triumphi curules* of Augustus are mentioned; the *ovatio* was different from such a triumph.[3] It seems, moreover, that the military tribunes never had any jurisdiction; but it was originally possessed by the censors and afterwards by the *praefectus urbi*, who probably also presided in the senate. This latter magistracy, too, had been abolished by the decemviral legislation, but now appears again. The consular power was thus weakened, just as was done afterwards when the Licinian law was carried: for when the consulship was divided between the patricians and plebeians, the praetorship was detached from it and constituted as a separate magistracy. It thus becomes intelligible why the plebeians preferred the election of military tribunes, even though they were not taken from their order, for the power of those magistrates was inferior to that of the consuls. According to Livy's account, it was always the senate which determined whether consuls or military tribunes should be elected; but it is more probable that this question was decided by the curies; confusion here may have arisen from the ambiguity of the word *patres*. The military tribuneship, however, presents surprising changes in number, for sometimes, though rarely, we find three, more frequently four, but from the year A.U. 347 or A.U. 348 regularly six, wherever they are mentioned, and in one year eight, the two censors being included. When there are four, one of them usually is the *praefectus urbi*, so that in reality there are only three. The right of the plebeians to be elected military tribunes was never disputed, but after the first election it was

---

[3] It is a mysterious statement which occurs in Livy and elsewhere, that a special law was passed for a dictator, *ut ei equum escendere liceret*. This is explained by saying that a dictator was not entitled to appear on horseback, whereas the *magister equitum* did possess this privilege. It is possible that the dictator was not only entitled to use a chariot, but that he was not allowed to appear otherwise than in a chariot, especially on his return from battle. An allusion to this is contained in a verse in Varro: *Dictator ubi currum insedit vehitur usque ad oppidum. Oppidum* according to Varro is the city wall (also a place surrounded with a wall, in opposition to *pagus* and *vicus*).—N.

nearly always frustrated, though by what means is incomprehensible, for Livy's account, which I have already mentioned, is foolish. It is possible indeed that an arrangement was made, and that the patricians said: "We grant the institution of a weaker magistracy, but then they must be elected from among our body exclusively;" or that it was in ancient times a privilege of the presiding magistrate not to accept any votes (*nomina non accipere*) which for various reasons could be rejected; or it may be that when six military tribunes were elected, the curies conferred the *imperium* only upon the patricians, and refused it to the plebeians. But on this last supposition, it is inconceivable how the plebeians should have acquiesced in it. We are here unfortunately without the guidance of Dionysius, who though he did not comprehend the relations, yet gave faithfully what he found in his authorities: if we had his account, the whole period would undoubtedly be much clearer to us. But we are confined to Livy, and on many points we cannot hope to obtain any certain information. After the last change, when the number of military tribunes became regularly six, we repeatedly find a majority of plebeians among them, and the regulation evidently was, that the number six should always be complete, and that they should be chosen without distinction from both orders. There is every appearance, that when this change was introduced, the election was transferred from the centuries to the tribes. Everything therefore depended upon the honesty of the president, and upon his accepting the votes or not. The sad policy by which Italy became great in the fifteenth and sixteenth centuries, now appears in Roman history, especially in the divisions of the college of tribunes; and this is, to some extent, the reason why the development of Rome was for a time compromised.

A period in which successful wars are carried on, as was the case with Rome from this time down to the Gallic calamity, is extremely well calculated to make the subjects of a state submit to things which they would not otherwise tolerate. The name of the Roman republic was surrounded with glory, great conquests and much booty were made, the plebeians as well as the patricians felt comfortable, and although the rulers were not popular, yet things were allowed to go on as they were. Rome thus recovered from the decline into which she had sunk ever since the *regifugium.* The grant of the connubium between the two orders also must have exercised a mighty influence: the families became more closely connected and attached to one another; a patrician born of a plebeian mother when sitting in the senate stood on a footing of equality with the plebeians, and perhaps did many a thing to please them. The number of plebeians in the senate may not have been very great, but the mere fact of their being there, even without influence, was agreeable to the whole body of plebeians.

The censorship being a permanent magistracy, and apparently the highest, had a lustre which far surpassed that of the military tribuneship. If we suppose that it was instituted by the twelve tables, it becomes clear why Cicero, in his work *De Legibus*, represents the censors as the first magistracy; he probably copied it from the twelve tables, and only omitted a few things; for in the twelve tables they had still more attributes. In the earlier times the consuls are said to have performed the functions of the censors, and this is very probable, considering the almost regal power of the consuls; but it is surprising how they can have discharged their enormous duties. The Greek states of Sicily and Italy, likewise had their τιμηταί (Athens had none), but in no part of Greece were their powers as extensive as at Rome. According to the Roman law, the censors had to conduct the census, and to determine a person's status in society. Accurate lists were kept of the property, births and deaths of the citizens, as well as of those who were admitted to the franchise. But we must distinguish between two kinds of lists. One class consisted of lists of persons arranged according to names. Q. Mucius, for example, was registered under the *tribus Romilia* with his name, his whole family, and his taxable property. His sons, who had the *toga virilis*, probably had a *caput* of their own. The other lists were of a topographical kind, and contained a tabular view of landed estates according to the different regions, e. g. the *tribus Romilia* in all its parts. The ancients, in general, had much more writing than is commonly imagined; all was done with a minuteness which was part of their political forms. I once saw in London the registers of an Indian province—of course in a translation, for I do not understand one word of the Indian language—which were drawn up with a minuteness of which we can scarcely form an idea. The same was the case with the ancients. The registers of property at Athens were very minute, and so also even in later times were the Roman contracts before the curiae. The division of the *jugera* was very accurately recorded in the lists of the Roman censors; the *caput* of each individual contained his descent, tribe, rank, property, etc. The censors at the same time had the right of transferring persons, for the purpose both of honouring and of disgracing them: but what were the offences which the censors punished with ignominy (*ignominia* is the real expression)? Every one at Rome was expected to answer the definition of his status. A plebeian was necessarily a husbandman, either a landed proprietor or a free labourer. This is established by positive testimony, and still more in a negative way, for no one could be a plebeian who was engaged in craft or a trade. Whoever so employed himself was struck from the list of his tribe, which accordingly was not so much a personal *ignominia*, as a declaration that a person had passed over from one side to the other. But whoever neglected his farm, was likewise struck out from his tribe, i. e. it was declared that he was *de facto* not a husbandman. An *eques* who kept his horse badly was similarly treated, and this was the *notatio censoria*, by which a person was degraded to the rank of an *aerarius*, being considered unworthy to hold his property. An *aerarius*, on the other hand, who distinguished himself, and acquired landed property, was honoured by being registered among the plebeians; and a plebeian who distinguished himself was entered in the centuries of the plebeian equites. But the censors certainly could not raise strangers to the rank of citizens; for this was a point concerning which there were established laws, or else the assembly of the people conferred the franchise by an extraordinary act. A state whose varying elements present great differences, where the plebes does not form a close body but may complete itself, and contains the aristocratic elements of plebeian equites who are not restricted by the census, must necessarily have some magistrate for the purpose of assigning to every individual his rank; for such an honorary class of men as the equites could not be close or immutable, just because it was an honorary class. We may say that the power of deciding respecting it might have been left to the people; but this would not only have been tedious but also

perverse, since it might be presumed that the censors, who
were chosen from among the most distinguished men, and had
to bear all the responsibility—one of them having even
power to oppose the acts of his colleague—would act much
more fairly and justly, than if the whole people had been
called upon to decide. The proper filling up of vacancies
in the senate also required a careful superintendence. It was
originally an assembly of the gentes, in which each gens was
represented by its senator: but when gentes became extinct,
three hundred were taken from the whole body of burghers,
one hundred from each tribe, so that as gentes became extinct,
one gens might have several representatives, while another
might become altogether incapable or unworthy of being
represented. At a later time the *lex Ovinia tribunicia*[4] interfered, in which it was declared, that out of the whole body
of the burghers, the worthiest should be taken without any
regard to the gentes. If this law belongs to the first period of
the censorship, it shews that at that time the senate still consisted of patricians only, and that the worthiest were taken
from all the three tribes. The account that even Brutus or
Valerius Poplicola introduced plebeians into the senate under
the name of *conscripti*, is a mere fable, or must be regarded
only as a transitory arrangement. About the time of the
secession of the commonalty there cannot have been a single
plebeian in the senate, and their existence there cannot be
proved till the middle of the fourth century. The senate now
became a body of men elected by the people, as the magistrates
obtained the privilege of voting in the senate, and the right of
being elected into it, when the new list was made up. This
right extended even to the quaestors. The throwing open of
the quaestorship to both orders in the year A.U. 346, appears
to me to have been the first occasion on which the plebeians
were admitted into the senate ; and when afterwards eight
quaestors were appointed every year, the arbitrary power of
the censors necessarily ceased. They could, indeed, exclude
plebeians, but the senate consisted of only three hundred members; and as the censors at the close of each lustrum always
had before them forty men with claims to a seat in the senate,
it is obvious that the senate might soon become a plebeian
rather than a patrician assembly. The power of the censors,

---

[4] Festus, s. v. *praeteriti senatores.*   Comp. *Hist. Rome*, vol. i. note 1163.—Ed.

therefore, like that of all the other magistrates, except the tribunes, decreased in the course of time. Formerly only a censor could stop the proceedings of his colleague, but afterwards the tribunes also presumed to interfere with the decrees of the censors. It was at one time believed to be impossible that the censor should have had the powers which were given them by the Ovinian law; or if such were the fact, that their powers were excessive. Originally, however, they actually had great arbitrary power; but as afterwards the two orders were no longer exclusively opposed to each other, but the government and the people, the latter limited the power of the former, and the censors too lost a part of theirs. The censorial power did not affect the patricians, for their books were closed; and according to the notions of those times about the auspices, no person could become a patrician not even by adoption, though afterwards cases certainly do occur.

The question now is: Were the censors allowed to exercise their power in regard also to the moral conduct of citizens? Could they mark a bad man with a *nota censoria*? I formerly answered these questions in the negative, excepting perhaps cases of decided villany; but in the recently discovered excerpts from Dionysius there is a passage, in which he manifestly speaks of the power of the censors to brand every moral baseness which could not be reached by the law, such as disaffection towards parents, between husband and wife, between parents and children, harshness towards slaves and neighbours. In the time of Dionysius, it is true, the ancient character of the censorship was no longer visible; but this is the very reason why we must suppose, that in describing the censorship he represented it such as it had been in past ages, rather than as it was in his own time, which was known to every one. It is therefore probable that the censorial power actually had that great extent of which, by our existing materials, we can still fix the limits. The censorship of Gellius and Lentulus in the time of Cicero was an irregularity[5]. Whether some tribes were *minus honestae*, and others *honestiores*, as early as the period we are now speaking about, cannot be determined; but in regard to later times, it is acknowledged that the *tribus urbanae*, and especially the Esquilina, were despised, while the Crustumina stood higher;

[5] Cic. *p. Cluent.* c. 42 ; Ascon. *in Orat. in Tog. Cand.* p. 84. Orelli.—Ed.

but it would be quite absurd to suppose the same thing for the earlier times.

The censors were at first elected for a *lustrum*, or a period of five years; and this seems to have been the period intended by the decemviral legislation for all magistrates, according to the whole character of that legislation, the principle of which was to apply cooling remedies against the political fever, elections being always most powerful in stirring up the passions. Whether Mam. Aemilius actually limited the censorial power to eighteen months, and was therefore branded with ignominy by his successors, or whether this is merely a tale which was contained in the books of the censors and intended to trace an existing law back to some individual, cannot be determined; though it is certain that there existed such books of the censors.

LECTURE XXVIII.

IN the year A.U. 315, a fearful famine broke out at Rome; many citizens threw themselves into the Tiber to escape from death by starvation. The prices of corn then were in general as fluctuating as in the middle ages, which gave rise to much speculation and hoarding up of grain, especially as in Italy corn can be kept for a long time under ground. The calamity came on unexpectedly; the *praefectura annonae* was then instituted, which seems to have been a transitory magistracy: L. Minucius Augurinus was the first appointed to the office. He did all he could to keep prices down: he ordered the existing stores to be opened, compelled the proprietors to sell the corn at a fixed price, and made purchases among the neighbouring nations; but his measures were too slow, and the means employed for the purpose were not sufficient. No effectual help was afforded but by a plebeian eques, Sp. Maelius. He at his own expense caused large quantities of grain to be purchased in Etruria and the country of the Volscians, and distributed the corn among the poor. We cannot indeed conceive that his private property could have been very large, but at such times even a little aid is welcome. A person who conferred such benefits

upon his fellow-citizens, became easily suspected in the states
of antiquity of acting from impure motives. Maelius accordingly was accused of trying to gain over the people, and by
their assistance the *tyrannis*. Minucius is said to have reported
to the senate that many plebeians assembled in the house of
Maelius, and that arms had been carried into it. No man can
presume to say whether this accusation was well founded or
not; but at any rate it would have been senseless for a man to
form a conspiracy, who was not distinguished for anything but
his wealth, and who would have been opposed no less by the
tribunes than by the patricians. But however this may be, he
was regarded as the head of a party, and in order to crush him,
the senate and the curies appointed L. Quinctius Cincinnatus
dictator, and he chose Servilius Ahala for his master of the
horse. In the night Cincinnatus occupied the Capitol and the
other fortified places, and on the next morning he set up his
curule throne in the forum, and sent Ahala to summon Maelius
before his tribunal. Maelius foresaw his fate, as no tribune
could protect him against the dictator; he accordingly refused
to appear, and concealed himself among the crowd of plebeians;
but Servilius Ahala seized and slew him on the spot. This act
is much admired by the ancients; but its merit is very doubtful,
as it may have been a mere murder. The *praefectus annonae*,
according to a very probable account, is stated to have renounced the *patres*, and to have gone over to the *plebes*, and
to have been appointed the eleventh tribune of the people. In
a few weeks, it is said, he succeeded in bringing down the
prices: this shows that the distress had been occasioned by artificial means rather than by actual scarcity. The corn contained
in the granaries of Sp. Maelius was taken by the senate and
distributed among the people. Moreover, according to Cicero,
Ahala was charged with murder before the plebes, and went
into exile: whether he was afterwards recalled, we do not know.
This also suggests a bad case. The house of Maelius was pulled
down. The Aequimaelium or place where it stood, was below
the Capitol, and is now quite buried under rubbish which
forms a hill at the foot of the Capitol: this point is of great
importance in Roman topography.[1]

[1] The story about Maelius very much resembles one of a Pasha of Aleppo.
During a great scarcity, he convened all the most distinguished persons, ordering
every one to state the amount of corn he possessed. He then rode to their store-
houses, and on measuring the corn found double the quantity that had been
returned, and he accordingly took away the surplus, and the dearth ceased.—N.

When the Valerian laws, as we have before seen, so far limited the ancient right of the consuls to force the people to obedience, that when they pronounced a person deserving of corporal punishment, he could appeal to the commonalty, a certain sphere of inflicting punishment not subject to appeal was necessarily left to the consuls, for otherwise their authority would have been entirely destroyed. This right of punishment consisted in the infliction of fines, which regulation also is ascribed to Valerius. But this is improbable, for the law of the consuls Tarpeius and Aternius, which was passed by the centuries, and by which the *multa* was fixed in heads of cattle, as is expressly stated by Cicero (*De Re Publica*), is framed in terms which are too precise. This could not have been the case, if the Valerian law had already determined the limitation, unless indeed the rulers had afterwards again been guilty of most arbitrary proceedings. I may remark in general that all that is said about the Valerii is of a doubtful character, as Valerius Antias looked upon himself as belonging to the Valerian gens, and invented a great many things to honour it; the Valerii themselves too were vain of popular favour. That law fixed two sheep and thirty heifers as the highest *multa*, concerning which Gellius makes a thoughtless remark, when he says that sheep were then so rare that two sheep were equal in value to thirty heifers, though immediately afterwards he himself mentions the value; that of a sheep as ten, and that of an ox as one hundred *asses*. The fact is simply, that the consuls gradually increased their fine so as to leave the return to obedience open: he who did not appear on the first summons, had to give one sheep, if he refused on the second, two sheep, then a heifer, etc. There is yet another circumstance, which we know from Cicero and which shows how little confidence can be placed in other accounts: it was not till twenty-five years later that the value of these things was fixed in money, and at a very moderate rate. Cicero justly regards this as an advance in the liberty of individuals.

The number of quaestors or paymasters who had formerly been elected by the king or the curies, and afterwards according to the law of Poplicola by the centuries, was increased from two to four, and they were to be partly patricians and partly plebeians. At first the patricians prevented the execution of this law, but afterwards the plebeians successfully established their claim. This progress was not merely a matter of honour, but a reality, inasmuch as it concerned the immediate interests of the plebeians, for they now had a share in the administration of the public purse, which accordingly was no longer a *publicum,* but an *aerarium.* By this means, as I have already observed, the senate also was opened to the plebeians, and nothing but the censorial power could remove them from it.

A further progress towards liberty was the fact, that, about twenty years after the decemviral legislation, the right to determine upon peace and war was transferred from the curies to the centuries. That the curies originally possessed this right, is established by the testimony of Dionysius, but as the plebeians alone were destined to serve in the ranks and the patricians deprived them of the booty, it was natural that the tribunes should demand for their order the right to determine, as to whether they wanted war or not, and the tribunician opposition to declarations of war was nothing but a reservation of the rights of the plebes. When the centuries had passed a resolution to declare war, the curies had of course to give their assent; and this they unquestionably always did, as the proposal proceeded from the senate, and as it is inconceivable that the senate and curies should not have been of one mind.

The existence of plebeian senators is clear beyond a doubt; it is expressly attested that P. Licinius Calvus sat in the senate, and hence when an *interrex* was to be appointed, it was not the *decem primi* alone that met — for through the admission of the plebeians they had lost their meaning — but all the patricians of the whole senate. This act was termed *patricii coeunt ad interregem prodendum,* and may have been established even by the laws of the twelve tables. We can easily understand that the Romans might know the laws of the twelve tables by heart, and yet not see that there was in them something different from what existed afterwards.

We have now seen how, from the time of the decemviral legislation down to the taking of the city by the Gauls, internal freedom was in a steady process of development, corresponding to the outward increase of dominion, which shows the necessary connection between the two.

The history of the Italian nations is known to us almost exclusively through the Romans; yet if we possessed it, it would supply us with the only means of understanding the external history of Rome; for the latter is frequently not only defective, but deceitfully corrupted. The decline of the state after the expulsion of the kings may have been the consequence partly of internal commotions, and partly of the feuds with the Latins; but afterwards the influence of the Etruscans from the north gave a fresh blow to Rome, and at the same time the extension of the Sabines and their colonies produced a great effect. The Romans called the latter Sabellians, for *Sabellus* is the ordinary adjective along with *Sabinus* like *Hispanus* and *Hispellus*, *Graecus* and *Graeculus*, *Poenus* and *Poenulus*, *Romus* and *Romulus ;* it was not till later times that the termination *lus* assumed a diminutive meaning. *Sabellus* is perfectly equivalent to *Sabinus*, except that, according to common usage, Sabelli denotes the whole nation, and Sabini only the inhabitants of the small district which bears that name. These extensions of the Etruscans and Sabines, then, were the principal cause of the decline of Rome, and without them the wars of Porsena would not have taken place. If the Etruscans had spread in another direction, and if the Sabellians had not been themselves pressed upon and obliged to advance, the Ausonian tribes, especially the Aequians, would not have been driven to make conquests.

The period of Etruria's greatness falls in the middle of the third century after the building of the city, according to the testimony of Cato that the Etruscan colony of Capua or Vulturnum was founded about the year A.M. 260, that is, about the time when the Romans were so hard pressed by the Veientines. At that time the Etruscans, or, as the Greeks call them, the Tyrrhenians, were the most formidable conquerors; but a crisis took place in the destruction of their navy by the Cumaeans who were assisted by Hiero, about the end of the third century. We can speak of this change only in general terms, for unfortunately all the detail is lost. A mighty part of the history of man is here buried in darkness. About the same time their power was broken on the Tiber also.

The Sabines often appear as enemies of the Romans in the opposite direction, during the latter half of the third century; the earlier accounts of the victories of Valerius over them are quite apocryphal. We will not attempt to decide whether they were dangerous to the Romans, but there can be no doubt that wars were fought with the Sabines as with the other tribes in the neighbourhood; all the detail, however, consists of poetical fictions. But towards the end of the third century, history becomes clearer and clearer, and we can perceive traces of the ancient annals. The last Sabine war is that which was carried on by Valerius and Horatius in the first year of the restoration of the consulship; it is related too minutely to deserve credit in all its parts, but it is certain, that, during the subsequent period of nearly one hundred and fifty years down to the time of Curius, the Sabines did not carry on any war against the Romans. This must have had its peculiar reason; and I perceive this reason in a treaty of which not a trace is left, but by which isopolity was established between the two nations: the existence of that isopolity is attested by Servius in his commentary on Virgil.

About the year A.U. 310, the formation of the Campanian people is mentioned, for it is said that at Vulturnum or Capua the Etruscans admitted Samnites as *epoeci*, and shared their territory with them. This is a proof of the progress of the Sabines in those parts, for the Samnites were a Sabine people. The Aequians and Volscians discontinued their attacks upon Rome, and the Sabine wars ended: hence we here recognise the time when the migration of the Sabines to the south ceased, and they left off pressing the Ausonian mountaineers. The Etruscans stopped all at once, as is naturally the case with a people governed by an oligarchy: when such a people comes to a state of rest, it never puts itself in motion again, or acquires fresh life: at least history furnishes no example of the kind. In this manner we may connect the events which the Romans have recorded in a very confused manner.

During the period from A.U. 306 to 323, there was almost a total cessation from wars; the account of the insurrection at Ardea, in which the Romans were called upon for assistance, has something so strange about it, that we can place no reliance on it: we have here a complete repetition of the story of Cincinnatus surrounding the hostile army. But in the year 323 the war broke out afresh and seriously. We do not know whether the Antiatans took part in it; but there is no doubt that Ecetra did. They then met the Aequians on mount Algidus. The Roman armies fought against them between Velitrae, which was Volscian, Tusculum, and the Alban

mount: but a battle was lost, whereupon A. Postumius
Tubertus was appointed dictator. This war is perfectly historical and accurately described; but whether it is true that
A. Postumius gave weight to his imperium in the minds of
those who fought under him, by inflexible severity towards
his own son, may remain undecided; the prevailing opinion
is, that Manlius followed his example, but from the expression
imperia Manliana no inference can be drawn; Livy's attempt
to prove the contrary is, at all events, futile. Postumius led
the whole strength of the republic and her allies against the
enemy; he gave one army to the consul, and took the other
for himself; the former was stationed on the road to Lanuvium,
the latter on that to Tusculum, near the point where these
two roads crossed each other. The Volscians and Aequians
were stationed in separate camps, one of which was opposed
by the consul, and the other by the dictator, but the two
armies were near each other. The enemy attacked the consul's
camp in the night; but the dictator being prepared, sent a
detachment to take possession of the Volscian camp, which was
almost entirely abandoned, and he himself led the greater part
of his army to the assistance of the consul, and attacked the
enemy in the rear. The latter were completely cut to pieces
with the exception of a small band of men, who, under the
command of the brave Vettius Messius, fought their way
through the Romans.

This battle is one of those which exert an influence upon
the history of the world: it broke the power of the Volscians
of Ecetra and of the Aequians; the massacre must have been
immense. The Aequians forthwith sued for peace, and obtained
it for eight years; from this moment they ceased to be formidable. After this time the Romans were constantly extending
their dominion, and recovered the places which had been taken
from them in former wars by the Volscians and Aequians.
Among them we have express mention of Lavici[2], formerly
one of the great Latin towns, Bolae or Bola, Velitrae, Circeii,
Anxur, Ferentinum, which had formerly belonged to the
Hernicans and must now have been restored to them, since it
re-appears among their towns. In this manner, the Romans
advanced as far as the boundaries of Latium in the narrower
sense, that is just as far as they had penetrated under the kings.

---

[2] *Labici*, which we commonly read in Livy, is a mistake of the fourth and
fifth centuries for *Lavici*. The opposite mistake, *Vola* instead of *Bola* occurs in
the early editions. — N.

In the same way Setia, Norba, Cora, and Signia must have been recovered, and as the Romans and Latins now no longer stood on a footing of equality, they must have come under the sole dominion of Rome. In the country of the Aequians, the Romans advanced to lake Fucinus. The subjugation of the Volscians rendered it possible for them to carry on the fearful war against Veii. In consequence of these conquests, many poor people were provided for, by means of Roman colonies established at Lavici and Velitrae; and the colony at Circeii was probably made a Latin one.

After a long interval, the agrarian law was seriously brought forward again in the year A. U. 345; it had been previously mentioned only once, but slightly. The cause of this silence in the preceding years is not quite clear; some assignments of colonies took place, but always in conjunction with the Latins and Hernicans, and without any beneficial consequences for those who did not wish to give up their Roman country and franchise. Times of contentment or of discontent in history correspond not so much to the political development of rights, as to prosperity in general: in happy circumstances man likes to enjoy life without thinking much of his political condition. Such a period occurred in Germany previously to the thirty years' war, when every thing rose in value, and the internal condition of the country was tranquil: the same was the case in France under Henry IV. Such also, on the whole, was the condition of Rome at the time under consideration, and this was perhaps the principal reason why no violent internal commotions occurred for so many years. If, however, during such a period new powers have been developed, then new claims also arise, which are put forth at once and with vehemence: this was now the case with the agrarian law. Till now, the patricians had with great cunning succeeded in excluding the plebeians from the honors which belonged to them; consuls were often elected instead of military tribunes, and the number of the latter was frequently not complete; but now the plebeians began to insist upon certain claims. The humiliation of Rome abroad occasioned by the wars of the Etruscans and Volscians had ceased, new conquests quickly raised the city to a great height, and under these circumstances the tribunes exerted their powers for the advantage of the members of their own order. The conquest of Lavici afforded the first opportunity for such measures, and its consequences must have been far greater than those described by Livy: a colony was demanded for that place, but the Roman senate refused it. The Cassian law was now never mentioned, but the tribunes brought a new *lex tribunicia agraria* before the tribes: it was demanded that the public land should be divided, and that the portion of it possessed by the patricians should again become subject to a tax; the latter had originally been a regulation in all agrarian laws, but the patricians had contrived to neglect this obligation with impunity. These demands of the tribunes were not complied with indeed, but they led to the foundation of several colonies of Roman citizens, that is purely Roman colonies, whence they are called *coloniae Romanae*. After the taking of Bolae, an unfortunate military tribune, M. Postumius, had sold all the booty for the benefit of the publicum (*publicum redigere*, for the *publicum* was the separate treasury of the curies). This so infuriated the soldiers, that they rose against the quaestor and slew him. The military tribune, who tried the offenders for this crime, drove them to despair; in consequence of which they rose against him also, and imbrued their hands in his blood, the only instance of the kind that occurred before the time of Sulla. The senate treated the matter leniently, for the guilt was too evident. The consequences of this insurrection must have been very great, though Livy says nothing about them, for from this time forward we never find less than six military tribunes, and their election seems to have been transferred at that time from the centuries to the tribes, for otherwise it would be very careless of Livy to speak of a *tribus praerogativa*. The curies, however, still continued to confer the imperium upon those who were elected.

Rome now directed her arms against Veii, which was situated at the distance of about twelve miles and measured nearly five miles in circumference; its territory must have extended to the very foot of the Janiculum. This city was a thorn in the side of Rome, which could not become great until this rival was conquered. Fidenae which is called an Etruscan city but was really Tyrrhenian, is described from the earliest times, and even in the reign of Romulus, as involved in war with Rome; it was situated on the Tiber five miles above Rome, and had at an early period been occupied by Roman colonists, who had been repeatedly expelled but were always

restored. It was either in A. U. 320 or 329[3], when the Fidenatans again rebelled against the Roman colonists and expelled
them. We must conceive these colonists as a settled garrison, who
had their own farms. Three Roman ambassadors appeared at
Fidenae to demand reparation and the restoration of the
colonists. This demand appeared to the Fidenatans so out-
rageous, that they slew the Roman ambassadors, and threw
themselves into the arms of Lars Tolumnius, king of Veii; for
all the Etruscan towns were governed by kings elected for life.
Tolumnius marched across the Tiber to their assistance; and as
the Romans, after the conquest of the Aequians and Volscians,
had now become formidable neighbours, the Capenatans and
Faliscans, two Oscan tribes which had maintained themselves
in those districts against the Tyrrhenians, likewise came to the
assistance of the Fidenatans. This army posted itself five miles
from Rome on the other side of the Anio and created great
terror in the city. A dictator was appointed, who chose the
military tribune A. Cornelius Cossus for his master of the horse.
The Romans fought a successful battle, and Cornelius Cossus
with his own hands slew the Veientine king, who was charged
though probably unjustly, with having murdered the Roman
ambassadors.[4] After this victory, Fidenae was taken and razed
to the ground, and its territory became *ager publicus*. With
the Veientines a truce was concluded; and it must have been
welcome to the Romans to have peace in that quarter, until
they should have completely broken the power of the Aequians
and Volscians.

When the truce was drawing to its close, the Veientines sent
ambassadors to all the other Etruscan towns to solicit their
assistance against the Romans; but it was refused, because
another and far more dangerous enemy had appeared in the
Apennines, and after the fashion of a Turkish invading army
destroyed everything that came in their way: these were the

[3] Two wars are here related, but they are, according to all appearance, trans-
posed; the minute account of one at least is out of place, and probably belongs
to the year 329, although hostilities may have occurred in 320 also; this at all
events is the Chronology of Diodorus, to which we must adhere.—N.

[4] The Emperor Augustus directed Livy's attention to the fact, that Cossus, on
the ground of having gained the *spolia opima* on that occasion, set himself up as
consul, for that on his armour he called himself consul. This is a later addition
in Livy, and stands quite apart from his narrative, for otherwise he ought to
have placed the event seven years later.—N.

Gauls.   The Etruscans advised the Veientines by all means to maintain peace with the Romans; but the demands of the latter may have been very high; they may have claimed the sovereignty of Veii, so that the Veientines were compelled to decide upon war.   If we compare the account of the first Veientine war which occurred seventy years before, we find the Veientines at that time supported by all the powers of Etruria, whereas now they were confined to the protection of the Capenatans[5] and Faliscans; it was only in one campaign that the Tarquinians came to their assistance; the Caerites were on friendly terms with the Romans and therefore remained neutral: the Etruscans indeed were masters of the place, but the population may have been still essentially Tyrrhenian.   In short, the war was limited to the Veientines and their immediate neighbours.   Rome was obliged to make the greatest efforts, and was supported by the Latins and Hernicans.

LECTURE XXIX.

THE ridicule which Florus casts upon the *bella suburbana : De Verulis et Bovillis pudet dicere sed triumphavimus*, is that of a rhetorician, and we cannot quarrel with him for finding those occurrences uninteresting.   Wars carried on in a limited territory cannot indeed have the same interest, as, for example, the Hannibalian war, but still we may see in them the development of the strength of Rome.   We will not despise this Veientine war, yet we shall not describe it as minutely as Livy does, but confine our account to a few brief outlines.   The feelings and sentiments with which the Romans undertook it deserve our admiration, for, considering their circumstances, the difficulties were as great as those which they had to encounter at the beginning of the first Punic war; it was only by continued perseverance that they could hope for a favorable issue.   A city situated at so short a distance, and so well fortified as Veii

---

[5] The Etruscan town of Capena was probably as near to Rome as Veii, though its site cannot be determined, because it disappears from history at an early time; but it was certainly situate between Veii, Falerii, and the Tiber.—N.

could be conquered only by a blockade or siege; for whenever the Veientines felt that they were too weak in the open field, they retreated within their walls, against which the Romans were powerless. It was necessary, therefore, either to blockade the town so as to compel it to surrender by hunger, and if necessary by fortifications and undermining, or the Romans had to try to reach it by inflicting calamities upon it, that is, they might fortify a place in the neighbourhood (ἐπιτείχισις), as Decelea was fortified in the neighbourhood of Athens, and thence destroy everything far and wide, preventing all cultivation of the fields, so that the hostile city would be thrown into a state of distress, which it must endeavour to avoid in every possible way. But in order to do this, the Romans would have been obliged to change their mode of warfare, and moreover they had to fear the neighbouring towns of Capena and Falerii. Hitherto they had only made short campaigns during a few summer months, which often lasted only from ten to twelve, nay, sometimes not longer than six days, especially during the time of the republic, for under the kings i must have been different. There were from the earliest times certain months destined for war, during which neighbouring tribes ravaged each other's territories: such was the case among the Greeks, and such is still the practice of the Asiatics. Russia and Persia fight every year for a few months on the frontiers of Georgia; and in the laws of Charlemagne the time is fixed during which nations are bound to serve in the field. In the intervals, intercourse between the countries was more or less free, and at the times of festivals especially it was quite free, as, e.g. during the common festivals of the Etruscans at the temple of Voltumna, and of the Ausonian nations at the temple of Feronia. The soldiers could be kept in the field for a limited time only, and when that was over they dispersed.

The means of Rome for keeping up a great army had been much reduced since the Etruscan and Volscian wars. In former times, the armies had been paid out of the tithes which were paid by the possessor of the ager publicus, but since the ager publicus had been lost, every one went into the field as an οἰκόσιτος, that is, he brought his provisions with him from home, and whatever more was required, he obtained by foraging; if this could not be done, the army was obliged to return home. Hence we hear so little of sieges. But now when the

war was to be conducted seriously, and as arms were not to be
laid down till Veii should be subdued, it became necessary to
pay the soldiers. This determination was perhaps connected
with the proposal to recommence levying the tithes upon the
ager publicus, and to pay the soldiers out of their produce.
But what seems to confirm the supposition that a stipendium
was generally paid even from the earliest times, is the statement that in the census of Servius Tullius, the *equites* received
2000 *asses:* if so, why should not the *pedites* also have received
something? I conjecture that they were paid 100 *asses,* whether the war lasted a longer or a shorter period: and out of this
sum the soldier had to provide himself with arms and provisions. So long as this was the case, wars of conquest were
impossible, for in them the soldiers must be entirely maintained
by the state, and this latter is the arrangement which was made
when, according to tradition, the Roman soldiers first received
a stipendium. It would be wrong to suppose that before that
time they had no pay at all; but the difference between receiving a small sum once for all, or a small daily pay is considerable.
We may take it for granted, that the aerarii, being exempt
from military service, were at all times obliged to pay a war-
tax for the *pedites,* as the *orbi orbaeque* did for the equites; for
it is impossible that the double burden of serving with his life
and his property should have fallen on the plebeian.

The pay of the Romans then, from early times, was 100
asses per month for every man, and this pay was proportioned
to their wants. Such pay was invariably given at Athens
after the time of Pericles, but probably not earlier. The pay
of an Athenian hoplite was enormous, but at Rome, where
the allies did not pay any contributions, it was necessarily
smaller. One hundred *asses* continued in later times to be
the monthly pay. When the *asses* were made too light, they
were calculated in silver in the proportion of one to ten.
Every three days the soldier received a denarius (the value of
a drachma), that is, daily two oboli. The stipendium was
regarded as a unit, but was afterwards multiplied (*multiplex
stipendium.* Domitian added a *quartum stipendium*). This,
however, is at all times to be understood only of one month.
The excellent Radbod Hermann Schele errs in supposing, on
the authority of writers who are worth nothing, that the
stipendia were annual, which is in itself impossible, and would

have answered no purpose. In this supposition, he was for once deserted by his practical good sense. The pay was given only for the time during which the soldiers were actually in the field. If the war lasted a whole year, pay was of course given for a year. Livy, in making Appius Claudius say, *annua aera habes, annuam operam ede*, merely makes him express his own erroneous opinion.

This innovation was of extraordinary importance to the republic; for without a national army, Rome would never have become great. Now if it had been possible to give the pay without imposing a tax, it would have been fortunate indeed; but if the patricians did not pay the tithes on the ager publicus, or if the revenue of the state was not sufficient, the plebeians must have felt the war very oppressive, for it then became necessary to obtain the pay by a property-tax, and it might so happen that the service in the army lasted a very long time. This injustice, however, was necessary. The plebeians had formerly not been taxed, probably because they had not been able to pay; but during the last twenty years, Rome had been ever increasing in prosperity, so that it was now possible to tax the plebeians, although it gave rise to new distress, which led again to the old oppression exercised by creditors on debtors. An army, however, might now be kept in the field all the year round. At the same time a change was made in the armour. Livy says, *postquam stipendiarii facti sunt, scuta pro clupeis habebant;* seeming to suppose that this change was occasioned by the introduction of pay for the soldiers. The first step to it may certainly have been taken even previously to the Gallic wars.

The Romans began the last Veientine war with the determination to conquer Veii. The republic, which now again extended as far as Anxur, began to feel her own strength, since she had gained the victory over the Aequians, and was at least on friendly terms with the Sabines. How far the Latins took part in this war is uncertain, but it is likely that their co-operation did not extend beyond the Tiber. It is not an improbable statement, that soon after Anxur, Circeii also was recovered by the Romans; so that the only place which still maintained its independence as a Volscian state was Privernum, a town at the foot of the hills. The weakness of the Ausonian nations was the result of the extension of the

Samnites, and must have inclined those nations to keep peace with Rome. The Romans thus had time to make a permanent conquest of countries which probably they had no longer to share with the Latins.

The preceding war with the Veientines had been succeeded by a truce of twenty years. The Etruscans, like many other nations of antiquity, were accustomed to conclude their wars by a mere truce for a certain number of years, and these years consisted of ten months. A proof of the latter assertion is the fact, that in nearly all instances, hostilities break out sooner than could have been expected if the years had been years of twelve months, but never earlier than would have been the case if the years were reckoned equal to ten months. The truce between Rome and Veii had been concluded in A.U. 330, and is said to have ended (*induciae exierunt*) in A.U. 347. The use of this year of ten months was very common among the Romans: it was the term established for mourning and for all money transactions. In the sale of corn, ten months' credit was a matter of course. Loans for a number of years were unknown, and all business was done only for short periods, being founded on personal credit like debts arising from bills of exchange. The Veientines, contrary to their former practice, endeavoured to avoid the war by every possible means. There can be no doubt, that probably in consequence of its situation, Veii had formerly been the head of many Etruscan towns; for in previous wars its power appears very great. But the invasion of the Gauls caused the towns south of the Apennines, such as Arretium, Faesulae, and others, to be called upon to assist their countrymen beyond the mountains. This assistance was useless; the loss was great, and Etruria wasted her life-blood in the plains of Lombardy. Tarquinii and Capena alone supported Veii; the Aequi Falisci did the same, though not as an Etruscan people, but because they looked upon Veii as their bulwark.

The Romans at first believed they could bring the war to a speedy termination. They built strong forts in the Veientine territory, just as Agis did in Attica during the latter period of the Peloponnesian war; and issuing from those forts, they prevented the Veientines from cultivating their fields, or burnt the ripe crops, so that distress and famine soon shewed themselves in the city. This system of warfare is designated on this occasion by the word *obsessio*. The Romans only once undertook to carry on a siege according to the simple manner of the time. Between two forts, a line parallel to the wall of the city was formed, consisting of accumulated rubbish, sacks of sand and faggots, and on both sides of it wooden fences (*plutei*) were erected to give consistency to the rampart. It was pushed nearer and nearer to the city, an operation which presented the main difficulty. These works were raised to about the same height as the wall, to which bridges and scaling ladders were applied (*aggerem muro injungebant*), and then the engines were brought up; at first battering-rams, but in later times catapulta and ballistae, for these engines, which were not yet known at Rome, were invented at Syracuse for Dionysius. The besieged endeavoured to destroy the works of the besiegers by undermining them. But the neighbouring tribes defeated the Romans, and destroyed their works; and from that moment several years passed away without the Romans again pitching their camp at Veii.

The war of Veii presented to the ancients a parallel to the Trojan war; the siege was believed to have lasted ten years; and the taking of the city was as marvellous as that of Troy by the wooden horse. But the account of the whole war is not fictitious: the ancient songs took up isolated historical points, which they worked out and embellished, and this constitutes the difference between them and the lays of the earliest history. An annalistic narrative which is by no means incredible, runs parallel to these lays. The defeat of the tribunes Virginius and Sergius is historical, but the detail about the Alban lake and the like belong to poetical tradition, and must be taken as the ancients give them: whether they were composed in prose or in verse is a matter of no consequence. The story runs as follows:—

After Rome had already worn herself out in the struggle with Veii for upwards of seven years, and in the midst of the most profound peace with the Aequians and Volscians, a prodigy appeared. The Alban lake, the waters of which had always been below the edge of the ancient crater, began to rise, and threatened to overflow the country: this is the general substance of the ancient story, for in regard to the detail the accounts contradict one another; according to Dionysius and Dion Cassius (in Zonaras), a stream of water flowed from the lake straight towards the sea, while according to others, the lake only threatened to overflow its borders. The Romans knew not what to do; they had fixed their posts near Veii; whenever there was no fighting, they observed a kind of truce: on one of these occasions, an Etruscan aruspex ridiculed the Romans for taking so much trouble to make themselves masters of Veii: so long as they were not masters of the Alban lake, said he, they could not take Veii. One Roman took notice of this remark, and under the pretext of a *procuratio rei domesticae* invited the aruspex to the camp. When he came, the Romans arrested him, and compelled him to say what was to be done. He answered that they must let off the waters of the Alban lake, so that they might be conducted through one of the neighbouring rivers to the sea. The same answer was given by the god of Delphi. The Romans now undertook the work and finished it. When it was nearly completed, the Veientines sent an embassy to entreat the Romans to receive their city *in deditionem;* but the Romans would not listen to the proposal, for they knew that the talisman was broken. The Veientines did not contradict this, but said that it was also written in their books that if Veii should be destroyed, Rome would likewise soon be taken by barbarians, and that this part of the prophecy had been concealed from them by the aruspex. The Romans determined to run the risk, and appointed Camillus dictator; he called upon all the people to take a part in securing the booty, and undertook to storm the city: all duties towards the gods were discharged, and human prudence now did its work. Camillus formed a subterraneous passage which led to a spot under the arx of Veii, and from that point a passage was made to the temple of Juno; for fate had determined that whoever should offer up the sacrifice in the arx of Veii, should win the victory. The Romans penetrated into the temple, slew the Etruscan king, and offered up the sacrifice. At this moment the walls of Veii were scaled by the Romans on all sides.

This is very pretty poetry, and if we examine the historical nonsense of this account, we cannot hesitate for a moment to believe in the existence of a poem. The arx of Veii is still discernible[1]: it is situated near the *aqua rossa*, almost entirely surrounded by water, and is of a moderate height: the rock consists of tufo. The Romans would have been obliged to make their tunnel under the river, and to construct it so cunningly that no one should perceive it, and that at last they would only just have had to lift up the last stone in the temple and to rise above ground as through a trap-door.

The fact was probably this. There were two kinds of sieges: the first was the one described above, which consisted in throwing up a mound of earth against the wall: according to the second method, the walls were undermined with immense labour, so that they rested only on a scaffolding of beams, which was then set on fire, and thus the downfall of the walls was caused. Battering rams probably do not occur previously to the Peloponnesian war, and among the Romans not till a still later time. If Veii was actually taken by a cuniculus, it must be understood to have been by undermining the walls.

The letting off of the water of the Alban lake must certainly belong to this period; for there is no reason for supposing that a work of an earlier date was inserted here. The subterraneous passages through which the water was carried off had probably become obstructed, and Latium was in danger of being inundated; it is possible that use was made of the credulity of the people to induce them to undertake this gigantic work, but I believe that when the senate declared the work to be necessary, there was no want of obedience. It must be supposed that the Alban lake, like the Fucinus and all other lakes formed in the craters of volcanoes, discharged its waters by subterraneous passages, which may have been filled up in consequence of earthquakes. Livy, at a somewhat later time, speaks of a severe winter during which the Tiber was covered with ice, and says that epidemics were very prevalent in the following summer: the newly discovered excerpts from Dionysius place the building of the tunnel in the year after that severe winter. Livy relates, that during that winter the snow was seven feet deep and that the trees were destroyed by frost; a statement closely resembling the records of the annals, and quite credible, although the ancient annals perished in the conflagration, for such a winter must have been remembered by every one.

---

[1] It is a mere accident that I never was at Veii, but I have an accurate knowledge of the locality from maps and drawings.—N.

The winter of A. U. 483 was equally severe, for snow covered the forum for forty days. The early history of Rome would indicate that the mean temperature of the air was then much lower than it is now.[2] In the history of Rome and Greece, such unusual phenomena in the weather are nearly always followed by fearful earthquakes: an eruption of Aetna occurred about that time (A. U. 354). Vesuvius was then at rest, but the earthquakes were fearful, and it is possible that by one of them the outlets of the Alban lake were obstructed. In general all lakes which have no outlet, have remarkable periods in the increase and decrease of their waters. Lake Copaïs had even artificial tunnels to let off the water into the sea of Euboea: these were afterwards obstructed, and in the time of the Macedonians all Boeotia was not able to raise the money necessary for cleansing them; in consequence of which the waters rose and inundated the country far and wide. After that time probably nothing was done to remedy the evil; it is very likely, as Aristotle observes, that the quantity of water in Greece was decreasing; lake Copaïs is at present a mere swamp and in reality no longer deserves the name of lake, but resembles the bogs in our moors.

What the Romans did to prevent the overflow of the water is extraordinary: the tunnel still exists uninjured of the length of 2,700 paces or nearly three Roman miles[3], and the water of the lake is reduced to a proper height. The advantages of letting off the water are great even now, although the country around is uncultivated and covered with shrubs and bushes, since it supplies water for domestic purposes to the Campagna of Rome: and although this water is not very good, still it is better than that in the wells of the Campagna. The tunnel resembles the greatest Etruscan works: the entrance

---

[2] Compare, on the other hand, *Hist of Rome*, vol. iii. n. 1034. I was unwilling to suppress the above passage occurring in the Lectures of 1826-7. According to Arago, the winter in Tuscany is less cold and the summer less hot than formerly. See Berghaus, *Länder und Völker*. i. p. 248.—ED.

[3] This statement belongs to the Lectures of 1828-9, and is the same in all the manuscripts, but in 1826-7, Niebuhr said that the length of the tunnel had not been measured, but that it was estimated at 7,500 feet or two and a half Roman miles. In his *Hist. of Rome*, ii. p. 508, the length is said to be 6000 feet. Abeken (*Mittelitalien*, p. 179) says: "The tunnel runs into the south-western side of the lake and is nearly 4000 feet long." The measurement given in the text seems therefore to be based upon an error.—ED.

from the lake into it is like the vault of a temple executed in
the grandest style, whence we see that the Romans now again
built in the same manner as under the kings: this is characteristic of the age of Camillus.   The tunnel is cut for the most
part through a hard mass of lava, only a small portion running
through peperino which is more easily worked, and forms a passage nine palms high and five palms broad. By this work, which
has never yet required reparation, the lake, it seems, is permanently confined to a limited height: it was previously about
100 feet higher than the level to which it was then reduced.
It is an interesting point to know how such a work was executed. Considering the imperfection of instruments in those
times when the compass was yet unknown, it must have been
extremely difficult to find the correct point at a distance of
more than two miles; and even now it would be attended with
great difficulties, for the architect must know to a line how
high he may build in order to find the inclined plane for the
watercourse. It is well known in the country and is also recorded in some books, that on the whole line from the lake to
the point in the plain whither the water was to be conducted,
there exist to this day open wells into which people descend to
cleanse the tunnel; but these openings were not made merely
to enable the mud to be removed—the lake is not muddy—
but also to calculate the depth and let in air. By means of
these wells, the Romans were enabled accurately to calculate
the line as far as the issue.   In our days people have so little
practice in levelling, that till very recently it was not known
that the lake of Nemi lies higher than that of Alba.[4] The
construction of these wells rendered it possible to employ a
great many men at once, and to complete the work with tolerable speed: from the bottom of each well two parties of workmen might work in opposite directions and so as to meet other
parties commencing at the bottom of other wells.   In this
manner the tunnel was formed till it came close up to the lake,
the entrance to which was undoubtedly made by means of a
stone-borer of the thickness of a little finger, since the wall of
basalt need not have been thicker than two cubits to resist the
whole pressure of the lake.   The small opening being made,
the water ran off very gradually, so that the workmen had
time to be pulled up through the wells. When this was done,

---

[4] It must be remembered that this was said in the year 1828.

the wall between the lake and the tunnel was knocked down,
and the entrance facing the lake was made in such a manner
as to prevent trees and the like from being carried into the
tunnel; the arch was then embellished and wrought into a
magnificent portico, like the entrance to a temple. This structure eclipses all the works of Egypt: they are wonderful but
useless; this is practical and useful.

LECTURE XXX.

THAT Veii was taken by storm is certain: the people were
destroyed, and the city was methodically plundered. It is
related, that the whole Roman population was let loose upon
the place for the purpose of plundering it; but this can refer
only to the men capable of bearing arms, and was done partly
on account of the proximity of Rome, and partly because in
the long protracted war all had taken a part in it. The fate
of the inhabitants of Veii was the same as that which befell so
many people of antiquity: whoever escaped from the sword,
was led away into servitude. When the city fell into the
hands of the Romans, it was empty. We readily believe that
it was a more beautiful place than Rome. The latter has an
excellent situation, but its picturesqueness is connected with
many disadvantages, for the territory round the city is exposed
to frequent inundations, and the intercourse within was very
difficult for carriages and other conveyances, on account of the
many hills and valleys. Veii, on the other hand, with the
exception of its arx, was situated in a plain, and probably had
beautiful and wide streets: no wonder therefore that the
Romans were loth to destroy the handsome city.

Immediately after the conquest, quarrels arose between the
government and the plebes who demanded a distribution of
the territory, while the former claimed the whole for themselves alone; but such a thing was no longer possible. Another
difficulty was occasioned by the beauty of Veii, for it was
thought a pity that it should remain deserted: it may easily
be conceived that when it was proposed to distribute the ter-

ritory, it was at the same time wished that those who were in want of houses should have habitations assigned to them at Veii. A tribune of the people proposed that if the patricians thought the plebeians too low to live together with them, the plebes with their magistrates should emigrate to Veii: it would be folly to believe that the proposal was such as Livy describes it, viz.: that half of the senate and the people should remove to Veii. But even the other proposal calls forth doubts, for the scheme would have been highly unreasonable, and the objections which Livy raises against such a tearing up of the republic are very important, and after all, a complete separation would have been impossible. It would have been dangerous even to discuss the sending of a great colony with a local government to Veii. But an arrangement was made: the patricians secured the greater part of the territory for their occupation, but the plebes also obtained a portion, and not only each for himself the usual seven *jugera forensia*, but also something in consideration of his children. According to Diodorus, each family received twenty-eight *jugera;* but if this is true, the territory of Veii must have been enormous. The aerarii had no share in these assignments, but those among them who were clients of patricians received allotments on the farms of their patrons.

The sequel of these events shows, that at that time the territory of Veii and Capena, and of the Etruscan cities in general, comprised large tracts of country with subject towns, which, during the war threw themselves into the arms of the Romans: those who did so were undoubtedly the ancient inhabitants of those places, who saw in the Romans their deliverers.

The conquest of Veii was one of the most decisive events in history, for it delivered Rome from a counterpoise which checked her development. As all the east of Latium was at peace, the Romans irresistibly penetrated into Etruria, the Etruscans being obliged in the mean time to exert all their powers in the Apennines to keep off the Gauls. But the war was also carried on against the Faliscans: to judge from their name they were Voliscans, whence Virgil calls them Aequi Falisci. According to Strabo, they had a peculiar language, and were a nation different from the Etruscans. The war of Camillus against them is known to us all from our childhood; the tale, that by his generosity he influenced them so much, that they accepted the treaty of friendship with the Romans, has great internal improbability: the story of the schoolmaster's treachery I may leave uncriticised. The war was moreover directed against the Vulsinians, in whose territory the Romans made conquests and with whom they concluded an advantageous peace. The Romans had then penetrated even beyond the Ciminian forest, which afterwards in the great war of Fabius presents so frightful an appearance. The separation of countries by this forest does not seem to have been very strongly marked at that time, but afterwards it appears to have been intentionally allowed to grow wild, that it might form a boundary, just as a forest divides the Austrian from the Turkish part of Dalmatia. Capena is not afterwards mentioned in history, and must therefore have been destroyed either by the Romans after the taking of Veii or by the Gauls: it is an historical fact, that subsequently to the Gallic calamity the surviving Capenatans became Roman citizens.

After these victories, Camillus shone as the greatest general of his age; but he was nevertheless accused of having appropriated to himself sundry valuable things from the Veientine booty, especially the brass gates of the temple of Juno, and of having declared too late his obligation to dedicate the tenth part of the booty to the Pythian Apollo. It would be an unprofitable labour to speculate on the guilt or innocence of Camillus; but we must not forget that every Roman general was entitled to set apart a portion of the booty to himself.[1] We cannot decide whether Camillus took more than he was legally allowed or not; what one person does on a small scale another does on a large. We must not believe that Camillus committed the crime in secret, for he undoubtedly ordered the gates to be fitted to his own house; if he had wished to make use of the metal they would have been melted down long before. The real cause of the hatred against Camillus was of a political kind, for down to the end of his life he stood at the head of the most stubborn patrician party; the plebeians were ever becoming stronger and more powerful, and the ease of prosperity had produced a certain desire for excitement: Camillus was accused because a considerable party was against him, and he was sentenced to pay a sum of 15,000, or according to others 100,000

[1] Compare the speech of Fabricius in Dionysius (p. 77, ed. Sylb.)—N.

or even 500,000 *asses*. He did not wait for the sentence but went into exile to Ardea. Livy says that previously to the trial he implored his clients and tribules to do their utmost to obtain his acquittal (this would prove that he was tried before the centuries, for the tribes cannot possibly be meant): they are said to have declared that they would pay his fine, but not acquit him: this would clearly prove his guilt. According to Dionysius, his gentiles and clients actually paid the fine and he went into exile from vexation. I believe however that he was condemned by the curies, because when he was to be recalled, the curies assembled in the Capitol to repeal the decree of banishment; for the curies could assemble only at Rome, and this would prove likewise that he was found guilty,—a thing then not uncommon with great men.

At that time no Roman foresaw the calamity which was threatening them. Rome had become great, because the country which she had conquered was weak through its oligarchical institutions; the subjects of the other states gladly joined the Romans, because under them their lot was more favorable, and probably because they were kindred nations. But matters went with the Romans as they did with Basilius, who subdued the Armenians when they were threatened by the Turks, and who soon after attacked the whole Greek empire and took away far more than had been gained before.

The expedition of the Gauls into Italy must be regarded as a migration, and not as an invasion for the purpose of conquest: as for the historical account of it, we must adhere to Polybius and Diodorus, who place it shortly before the taking of Rome by the Gauls. We can attach no importance to the statement of Livy that they had come into Italy as early as the time of Tarquinius Priscus, having been driven from their country by a famine: it undoubtedly arose from the fact, that some Greek writer, perhaps Timaeus, connected this migration with the settlement of the Phocaeans at Massilia. It is possible that Livy even here made use of Dionysius, and that the latter followed Timaeus: for as Livy made use of Dionysius in the eighth book, why not also in the fifth? He himself knew very little of Greek history[2]; but Justin's account is here evidently opposed to Livy. Trogus Pompeius was born in the neighbourhood of Massilia, and in writing his forty-third book, he

[2] Comp. *Hist of Rome*, vol. iii. n. 485.

obviously made use of native chronicles, for from no other source could he derive the account of the *decreta honorifica* of the Romans to the Massilians for the friendship which the latter had shown to the Romans during the Gallic war; and from the same source must he have obtained his information about the maritime wars of Massilia against Carthage. Trogus knows nothing of the story that the Gauls assisted the Phocaeans on their arrival; but according to him, they met with a kind reception among the Ligurians, who continued to inhabit those parts for a long time after. About the year A.U. 350, that is, about fifteen years before, Livy himself says, *gentem invisitatem, novos accolas, Gallos comparuisse.* Even the story of the Lucumo who is said to have invited the Gauls is opposed to him, and if it were referred to Clusium alone, it would be absurd. Polybius places the passage of the Gauls across the Alps about ten or twenty years before the taking of Rome; and Diodorus describes them as advancing towards Rome by an uninterrupted march. It is further stated, that Melpum in the country of the Insubrians was destroyed on the same day as Veii: without admitting this coincidence, we have no reason to doubt that the statement is substantially true; and it is made by Cornelius Nepos who, as a native of Gallia Transpadana, might possess accurate information, and whose chronological accounts were highly esteemed by the Romans. There was no other passage for the Gauls except either across the Little St. Bernard or across the Simplon: it is not probable that they took the former road, because their country extended only as far as the Ticinus, and if they had come across the Little St. Bernard, they would naturally have occupied also all the country between that mountain and the Ticinus. The Salassi may indeed have been a Gallic people, but it is by no means certain; moreover between them and the Gauls who had come across the Alps the Laevi also lived; and there can be no doubt that at that time Ligurians still continued to dwell on the Ticinus.

Melpum must have been situated in the district of Milan. The latter place has an uncommonly happy situation: often as it has been destroyed, it has always been restored, so that it is not impossible that Melpum may have been situated on the very spot afterwards occupied by Milan. The Gallic migration undoubtedly passed by like a torrent with irresistible rapidity: how then is it possible to suppose that Melpum resisted them

for two centuries, or that they conquered it and yet did not
disturb the Etruscans for two hundred years? It would be
absurd to believe it, merely to save an uncritical expression of
Livy. According to the common chronology, the Triballi who
in the time of Herodotus inhabited the plains, and were afterwards expelled by the Gauls, appeared in Thrace twelve years
after the taking of Rome (according to a more correct chronology it was only nine years after that event). It was the same
movement assuredly which led the Gauls to the countries
through which the middle course of the Danube extends, and
to the Po: and could the people who came in a few days from
Clusium to Rome, and afterwards appeared in Apulia, have
been sitting quiet in a corner of Italy for two hundred years?
If they had remained there because they had not the power to
advance, they would have been cut to pieces by the Etruscans.
We must therefore look upon it as an established fact, that the
migration took place at the late period mentioned by Polybius
and Diodorus.

These Gauls were partly Celts, and partly (indeed principally) Belgae or Cymri, as may be perceived from the
circumstance, that their king, as well as the one who appeared
before Delphi, is called Brennus. Brenin, according to Ade-
lung, in his *Mithridates*, signifies in the language of Wales
and Lower Brittany, a *king*. But what caused this whole
emigration? The statement of Livy, that the Gauls were
compelled by famine to leave their country, is quite in keeping with the nature of all traditions about migrations, such as
we find them in Saxo Grammaticus, in Paul Warnefried from
the sagas of the Swedes, in the Tyrrhenian traditions of
Lydia, and others. However, in the case of a people like the
Celts, every specific statement of this kind, in which even
the names of their leaders are mentioned, is of no more value
than the traditions of other barbarous nations which were
unacquainted with the art of writing. It is indeed well
known that the Celts in writing used the Greek alphabet, but
they probably employed it only in the transactions of daily
life; for we know that they were not allowed to commit their
ancient songs to writing. There was, however, among the
Celts a tradition which we find in Ammianus Marcellinus,
that Britain was one of their earliest seats. Now we meet
with them in different parts of Britain, Ireland, and Spain,

and in two places of Portugal, for the Celtici and Celtae in Portugal, who lived in Algarbia and Alemtejo, and between the Minho and Douro, were pure Celts. The Celtiberians in Spain were a mixture of Celts and Iberians, and dwelt in the very heart of the mountains between Saragossa and Madrid, which are connected with the Pyrenees.[3] There was the same tradition about those Celts in Spain as about their appearance in Italy, for they were said to have been driven thither by a famine, and then to have made conquests and spread over the country. Here again we have a confusion of the polarity in history. Wherever there is a national migration, we never find the invading people settled in scattered groups. The dispersed inhabitants of such countries, especially in mountainous districts, are usually remnants of the ancient population, the bulk of which has either emigrated or become changed. Among the Celtiberians the Iberians predominated, but the Celts were the native people, united with the Iberians who immigrated from Africa. The language which arose from this union may have been a mixture of the two, but the names of places are Iberian. Similar changes of a great tribe do sometimes occur in history. The Wends in Germany, who were originally Slavonians, though the colonies founded among them were not of much consequence, and there was neither a German conquest, nor German princes, yet for the most part adopted the German language.

LECTURE XXXI.

THE existence of the Aquitanians in Gaul, is a proof of the migration of the Iberians, for we are told by Caesar that they were pure Spaniards; and there is no reason for supposing that this migration took place at a late period, for the Basques still live north of the Pyrenees. We have, moreover, the statement of Scylax, that the people of Gaul, from the Pyrenees to the river Rhodanus, was composed of Iberians and Ligurians. The Celts at one time were masters of all

[3] The mountains of southern Spain are connected with those of Africa. — N.

Spain, with the exception of Andalusia; and besides Spain, they occupied the south of France, Ireland, and a part of England. The boundary of the Iberians cannot be accurately fixed in the north, though in the earlier times it was the Sierra Morena. In the south we find them in southern Spain, in the Balearean islands, Sardinia, Corsica, and Western Sicily; and lastly also in Africa.

The Cymri or Belgae were a people different from the Celts, though akin to them. This difference, concerning which I expressed my opinion years ago, is of great importance, and is now generally acknowledged. It is not a new discovery; I have only brought forward facts which were previously overlooked. Caesar's idea that the Belgae were a mixture of Germans and Celts is erroneous. They were perfectly distinct from the Germans, although a small number of words in their language are Germanic. In Caesar's time they were unquestionably Cymri, somewhat mixed with Germans, who had joined them in their migration. A part of Britain too was inhabited by Cymri, who were probably the earlier inhabitants, having afterwards been expelled by the Gael. The latter were pressed on by the Iberians, the Cymri by the Gael, and the Germans by the Cymri, who then inhabited the north of France and the low countries, which were subsequently inhabited by Celts.

The south of France from the Pyrenees, Lower Languedoc, and the valley of the Rhone, Piedmont, and Lombardy, as far as the Etruscans, were occupied by the Ligurians, a great European nation. Scylax states, that Lower Languedoc had a mixed population of Iberians and Ligurians, and in later times, which cannot be chronologically determined, the Celts drove the Iberians from Spain as far as the Garonne, and the Iberians forced the Ligurians to retire as far as the district of Aix in Provence, an event which may be recognised from its consequences. By this impulse the Gauls and Cymri together were compelled to emigrate: some Cymri retreated before the Gauls and went away, but others joined them. The Gauls and Cymri were very different from one another, for their language and grammar are quite distinct. The two great migrations under Bellovesus and Sigovesus, which are mentioned by Livy, must be regarded as true, although the leaders are perhaps nothing but personifications. The one directed

towards Italy, between the Alpine tribes of the Etruscans and
the Ligurians, overran the Etruscan towns in the plain of
Lombardy; the other extended north of the Alps. The
Raetians, Lepontians, Camunians, Stonians, and other Alpine
tribes in the Tyrol and the Southern Alps, as far as Verona,
maintained their ground like islands among the invading
Gauls, who poured in around them like a sea; so that their
situation reminds us of that of the three Celtic tribes in Spain.
The migration of which the Helvetii were a remnant, has
been sufficiently explained in my Essay on the Scythians and
Sarmatians.[1]   It first appears about the Black Forest, where
it rested for a while, and thence proceeded towards the middle
Danube, Hungary, and Lower Slavonia.   There the migratory
hordes undertook the difficult conquest of the high mountains,
and then spread over Macedonia, Thrace, and Bulgaria.
They also advanced across the Danube as far as the Dnieper,
but being repelled by the Sarmatians, they again threw themselves upon Europe. This is the only known instance in which it
is clear, that the torrent of a migrating people rolls on till it
meets with insurmountable obstacles, and then returns with
the same rapidity.   At the time when Herodotus wrote (about
A.U. 320), the people on the middle and lower Danube still
lived undisturbed in their ancient seats.   The Scythians
inhabited Moldavia and Wallachia as far as Transylvania.
Slavonia and Lower Hungary were inhabited by the Agathyrsi
and Triballi.   But nine years after the taking of Rome by the
Gauls, the Triballi appear in the neighbourhood of Abdera in
Thrace, and afterwards we find them on the southern part of
the Danube in Bulgaria.   The Scythians, on the other hand,
were confined to Bessarabia as early as the time of Philip; and
in the time of Alexander, the Getae were in possession of
Moldavia and Wallachia.   The nation that brought about this
change was the Gauls, and that in the same migration during
which they poured in upon Italy.

   Scylax (Olymp. 106) was aware that there were Gauls at
the head of the Adriatic, which was afterwards inhabited by
the Carnians and Noricans; they were, according to him, a
remnant of the Gallic migration, and a part of the Gauls who
had advanced farther dwelt in Sirmium; thence they crossed
the Danube under the name of the Bastarnians, and forced the

---

[1] In the *Kleine Hist. Schriften, Erste Sammlung*, p.352, etc.

Getae to throw themselves into Hungary and Transylvania; afterwards they spread in the Ukraine. From the important inscription of Olbia published by Köhler, we see that the Galatians, and along with them the Sciri (afterwards a German people), lived about the Dnieper, and this fact agrees well with the disappearance of the Scythians at that time. For there was also an eastern migration of the Sarmatians, a people whom Herodotus knew only beyond the Tanais; Scylax, who lived seventy years later, speaks of them as living on the western side of that river: in the inscription of Olbia they appear east of the Dnieper, and under Augustus they destroyed the Greek towns in Wallachia. This movement afterwards caused the migration of the Cymri or Cymbri, for the Cymri always took part in the migration of the Celts: among them were the Bastarnae, who lived in the south of Poland and in Dacia, and were expelled by the Sarmatians: J. von Müller was the first who saw the truth of the statement of Posidonius, that the Cimbri did not come from Jütland but from the East; he did not see however that they were originally Belgic, or, as the Greeks call them by a more general name, Κέλται. It is foolish to claim the victories of the Cimbri as having been gained by the German nation.

These migrations extended in Germany as far as the river Mayn and the forest of Thüringia, nay even Bohemia was inhabited by Celts previously to the time of Caesar, and some of their tribes existed in that country as late as the time of Tacitus, for the Gothini still continued to speak Gallic; and the Noricans in Austria were of the Celtic race. The Raetians were Etruscans, and the Vindelicians Liburnians. The Helvetii conquered the greater part of Switzerland, but the country about the St. Gothard remained in the possession of the ancient inhabitants. The Gauls penetrated into Italy only through a limited part of the Alps, probably across the Simplon, and the Valais was the sole bond between the Gauls in Italy and their kinsmen north of the Alps. As far as Aosta the ancient inhabitants maintained themselves, for the Salassians, Taurinians and others were Ligurians, and the people at the foot of the St. Gothard were Etruscans. The Ligurians were a very warlike people and kept their ground on both sides of the Alps; the Allobroges, however, were pure Celts. Hence Gallia Cisalpina in our maps is much too large, and that even in

D'Anville's map. Piedmont formed no part of it; it comprised only the Austrian territory of Milan, Bergamo and
Brescia, Lombardy south of the Po as far as the Adriatic, and
north of the Po to about the lake of Garda. Thus all the
country occupied by them was in the plain, and this is another
reason why their migration cannot have lasted as long as Livy
states.

During this Gallic migration we are again made aware how
little we know of the history of Italy generally: our knowledge
is limited to Rome, so that we are in the same predicament
there, as if of all the historical authorities of the whole German
empire we had nothing but the annals of a single imperial city.
According to Livy's account, it would seem as if the only object
of the Gauls had been to march to Rome; and yet this immigration changed the whole aspect of Italy. After the Gauls had
once crossed the Apennines, there was no further obstacle to
prevent their marching to the south of Italy by any road they
pleased; and it is in fact mentioned that they did proceed
farther south. The Umbrians still inhabited the country on
the lower Po, in the modern Romagna and Urbino, parts of
which were occupied by Liburnians. Polybius says that many
people there became tributary to the Gauls, and that this was
the case with the Umbrians is quite certain.

The first historical appearance of the Gauls is at Clusium,
whither a noble Clusine is said to have invited them for the
purpose of taking vengeance on his native city. Whether this
account is true, however, must remain undecided, and if there
is any truth in it, it is more probable that the offended Clusine
went across the Apennines and fetched his avengers. Clusium
has not been mentioned since the time of Porsena; the fact of
the Clusines soliciting the aid of Rome is a proof how little
that northern city of Etruria was concerned about the fate of
the southern towns, and makes us even suspect that it was
allied with Rome; however, the danger was so great that all
jealousy must have been suppressed. The natural road for the
Gauls would have been along the Adriatic, then through the
country of Umbrians who were tributary to them and already
quite broken down, and thence through the Romagna across
the Apennines. But the Apennines which separate Tuscany
from the Romagna are very difficult to cross, especially for
sumpter horses; as therefore the Gauls could not enter Etruria

on that side, which the Etruscans had intentionally allowed to
grow wild, and as they had been convinced of this in an unsuccessful attempt, they crossed the Apennines in the neighbourhood of Clusium, and appeared before that city. Clusium
was the great bulwark of the valley of the Tiber; and if it
were taken, the roads along the Tiber and the Arno would be
open, and the Gauls might reach Arezzo from the rear: the
Romans therefore looked upon the fate of Clusium as decisive
of their own. The Clusines sued for a treaty with the mighty
city of Rome, and the Romans were wise enough readily to
accept the offer: they sent ambassadors to the Gauls ordering
them to withdraw. According to a very probable account, the
Gauls had demanded of the Clusines a division of their territory as the condition of peace, and not, as was customary with
the Romans, as a tax upon a people already subdued: if
this is correct, the Romans sent the embassy confiding in
their own strength. But the Gauls scorned the ambassadors,
and the latter, allowing themselves to be carried away by
their warlike disposition, joined the Etruscans in a fight
against the Gauls: this was probably only an insignificant
and isolated engagement. Such is the account of Livy,
who goes on to say, that the Gauls, as soon as they
perceived this violation in the law of nations, gave the
signal for a retreat, and having called upon the gods to avenge
the wrong marched against Rome. This is evidently a mere
fiction, for a barbarous nation like the Gauls cannot possibly
have had such ideas, nor was there in reality any violation of
the law of nations, as the Romans stood in no kind of connection with the Gauls. But it was a natural feeling with the
Romans to look upon the fall of their city as the consequence
of a *nefas*, which no human power could resist. Roman
vanity also is at work here, inasmuch as the Roman ambassadors are said to have so distinguished themselves, that they
were recognized by the barbarians among the hosts of Etruscans. Now according to another tradition directly opposed to
these statements, the Gauls sent to Rome to demand the surrender of those ambassadors: as the senate was hesitating and left
the decision to the people, the latter not only rejected the demand, but appointed the same ambassadors to the office of military tribunes, whereupon the Gauls with all their forces at once
marched towards Rome. Livy here again speaks of the *populus*

as the people to whom the senate left the decision: this must
have been the patricians only, for they alone had the right to
decide upon the fate of the members of their own order. It is
not fair to accuse the Romans on that occasion of dishonesty;
but this account assuredly originated with later writers who
transferred to barbarians the right belonging to a nation standing in a legal relation to another. The statement that the
three ambassadors, all of whom were Fabii, were appointed
military tribunes, is not even the usual one, for there is another
in Diodorus, who must here have used Roman authorities
written in Greek, that is, Fabius; since he calls the Caerites
Καίριοι and not Ἀγυλλαῖοι. He speaks of a single ambassador,
who being a son of a military tribune fought against the Gauls.
This is at least a sign how uncertain history yet is. The
battle on the Alia was fought on the 16th of July: the military
tribunes entered upon their office on the first of that month;
and the distance between Clusium and Rome is only three
good days' marches. It is impossible to restore the true history,
but we can discern what is fabulous from what is really historical.

An innumerable host of Gauls now marched from Clusium
towards Rome. For a long time the Gauls were most formidable to the Romans, as well as to all other nations with whom
they come in contact even as far east as the Ukraine; as to
Rome, we see this as late as the Cisalpine war of the year A.U.
527. Polybius and Diodorus are our best guides in seeking
for information about the manners of the Gauls, for in the time
of Caesar they had already become changed. In the description of their persons we partly recognise the modern Gael, or
the inhabitants of the Highlands of Scotland: huge bodies,
blue eyes, bristly hair; even their dress and armour are
those of the Highlanders, for they wore the checked and
variegated tartans (*sagula virgata*, *versicoloria*); their arms
consisted of the broad unpointed battle-sword, the same
weapon as the claymore among the Highlanders. They had
a vast number of horns, which were used in the Highlands for
many centuries after, and threw themselves upon the enemy in
immense and irregular masses with terrible fury, those standing
behind impelling those stationed in front, whereby they became
irresistible by the tactics of those times. The Romans ought
to have used against them their phalanx and doubled it, until

they were accustomed to this enemy and were enabled by their greater skill to repel them. If the Romans had been able to withstand their first shock, the Gauls would have easily been thrown into disorder and put to flight. The Gauls who were subsequently conquered by the Romans were the descendants of such as were born in Italy, and had lost much of their courage and strength. The Goths under Vitiges, not fifty years after the immigration of Theodoric into Italy, were cowards and unable to resist the 20,000 men of Belisarius: showing how easily barbarians degenerate in such climates. The Gauls moreover were terrible on account of their inhuman cruelty, for wherever they settled, the original towns and their inhabitants completely disappeared from the face of the earth. In their own country they had the feudal system and a priestly government: the Druids were their only rulers, who avenged the oppressed people on the lords, but in their turn became tyrants: all the people were in the condition of serfs,—a proof that the Gauls, in their own country too, were the conquerors who had subdued an earlier population. We always find mention of the wealth of the Gauls in gold, and yet France has no rivers that carry gold-sand, and the Pyrenees were then no longer in their possession: the gold must therefore have been obtained by barter. Much may be exaggeration; and the fact of some noble individuals wearing gold chains was probably transferred by ancient poets to the whole nation, since popular poetry takes great liberty especially in such embellishments.

Pliny states that previously to the Gallic calamity, the census amounted to 150,000 persons, which probably refers only to men entitled to vote in the assemblies, and does not comprise women, children, slaves and strangers. If this is correct, the number of citizens was enormous; but it must not be supposed to include the inhabitants of the city only, the population of which was doubtless much smaller. The statement of Diodorus that all men were called to arms to resist the Gauls, and that the number amounted to 40,000, is by no means improbable: according to the testimony of Polybius, Latins and Hernicans also were enlisted. Another account makes the Romans take the field against the Gauls with 24,000 men, that is, with four field-legions and four civic legions: the field-legions were formed only of plebeians, and served, according to the order of the classes, probably in maniples; the civic legions contained all those who belonged neither to the patricians nor to the plebeians, that is, all the aerarii, proletarii, freedmen, and artizans who had never before faced an enemy. They were certainly not armed with the pilum, nor drawn up in maniples; but used pikes and were employed in phalanxes. Now as for the field-legions, each consisted half of Latins and half of Romans, there being in each maniple one century of Romans and one of Latins. There were at that time four legions, and as a legion, including the reserve troops, contained 3,000 men, the total is 12,000; now the account which mentions 24,000 men, must have presumed that there were four field-legions and four irregular civic ones. There would accordingly have been no more than 6,000 plebeians, and, even if the legions were all made up of Romans, only 12,000; if in addition to these we take 12,000 irregular troops and 16,000 allies, the number of 40,000 would be completed. In this case, the population of Rome would not have been as large as that of Athens in the Peloponnesian war, and this is indeed very probable. The cavalry is not included in this calculation: but 40,000 must be taken as the maximum of the whole army. There seems to be no exaggeration in this statement, and the battle on the Alia, speaking generally is an historical event. It is surprising that the Romans did not appoint a dictator to command in the battle; it cannot be said indeed that they regarded this war as an ordinary one, for in that case they would not have raised so great a force, but they cannot have comprehended the danger in all its greatness. New swarms continued to come across the Alps; the Senones also now appeared to seek habitations for themselves; they, like the Germans in after-times, demanded land, as they found the Insubrians, Boians and others already settled; the latter had taken up their abode in Umbria, but only until they should find a more extensive and suitable territory.

The river Alia possesses no remarkable feature, and one might almost be inclined to believe that the aspect of the country in that district has changed. It is only by the distances being mentioned that we can determine the river called Alia. The ancients describe it as a river with high banks, but the modern river which must be identified with it, has no such banks. The name has entirely disappeared. In summer all the rivers of that country have very little water, and the position behind it was therefore of little avail. The Romans committed the great mistake of fighting with their hurriedly collected troops a battle against an enemy who had hitherto been invincible. The hills along which the right wing is said to have been drawn up are no longer discernible, and they were probably nothing but little mounds of earth[2]: at any rate it was senseless to draw up a long line against the immense mass of enemies. The Gauls, on the other hand, were enabled without any difficulty to turn off to the left. They proceeded to a higher part of the river, where it was more easily fordable, and with great prudence threw themselves with all their force upon the right wing, consisting of the civic legions. The latter at first resisted, but not long; and when they fled, the whole remaining line, which until then seems to have been useless and inactive, was seized with a panic. Terror preceded the Gauls as they laid waste everything on their way[3], and this paralysed the courage of the Romans, instead of rousing them to a desperate resistance. The Romans therefore were defeated on the Alia in the most inglorious manner. The Gauls had taken them in their rear, and cut off their return to Rome. A portion fled towards the Tiber, where some effected a retreat across the river, and others were drowned; another part escaped into a forest. The loss of life must have been prodigious, and it is inconceivable how Livy could have attached so much importance to the mere disgrace. If the Roman army had not been almost annihilated, it would not have been necessary to give up the defence of the city, as was done, for the city was left undefended and deserted by all. Many fled to Veii instead of returning to Rome: only a few, who had escaped along the high road, entered the city by the Colline gate. Rome was exhausted, her power shattered, her legions defenceless, and her warlike allies had partly been beaten in the same battle,

[2] It is very difficult to recognise the places in Lombardy where the battles of 1799 were fought, because the roads have since been laid differently. The same is the case at Lützen, Breitenfeld, and Leuthen; nay, even at Prague and Collin it is not an easy matter to identify the fields of battle. — N.

[3] The Gauls destroyed all the towns in Gallia Cispadana, and they themselves lived only in villages. When subsequently the Romans conquered the country of the Insubrians, they found no trace of the ancient population. — N.

and were partly awaiting the fearful enemy in their own countries. At Rome it was believed that the whole army was destroyed, for nothing was known of those who had reached Veii. In the city itself there were only old men, women, and children, so that there was no possibility of defending it. It is, however, inconceivable that the gates should have been left open, and that the Gauls, from fear of a stratagem, should have encamped for several days outside the gates. A more probable account is, that the gates were shut and barricaded. We may form a vivid conception of the condition of Rome after this battle, by comparing it with that of Moscow before the conflagration: the people were convinced that a long defence was impossible, since there was probably a want of provisions. Livy gives a false notion of the evacuation of the city, as if the defenceless citizens had remained immovable in their consternation, and only a few had been received into the Capitol. The determination, in fact, was to defend the Capitol, and the tribune Sulpicius had taken refuge there, with about 1000 men. There was on the Capitol an ancient well which still exists, and without which the garrison would soon have perished. This well remained unknown to all antiquaries, till I discovered it by means of information gathered from the people who live there. Its depth in the rock descends to the level of the Tiber, but the water is now not fit to drink. The Capitol was a rock which had been hewn steep, and thereby made inaccessible, but a *clivus*, closed by gates both below and above, led up from the Forum and the *Via Sacra*. The rock, indeed, was not so steep as in later times, as is clear from the account of the attempt to storm it; but the Capitol was nevertheless very strong. Whether some few remained in the city, as at Moscow, who in their stupefaction did not consider what kind of enemy they had before them, cannot be decided. The narrative is very beautiful, and reminds us of the taking of the Acropolis of Athens by the Persians, where, likewise, the old men allowed themselves to be cut down by the Persians. Notwithstanding the improbability of the matter, I am inclined to believe that a number of aged patricians—their number may not be exactly historical—sat down in the Forum, in their official robes, on their curule chairs, and that the chief pontiff devoted them to death. Such devotions are a well-known Roman custom. It is certainly not improbable that the Gauls were amazed when they found the city deserted, and only these old men sitting so immoveable, that they took them for statues or supernatural visions, and did nothing to them, until one of them struck a Gaul who touched him, whereupon all were slaughtered. To commit suicide was repugnant to the customs of the Romans, who were guided in many things by feelings more correct and more resembling our own, than many other ancient nations. The old men, indeed, had given up the hope of their country being saved; but the Capitol might be maintained, and the survivors preferred dying in the attempt of self-defence, to taking refuge at Veii, where after all they could not have maintained themselves in the end. The sacred treasures were removed to Caere, and the hope of the Romans now was, that the barbarians would be tired of the long siege. Provisions for a time had been conveyed to the Capitol, where a couple of thousand men may have been assembled, and where all buildings, temples, as well as public and private houses, were used as habitations. The Gauls made fearful havoc at Rome, even more fearful than the Spaniards and Germans did in the year 1527. Soldiers plunder, and when they find no human beings, they engage in the work of destruction; and fires break out, as at Moscow, without the existence of any intention to cause a conflagration. The whole city was changed into a heap of ashes, with the exception of a few houses on the Palatine, which were occupied by the leaders of the Gauls. It is astonishing to find, nevertheless, that a few monuments of the preceding period, such as statues, situated at some distance from the Capitol, are mentioned as having been preserved; but we must remember that *travertino* is tolerably fire proof. That Rome was burnt down is certain; and when it was rebuilt, not even the ancient streets were restored.

The Gauls were now encamped in the city. At first they attempted to storm the clivus, but were repelled with great loss, which is surprising, since we know that at an earlier time the Romans succeeded in storming it against Appius Herdonius. Afterwards they discovered the footsteps of a messenger who had been sent from Veii, in order that the state might be taken care of in due form; for the Romans in the Capitol were patricians, and represented the curies and the government, whereas those assembled at Veii represented the

tribes, but had no leaders. The latter had resolved to recall
Camillus, and raise him to the dictatorship. For this reason
Pontius Cominius had been sent to Rome to obtain the sanction of the senate and the curies. This was quite in the spirit
of the ancient times. If the curies had interdicted him *aqua
et igni,* they alone could recall him, if they previously obtained
a resolution of the senate authorising them to do so; but if he
had gone into voluntary exile, and had given up his Roman
franchise by becoming a citizen of Ardea before a sentence
had been passed upon him by the centuries, it was again in
the power of the curies alone, he being a patrician, to recall
him as a citizen; and otherwise he could not have become
dictator, nor could he have regarded himself as such.

LECTURE XXXII.

It was the time of the dog-days when the Gauls came to Rome,
and as the summer at Rome is always pestilential, especially
during the two months and a half before the first of September,
the unavoidable consequence must have been, as Livy relates,
that the barbarians, bivouacking on the ruins of the city in the
open air, were attacked by disease and carried off, like the
army of Frederick Barbarossa when encamped before the castle
of St. Angelo. The whole army of the Gauls, however, was
not in the city, but only as many as were necessary to blockade
the garrison of the Capitol; the rest were scattered far and
wide over the face of the country, and were ravaging all the
unprotected places and isolated farms in Latium; many an
ancient town, which is no longer mentioned after this time,
may have been destroyed by the Gauls. None but fortified
places like Ostia, which could obtain supplies by sea, made a
successful resistance, for the Gauls were unacquainted with the
art of besieging. The Ardeatans, whose territory was likewise
invaded by the Gauls, opposed them, under the command of
Camillus[1]; the Etruscans would seem to have endeavoured to

[1] A difficult passage in Ovid's *Metamorphoses* must perhaps be referred to
this war: he says, that out of the ruins of the town of Ardea, which had been

avail themselves of the opportunity of recovering Veii, for we are told that the Romans at Veii, commanded by Caedicius gained a battle against them, and that, encouraged by this success, they began to entertain a hope of regaining Rome, since by this victory they got possession of arms.

A Roman of the name of Fabius Dorso, is said to have offered up in broad daylight, a gentilician sacrifice on the Quirinal; and the astonished Gauls are said to have done him no harm—a tradition which is not improbable.

The provisions in the Capitol were exhausted, but the Gauls themselves being seized with epidemic diseases became tired of their conquests, and were not inclined to settle in a country so far away from their own home. They once more attempted to take the Capitol by storm, having observed that the messenger from Veii had ascended the rock, and come down again near the Porta Carmentalis, below Araceli. The ancient rock is now covered with rubbish, and no longer discernible. The besieged did not think of a storm on that side; it may be, that formerly there had in that part been a wall, which had become decayed; and in southern countries an abundant vegetation always springs up between the stones[2], and if this had actually been neglected it cannot have been very difficult to climb up. The Gauls had already gained a firm footing, as there was no wall at the top. The rock which they stormed was not the Tarpeian, but the arx—when Manlius who lived there was roused by the screaming of the geese: he came to the spot and thrust down those who were climbing up. This rendered the Gauls still more inclined to commence negotiations; they were moreover called back by an inroad of some Alpine tribes into Lombardy, where they had left their wives and children: they offered to depart if the Romans would pay them a ransom of a thousand pounds of gold, to be taken no doubt from the Capitoline treasury. Considering the value of money at that time,

---

laid waste by the barbarians, there arose a heron. Modern commentators have incorrectly referred this destruction to the Hannibalian war; it might be an allusion to some Samnite war, in which Ardea was destroyed, as we may perhaps infer from Strabo, who says that the Samnites carried their conquests as far as Ardea; but the Samnites were surely not called barbarians: we probably have here the reverse of the tradition given in the text, that the Ardeatans under Camillus conquered the Gauls.—N.

[2] Virgil says: *Galli per dumos aderant*, and Livy too speaks of *virgulta*.—N.

the sum was enormous: in the time of Theodosius indeed, there were people at Rome who possessed several hundred weights of gold, nay, one is said to have had an annual revenue of two hundred weights.   There can be no doubt that the Gauls received the sum they demanded, and quitted Rome; that in weighing it, they scornfully imposed upon the Romans is very possible, and the *vae victis* too may be true: we ourselves have seen similar things before the year 1813.   But there can be no truth in the story told by Livy, that while they were disputing Camillus appeared with an army and stopped the proceedings, because the military tribunes had had no right to conclude the treaty.   He is there said to have driven the Gauls from the city, and afterwards in a two-fold battle to have so completely defeated them that not even a messenger escaped.   Beaufort, inspired by Gallic patriotism, has most excellently shown what a complete fable this story is.   To attempt to disguise the misfortunes of our forefathers by substituting fables in their place is mere childishness.   This charge does not affect Livy indeed, for he copied only what others had written before him; but he did not allow his own conviction to appear as he generally does, for he treats the whole of the early history with a sort of irony, half believing, half disbelieving it.

According to another account in Diodorus, the Gauls besieged a town allied with Rome (its name seems to be miswritten but is probably intended for Vulsinii), and the Romans relieved it and took back from the Gauls the gold which they had paid them; but this siege of Vulsinii is quite unknown to Livy.   A third account in Strabo and also mentioned by Diodorus does not allow this honour to the Romans, but states that the Caerites pursued the Gauls, attacked them in the country of the Sabines and completely annihilated them.   In like manner the Greeks endeavoured to disguise the fact, that the Gauls took the money from the Delphic treasury and that in a quite historical period (Olymp. 120).   The true explanation is undoubtedly the one found in Polybius, that the Gauls were induced to quit Rome by an insurrection of the Alpine tribes, after it had experienced the extremity of humiliation.   Whatever the enemy had taken as booty was consumed, they had not made any conquests but only indulged in plunder and devastation; they had been staying at Rome for seven or eight months, and could have gained nothing further than the Capitol and the very money which they received without taking that fortress. The account of Polybius throws light upon many discrepant statements, and all of them, not even excepting Livy's fairy-tale-like embellishment, may be explained by means of it. The Romans attempted to prove that the Gauls had actually been defeated, by relating that the gold afterwards taken from the Gauls and buried in the Capitol, was double the sum paid to them as a ransom; but it is much more probable that the Romans paid their ransom out of the treasury of the temple of the Capitoline Jupiter and of other temples, and that afterwards, double this sum was made up by a tax, which agrees with a statement in the history of Manlius, that a tax was imposed for the purpose of raising the Gallic ransom: surely this could not have been done at the time of the siege, when the Romans were scattered in all parts of the country, but must have taken place afterwards for the purpose of restoring the money that had been taken. Now if at a later time there actually existed in the Capitol such a quantity of gold, it is clear that it was believed to be a proof that the Gauls had not kept the gold which was paid to them.

Even as late as the time of Cicero and Caesar, the spot was shewn at Rome in the Carinae, where the Gauls had heaped up and burned their dead; it was called *busta Gallica*, which was corrupted in the middle ages into Portogallo, whence the church which was built there was in reality called *S. Andreas in bustis Gallicis*, or according to the later latinity *in busta Gallica*,—*busta Gallica* not being declined.

The Gauls departed with their gold which the Romans had been compelled to pay, on account of the famine that prevailed in the Capitol which was so great that they pulled the leather from their shields and cooked it, just as was done during the siege of Jerusalem. The Gauls were certainly not destroyed. Justin has preserved the remarkable statement that the same Gauls who sacked Rome went to Apulia, and there offered for money their assistance to the elder Dionysius of Syracuse. From this important statement it is at any rate clear, that they traversed all Italy, and then probably returned along the shore of the Adriatic: their devastations extended over many parts of Italy, and there is no doubt that the Aequians received their death-blow at that time, for henceforth we hear no more of the hostilities of the Aequians against Rome. Praeneste, on the other hand, which must formerly have been subject to the Aequians, now appears as an independent town. The Aequians, who inhabited small and easily destructible towns, must have been annihilated during the progress of the Gauls.

There is nothing so strange in the history of Livy as his view of the consequences of the Gallic calamity; he must have conceived it as a transitory storm by which Rome was humbled but not broken. The army according to him was only scattered, and the Romans appear afterwards just as they had been before, as if the preceding period had only been an evil dream, and as if there had been nothing to do but to rebuild the city. But assuredly the devastation must have been tremendous throughout the Roman territory: for eight months the barbarians had been ravaging the country, every trace of cultivation, every farmer's house, all the temples and public buildings were destroyed; the walls of the city had been purposely pulled down, a large number of its inhabitants were led into slavery, the rest were living in great misery at Veii; and what they had saved scarcely sufficed to buy their bread. In this condition they returned to Rome. Camillus as dictator is called a second Romulus, and to him is due the glory of not having despaired in those distressing circumstances. After the time of the Volscian war, Rome had no longer been able to concede to her former allies, who were then in a state of weakness, the same rights as before: they had been subjects of Rome for nearly seventy years, though Rome was very mild in the use of her power. But all those people who had suffered less than Rome, now renounced her supremacy, and this is the *defectio Latinorum qui per centum fere annos nunquam ambigua fide in amicitia populi Romani fuerant*, of which Livy speaks: nothing is more natural than that they should assert their independence. It would be very lamentable if unnatural regulations had an invincible power, rendering it impossible for that which is in accordance with nature finally to become established. It is quite a different question how it necessarily came to pass that shortly before the Gallic invasion the Romans in reality had the supremacy; this certainly was the case, as under similar circumstances among the seven Dutch provinces, although all had perfectly equal rights, yet Holland in fact stood at their head, and occupied the rank which belonged to it in virtue of its wealth and population. In like manner, Rome might be regarded as the head of the confederacy, but only so long as she was in possession of all her power.

There is an ancient tradition that during the famine, the aged were killed in order to save them from the pangs of death by starvation, and to preserve the little means which yet remained for those who were to perpetuate the republic. Things were almost as bad as at the destruction of Magdeburg, where the number of inhabitants was reduced from 30,000 to 3,000. Even after it was rebuilt, Rome must for several generations have been only a shadow of what it had been previously to its destruction. It is quite natural that the people should have been desponding, and that the tribunes should have insisted upon abandoning Rome and settling at Veii. It is the merit of Camillus that he resisted this pusillanimous despondency, and he was on that occasion supported by his high aristocratic sentiments. It required great acuteness to hit upon the right plan: the gods had abandoned Veii, and Juno had loudly declared that she would not inhabit it, but Rome. The discussions upon this subject in Livy have a peculiar charm. I do not mean to say, that Rome would not have been able to strike new roots at Veii, but it is more probable that it would have entirely perished; the Latins would have made themselves masters of the left bank of the Tiber, and perhaps a Volscian or Latin colony would have been established on the seven hills. The situation of Rome on a river between three nations had been chosen by Providence for her greatness; its advantages are obvious: but at Veii the Romans would perhaps have become Etruscans. The senate now acted like a severe father: after it had passed the resolution to rebuild Rome, which was very hard for the poor, an order was issued that, for the purpose of restoring Rome, Veii should be destroyed. The senate, it is said, gave gratis, tiles, stones and other building materials, all of which were to be found at Veii, the buildings of which were the property of the Roman republic. The materials had now to be carried to Rome. The new habitations were badly built huts, and it was only gradually that better houses were erected. The senate gave the people leave to build as they pleased, for according to Roman principles all private property had during the confusion reverted to the state, which now gave permission to occupy it anew. The walls were restored, and the dangerous place in the Capitol where the Gauls climbed up, was strengthened by

a substructure of square blocks. It was not till the time of
Augustus that Veii was restored as a military colony, but it
was only a small place like Gabii, Lavici and others.

The longer I have been engaged in these investigations, the
more satisfaction have I derived from them. I am conscious
of having searched after truth without allowing myself to be
dazzled by authority. When I find that statements which I
had absolutely rejected, are after all, correct in a certain sense,
and that they have become imperfect only through want of
knowledge or through having fallen into oblivion, I am always
greatly rejoiced. This has happened to me frequently, and
especially in regard to the history of the Roman rate of interest
and the laws about usury. If I am to state what I think, I
must say that before my time these subjects were in the
greatest confusion. During the eighteenth century, the
antiquities of the Roman law, especially the *jus publicum*,
were sadly neglected: I except Schulting. Heineccius, a man
deserving of all honour, possessed great talent and learning,
but did not know what course to take; he laboured under the
same mistake as the men of the sixteenth century whose
disciple he was, and had no independence of judgment. A
variety of opinions have been published on the Roman rate of
interest: among others Hugo of Göttingen has written upon
the subject: he came forward as the founder of a new school
of learned jurisprudence; he was a man of excellent taste,
and took great interest in these questions, but did not possess
the solid learning which is required for such discussions.
Savigny and I were long ago convinced, that what Hugo had
written on the rate of interest was worth nothing, and that
the whole subject must be investigated anew. Savigny did
not undertake the task, but I was led to it in the course of
my investigations into Roman history: my results have been
confirmed by Schrader of Tübingen, and my opinions are now
generally adopted.[3] Roman contracts of loan were concluded
for years of ten months each, and one ounce was paid as
interest upon one *As*, that is, one twelfth part of the capital,
which is as much as ten per cent. in a year of twelve months.

---

[3] As an artist opens his pupil's eye and trains it best by working in his presence, so it is in science also: he who has searched all his life certainly does a
service to his disciples if he shows to them the manner in which he made progress, and sometimes also how he was obliged to retrace his steps.—N.

Hugo thought that one twelfth was paid for every mon th which proves that he had no perception of what is possible in the affairs of practical life. Jurisprudence, in general, has two sides: the one is science or theory, and the other the practice of ordinary life; in regard to the latter, we Germans are in a wrong way: in other countries things are better, inasmuch as the knowledge of theory goes more hand in hand with the relations of practical life. It is quite remarkable that there are teachers of law, who have no knowledge of actual affairs, which appears to me as absurd as if a man were to come forward to teach medicine without having any notion of disease. A practical knowledge must support historical jurisprudence, and if any one has got that, he can easily master all scholastic speculations. The later Roman law of debt was taken entirely from the Greek law, and the calculation of the *syngrapha* and *centesimae*, such as it existed in the time of Cicero, arose from the condition of things established in the Greek cities of Athens, Rhodes and Alexandria. We read in Tacitus, that the *foenus unciarium* was introduced by the laws of the twelve tables, and in Livy that it was established at the beginning of the fifth century. These statements have been considered an inexplicable contradiction, and I too formerly believed that Tacitus was mistaken; but I am now of a different opinion. We must here make a distinction: it does not follow from Livy's account that the *foenus unciarium* was not mentioned in the twelve tables. Down to the time of the Gallic invasion we hear of no complaint about usury, but afterwards, when every one was obliged to build, the law of usury was probably abolished, in order to enable every one to obtain money on any terms. Hence arose a dreadful state of debt; and forty years later the ancient laws of usury were re-established. Livy is therefore probably correct in saying that at one time the taking of interest was entirely forbidden. In the year 1807, some friends of mine in opposition to my urgent remonstrances, carried a decree by which the laws of usury were abolished in Prussia; but the consequences were very unfortunate. Afterwards the money could not be paid, and then *faciebant versuram*, that is, the interest was added to the capital.

It is unaccountable how men could be found at that time to advance the money; it is true people were content with satisfying their most pressing wants, and for this reason the senate

allowed them to build as they pleased; but however much the
state might do to facilitate the building, still the restoration
must have been immensely expensive. I believe that the
means were obtained through the clientela: the grand determination to restore Rome, which had been made by the senate in
the consciousness of her immortality, was very imposing and
must have made people believe that the strength of the state
was unexhausted; and thus capitalists in various parts of Italy
may have been tempted to go to a place where they might
expect to make enormous profits: the patricians had probably
not been able to rescue such immense capitals from the Gallic
calamity. When therefore a Syracusan or a Neapolitan came
to Rome with ready money, he was not allowed to lend it
himself, and accordingly became the client of a patrician who
concluded the nexum for him. In this manner the condition
of the commonalty down to the passing of the Licinian law
was extremely wretched, and it was unfair that the order
which enjoyed so many advantages in the state, should
also derive a usurious interest from their less fortunate fellow-
citizens.

LECTURE XXXIII.

IF Rome alone had been destroyed by the Gauls, as the
reader of Livy must believe, unless he rises to a higher point
of view, it would be inconceivable how Rome could have
maintained herself against the neighbouring nations, which
had seized the opportunity of shaking off her yoke. But her
neighbours like herself had undoubtedly deeply felt the calamity,
even supposing that they defended their towns, and that many
may have warded off devastation by a heavy war-tax. The
condition of a great part of Italy reminds us of the time which
followed immediately after the termination of the Thirty Years'
War, when new wars broke out forthwith. I shall give you only
brief sketches of these events. We clearly see that the Etruscans rose against the Romans, and that this affair terminated
favorably for the latter. Sutrium and Nepet were then the

Roman frontier towns towards Etruria,—all the rest, including Falerii, was lost,—and even these towns were sometimes besieged and actually taken; when the Romans had reconquered them they formed them into colonies. The war was carried on mainly against the Tarquinians and Vulsinians. The fact of the Etruscans endeavouring to recover the conquests made by the Romans, shews that the Etruscan confederacy also was then in a state of dissolution, for the northern Etruscans were fighting against the Gauls, while the southern ones attacked Rome. In the accounts of our historians, however, these Etruscan wars are still as full of fabulous statements as the former ones. At this time we everywhere, even in Greece, see a dissolution of the ancient confederacies, and a tendency to unite into larger states. The condition of Latium was such, that we may say there was no longer any bond to keep the confederacy together. Antium, Velitrae and Circeii, whose colonists were either expelled or made common cause with the Latins and Volscians, as well as the Hernicans, were separate from Rome, and scarcely the nearest towns such as Tusculum and Lanuvium remained faithful to her. Praeneste now became an important place: the Praenestines and Tiburtines seem at that time to have been allied, and Praeneste may perhaps have been the head of a portion of the Aequians. The boundary between the Aequians and Romans ceased to be at Praeneste, and extended beyond it. Political relations in the ancient world change with extraordinary rapidity, as is most manifest in Arcadia, where the three principal tribes are in the end completely lost sight of. The union of Latium was dissolved, and a portion of the Latins along with Velitrae and Antium rose against Rome, and so also did Praeneste with a portion of the Aequians. The period of Rome's supremacy was gone, Veii alone was a permanent gain, and the Romans now admitted Etruscan places, which had already possessed the franchise without the suffrage, to the full privilege of citizens, and formed them into four new tribes, the number of which thus became twenty-five. Livy erroneously states, that the new tribes were formed of those who revolted to Rome in the earlier wars: this is impossible, for the Romans always formed their new tribes of a much larger number of individuals than was contained in the ancient ones, since it was only in this manner that they could truly unite with them, and yet

that the influence of the new tribes in the assembly might be
limited, although individually all tribesmen were on a footing
of perfect equality. I for my part am convinced that all these
new tribes had formerly been sovereign towns with their territories. The territories of Veii, Capena, Vulsinii and others,
undoubtedly acted the part of mere spectators in the wars of
their ruling towns, and surrendered to the Romans as soon as
they appeared, without any resistance, because to whatever
state they belonged their condition was equally good or bad:
many also were neutral, as under similar circumstances we see
was the case, in the war between Spain and the Low Countries,
with the towns of Brabant, which paid taxes to both the belligerent powers that they might remain unattacked. By the
destruction of a town its territory became subject to Rome, and
it was unquestionably to these people that Rome now granted
the full franchise, and thus recruited the reduced number of
her citizens. The Etruscan cities undoubtedly maintained a
very passive attitude during this change. Rome was wise
enough to grant to her new subjects the full plebeian franchise:
her case was like that of Jerusalem when Ezra and Nehemiah
returned from Babylon and rebuilt the city.

Plutarch and Macrobius mention a tradition respecting the
reduced state of Rome, which, however, as reported by them,
seems to be unhistorical. The city was yet without walls,
when some of the neighbouring and very insignificant places,
such as Fidenae and Ficulea appeared with their armies, and
compelled the Romans to give hostages. But the hostages,
instead of being noble virgins, were female servants; and their
leader, a Greek slave named Philotis, imitated the example of
Judith, for while the troops were celebrating their unwonted
success, and were intoxicated, she gave a signal to the Romans
with a torch, whereupon they rushed forth and annihilated
their enemies. This event was placed in the month of Quinctilis, consequently four months after the evacuation of the
city; and the tradition shews at all events how much Rome
was conceived to have been reduced.

After the formation of the four new tribes Rome had again
an extensive territory, which formed the basis of her recovery.
At the end of this period, affairs on the left bank of the Tiber
continued to be in the same state of dissolution as before. On
the right bank all the territory belonged to Rome as far as

Sutrium and Nepet, which were frontier fortresses, and beyond which the Ciminian forest was allowed to grow wild for the purpose of protection. Whenever *ager publicus* is mentioned at this time, it must be conceived to have been almost exclusively in those districts. The relation of isopolity probably existed only with the nearest Latin places, Tusculum, Lanuvium, and Aricia. I cannot here relate to you all the events of that period; the detail would be entirely useless. Lectures like the present should only dwell upon events which are important in themselves and in their consequences. Livy's case was different since he wrote for his own countrymen.

Of far more importance to us are the events which occurred in Rome itself. Avarice and usury were among the darling sins of the Romans; and the less they were checked, the more oppressive they became. Had the system of usury not been so excessive, the revolution which now began would have been accompanied with less violence. A few years after the evacuation of the city, the distress was so great that Livy was ashamed to reveal it to the world, perhaps even to himself. M. Manlius rose to protect the unhappy. He does not derive his name Capitolinus from having saved the Capitol, but because he lived there; for T. Manlius, probably his father, appears in the Fasti with this name twenty years earlier. The saving of the Capitol was not the only brilliant feat performed by Manlius. He was acknowledged to be one of the most illustrious military heroes; and the fact of his name not being mentioned in the Fasti throws light upon his position. He is universally said to have had *consilia regni affectandi*, but Livy states that the annals contained no evidence to support this charge, except that meetings were held in his house, and that benefits had been conferred by him upon the plebes. It may be that he was indignant at the ruling party, because he had not been rewarded for his service; but it is also possible that his great soul was stirred up by ungovernable ambition, and that he indulged in the hope of rewarding himself with a crown. All his actions were of a kind which the purest and most benevolent mind might have suggested without being under the influence of ambition. Citizens were every day assigned to their creditors as slaves for debt. Manlius paid for them what they owed, especially for old soldiers, and by the sacrifice of his whole property he restored them to their families. He is also said to have accused the patricians of having appropriated to themselves the money which had been recovered from the Gauls. This suspicion must have arisen from the imposition of the tax for the purpose of restoring the gold which had been paid to the Gauls, since the levying of a tax under such circumstances, though it was destined for the gods, was not free from harshness and fanaticism. Manlius, who thus gained immense popularity, became the object of the greatest hatred to the ruling body. Instead of profiting by his hint and relieving the distress, the patricians obstinately insisted on their rights, and thus arose a contest between beneficent ambition on the one hand, and the most stubborn oligarchy on the other, as in Ireland in the year 1822, where, when the cattle were bled, the poor fought for the blood in order to satisfy their hunger, and where the landlords nevertheless insisted on their legal claims. The natural consequence was a very general feeling, that any change would be better than such a government, and that Manlius as a usurper might be as useful as many a Greek tyrant. This state of things undoubtedly became very dangerous. When a government is in a bad course, and unwilling to retrace its steps, it drives men to sin, and has much to answer for before God and man. The Roman government was in this predicament, and ordered Manlius to be arrested; but this led to nothing, for a general sympathy manifested itself for him, who until then had committed no crime. The plebes put on mourning, and assembled in crowds at the gate of his dungeon. The government therefore was obliged to set him free. It had acted rashly, and as Manlius was now provoked, it thought that he was sure to take wrong steps, and that it would thus obtain an opportunity of crushing him. Manlius had a difficult part to act. Under such circumstances men often begin their career with the purest intentions, but gradually fall into frightful aberrations. I believe that Manlius did not start with the idea of making himself the tyrant of his country; but when the men of his own order reviled him, and misinterpreted his pure intentions, the germs of his actions became poisoned, and this might lead him to 'the detremination to set himself up as tyrant; but no evidence of that supposition is to be found. The tumult in the mean time increased, and Manlius, enraged, and proud because he

had conquered, demanded that a portion of the domain land
should be sold, and that the produce should be employed in
paying the debts of the poor: a fair demand, as the state was
the proprietor of the domain land. But the oligarchs were
bent upon reserving the possession of it for themselves, and
rejoiced at the wretchedness of the plebeians. The distress
rendered the dependence of the plebeians very great. So long
as the *praefectus urbi* had it in his power to assign a debtor to
his creditor, every man was in danger of losing his freedom.
It may be that dangerous thoughts gained from day to day
greater ascendancy over the mind of Manlius, and thus at
last the patricians ventured to accuse him. Two tribunes
declared for the senate; and according to Zonaras, Camillus
was appointed dictator for the occasion. Under the terrors of
the dictatorship, Manlius was summoned before the assembly
of the centuries, but no one dared to imprison him again. On
giving security, he was allowed to retain the enjoyment of his
liberty; and on the appointed day he appeared and defended
himself, which is the strongest argument for his innocence,
since he might have withdrawn from the city. He referred
to his great military achievements and services as a proof of
his sentiments; he brought forward the spoils of thirty enemies
whom he had slain, and forty marks of honour which he had
received in war; he appealed to the citizens whom he had
saved, and among them even to the *magister equitum;* he
pointed to the Capitol, which could be seen from the Campus
Martius—and the centuries acquitted him. But the oligarchy
was not satisfied with this, and the senate summoned him
before the curies (*concilium populi*), who as his peers were
to try his case in the Petelinian grove, a fact which Livy and
all his followers have misunderstood. As the *concilium populi*
is rarely mentioned, Livy thought of a tribunician accusation;
but at the same time he cannot deny that the patrician *duumviri* were his accusers. The meeting was in the Petelinian
grove, not because the Capitol could not be seen from that
spot, but because his enemies felt an aversion to pronouncing
the sentence of death in the city, and yet were obliged to
meet in a consecrated place. Manlius was condemned and
thrown down the Tarpeian rock. This catastrophe, like the
death of Sp. Cassius, produced for a few years a death-like
stillness at Rome; but the patricians had nevertheless to atone

for their crime, as was always the case, although the full vengeance did not fall upon them, for down to the time of C. Gracchus, who called the murderers of his brother to account[1], the rulers who committed such a crime were not made personally responsible for it; and to this forbearance Rome owed the preservation of her liberty. From the blood of Manlius arose men, whose object was not to avenge him, but to accomplish what he had desired. Licinius and Sextius had perhaps (nay probably) been his friends, and his ignominious death gave them courage to defy all dangers in accomplishing their great work. Inspired by his example, they performed their task without shedding one drop of blood.

It was about ten or eleven years after the destruction of the city, that two tribunes of the people, C. Licinius, and L. Sextius, placed themselves at the head of their order, with a firm determination to place at length the relation of the two orders on a just footing: it was not their intention that the patricians, as a distinct order, should perish, but the plebeians were to stand by their side with equal rights, and the state, according to the original idea, was to be a double state, of two perfectly equal communities. The military tribunes, according to our authorities, were again nearly always patricians, which is inconceivable: something must be wanting here; but the excerpts *De Sententiis* from Dion Cassius, unfortunately contain nothing about this period. The patricians were satisfied with the military tribuneship, and did not want any consuls. There is a foolish story explaining the motive that induced Licinius to come forward in this manner; but it was easy for Beaufort to shew that it is nothing but a fiction. M. Fabius Ambustus is said to have had two daughters, the one married to the patrician Sulpicius, and the other to C. Licinius. Sulpicius was military tribune, and as usual returned home with the lictors; the younger sister was staying with the elder, and being frightened by the noise, was ridiculed by her sister, who said that it was natural to be sure that the noise should alarm her, since she was married to a man who could never attain to this honour. Beaufort has justly remarked, that the children of

---

[1] Mirabeau said at Marseilles in the year 1789, that C. Gracchus called to heaven to avenge the blood of his brother, and that out of that blood Marius arose; but Gracchus was an innocent and holy man, while Marius was a tyrant. — N.

M. Fabius Ambustus could not possibly be unacquainted with this mark of honour, and it is an equally unhistorical statement, that the younger Fabia entreated her father and husband to procure it for her also, inasmuch as the military tribuneship was open to the plebeians as much as to the patricians, and M. Fabius Ambustus himself afterwards appears among those who lent a helping hand in the attempt to overturn the Licinian laws. The whole story is a miserable piece of scandal, invented by a party which was annoyed at the success of the plans of its opponents. The motives of men are often really despicable, but there is no reason for coming to such a conclusion generally, and we ought not to trace every thing great to mean and contemptible motives. Livy merely copied the tale from others, and in his haste and want of a vivid conception of the circumstances, he wrote it down, not intending to represent it as a real history, but only as a pretty story: his soul was pure and noble, and although his patrician predilections sometimes lead him astray, he nevertheless speaks truly when he says in his preface, that he was impelled by an irresistible power to search after that which was great in the early times.

But whatever may have been the occasion, the object was plain enough, namely to remove the existing abuses by a thorough reform. The reform proposed by Licinius and Sextius had two great ends; and to relieve the momentary distress was their third object. The first bill which they brought forward, ordained that no more military tribunes should be elected, but consuls, one of whom should necessarily be a plebeian. The patricians, notwithstanding their small numbers, were still predominant in the government, and for a long time endeavoured to prevent the passing of the bill, until in the end the matter was so managed that all their intrigues became useless: these very intrigues rendered it necessary to bring forward the bill in its absolute form. The tribunes could not have said that the worthiest should be elected from the two orders, for as the curies still had to sanction the elected magistrate, and could refuse their sanction to a plebeian, it was necessary to fix the appointment of one plebeian as indispensable. The division, moreover, was important for the patricians themselves, for as soon as the plebeians acquired power in the senate, they would have elected two men from their own order. It was not till two hundred years later, that the plebeians actually acquired this preponderance, when the extreme diminution in the number of patricians became sensibly apparent, the patrician being to the plebeian nobility in the ratio of one to thirty. The second law established the principle that the plebeians should have a share in the possession of the *ager publicus,* as well as the patricians, and that, in accordance with the Cassian law, a portion of it should be given to them in full ownership, to indemnify them for the past; in future it was to be a rule that one part of it should always be assigned to the patricians as their possession, and another be distributed among the plebeians as their real property. No individual was to possess more than 500 jugera; the surplus was to be divided among the plebes in lots of seven jugera, and no one was to be allowed to keep more than a certain number of cattle on the common pasture, during the summer in the mountains, and during the winter in the meadows near the city. The third bill contained the temporary measure regarding the debts of the plebeians: the interest which had been added to the capital was to be cancelled, and the rest was to be paid back by three annual instalments, each year being reckoned at ten months, and undoubtedly without interest. This was indeed something like a general bankruptcy; but the matter could not be settled otherwise, and the creditors had assuredly made sufficiently large profits by their former usury. The tribunes in this case did for individuals, what Sully, after the unfortunate times of the League did for the state, in diminishing the amount of debt: he cancelled the usurious interest already paid, and allowed the remaining capital to stand at the ordinary rate of interest. It was in consequence of this violent measure that France reached its high state of prosperity under Louis XIII, while previously the farmers of finance and the usurers had alone fattened upon the marrow of the nation. There is no doubt that at Rome too, it was only the worst individuals that suffered by the law: a gentler remedy would have been desirable, but none was to be found, and without some remedy the state would have perished.

The patricians not only opposed these rogations with a fixed determination not to yield, but they also exerted all their influence at the elections, in order that the tribunes, who for ten years were re-elected year after year, might have opponents in

their own college. The whole history of these occurrences is
buried in utter darkness, and we cannot say from what quarter
the opposition came, nor wherein the difficulty lay. Whether
the tribunes themselves formed the opposition, or whether the
patricians contrived to produce indifference and hostility among
the commonalty, or whether the laws were passed as rogations
by the centuries, so that only the senate and the curies refused
their sanction,—all these are questions which we cannot answer,
but the state of things was probably different at different
times.

LECTURE XXXIV.

OUR authorities state that the tribunes Licinius and Sextius,
for the purpose of carrying their laws, opposed the election of
new magistrates with such perseverance, that for five, or according to others for six years, no curule magistrates were
elected. This is one of those accounts which we may often
read, without being able at first to believe that they can be
inventions; in all the Fasti we find five years, during which
neither consuls nor military tribunes are mentioned, but only
the tribunes of the plebes, Licinius and Sextius; their colleagues,
who surely should have been recorded along with them, are
not named. Such also was the case in Junius Gracchanus,
from whom the statement was adopted by Joannes Lydus, but
it is nevertheless false. There is no doubt that the tribunes
for a time stopped the election of curule magistrates, whereby
the Fasti were thrown into disorder; but what would have
been the confusion, if this had happened for five successive
years! Interreges were indeed sufficient for times of peace,
but they could not have led an army into the field: and would
the neighbours of Rome have left her undisturbed during such
a state of internal dissolution? The story appears to have arisen
in the first place from the certain knowledge that during the
whole struggle the tribunes actually opposed the elections, and
yielded only at times of the most urgent necessity, when a war
absolutely demanded the appointment of curule magistrates;

the periods therefore during which there were no magistrates were always short, the elections being only put off. In the second place, the ancients imagined that Rome was taken by the Gauls, in the archonship of Pyrgion[1], Olymp. 98. 1, as they read in Timaeus, whose statement they regarded as authentic, not considering that his knowledge of the fact was not as certain as his statement was positive. Fabius wrote his work fifty Olympiads later, Olymp. 148. 1 = A.U. 565 according to Cato; he knew very well how people then reckoned in Greece, and he also knew that two hundred years previously Rome had been taken by the Gauls: he accordingly calculated backwards, but the Fasti did not agree, six or seven years being wanting between the taking of Rome and the Licinian rogations; some time might be occupied by the interreges, who had supplied the place of consuls, but all the years could not be filled up in this manner. After the Gallic calamity, the consuls were elected on the kalends of Quinctilis, and in his time, perhaps on the kalends or ides of Augustus, for the elections always took place on one of these two days of a month; by this means the calculation of the years changed its starting point. The result is, that what is senseless, is also untrue, and the Gallic conquest must be placed considerably, at least four years, later than the date usually assigned to it. Now, the first authors who promulgated our account, certainly did not mean to say that, during five years, the tribunes were the only magistracy: they combined the Greek date and the Roman statements, but did not know how to find their way in the Fasti, — hence, in the Fasti of Varro, dictatorships are inserted, which are said to have lasted for a whole year, but they likewise are wrong; they arose merely from the shifting of the consular years;— the ancient authors then went beyond the restoration of the consulship in A.U. 388, fixed there the impossible anarchy of five or six years, and inserted the tribunes of the people, to whom however, instead of ten years, they assigned far too many. The interpolator found in the Fasti the title *tribuni*,without any further attribute to indicate the curule magistrates, and therefrom he inferred the opposition to the elections, which Livy has spun out so much.

---

[1] Συμφωνεῖται σχεδὸν ὑπὸ πάντων, says Dionysius; this σχεδὸ proves that all were not agreed, and I believe that the excellent Cincius assigned it to a different year, perhaps to Olymp. 99. 1 or 2.—N.

There can be no doubt that during these contests the Roman magistrates were always military tribunes, and almost invariably patricians, on one occasion only half their number consisted of plebeians, and the presidents at the elections generally refused to accept any votes for plebeian candidates. The exasperation of the people rose from day to day, and went so far that in the end the outbreak of a civil war was feared. Under the dictatorship of Manlius the tribunes carried a law, which they had perhaps proposed along with others, that half the decemvirs, who were entrusted with the keeping of the Sibylline books, should be elected from the plebeians, in order to prevent false assertions on the part of the patricians respecting the prodigies. Another great advantage was gained by the dictator P. Manlius raising a cousin of the tribune Licinius to the office of *magister equitum*: this was certainly in accordance with the ancient custom, for the plebeians too had their *equites*, and Brutus in his time had been *tribunus celerum*. When none of the tribunes made any further opposition, and the tribes had passed the rogation of Licinius, matters came to extremities, because the senate, consisting almost entirely of patricians, refused to give its sanction. The commonalty shewed much less obstinacy in endeavouring to carry the law respecting the consulship, which was of the highest importance to the plebeian nobility, than in passing the other laws. The senate here again tried its old tactics, attempting to get out of its difficulties by temporary concessions. But Dion Cassius relates that the tribunes of the people, in order to carry all their laws at once, combined them in one bill, and Licinius is reported to have said, that if they would not eat, neither should they drink.

In all free states there are families in which certain political views and principles are hereditary, for there a man is born in a political party as he is born in a particular church. Roman history furnishes many examples of this kind: the first tribune of the plebes was a Licinius; a Licinius was the first who led the people in their insurrection on the Sacred Mount; and 420 years later it was again a Licinius, who after the death of Sulla vindicated the rights of the tribuneship, so that the Licinii always remained the foremost among the plebeian families. The same observation may be made in regard to the Publilii and Sicinii. It may at first seem a strange limitation of

individual freedom to be thus dependent on the principles of
one's forefathers, as if it were an external obligation, but a little
experience shews that it is the foundation of the firmness and
strength of a nation. But to return to our narrative: Licinius
then combines his various laws that all might stand or fall at
once. Nothing is more glorious in Roman history than that
the commonalty though far superior to their opponents in
strength and numbers bore their machinations with the greatest
composure and patience and without committing any illegal
act, although the struggle lasted for a series of years.

The aged Camillus—he was now eighty years old—was appointed dictator: his blood had not yet been cooled, the ancient
party-spirit and animosity still survived in him, and when
called upon by his order he fancied he could do what was in
reality impossible. The plebeians did not dare to resist the
dictator, but with extreme wisdom resolved that if Camillus as
dictator should undertake anything unlawful against them,
they would accuse him after the expiration of his office and
propose that he should be fined 500,000 *asses*. This declaration paralysed Camillus, and the senate was afraid to let matters
come to extremities. Camillus found that he could do no more
than Cincinnatus ninety years before, who had to avenge a dis-
graced son. The patricians began to reflect, and Camillus
himself advising them to yield, made a vow that he would
build a temple of Concord if he should succeed in reconciling
the two orders. This temple was consecrated though not till
after the death of the great man. The Romans of a later time
thought its ancient magnificence too mean; in the reign of
Augustus its place was supplied by another, and Trajan built
a still more magnificent one instead of the second. Down to
the year 1817 its site was sought for in a wrong place: it stood
in a corner below the Salita which leads from the arch of Sep-
timius Severus to the Capitol; several votive tablets were
found there behind the church of S. Servius, which Pope Cle-
ment VII. erected on the site of a more ancient church. The
pillars of the later temple were of Phrygian marble, wrought
with extraordinary elegance. Trajan loved to dwell in past
ages: he coined Roman denarii, bearing on one side his own
head and on the reverse the emblems of great families which
had become extinct (for in the earlier times the right of coining
was not an exclusive privilege of the state): and there still

exist a considerable number of these *nummi restituti*. It was the same feeling which prompted him to restore the ancient temple of Concord, for the spot on which the golden age of Rome had begun was sacred to him as it was to his friends Pliny and Tacitus. Its site is now clear of rubbish and is a classical spot in Roman topography,—the symbol of a free and equal constitution.

The reconciliation was brought about in this manner: it was agreed that one of the consuls should be a plebeian and the other a patrician; the ancient consulship, however, such as it had existed previously to the decemvirate, was not to be restored, but the praefect of the city was to be a permanent and new curule magistrate under the name of *praetor urbanus*.[2] This *praefectura urbis* had existed even before the decemviral constitution, and was to have received a different character in that constitution; there were now many reasons for the patricians not allowing it to fall into the hands of the plebeians, because the whole possession of the *ager publicus* was dependent upon it. If for example a father bequeathed 400 jugera to his son, who already possessed 400 jugera, a conscientious praetor might take from him the 300 above the legal quantity; but if a praetor was determined to render the law ineffectual, he assigned the bequest to the son and would not listen to the charge that he already possessed more than the law allowed. In addition to this, it must be remembered that the laws were still under the superintendence of the pontiffs, and that accordingly the patricians, who alone were eligible to the pontificate, might say that they were exclusively entitled to be invested with the praetorship. Another no less important right of the praetor was that of appointing the judices. The centumviri, who were elected by the tribes, had to decide in questions of property, but all criminal cases were brought before the praetor. When the crime was a *delictum manifestum*, the perpetrator was dragged before his tribunal *obtorto collo*, and the praetor at once determined the punishment; but when the matter was disputed, the praetor delegated a *judex*, and directed him to decide the case in this or that manner according to the result of the investigation; there is no doubt that he himself also might act as *judex*, but he alone could not possibly have

[2] This name was not devised to distinguish him from the *praetor peregrinus*, a point in which I myself was formerly mistaken as well as many others.—N.

managed all the cases that were brought before him. These *judices* or judges, then and for a long time afterwards, were chosen from among the senators; and hence it was of great consequence to the patricians to reserve for themselves the exclusive right to the praetorship. This circumstance also shews the importance of the measure brought forward by Gracchus. The patricians retained the possession of the praetorship for thirty-two years; but when a great portion of the *ager publicus* had passed into the hands of the plebeians, when consequently the praetor changed his character, commanded armies, and often performed the functions of a consul, the office could no longer be withheld from the plebeians. It should, moreover, be observed that the praetor was called the colleague of the consuls and that he had six lictors, as the two consuls together had twelve.

It is further mentioned that the curule aediles were then for the first time appointed for the purpose of conducting the public games; the plebeian aediles are said to have refused to give expensive games for the celebration of the peace, and as some patrician youths generously undertook to do so, the new office is stated to have been instituted to honour them. Even in the first edition of my Roman history I shewed the folly of this opinion; the curule aediles were neither more nor less than what the ancient *quaestores parricidii* had been: they brought public accusations before the popular courts in cases of poison, sorcery, and the like. Their jurisdiction was quite different from that of the praetors, and when the law had not fixed a particular punishment for a crime, they determined the punishment according to the nature of the offence. On this subject the ancients entertained different notions from ourselves. I know the advantages of our own times, and he whose soul is completely absorbed in one period is not fit for any other. A person who looks with fondness upon past ages and would fain recall them, is not a *homo gravis*, but is diseased in his mind. I would rather see a man preferring the present to the past; but the legislative conceit of our age is very injurious, for legislators imagine that they can determine everything. I was once present in a country when the discovery was made that there existed a conspiracy of men who dug up corpses from their graves after they had been buried for many years, and as the law had made no provision for such a crime the monsters escaped with impunity. One year after the institution of the curule aedileship the plebeians gained access to it also, and for a period of 130 years there were alternately one year two patrician, and the next, two plebeian aediles. The *ludi Romani* were increased by a fourth day for the plebeians, who had before had their own games. From the statements made by Dionysius after Fabius at the end of his seventh book, it is clear that until the time to which those statements refer, the state had annually provided a large sum of money to defray the expenses of those games, but that in consequence of the unfortunate events in the first Punic war, the expenses were thrown upon individual citizens. The games were thenceforward given at the expense of individuals, and the curule aedileship became a *liturgy* in the Greek sense: the aediles obtained access to all the great offices, but in return they were obliged to defray out of their own means the expenses of the games.

The plebeian aediles were a general Latin magistracy, as is evident from the fact of their being mentioned as existing in Latin towns; but we cannot say whether the curule aedileship had existed before as such a local magistracy among the patricians, or whether it was then newly created. These curule aediles have hitherto always been considered as a sort of police magistracy; it is true, to some extent they were so, and in so far, they competed with the plebeian aediles; but their real office did not consist in the superintendence of the corn trade, public buildings and the like, in which they cannot be distinguished from the plebeian aediles, but they were the ancient *quaestores parricidii* who instituted their inquisitions before the people, as I have proved by several examples. I suspect that the *triumviri capitales* were a detached branch of the aedilician power. The aediles had no lictors and no imperium. Now, how did it happen that these new magistrates were elected in the *comitia tributa?* It seems probable that at first they were elected alternately by the *comitia tributa* and *curiata*, and that the *comitia* which did not elect had to sanction the election; but when the Maenian law reduced the sanction of the curies to a mere matter of form, the election was altogether transferred to the tribes. The inferior magistrates, such as the *triumviri monetales*, *quatuorviri* and others, were not instituted till after the Hortensian and Maenian laws, when the curies had ceased to meet, and the election was altogether transferred to the tribes. As regards the praetor, there can be no doubt that, like the consuls, he was elected by the centuries; for it is said that he was elected *iisdem auspiciis*, and the auspices were taken only for the *comitia* of the centuries and curies. Thus the few points which are known help us in explaining what is mysterious in the history of the Roman constitution.

LECTURE XXXV.

ACCORDING to Joannes Lydus (that is, according to Gracchanus), the government at the close of these disturbances was for a time in the hands of triumvirs. I shall endeavour to explain this elsewhere, but the fact itself is quite credible. The circumstance that Varro in his work inscribed to Pompey, *De Senatu habendo*, mentioned the *triumviri reipublicae constituendae* among those who had the right to convoke the senate, is a strong argument in favour of it: the later triumvirs probably adopted the title with reference to this early magistracy. I will however not deny that the first military tribunes were likewise called *triumviri reipublicae constituendae* in the ancient records.

When the Licinian laws were passed and the first plebeian consul had been elected, circumstances arose which threatened to throw everything back again into confusion, for the patricians refused to sanction the plebeian consul. It was only with great difficulty that matters were settled: the patricians in the end yielded and recognised L. Sextius as plebeian consul. In this manner the lawful and necessary revolution was brought to a close: it had proceeded like the normal changes in the human body when a youth passes into the age of manhood. We cannot wonder that the peace was not cordially meant; the patricians yielded only to necessity, and with the firm determination to recover what was lost as soon as an opportunity should offer. The struggle was renewed about eleven years later, in A.U. 399 according to the Catonian era which is adopted by Livy also[1]; the patricians again succeeded in obtaining

---

[1] Chronology is here very uncertain on account of the shifting of the time at which the magistrates entered upon their office ; it was not till the time of the Punic wars that the consuls regularly entered upon their office in spring, and during the latter period of the republic on the first of January.—N.

possession of both places in the consulship, and continued the contest until A.U. 413, usurping during more than one third of that period the consulship for themselves exclusively. But in the end they were obliged to yield with disgrace, and during the struggle itself they had to make concessions to the plebeians, which the latter would not have demanded with such vehemence, if the peace had been honestly observed.

The beginning of the period which now opens is marked by very few events; it may be, as Livy says, that no wars were carried on, in order not to give the plebeian consul any opportunity of distinguishing himself, but it is also possible that this is merely a conjecture of his. All the care of the Romans was directed to their internal affairs, for it is natural to suppose that the innumerable arrangements which the Licinian law rendered necessary engrossed all their attention. The whole of the *ager publicus* had to be measured and divided, a commission was engaged in regulating everything connected with the debts, and a variety of other business had to be settled. The general assignment of land to the plebeians must be regarded as the cause of the rebuilding of the city. We shall not easily find so speedy a recovery in history, for Rome appears regenerated, although almost every year is marked by wars: a part of the debts remained, and the law of *nexum* was not abolished, but it became less and less oppressive. The changes produced by the Licinian laws must have been much more extensive than we are aware, and the chest of the patricians now probably became the common treasury of the republic. The time was outwardly one of tranquillity, the Latins, separated from Rome, lived in peace, and none but isolated towns, such as Tibur and Praeneste were hostile, and that more from mistrust than from any other special reason. The Tarquinians were the only enemies that really threatened Rome. In the year A.U. 393, thirty years after the first invasion, however, there appeared a new enemy at a distance, the Senonian Gauls. Whatever is said of an earlier appearance of the Gauls is contradicted by Polybius, who mentions all their expeditions, and calls this one the first subsequent to the destruction of Rome. It appears that after that event the Gauls marched into Apulia, and there concluded a treaty with Dionysius of Syracuse; after plundering the country they returned to their own homes, the modern Romagna and

Urbino. But a new host came across the Alps and advanced as far as the Anio. We must not suppose those Gauls to have been very warlike when they had the means of a peaceable existence. On the Anio, Manlius Torquatus is said to have fought in single combat with a Gaul and to have taken from him a golden chain: this seems to be historically established, and we have no reason to consider it as a fable; a great battle was not fought there, and the Romans though prepared were now on the alert and cautious. The Gauls then fixed themselves in those parts, took possession of the Alban mount and the hills of Latium, and sallying thence laid waste the Latin territory; they advanced beyond Tivoli[2] into Campania, nay, according to one account, even as far as Apulia; they must consequently have subdued the Samnites, and have marched through their long and narrow territory, as the Romans did afterwards.

These occurrences, like the Volscian war a hundred years before, were followed by consequences which were highly advantageous for Rome. The Romans themselves, as well as the Latins and Hernicans, arrived at the conviction that by separation they were exposing themselves to great danger. There was no hostility between the Romans and Latins, but between the Romans and Hernicans there was an open war, in which the Romans may have taken the strong town of Ferentinum: the war ended in a restoration of the ancient relation. The statement that the Hernicans surrendered, is false, for even half a century later they continued to receive one third of the booty, or a compensation in money until C. Marcius subdued them. The Latins and Hernicans united with Rome, and a new state was formed, as Livy relates in two passages[3] without recognizing the connection. There is every appearance that the Latins did not yet form a compact state: it was impossible for them to recover the position which they had formerly occupied, since a great many of their towns had been destroyed by the Aequians and Volscians or by the

---

[2] In the neighbourhood of Tivoli, I have discovered traces of several towns which are not generally known, and which may have been destroyed at that time. They are built upon hills in the form of squares and exhibit no traces of having been surrounded by walls. They shew how small were the towns, which were then scattered over Italy; they may have contained about fifty houses.—N.

[3] Probably vii. 12 and viii. 6 and 8; but there are also some other passages in which this is alluded to.—Ed.

Gauls. But the Volscians, their former enemies, were now likewise broken up into several states; the Antiatans seem to have stood by themselves, while other Volscian towns united themselves with Latium; they felt an urgent need of joining some other state, as they were hard pressed by the Samnites who were making conquests on the Upper Liris, had taken Fregellae, and remained in the possession of Casinum. Thus a new Latin confederacy was formed, which was joined by the Latin colonies and a part of the Volscians, for the Romans seem to have renounced all claims to supremacy over the Latin colonies; and Sutrium and Nepet on the left bank of the Tiber likewise joined the Latin league. Forty-seven tribes, it is said, took part in the sacrifice on the Alban mount: a statement which must be referred to this time when Latium stood by the side of Rome as a powerful state. Another portion of the Volscians was admitted to the Roman franchise, apparently to form a counterpoise to Latium, for two new tribes, situated on the Volscian frontier were formed, just as in the treaty of Spurius Cassius, the Latins had ceded to the Romans the Crustuminian territory. The year A.U. 397 is thus remarkable for the restoration of the ancient relation between Rome, Latium, and the Hernicans. Festus, in the article *Praetor ad portam*, which is derived from Cincius, speaks as if the Romans had always been in an equal alliance with the Latins ever since the fall of Alba. This is correct in regard to the periods from the peace of Sp. Cassius down to the year A.U. 290, and from A.U. 397 down to the consulship of Decius Mus, but the intervening period is overlooked. Cincius undoubtedly had the correct statement, but was probably misunderstood by Verrius Flaccus. The different times must here be very carefully distinguished; I myself have been in error for many a year in regard to this point.[4] A Roman and a Latin imperator had in alternate years the command of the united armies, he offered the sacrifice on the Capitol at Rome, and was saluted at the gate of the city.

[4] The triumph on the Alban mount which is first mentioned in the case of Papirius Maso, after the first Punic war, is commonly regarded as an arbitrary act of the generals, to whom the triumph at Rome was refused: but it assuredly was a recollection of the ancient usage, according to which the Latin commander triumphed on the Alban mount, and the Roman commander at Rome. At the time when there were no Latin generals, the imperator as general of the allies assumed the triumph on the Alban Mount, when the honour was refused to him at Rome.—N.

The new alliance of the three states undoubtedly arose from a fear of the Gauls who were very near, though they did not appear on the Tiber that year. It would be of no advantage to relate here the details of the war, you may read it in Livy, whose work you cannot study too much, both as scholars and as men who seek and love that which is beautiful. His faults, which we cannot deny, are like the faults of a bosom friend which we must know but towards which we ought not to be unjust, and which ought not to disturb our feelings. It was a fearful time for the Romans; the struggle with the Gauls continued till A.U. 406 and 407; and Latium and Campania more particularly were for thirteen or fourteen years continually ravaged by the barbarians. On one occasion they appeared at the Colline gate: the Romans successfully resisted them, or the fight remained at least undecided; it was the same spot where afterwards Sulla defeated the Samnites, and is now within the city. It is a continuation of the Quirinal hill which slopes downwards; on the left side there is a deep valley, and where the Quirinal comes down to the plain, other hills again arise, over which run the walls of the city: it was undoubtedly on these latter hills that the Gauls and Samnites were encamped. Whoever of you has the happiness to visit Rome may heighten it by making himself acquainted with these localities.

One of the changes which were brought about by this new alliance with the Latins, is expressly mentioned by Livy, and was, that New Latium was governed by two *praetors*, whereas Ancient Latium had been governed by a dictator, as we know from Cato (in Priscian). An alliance between the Romans and Samnites, which is likewise mentioned by Livy, belongs either to this or to a somewhat later time. We may indeed suspect that such connections existed between the Samnites and Romans even at an earlier period; but we cannot assert it with certainty, in consequence of the vagueness of a statement in Festus in the article *Numerius*. According to this passage, one of the Fabii, who after the battle on the Cremera was sent as a hostage to the Gauls, married the daughter of a Samnite of Beneventum. Now the connubium could not have existed without treaties. It is, however, possible, that this relation existed only between the Sabines and Romans, and that the former transferred it to their Samnite colonies. There may have been two motives for forming such an alliance. If fear of the Gauls led to it, it must have been concluded between the second and the third expedition of the Gauls, that is, between the one to the Anio and the one to the Alban mount; but according to a very probable conjecture, the alliance may have been the consequence of a jealousy of the power of Latium; for the latter country, by the addition of Volscians and Aequians, had become so powerful, that Rome had reason to be jealous. The Latins were in close contact with the Samnites on their frontier, and the latter were endeavouring to make conquests on the Upper Liris. Hence an alliance between Romans and Samnites was very natural: Rome and Latium were allied indeed, but without trusting each other. It is not necessary, however, to regard such a connection as a defensive alliance, of which, in fact, it bears no appearance whatever. It was a treaty rather than an alliance; and we must especially remember, that such treaties in antiquity usually contained an honest clause, fixing a line up to which each party was to be allowed to make conquests. Such was the treaty of Rome with Carthage, that of the Carthaginians under Hasdrubal in Spain, and that of the Romans with the Aetolians. The moral reflections with which the division of the new world made by pope Alexander VI. between Spain and Portugal has been censured, are idle declamations; for this division was nothing else than the fixing of limits to conquests which each party might make. In like manner, a boundary was fixed in the first real peace between the Romans and Samnites, and the fact of the limit not being determined with sufficient distinctness, gave rise to the second war.

Notwithstanding the general peace with the Latins, the Tiburtines acted in a hostile manner towards Rome. They seem to have formed an independent state, and took Gallic armies into their pay. A war with the Tarquinians led the Romans into Etruria along the sea coast. It was carried on with great exasperation. The Etruscans penetrated to the neighbourhood of Rome, but the plebeian consul, C. Marcius, completely defeated them, and compelled them to conclude a long truce.

The internal distress continued in consequence of the magnitude of the debts. One commission was appointed after another, terms were fixed, and the state had again to interfere.

The republic, which was now in the receipt of the tithes from the domain land, was so wealthy that it was in a condition to make some general regulation. The debts were examined by a commission, and all those who were involved, but could give security, received advances from the public treasury to pay their debts, a wise measure; for by paying back the capital the rate of interest was brought down, money accumulated greatly, and people were obliged to make the best use of it they could. On the other hand, it was determined that whoever had property should not be compelled to sell it, which would have lowered the price of land, but that he should be allowed to give up his property for the debt according to a fair valuation. In consequence of this measure the price of land necessarily rose, and the rate of interest again fell: the financial calculation was extremely wise and subtle. It produced permanent and excellent results, although fresh misfortunes were soon followed by fresh distress. Whenever the calamities of a period arise from extraordinary events, even the wisest ruler cannot prevent the pressure and misery that flow from it. The misfortune to which I allude is the third Gallic expedition in the year A.U. 405, which was far more formidable to Rome than the second. The Gauls appeared at the gates of the city, but the Romans did not dare to offer them battle. Their tactics were now greatly developed, yet they were wise enough to confine themselves to the defence of the city, although their territory was laid waste in consequence. The Gauls remained in Latium for a long time, and even during the winter. If we may believe the accounts of the Romans, the Gauls were in a situation similar to that of the Ostro-Goths under Radagasius, whom Stilicho confined among the Apennines[5], not far from Fiesole. They are said to have withdrawn to the Alban hills, that is to Monte Cavo. It is indeed possible, but highly improbable, that they should of their own accord have gone to snow-covered hills. It is clear that L. Furius Camillus, a nephew, not a son of the great Camillus, marched out against the Gauls, and distinguished himself as a general. He was indeed

---

[5] Even now the name given by the peasants to these mountains refers to that Gothic period.—N. (Monte Sasso di *Castro*, above Mugello, is the mountain to the name of which Niebuhr here refers, according to a conjecture of the Editor of the third volume of the Roman history, p.79, n.144.)

an obstinate patrician, who violated the peace between the two orders; but he was nevertheless *bono publico natus.* We see that the Romans and Latins together sent a great army into the field. They formed ten legions, a number which could not have been furnished by the Romans alone. The campaign against the barbarians was conducted with great skill, for the Romans did not fight a battle, but threw them into extreme distress by means of entrenchments. The statement of a grammarian that the Gauls concluded a treaty with the Romans must probably be referred to this time. They were allowed to depart, and having spread over Campania and plundered it, they proceeded farther south.

Many important changes took place in the beginning of the fifth century. We find it mentioned as early as the year A.U. 397, that the tribes declared war. This right at first belonged to the curies, afterwards to the centuries, and now to the tribes. It was natural, that as the vital power of the state increased, the old customs should be set aside: as, for example, to stop the proceedings of the assembly in consequence of lightning, or because a bird of ill-omen flew by, and the like. Such things had hitherto prevented an army being formed, or any resolution whatever being passed by the centuries; and it was reasonable to transfer the declaration of war, and other important matters, to the assembly of the tribes, an institution which from the beginning had been conceived in a purely practical sense, and adapted to the actual wants of the community.

LECTURE XXXVI.

THE extension of the rights of the plebeians is connected with the name of C. Marcius Rutilus, the first plebeian censor and dictator: he preserved the peace between the two estates; and in his case we perceive a change in the mode of electing a dictator which is alluded to by Zonaras, but entirely overlooked by Livy. Up to this time the dictator had always been elected by the patricians, that is, they elected one from among those candidates who were proposed, as is expressly attested by a passage in Livy: the last dictator elected by the curies was Sulpicius, for otherwise there would have been no reason to make particular mention of it. Livy merely copied thoughtlessly: he has many such statements, which seem superfluous, unless we know from other sources how to account for them. Three years later, we find a plebeian dictator whom the curies would never have sanctioned. The change consisted in this: the senate only determined that a dictator should be appointed, and the consul named him. This is also implied in the statement of Dionysius, which he applies to an earlier period, that the appointment of the dictator was for a time left to the discretion of the consul: I have sufficiently explained this subject in the first volume of the new edition of my Roman History. Thus in proportion as the curies lost power, the senate gradually acquired an influence which it had not formerly possessed. The traces of the very violent commotions, which took place at that time, are much obscured, but a mention of them is preserved in Cicero, who relates that Popilius Laenas, in his consulship, quelled a sedition of the plebes, whence he received a surname. I place this consulship immediately before the election of the plebeian dictator. In the year A.U. 400 the patricians succeeded in setting the Licinian law at defiance and continued to do so for a few years. Another great change took place, by which the appointment of a number of tribunes of the soldiers was assigned to the tribes.

In regard to Etruria, it is related that in consequence of a truce the town of Caere was obliged to give up a portion of its territory; a war therefore must have taken place with Caere, which had never happened before; this war is commonly much declaimed against as being ungrateful on the part of Rome, since during the Gallic war, Caere had protected the sacred treasures of the Romans: but we know nothing certain about it.

We have now come to the time when, as Livy says, *majora hinc bella narranda sunt*, for large masses meet each other in the field, and Rome has to fight with a great people which showed an heroic perseverance, possessed great generals and excellent armour (which the Romans themselves adopted from them), and had all the political virtues calculated to render a nation illustrious in the history of the world. The struggle for life

and death lasted for seventy years, and was interrupted only by
treaties of peace or rather by truces. The Samnites show how
much may be gained by a nation for its descendants by heroic
perseverance, even when in the end it succumbs; for the lot of
the Samnites was always more bearable than that of many other
nations which were subdued by Rome. Had their descendants
limited their wishes according to their actual circumstances,
had they not aimed, though with great heroism, at impossibilities, and not given themselves up to antiquated feelings, they
would not have perished, no not even under Sulla. At that
time their fate was fearful; but only because they had ceased
to take their own circumstances into consideration.

The great event which marks the transition of Rome from
the age of boyhood to that of youth, was the taking of Capua
under its protection; but the account of this event is very obscure, and has moreover been falsified by the Romans themselves.

When in antiquity we hear of a colony committing acts of
hostility against the mother country, we always think of rebellion and ingratitude: the ancients themselves, that is, our
authors, see in such an insurrection the strife of a daughter
against her mother. In some cases indeed this view is correct,
but in most of them, especially in the history of Italy, the
relation is quite different. We must remember how colonies
arose, how a portion of the territory was set apart for and
assigned to the colonists, the remainder being left to the
ancient inhabitants, and how the colonists then became either
the representatives of the ruling state, or, if they emancipated
themselves, an independent sovereign power. The Romans
always connected their colonies closely with themselves, and
the same appears to have been done by the Latins. The Greek
colonies have scarcely any resemblance to them in this respect.
The Greeks mostly sent their colonies into desert districts,
where they built new towns into which they afterwards sometimes admitted pale-burghers and aliens; but they remained
quite foreign to the nations among whom they settled, as was
the case in Libya, on the Black Sea, in Asia Minor, Thrace,
Gaul and Spain. It was only the Pelasgian nations in Italy
and Sicily that were akin to them, and hence the rapid growth
of the Greek colonies in those countries. The cause of sending out a colony was usually of a political nature; it generally

consisted of political malcontents or of the surplus of an over-populous place, and soon emancipated itself, retaining towards the mother-city only the duties of respect. The Roman colonies, on the other hand, were always in *patria potestate*, and were bound to perform certain duties.

The system of the Samnites, and perhaps of all the Sabine states, was different. As they had a quite different religion, different fundamental forms of division, and different armour, so they had a different law in regard to their colonies also. Strabo mentions the tradition of the Samnites respecting their origin; they were descended from the Sabines, and found Oscans in the country which they conquered. That whole country was inhabited by Oscans, while the coast was occupied by the Pelasgians who at one time, we know not when, spread over the midland district also. At first the Pelasgians probably dwelt from the Tiber as far as mount Garganus, but the Oscans, being pressed upon by the Sabines spread from the mountains of Abruzzo over those districts, which the Sabines, the ancestors of the Samnites, subsequently occupied, and penetrated to the southernmost parts of Italy, destroying in their progress the original population. Their colonization, therefore, was undertaken, not like that of the Romans, with a view to establish their dominion, but in consequence of a superabundance and fulness of life, whence we nowhere find any trace of a connection between the Sabine colonies and the mother-people. Thus it is with the Picentians, the Marsians, Marrucinians, Pelignians, Vestinians, and also with the Samnites. The last-mentioned people consisted of four tribes which formed a confederacy, the Pentrians, Caudines, Hirpinians, and probably the Frentanians. The Frentanians were afterwards separated from the rest, and in their stead another canton, probably the Alfaterians, between Surrentum and the Silarus, was admitted into the confederacy. From the Samnites, again, other tribes issued, as the Lucanians; and out of a mixture of the Lucanians with Oscan and Sabellian adventurers and freedmen, there arose the Bruttians. When the Sabines had established themselves in the middle valley of the Vulturnus, they extended into Campania also, the most highly favoured country of Italy; an Etruscan colony had existed there ever since the year A.U. 280. The earliest inhabitants of that country were undoubtedly Tyrrhenians, whence the origin of

Capua like that of Rome was referred to the Trojans; the
Tyrrhenians were subdued by the Oscans, and the latter again
by the Etruscans: under the latter, Capua is said to have been
called Vulturnum. The Oscan population must have been
very numerous, for it gave a different character to the whole
nation. But the greatness of the Etruscans lasted only a short
time, for on the Tiber they were declining as early as the year
A.U. 320, and consequently in Campania even much earlier.
Now it is not surprising that Capua, a mere settlement of an
oligarchic nation, could not maintain itself against a conquering people, as the subdued Oscans were not very zealous in the
defence of their masters. The Etruscans in Capua, therefore,
made an agreement, by which they admitted a Samnite colony,
the epoeci of their enemies, — a foolish arrangement which we
meet with very often in ancient history: in this manner the
Amphipolitans admitted the Chalcidians, and the latter afterwards expelled the ancient Athenian colony: many similar
examples are mentioned by Aristotle. Such towns, in which
the ruling body of citizens consisted of different nations,
rarely had the good fortune enjoyed by Rome, that their
separate elements became equalized. The Samnites conspired
against the Etruscans, and shortly afterwards, with a faithless-
ness and cruelty peculiar to all the Sabellian and Oscan nations,
murdered them and kept the town for themselves. Three
years later the Samnites spread as far as Cumae, and conquered
that city which had long been the most illustrious place in
Italy. The ruling population at Capua accordingly consisted
at first of Etruscans, and afterwards of Samnites, but with a
very numerous Oscan commonalty; for according to this
system of colonization, a branch of the conquering nation
received the sovereignty in the colony, one portion of the
ancient inhabitants in the towns became clients, and the others
remained free; whereas in the country, the population were
made serfs as in the conquests of the Franks and Longobards.
The relation of the Spanish colonies in Mexico likewise is of
a similar nature; for there too the ancient population has remained. Such was the condition of Capua. We are now
told in Roman history, that the Campanians requested succour
from the Romans and Latins against the Samnites; but how
could this colony have fallen out with the mother people?
This can be explained only in the following manner. The

commonalty, consisting of Oscans who were kept in a state of dependence by the Samnites, gained strength and increased: and while the Roman plebes gradually became united with the patricians, the commonalty of Capua broke out in open rebellion and crushed the Samnite patricians. This was the cause of the enmity between Capua and Samnium, but the Samnites at Capua do not appear to have been annihilated, but only to have lost the government: they are the Campanian equites mentioned by Livy, to whom the Roman citizens paid an annual tax, either as a compensation for the *ager Falernus*, or as a reward for their fidelity to Rome. The Romans were fond of keeping dependent people under an oligarchical government.

The Samnites at that time extended from the Adriatic to the Lower Sea. No ancient author describes their constitution, and it is only from analogy and a consideration of particular circumstances that we can form the following probable conclusions. They consisted of four cantons, which constituted a confederacy, perhaps with subjects and allied places; and there is every appearance that all four stood on a footing of perfect equality. Each of these cantons was sovereign, but united with the others by a league which was to last for ever; in what manner the administration of the confederacy was managed we know not. The weakness of the Samnites, in comparison with the Romans, arose from the fact of their not forming a single compact state, as the Romans did from the time when the Latins came under their supremacy. It was only in times of war that they united, though they must have had a permanent congress; its nature, however, is entirely unknown. Livy never mentions a senate of the Samnites; but Dionysius in his fragments speaks of their πρόβουλοι. They were probably the envoys of each tribe, perhaps similar to the ἀπόκλητοί of the Aetolians; but whether these envoys had the right to decide upon peace and war, or whether a popular assembly met for that purpose, as in the states of Greece, is uncertain; if, however, the latter was the case, each tribe had a vote, for in voting the ancients never paid any regard to the accidental number of individuals[1] belonging to a tribe.

[1] This observation removes the difficulty, which would otherwise arise, in explaining how the majority could decide a point in an assembly in which only

Latium received non-Latins into its confederacy; and in like manner Rome formed two new tribes out of the allied Volscians who lived near the Pontine marshes. At that time, therefore, Rome and Latium still acted in concord, each admitting a portion of the Volscians into its own confederacy and keeping the Hernicans apart. Now the relation existing among the Samnites was similar to that between Rome, Latium and the Hernicans, who were united, without any one of them having the supremacy, and had their common meetings; each of the Samnite peoples was sovereign, and united with the others only in regard to foreign countries. Nations which are threatened with destruction from without, scarcely ever rise to the healthy view that they must sacrifice the wishes of their separate elements in order to preserve their nationality: the people of Greece joining the Achaean league is the only instance of the true policy. At first the Romans and Samnites fought under equal circumstances, but the Samnites never saw the fundamental error of their constitution. I have not the least doubt, that if they had reformed their constitution, and had instituted one senate and a popular assembly, the whole war would have taken a different turn. But as it was, the supreme command belonged to different cantons at different times; sometimes a measure was carried by Bovianum, sometimes by the Pentrians, and sometimes by the Caudines: now one people was attacked, then another; the chief command passed from one people to another, and was probably given to the canton which was most threatened at the time, in order that it might be able to protect itself. The supreme magistrate of the confederacy bore the title of *Embratur* (*Imperator*), which is often mentioned in inscriptions. It is probable that each canton also had its *imperator*, and that when a tribe had the chief command, its imperator became the *imperator* or perhaps *praetor*, of the whole army. There is every appearance that their constitutions were thoroughly democratical, as might be expected among such mountaineers. They must have been

---

those persons voted who chanced to be present. Let us apply this to Rome: how was it that those who belonged to the very distant *tribus Velina* did not feel themselves wronged in comparison with the *Palatina*? The difficulty is removed, if we remember that each tribe had only one vote, so that on important emergencies the distant tribes sent their best men to the city, whereby the government became a representative one.—N.

completely amalgamated with the ancient population, since, even after the most fearful defeats, they always appear in large numbers and perfect harmony.

The extension of the Samnites towards the Liris was the circumstance which in A.U. 412 involved them in a war with the Romans. The Volscians were of no consequence: their power was broken, and they were for the most part allied or united with the Latins. The sway of the Samnites extended as far as Casinum, and they had subdued the Volscians as far as Sora and Fregellae, though sometimes they evacuated those districts. But they had also spread as far as Apulia, and conquered a great part of that country, as for instance, Luceria. We thus see that they were a nation greater than the Romans and Latins put together, and that their country was equal in extent to half of the modern Switzerland. I have already mentioned their alliance or treaty with Rome at the beginning of the fifth century; but unfortunately such treaties are observed only so long as ambition and the love of conquest are not much excited. I have no doubt that the two nations had agreed not to extend their power beyond the Liris; but the Romans may have repented that they had fixed such narrow boundaries for themselves. Had the Samnites taken Teanum, they would have been masters of all the districts between the rivers, and have subdued the country as far as the Liris. Livy himself admits that the Romans had no right to form an alliance with the Campanians.

It is said that the Campanians became involved in war with the Samnites, because the latter attacked the Sidicines of Teanum[2]: the Sidicines probably belonged to the same race as the Oscans; they inhabited Teanum, but were perhaps not confined to that town. They first applied to the Campanians, because the latter were no longer the allies of the Samnites, and because the Campanian plebes could not but consider it an advantage to gain the Sidicines as a protection against the Samnites in the north. Capua ruled over a number of towns all of which are said to have been Etruscan, though this is improbable; the territory over which its dominion extended

---

[2] The war between the Samnites and Sidicines shows that the dominion of the Samnites then extended as far as the upper Liris, so that its boundary in D'Anville is too narrow.—N.

was called Campania[3] which was not the designation of the
country which bears that name in our maps: it extended only
a little beyond the Vulturnus as far as Casilinum, in the south,
and Calatia and Saticula in the north; Nola, Neapolis, Pompeii, and Herculaneum did not belong to it; the territory
therefore was small, and the name denotes only the domain of
the citizens of Capua. In consequence of the fertility of their
country, the Campanians were wealthy and unwarlike; they
were anxious to prevent the attack of the Samnites, but being
unable to resist the mountaineers they were defeated. The
Samnites proceed to Mount Tifata, above Capua, and laid waste
the country all around. It was the ancient Oscan population
of Capua that carried on the war in spite of the Samnite
colony: their distress was very great, and it is likely that the
Samnites contemplated restoring the oligarchical constitution
of the colony: under these circumstances, the Campanians
applied to Rome, or probably to the diet of the Romans,
Latins, and Hernicans. This is evident, from statements
derived from L. Cincius; in Livy we perceive the intentional
obscurity of the Roman tradition about it. The Romans
themselves would have been greatly perplexed by this proposal,
as they were allied by treaty with the Samnites; hence the
Campanians placed themselves under the protection of the
whole confederacy. This *deditio* must not be imagined to be
that of a conquered people; for here we merely have one
nation which seeks protection, and another which grants it.
In such things, the Romans were always hypocritical observers
of the letter of the law, though in reality they might act in
direct opposition to the spirit of the laws of Numa and Ancus;
the only good result of this feeling, was, that they always
wished to have at least the appearance of justice on their side.
We must not, however, on this account, consider the ancient
Roman *fides* as altogether hypocritical, since their reverence
for law certainly did keep them from many an act of oppression towards the weak. They may be excused by the consideration that according to all appearance the Samnites were
becoming too great; it could be foreseen that, after all, the
treaty would soon be violated, and hence they would not allow

[3] Campania is the country of the Campanians, that is, the inhabitants of
Capua. On coins we read *Capani*, and in Plautus we find *Campas* instead of
Campanus.—N.

a favorable opportunity to pass by. The Romans, however, were too much tempted by the prospect of gaining the Campanians and all the people of that country by forming a treaty of protection with Capua. There is no question that they were not impelled by a desire to protect those who were in want of aid; they were overpowered by an evil spirit, and the exasperation of the Samnites .against them was perfectly just. The Romans sent an embassy to the Samnites, requesting them to conclude peace with the Sidicines, and not to lay waste the Campanian territory because Campania had placed itself under their protection. The Samnites proudly rejected this proposal; and now arose their gigantic struggle against the Romans, Latins, and Hernicans.

This Samnite war is the first in Roman history that is worthy of being related; whatever deduction we may make from the numbers stated by Livy, — which we may do the more safely, as the person of whom these deeds are narrated is a Valerius, and Valerius Antiat was a client of that family — yet the difference between these battles, and the earlier ones is obvious. In the year A.U. 412, three battles were fought, the first great battles, excepting that of A. Postumius Tubertus, on Mount Algidus, that are recorded in Roman history.

In this year the Licinian law was violated for the last time: both consuls were patricians, A. Cornelius Cossus, of whom but little is known, and M. Valerius Corvus, a man in whose favour an exception might have been made at any time. He was, as Pliny justly remarks, one of the greatest and happiest men, and Solon himself would have admitted it. He is one of the historical heroes of Rome, although the story about the origin of his surname belongs to poetry (Livy himself does not consider it historical): but it proves, that even as late as that time the heroes of Rome were the themes of song. No one will believe that in A.U. 406, a Gaul challenged the boldest Roman to a single combat, and that Valerius, then only twenty-three years old, conquered him, a raven flying against the enemy, and pecking at and tearing his face, so as to render the victory easy for the youth. His first consulship falls in his twenty-third year, the one in which he had slain the Gaul: it is probable that forty-six years later he was raised to his sixth consulship: he lived to nearly the age of one hundred years, and saw the complete subjugation of Italy. At that time it was still a matter of frequent occurrence, that men, after their consulship, were invested with the other curule magistracies; to these Valerius was repeatedly elected down to his latest days, and discharged the duties of all with the full vigour of his mind. He is the man who may give his name to the century he lived in; he was the idol of his soldiers, being not only one of the greatest generals, but swaying the hearts of his soldiers by his amiable and brotherly manners, without ever losing his authority over them: the soldiers saw in him the ablest of their equals. If we imagine ourselves placed by the side of his death-bed, and look back upon his life, full of important events, we shall have before our minds' eye a gigantic period which we cannot picture to ourselves with too much distinctness.

Rome sent two consular armies, one-half consisting of Romans, and the other of Latins, into Campania, which on the side of Samnium was quite open. Nola was even a Samnite colony, and Neapolis was allied with them. The two armies appear in entirely different circumstances. That of M. Valerius was in Campania, beyond the Vulturnus, and acted evidently quite on the defensive. The army of Cornelius Cossus, on the other hand, was destined to make a diversion into Samnium, Capua undoubtedly being the basis of that operation, since he penetrated into Samnium to the north of the Vulturnus, by the common road from Calatia to Beneventum. We cannot obtain a clear view of the events of the war, and can judge of their course only by drawing inferences from isolated facts. We find Valerius on Mount Gaurus, probably near Nuceria, so that the Romans entered Samnium on that side for the purpose of protecting Campania. There was another Mount Gaurus, not far from Cumae and Cape Misenum. If the latter is meant, the Romans must have been pressed by the Samnites into that corner, and having the sea and the Vulturnus in their rear, their victory would have been the result of despair.[4] This would clearly show, that at first the Romans sustained losses which are passed over by Livy, or the annalists whom he followed; but,

---

[4] In his *Hist. of Rome*, III. p. 119, Niebuhr speaks with much more confidence in favour of the second view; but it must be observed that that passage, with the same words, occurs also in the first edition (1812), whereas the opinion

at all events, the battle restored the balance. It was obviously the greatest of all that had yet been fought by the Romans, for though previous battles may have been bloody, yet they were not carried on with perseverance. When the Gauls had fought for a few hours, and to no purpose, they gave up the battle; and the Aequians, Volscians, and Hernicans were few in number. The Samnites, on the other hand, were arrayed against the Romans in equal numbers, and possessed equal determination, and thus they fought the whole day till night-fall without any decisive result, until the Roman equites, the *principes juventutis* (the Samnites had no cavalry, and that of the Romans was weak), dismounted, placed themselves before the lines, and fought with true heroism. The real nobility of the nation put all the rest to shame, but the latter now followed their leaders and were irresistible. The massacre was immense on both sides; the Samnites yielded, but only retreated. It was not a flight, but just as at Grossgörschen and Bautzen; and the conquerors followed them with the greatest caution. In the neighbourhood of Suessula, only a few miles from the battle-field, the Samnites made a fresh stand. Their camp and the wounded, of course, fell into the hands of the Romans. The victory gave to the latter more hopes than real advantages; but the main point was, that the battle was a happy omen for the whole war, which they had certainly begun with the prospect of a possibility of their being in the end completely annihilated.

The expedition of A. Cornelius Cossus into Samnium undoubtedly belongs to the beginning of the campaign. He seems to have been met by a general rise of the militia of the Samnites, whose general custom it was to act on the offensive with the army, and to leave their country to the defence of the people: the invading Romans had mostly to do with the country people who rose in arms. Samnium was then in full vigour and strength; the Roman commander incautiously entered the hostile country, which was unknown to him and very difficult to pass with an army. No enemy opposing him, he crossed from west to east the chain of mountains which

expressed in our text, is that given by N. in his lectures of 1828-9. The detailed description of the battle, however, belonging to the year 1826, is based upon the explanation which he had given at an earlier period. We make this observation to prevent misconceptions. — ED.

runs from north to south. There were only a few passes: the
first column was already in the valley, while the rear was yet
on the ridge of the mountain — this is what we can gather
from the confused account of Livy. The consul's intention
probably was to reach the road to Beneventum and the fertile
valley of the Calore, in order to separate the northern from
the southern Samnites. When in this situation, he observed
that the opposite hill was occupied, he halted: to retreat
through the defile was very difficult, and the Samnites were
advancing to occupy a height commanding the road. The
Romans were almost surrounded, for the Samnites were
already engaged in taking possession of the road in their rear.
While the Romans were thus situated, the tribune, P. Decius
Mus, who belonged to one of the greatest plebeian families,
offered to the consul to hasten up the mountain with one
cohort, and to take possession of the height which the Samnites incautiously had just abandoned, so that he could attack
them in their rear, and sustain the shock of the enemy, until
the Roman army should reach the ridge of the mountain through
the pass. This plan was carried into effect. Decius reached
the height which commanded the pass, before the Samnites,
who were now obliged to try to dispossess him; but he there
fought with his men like the Spartans at Thermopylae, in the
conviction that they must die, and with such perseverance, that
the Samnites gave up the attack for that evening. While the
Romans retreated to the road which had been abandoned, the
Samnites encamped with the determination to storm the height
the next morning. The battalion of Decius, however, was
quite surrounded; but in the night he ventured to sally down
the hill, and forced his way through the enemy, and thus with
the survivors of his band he returned to the consul. It is stated,
indeed, that on the day following the Romans again won a
great victory, but we cannot trust the account. The army of
Cossus is not after this time mentioned : he had probably become aware of the perilous nature of his expedition, or he was
called into Campania, because some loss had been sustained
there. On Mount Gaurus, Valerius was alone, but at Suessula
we find the two consuls united: those enemies who followed
the march of Cossus joined the Samnites. Both were encamped
opposite each other for a long time, but the Samnites being
superior in numbers, considered their cause too safe. Their

commander cannot have been a man of much talent; they ranged over the country indulging in plunder, especially as Valerius in his fortified camp seemed to show symptoms of fear. When the Samnites were thus scattered, Valerius suddenly attacked their camp and took it; he then quickly turned against the separate corps and routed them one after another, so that both consuls gained a brilliant victory and were honoured with a triumph.

LECTURE XXXVII.

THE Romans now experienced that times may be bright and prosperous, although a heavy pressure is weighing upon the people. Ever since the Licinian law, the misery of the mass of the citizens continued uninterrupted, and ever and anon new commissions were appointed to liquidate the debts, but without any good result. The wars demanded very heavy taxes, and the plebeians were obliged to fight in the battles, and at the same time to provide for their families: we have reason to believe that not half the men capable of bearing arms remained at home; and so bloody a war as that against the Samnites must have caused severe sufferings to many a family. In the second year of the war, when either the Latins had the supreme command, or, perhaps, a truce existed between the Romans and Samnites, a mutiny arose which very nearly came to an insurrection. Livy is obscure on this subject, but an excerpt of Constantine from Appian, in which we distinctly recognise Dionysius, throws much light upon it. The insurrection of the year A.U. 413, was brought about by the state of the debtors; Livy conceals this, and relates, that, while the Roman army was encamped in Campania, probably in consequence of a truce, the soldiers were tempted to make themselves masters of Capua. The Roman consul who undertook the command and found the army engaged in a manifest conspiracy, endeavoured to get rid of the ringleaders by sending them one by one in different directions, and then ordering each to be arrested. This mode of acting however excited their suspicions, and one cohort which was sent to Rome halted near Lautulae, between Terracina and Fundi, four or five miles from the former, in a desolate district between the hills and the sea, which was at all times the haunt of robbers and banditti. The hills there approach the sea almost as near as at Thermopylae, though they are not so steep: it is quite a narrow pass by which Latium and Campania are connected. There seem to have been warm springs in this place, so that even in the name there is a resemblance between it and Thermopylae. The country is now desolate, and when I was at Terracina I forgot to enquire for the springs, in consequense of which I was not able to find them. In the second Samnite war a battle was fought near Lautulae, which is one of the greatest battles recorded in history. When the cohort reached that place, it revolted and was joined by a number of others; the communication between Rome and the head quarters of the army was cut off; the messengers of the consuls were intercepted, and we must suppose that the whole army refused to obey its commanders. A number of persons who were enslaved for debt attached themselves to the insurgents, and what now happened was more terrible than any thing which Rome had yet experienced, for the insurrection became general, and the common people marched against the city in arms, though they did not injure the consul. This multitude was no longer the plebes of the Sacred Mount: it was an insurrection of the proletarians against the rich, and very like a revolt of the workmen in a factory against their employers. But fortunately for Rome, they were not yet quite impoverished: they still looked upon themselves as plebeians, and upon the most distinguished among the plebeians as their leaders, so that the latter might make use of them in reforming the constitution. It is surprising to find that they fetched T. Quinctius, a lame and aged patrician, from his estate in the territory of Alba, and made him their captain, just as the peasants in the peasant-war of Germany made Götz their leader: they then advanced towards the city which was thrown into great alarm by the approaching danger. The government no longer knew in whom to trust: everybody in the city armed himself as well as he could; but the civic legions would scarcely have been able to maintain themselves against the army. The heart of Valerius Corvus was bleeding at the prospect of a civil war; the plebs too was fortunately not quite demoralised; and he made an offer of reconciliation. The army likewise was moved; when they saw their relations armed in the city, they raised loud lamentations and were willing to listen to proposals of peace: both parties were loth to shed the blood of their brethren. The consequence of this moderation on both sides was a reconciliation, and a peace was concluded in which, according to Appian, that is, Dionysius, the debts were cancelled.

The cause of the insurrection, as it is described in this account, is in the highest degree improbable; the sending away of individuals could surely have lasted only a very short time, and it is quite inconceivable that a whole cohort should have been thus disposed of. The other account does not speak at all of an insurrection of the soldiers, nor of their intention to take Capua, but represents it as an internal commotion, as a secession, like those of the commonalty in former times, and as having arisen out of the distress of the numerous debtors, and the disputes between the patricians and plebeians, since the Licinian law had ceased to be observed. The plebeians seceded to the neighbourhood of Alba, where they were joined by cohorts from the army. The senate, it is said, levied troops, but there is no mention of the two armies having met, nor of the appointment of Valerius to the dictatorship of which Livy speaks: when matters had proceeded so far as to call for the interference of the sword, both parties determined to put a stop to the dispute at any cost.

These occurrences were followed by a great and essentially civic legislation, by which that of Licinius was completed. Whatever may have been the real history of this commotion, it must, at all events, have been more important than Livy's description would lead us to suppose. Up to that time the Licinian law respecting the consulship had been violated seven times in the course of thirteen years; but henceforward we hear of no more actual violations, although some absurd attempts still continued to be made. During that commotion some regulation must have been made which rendered it impossible for any attempts against the Licinian law to succeed; and clauses must have been added, perhaps as severe as those in the lex Valeria Horatia, by which the heaviest penalties were inflicted on him who should disturb the election of the tribunes of the people. It is, moreover, said to have been determined that both consuls might be elected from among the plebeians, but this seems to be a misunderstanding, and it can at any rate be proved that no such regulation was carried into effect. In the Hannibalian war, a special resolution was once passed that during the war both consuls might be elected from among the plebeians, but no practical application of this resolution was made, and it was not till the year A.U. 500, that the natural principle gained the upper hand; the patrician nobility had then become so insignificant, that it was impossible any longer to abide by the law of Licinius.

Another regulation mentioned by Livy is of great importance, and shews that the question was no longer merely about the difference between the two estates, but that the plebeian nobles had begun to have recourse to the oligarchical intrigues, which until then had been employed by the patricians alone, a proof that the one set of men was not better than the other. The law in question established two points, first that no one should hold two curule offices at the same time, and secondly that a person invested with a curule office should not be re-eligible to it till the expiration of ten years. The first provision could affect only the patricians in regard to the praetorship, and was probably made because it had often happened that a patrician consul had at the same time caused himself to be elected praetor, in order to obtain an influence over his colleague; in regard to the aedileship, it may have affected the plebeians also in alternate years. Livy says that the law was mainly directed against the *ambitio novorum hominum;* the second provision of the law had probably been brought about by the plebeians themselves, as a security against the overwhelming influence of members of their own order, for up to that time we always find the same plebeian names in the consulship, such as Popilius Laenas, C. Marcius, C. Poetelius, so that it was intended to prevent the exclusive lustre of a few plebeian families.

Livy was aware of the existence of two laws respecting military affairs which arose out of this insurrection. The first enacted that whoever had once been a tribune of the soldiers should not afterwards be made a centurion: it is said, that this law was enacted through the agency of a certain Salonius who had been thus degraded by his enemies. The consuls had it in their power to appoint the centurions: when a person had

been tribune, it was contrary to the feeling of the soldiers
that he should become a centurion, because a centurion was
only a subaltern officer. Six of the tribunes were annually
appointed by the tribes, and the rest by the consuls, but a
person could not be elected for two successive years by the
same authorities. During the year in which he could not be
tribune, he would be free from military service. Now Salonius
who had been tribune, and in that capacity seems to have been
in opposition to the consuls was appointed centurion by them:
the consuls thus degraded him while he was raised by public
opinion, and it was against such proceedings that the law was
directed. The regulations about the corps of officers are among
the most excellent adopted by the Romans. Slow and gradual
advancement and a provision for officers in their old age were
things unknown to the Romans. No one could by law have a
permanent appointment; every one had to give evidence of his
ability; the idea of a gradual rising from the ranks and of a
standing corps of officers was never entertained: a tribune of
the soldiers was elected for one year only, and if he shewed no
skill he was not re-elected; but he who was fit was elected
year after year, sometimes by the people, sometimes by the
consuls. It was, moreover, not necessary to pass through a
long series of subordinate offices; a young Roman noble served
as eques, and the consul had in his cohort the most distinguished to act as his staff; there they learned enough, and in
a few years a young man, in the full vigour of life, might
become a tribune of the soldiers. But besides this, due attention was paid to that respectable class of people who without
talent for higher posts were well fitted to train the soldiers.
Such persons became centurions, who may be compared to our
sergeants; all of them were people of common descent, they
had good pay and a respectable position, and in special cases
where a man shewed particular ability he might become
tribune. All the functions which, in modern armies, are
performed by a large number of subaltern officers, might just
as well be performed by an able sergeant. The military regulations of the Romans in all these points, are as admirable as
those concerning the training of the individual soldier.

The second law shews how Livy confounds everything: the
pay of the equites is said to have been diminished because
they had taken no part in the insurrection. If the mutineers

could have carried such a law, the state would have been lost.
I believe that this was the time when the equites ceased to
receive their 2000 asses from widows and orphans, and when
it was established that they should have a fixed pay,—a fair
change, but a disadvantage to the *eques publicus;* fair, I say,
because the state was able to bear the expense.

The curies, assembled in the Petelinian grove, now decreed
a full amnesty for all that occurred, and no one was to be
upbraided, either in joke or in earnest for his conduct. Livy
considers it to have been a decree of the centuries, *auctoribus
patribus,* but from the trial of Manlius it is clear, that only the
curies assembled in the Petelinian grove.

Hereupon the Romans concluded peace with the Samnites:
even the year before, they had received from them a compensation for pay and provisions, or they received it now. The
peace was concluded by the Romans alone, and that with a bad
intention, for they had undertaken the war conjointly with
the Latins, whom they now left to shift for themselves. They
gave up Capua to the Samnites, and left the conquest of
Teanum to their choice, but the Sidicines threw themselves
into the arms of the Latins, and concluded a separate alliance
with the Volscians, Auruncans, and Campanians. Such things
have occurred in modern times also, as for example, the alliance
between Prussia and Russia under Frederick the Great, and
Peter the third, in the Seven Years' War. The Latins now
continued the war, *suo Marte,* which Livy, in accordance with
his peculiar views, regards as an act of injustice on their part,
as if they had thereby offended against the majesty of the
Roman people. They made war upon the Pelignians, from
which we see that the Aequians belonged to them, since otherwise they could not have come in contact with the Pelignians:
the latter allied themselves with the Samnites, and the Samnites
required the Romans either to act as mediators, or to give
them succour; for the peace with them had immediately been
followed by an alliance. The alliance of Rome with the Latins
and Hernicans had now come to a crisis; the Hernicans were
either neutral, or, as is more probable, were still allied with
the Romans, since Livy and the Capitoline Fasti do not mention
them among those who triumphed over Maenius. Such confederacies may exist among nations, none of which is as
ambitious and powerful as Rome then was: but now three

things were possible; they might either separate and remain friends, or form a union like that of Great Britain and Ireland, or lastly, decide by force of arms which was the strongest; for to continue together, side by side, was impossible. Even the year before, the war had not been carried on in common, and the Latins had gone into the field under their own banners. Hence it was now resolved to negotiate. The Latins had a more solid constitution than the Samnites, and were governed like the Romans; they had two praetors as the Romans had two consuls; and they must have had a senate, since there is mention of the *decem primi*, who were evidently the deputies of so many towns. These *decem primi* went to Rome, and there made the very fair proposal that the two states should unite. The senate was to be raised from 300 to 600; the popular assembly was to be increased (so that it would probably have been necessary to increase the twenty-seven Roman tribes to thirty, and to allow the Latin towns to vote as so many tribes), Rome was to be the seat of the government; and every year one of the consuls was to be a Roman, and the other a Latin. Had the Romans accepted this proposal, Rome and Latium would in reality have become equal; but every Roman would have felt his own influence weakened. A Latin consul was repugnant to the Romans; for in all republics, however democratical they may be, there is a spirit of exclusiveness, of which we have a striking example in the history of Geneva, where we find *citoyens*, *bourgeois*, *natifs*, that is, the children of the metoeci or *habitans*, and lastly *habitans*, all of which classes acquired the franchise one after another. The canton of Uri is the most oligarchical of all. The plebeians as well as the patricians were indignant at the proposal; as there was to be only one Roman consul, the question would have arisen, is he to be a patrician or a plebeian? they would more easily have adopted a proposal to have four consuls. The embassy of the Latins, as Livy says, was received with general indignation, not because the Romans were ignorant that the impending struggle would be a contest for life and death, but because vanity and selfishness outweighed this consideration. It is related that the consul, T. Manlius, declared that he would cut down with his own hand the first Latin who should appear in the Roman senate. The story moreover has this poetical addition, that while the discussions were going on in the Capitol, there arose a tempest, accompanied by a heavy fall of rain, and that the Latin praetor, in descending the hundred steps of the Tarpeian rock, fell down, and was picked up a corpse; the unpoetical spirit of later narratives has changed his death into a fit of fainting.

The Sabines with their ancient reputation for justice had sunk into a torpor and had lost all importance; the northern confederacy of the Marsians, Pelignians, Marrucinians and Vestinians, brave as they were, had no other wish than to live quietly among their mountains. The Romans were allowed to march through their territory, and as they were allied with the Samnites, the latter expected that the Latin war would afford them an opportunity of taking Capua and Teanum. If the Romans had dreaded to allow their territory to be ravaged by the Latins, they would have been obliged to maintain themselves on the defensive, or to carry on tedious sieges of the Latin towns. But the Roman commanders here shewed their greatness : they formed a most masterly plan, made up their minds to the very boldest undertakings, called out the army of reserve in the city, and abandoned their territory up to the very gates of Rome to the Latins. Their army marched through the Sabine and Marsian territory, taking a circuitous route in order to join the Samnites, and in conjunction with them proceeded towards Capua. If the Latins had abandoned the Campanians to their fate, and had gone to meet the Romans on their march, in the country of the Aequians, they might perhaps have defeated them in those impassable districts. But a great general places his enemy where he wishes to have him : the daring boldness of the Romans is a proof of the excellence of their generals, Manlius and Decius, who, like all great generals, had formed a correct estimate of their enemies, and trusting to the accuracy of their estimate, ventured to lead their army by that circuitous road. Had the Latins moved rapidly, they might have laid waste the whole Roman territory, appeared at the gates of Rome eight days before the Roman army could have returned, and effected an easy retreat to their fortresses ; but the Roman generals probably knew that their enemies were timid and without great leaders, and therefore left the road to Rome unprotected. The Latins listened to the complaints of the Campanians, and perhaps imagined that the Roman army might be annihilated then at one blow, since it could not return. Their forces justified them in this expectation, and the decision of the contest hung upon a thread; for there was as much probability of their conquering as of being conquered. The Romans undoubtedly had enlisted all the men they could muster, but they were, notwithstanding, inferior to the Latins in numbers: it is quite certain that they were joined by the Samnites, though the Roman annals endeavoured to conceal that fact by stating that the Samnites did not arrive till after the battle. The Latins and their allies, the Volscians, Aequians, Sidicines, Campanians and Auruncans were encamped on the eastern side of Mount Vesuvius; it is uncertain, whether Veseris, where the battle was fought, is the name of a place or of a river. The two armies faced each other for a long time, dreading the day which was to decide their fate. If the Latins had had an able commander they might, even after a defeat, have been better off than the Romans, as they might have withdrawn to Capua, and protected themselves behind the Vulturnus and Liris, and there collected reinforcements from their own country. The Romans, moreover, in a military point of view were not superior to the Latins; one Roman and one Latin century had always formed a maniple in the Roman legion, so that the constitution of the two armies was the same. Under these circumstances, the consul forbade, under penalty of death, all skirmishes, on account of the importance of the moral impression that might thence result, trifling events easily producing a prejudice regarding the issue of a battle, and not on account of the acquaintance of the Roman soldiers with the enemy, as Livy states. In like manner, it was forbidden in the Russian army to accept the challenge of the Turkish spahis. The stricter the command was, the more did the Latin horsemen provoke the Romans[1], and this gave rise to the single combat between Geminius Metius of Tusculum and the son of the consul Manlius. This occurrence is beautifully described by Livy, with the heart of a Roman and the power of a poet: the father in order to enforce obedience ordered his unfortunate but heroic son to be put to death. There is yet another circumstance which Livy mentions but cursorily[2]: there can be no doubt that in the ancient tradition

---

[1] The Roman cavalry was always the worst part of the army, and inferior, for example, to that of the Ætolians.—N.

[2] VIII. 8; towards the end.—ED.

there was, besides Manlius, a centurion who gained the victory
for the *pedites*, as the son of the consul did for the *equites*.

The long time which passed away before the battle began is
a decided proof that the Samnites joined the Romans. Both
parties commenced the fight with sad forebodings; and the two
consuls, moreover, had had a vision prophesying a disastrous
issue by informing them that one army and the commander of
the other were forfeited to the gods of the dead: the two consuls therefore agreed that the commander of that wing[3], which
should first be in danger should devote himself to the infernal
gods. Each of them offered up a sacrifice: that of Decius was
unfavorable, but that of Manlius promised success. It is mentioned on this occasion, as on many others relating to sacrifices,
that the liver had no *caput:* the caput is the same thing as in
Italian is still called *capo*, that is, the part where the liver is
connected with the diaphragm; and the *caput* being wanting
means that there was no trace of the connection. The liver
presents the greatest varieties, even in animals which are perfectly healthy. The heart and lungs afford no means for forming prophecies, while the liver in almost every case has some
abnormity. Decius, then, went into battle with the intention
of sacrificing himself; but the resolution must have been made
even before he left Rome, since the pontifex accompanied him
for the purpose of dedicating him to the gods.

The Roman legion at that time consisted of five battalions,
hastati, principes, triarii, rorarii and *accensi.* Among them
were three battalions of the line, mixed with light-armed troops,
and one battalion of light troops, the *rorarii* with one third of
the *hastati.* Nearly two thirds of the *hastati* had, from the
earliest times, been armed with lances; the *principes* had *pila*
as early as the time we are here speaking of, but the *triarii* still
had lances. These formed the troops of the line; but the *feren-
tarii* were light troops with slings, and one third of the *hastati*
also were light troops armed with javelins. They were placed
in front at the beginning of a battle, just like the ψιλοί of the
Greeks, and afterwards withdrew through the lines, and placed

---

[3] It is a general mistake of modern writers to compare the *cornu dextrum* and
sinistrum with arrangements of our own armies, and consequently to suppose
that there also existed a central battalion (*corps de bataille*); but a Roman army
consisted only of those two halves (*cornua*). All modern writers on tactics, with
the exception of Guischard, are mistaken on this head.—N.

themselves behind them, but always advanced again as soon as
the enemy retreated. These three battalions stood in single
maniples with intervals, as at Zama, but cannot possibly have
been drawn up *en échelons*, since so large an interval in one
line as that described by Livy is practically impossible, for the
cavalry would immediately have broken through it; they were
probably drawn up in the form of a quincunx, and in this
manner the intervals may be conceived.   Now as all the Roman
military arrangements were calculated to support the efforts of
individuals as long as possible, and not to form solid masses like
those of the Greeks, the first two battalions were drawn up as
near as possible to the enemy and under the protection of the
light troops.   Every Roman soldier was perfectly trained in
the art of fighting.   According to later regulations, the soldiers
began with the pilum.   The Roman soldiers were drawn up
in ten lines with large intervals, and when they were drawn up
close, the first battalion advanced, stopped and then threw the
fearful pila, which penetrated through the coat of mail, and of
which each soldier had several.   After the first charge, the
soldiers who had first thrown the pila retreated two steps, while
those who stood behind them advanced two steps, and occupied
places in the line by their side ; the first line then withdrew
and formed the tenth line, and thus all the ten lines had their
turn for making use of their pila. This mode of attack, which is
the only true and possible one, was formidable for the enemy.
If we consider this quiet mode of advancing and retreating, we
can understand why the battles lasted so long, and why the
combatants did not at once come to close quarters ; one hour
must undoubtedly have elapsed before all the pila were thrown,
and then the fight with swords began, during which the lines
again took it in turns: those who stood behind were not idle,
for when the foremost fell or were fatigued, those in their rear
advanced and took their places; and thus a Roman battle might
have lasted a long time.   To fight successfully in such a battle
the soldiers must be trained and drilled in the excellent manner
of the Romans: the dust and the war-cries were not disturbing
as smoke and the thunder of cannon.   When the hastati had
done fighting, they withdrew behind the principes who then
commenced: when they were overpowered, they fell back upon
the triarii, who at that time formed a kind of reserve, which,
however, was obliged to take part in the fight.   Besides these

four battalions, the three battalions of the line, and the one
with light armour, there existed a fifth consisting of the accensi
who were without armour, and whose business it was to step
in and take the armour of those who had fallen; the accensi
and velati were the two centuries that were added to the fifth
class, but did not come up to its census. It is clear that Manlius in that war did something which had never been done
before: he armed the accensi, made use of them instead of the
triarii to strengthen the lines, and reserved the triarii for the
decisive moment, and by this means he saved himself. Livy
states that the Latins mistook the accensi for the triarii, which
is impossible; but the accensi likewise may have been armed
with spears and have advanced as phalangites. The Latins
followed their old routine, and their battle-line consisted of the
most ordinary elements. The wing commanded by Decius
fought without success and the Latins conquered, whereupon
Decius ordered himself to be devoted to death by the pontiff
M. Valerius. This devotion inspired the whole army with
fresh courage and was at the same time believed to have a
magic effect upon it, since the consul had atoned for the whole
nation, which was now considered invincible. Hence, as tradition states, fate turned all at once : the legions rallied and
gained the most complete victory.

LECTURE XXXVIII.

If Rome had succumbed in this war, the whole Roman army
would have been annihilated; but the Latins could not have
derived the same advantages from their victory as were gained
by the Romans: as Latium itself had no unity and was without a great central point, the sovereignty of Italy would have
been undecided between it and Samnium. There is every
probability that Italy would then have fallen under the dominion of foreigners; it would perhaps have become a permanent
prey of Pyrrhus or of the Carthaginians, and the Gauls would
have ravaged it incessantly. Had the Italian nations been
wise, the same state of things might have been developed as

we afterwards find in existence, but it would have taken place
without violence and destruction. Rome conquered Italy, but
this subjugation is nevertheless the most desirable thing that
could have happened to Italy.

   The defeat of the Latins in the battle described in the
previous Lecture must have been complete, and so decisive,
that all were seized with a panic. Capua evidently submitted
at once, and the defeated did not even attempt to protect
themselves behind the Vulturnus, but at once retreated across
the Liris. Notwithstanding the general flight, however, a new
army formed itself at Vescia, an Ausonian town near the
Vescinian hills, and probably the modern S. Agata di Goti;
there are indeed no ruins, but many sepulchral monuments; it
is situated on the natural road from the Liris to the Vulturnus,
the mountains being on the left of the road to Naples. The
flight of the Latins therefore cannot have been as disorderly
as Livy describes it. There the survivors assembled and were
reinforced by the contingents of the ancient Latin and Volscian
towns; the Volscians on the sea-coast and the Liris, the
Auruncans and Sidicines, that is, the whole country between
the Liris and Vulturnus was united, and offered a final battle
to the Romans near Trifanum, on the Liris, between Sinuessa
and Minturnae. The Romans immediately, and even before
completing their march, attacked the enemy, and gained a
decided victory, but with great loss: this second defeat of the
Latins completed the destruction of all their resources, especially as they had the broad Liris in their rear. The contingents
dispersed to their respective homes in order to defend them.
The Romans made immediate use of their success, and advanced
through the territory of the Latins towards Rome. Now
whether, as Livy relates, Latium was completely subdued as
early as that time, or afterwards, cannot be determined with
any certainty, for the Latins again appear as enemies in the
following year. There are many circumstances in antiquity of
which we can say, that they must have been such or such; but
this is not the case with events which are accidental: *le vrai
n'est pas toujours vraisemblable*. I will therefore not assert positively whether the Latins, in their first consternation, laid
down their arms and afterwards took them up again. But
however this may be, the senate pronounced the sentence, and
with lofty confidence in the certainty of success resolved that

the *ager publicus* of the Latin state, the Falernian district of the Campanians, and part of the *ager Privernas* (Privernum seems not to have joined the Latin league) should be confiscated and assigned to the plebeians *viritim,* that is to every one who wore the *toga pura;* assignments beyond the Vulturnus would have been of no value to the Romans. The allotment, however, was made on a small scale, owing to the plebeian nobles having intrigued with the patricians against the multitude. An annual revenue of 450 denarii was assigned to the Campanian equites, probably as a compensation for the ager Falernus, and this sum had to be paid by the commonalty of Capua; it has already been observed that these equites consisted of the Samnites of the ancient colony, who anxious for their own interest, had not taken any part in the war. In the year following, the Latins again appeared in arms, probably because the Romans, after receiving their deditio, had driven them to despair by the fearful punishment inflicted upon them. We know, from several examples, with what cruelty the Romans acted towards a revolted people, witness Pleminius at Locri, in the Hannibalian war; hence we may imagine that the garrisons of each town were allowed every possible license, and such a place had to suffer all the horrors of a town taken by the sword. The Romans now made war against the Latins from the nearest points of their own territory: the insurrection existed only in the ancient Latium proper, at Tibur, Praeneste, and Pedum on the one hand, and at Aricia, Lavinium, Antium and Velitrae on the other; Velitrae was originally Latin, afterwards Volscian, and in the end it received a Roman colony; Tusculum and Ardea were Roman. These places form two masses, each of which endeavoured to defend itself. The two consuls Ti. Aemilius Mamercinus and Q. Publilius Philo fought against them. Publilius had frustrated an attempt of the Latins to maintain themselves in the field[1] ; while Aemilius besieged Pedum. There the Tiburtines, united with the people of Pedum, had fortified themselves, and the year passed away without any success. For reasons which are unknown to us,

---

[1] In one of the MSS. we find in *Campis Tincetanis* instead of " in the field;" but this has evidently been entered after the Lecture by a student who had left a gap during the Lecture, and Niebuhr probably alludes to the Campi Fenectani mentioned by Livy.—ED.

a dictator was now appointed; and Aemilius took this opportunity of conferring that dignity upon his colleague Publilius.

There now followed a cessation of hostilities, whether in consequence of a truce or from other causes, is utterly unknown, and a course of internal legislation to curtail the rights of the patricians engrossed every body's attention: this was the necessary result of circumstances, and does not deserve the blame which Livy attaches to it. The first law enacted, that henceforth one of the censors should necessarily be a plebeian; this had in fact existed even before, for we know that C. Marcius was the first plebeian censor; but it now became law, and was always observed: the second enacted that bills which were to be brought before the centuries should previously be sanctioned by the patricians whatever decree the centuries might think it right to pass. Formerly the consuls had the initiation in legislation; afterwards the praetor also had the same privilege, since he likewise might preside in the senate and make proposals, his power being an emanation from that of the consuls; but the aediles, though they had the *sella curulis*, did not yet possess this right. A resolution passed by the senate on the proposal of a magistrate was not yet law, but had to be brought before the centuries and then before the curies; this mode of proceeding arose at the time when the comitia of the centuries were instituted. The senate was formerly a patrician committee, and even now, the majority was undoubtedly patrician, though the plebeian element was already very strong. One hundred and ten years had elapsed since the decemvirate, and during that period many patrician houses must have become extinct, and others must have passed over to the plebes. From Von Stetten's history of the noble families of Augsburg we see, that out of fifty-one families, thirty-eight became extinct in the course of 100 years, and that even then the surviving families made the same claims, which a hundred years before the fifty-one families had been unable to establish. There was accordingly no reason for leaving to the patricians of Rome the *veto* which they had had before; and its abolition saved a great many unnecessary disputes. The more the patricians became reduced in numbers, and the more the ground tottered under their feet, the greater was their jealousy and the ill humour which they introduced into the most important affairs of the state. The change made by Publilius, therefore, was very reasonable and necessary. But nothing was ever formally abolished at Rome; when old institutions were no longer found useful, they were allowed to continue to exist as forms which could do no harm. Hence it was now enacted, that whenever the senate was going to pass a decree, the curies should sanction it beforehand. It is probable that this sham sanction was given, as in later times, by the lictors who were employed to represent the curies. The third law was, *ut plebiscita omnes Quirites tenerent*, and as I have explained before, affected such resolutions of the government (ψηφίσματα) as were to be sanctioned by the tribes instead of by the centuries. This, too, was a mere matter of form, for whenever the tribunes, who had previously consulted the consuls, were agreed among themselves, the plebes never refused their sanction.

The following year, A.U. 417, was decisive, the army of Pedum with its neighbours and the inhabitants of the sea-coast being completely defeated by L. Furius Camillus and C. Maenius, and Pedum being taken by storm. C. Maenius is described by the ancients as the man who brought about the decision of the war: he gained a victory on the river Astura, the site of which is unknown; a place of that name was situated between Circeii and Antium. It is quite certain that Maenius conquered the enemies on the sea-coast, and Camillus those in the interior; and an equestrian statue was erected to the former as the conqueror of the Latin people. Henceforth no Latin army appeared in the field, and each of the towns capitulated for itself. Livy's account of this seems to be extremely satisfactory, and the difficulties involved in it escaped me for many years; but if we compare it with other authentic statements, it is by no means really satisfactory; for he assigns some events to too early a time, others are passed over, others again are described very vaguely, and lastly he makes no distinction between the free and the dependent municipium. Hence our knowledge of the relations of the Latin towns to Rome is very imperfect. The whole of the Latin state was broken up; but the Roman senate determined to preserve the separate towns and render them subservient to the interests of Rome: a plan which was carried out in different ways but with extraordinary wisdom. Tusculum had from early times been in the enjoyment of the Roman franchise, though not in its full extent, but now its inhabitants received the full franchise; which was conferred

upon the inhabitants of Lanuvium and Nomentum likewise,
who thus became full citizens like the Tusculans, their population being entered in the census lists as plebeians, and admitted
into the tribes: the Tusculans were incorporated with the *tribus
Pupinia*[2], the Lanuvians and probably the Veliternians were
formed into a new tribe, apparently the Scaptia; whether the
people of Nomentum constituted the *tribus Maecia* is uncertain.
The Aricines, too, are mentioned by Livy among those who
received the franchise; but according to an authentic account,
they were, even some years later, in the condition of a dependent municipium. In this manner the places above mentioned
attained great honours, and no town produced so many illustrious plebeian families as Tusculum, though it was quite a
small place; I need only mention the Fulvii, Porcii, Corunca-
nii, Curii, and others[3]: certain places are particularly celebrated
for the number of great men they have produced. At
Lanuvium there was scarcely more than one family that
acquired any celebrity.

Other Latins likewise became citizens but not *optimo jure*,
and this is the beginning of the class of citizens *sine suffragio*,
which afterwards greatly increased and acquired a peculiar
importance. The isopolites of the ancient times were municipes, and when they settled at Rome, they might exercise all
the rights of Roman citizens, their position being similar to
that of the citizens of the territory of Florence, previously to
the year 1530. Those places which had received the *civitas
sine suffragio*, now stepped into this relation of isopolity. There
was this difference, that formerly those only were municipes,
who came to Rome, but whose native place was perfectly
independent in its political relations with neighbouring communities: this now ceased, and the separate towns which
became municipia were perfectly dependent in all their foreign
relations, whence Festus in his definition makes them form the
second class of municipia. Such municipia had the connubium
with Rome and their own magistrates; their inhabitants might
acquire landed property in the territory of Rome, but were
quite dependent upon Rome, like a son adopted by *arrogatio*,
or a woman *quae in manum convenerat;* and in their relations
with others they had no *persona*. Their rights in regard to

---

[2] Also *Popinia*; see Festus, *s. v.* Pupinia tribus p. 233 ed. Müller.—Ed.
[3] This is a remark of Cicero.—N.

Rome were rights of conscience on the part of the Romans; they might acquire the Roman franchise by being personally admitted by the censors, but not being contained in the tribes, they did not serve in the legions: they were however obliged to furnish troops, not as allies (*socii*), but as *Romani* in separate cohorts. We may now ask whether they were required to pay the tributum, that is whether in case of the levying a tributum being decreed at Rome, they had to pay according to the Roman census; and whether they had the right of sharing with the Roman people burthens and advantages, or whether their census was taken in their native places; the latter is probable, because they furnished and paid their own troops, and because the tributum was connected with the tribes. There cannot of course be any doubt as to their obligation to contribute. They unquestionably had a share in the public land, and whenever the Romans received a general assignment, those places too had a district assigned to them, with which they might do as they pleased. In this manner only can we conceive how Capua, after the war of Pyrrhus, could acquire such an extensive possession.

The decision of the fate of Latium was an important epoch to the Roman state, for it gave rise to an entirely new class of municipia. The consequence was that many Romans purchased estates in those districts; but an inconvenience soon arose, inasmuch as these Romans had to submit to courts of justice composed of people who ranked much lower than themselves. This was afterwards remedied by the institution of a praefectura, which the ancients, and especially Livy, misinterpret, as if the praefectures had kept those towns in a complete state of dependence, whereas their real object was to administer justice to those who were full citizens of Rome. Such places were called *fora* or *conciliabula*, which is the same as what is called in America a town-house in any particular township: they were both markets and places for the administration of justice. A Roman, for example, who bought a slave at Capua according to Capuan law, had no right to call the slave his own at Rome; but when the purchase had been made in the presence of the praefect and according to Roman law it was unassailable.

The fate of the other Latin towns was very severe. The ancient senators of Velitrae, probably of Volscian descent, were led into exile beyond the Tiber, together with a large

number of their fellow citizens, and a new colony was sent to
Velitrae. A port colony was established at Antium; its
inhabitants received the inferior Roman franchise, and the
Roman colonists by settling there entered into the same relation.
The Antiatans were deprived of their armed ships (*interdictum
mari*), for the Romans hated piracy; and this was the easiest
way of getting rid of it, it being indifferent to the Romans
whether the commerce of the Antiatans suffered or not.
Among the remaining places, the connubium and commercium,
as well as the common diets (*concilia*), were forbidden, just as
in Achaia, Phocis, and Boeotia. No person belonging to one
place was allowed to purchase land in another; but each town
had its fixed burthens, so that if in one of them, in consequence of any calamity the price of landed property fell, the
distress was very great, for the people of that place could sell
only among themselves or to Roman citizens, the commercium
existing with the Romans alone. This was the cause of the
decay of those places, for as Romans settled in them the distress became greater and greater, so that some of them entirely
perished. Praeneste and Tibur alone maintained themselves:
they were *agro multati*, but in the time of Polybius they again
appear in possession of the ancient *jus municipii*. From Livy's
account it might be inferred, that the ancient alliance with the
Laurentines had been preserved; and it is very possible that
the same was done in the case of Praeneste and Tibur, so that
they would have retained the right of municipium although
their domain land was taken from them. Both possessed large
and fertile territories, and must have had great vital power and
energy: Praeneste tried more than once to shake off the Roman
yoke. The punishment of isolation was also inflicted on all
those places which at the close of the fourth century were in
alliance with Latium; it extended moreover to the Aequians,
who had undoubtedly been members of the Latin confederacy.
The concilia remained forbidden, for the *feriae Latinae*,
formerly the general diet, became a mere shadow, a conventus
(πανήγυρις) for the celebration of the games.

Henceforth the Romans applied this system wherever they
wanted to break a conquered people, as they afterwards did in
Achaia. The towns thereby became entirely separate; the
feeling of unity died away, they looked upon each other as
strangers, and such a separation is usually followed by hostile

feelings, as in Southern and Northern Dithmarsch. The Romans were obliged to have recourse to this Machiavellian system, as they placed no garrisons in the towns. It was in this manner, that the grand duke Peter Leopold of Tuscany, who kept no troops, separated his subjects and thereby demoralised them.

The Latin colonies, it appears, were separated from the rest of Latium, whereas they formerly had been more closely connected with Latium, and were not in any direct relation with Rome; they now became a peculiar class of subjects, which had not hitherto existed at all. From this time forward Rome founded Latin colonies on her own account, and they deserve the admiration with which Machiavelli speaks of them, for they were the invention of great political tact. They were increased to the number of thirty, just as there had formerly been thirty Latin towns. The origin of these colonies was in the contract between the two nations: a district conquered by both in common used to be divided between them; but districts which could not be thus divided, were set apart for colonies. Rome indeed founded several colonies of her own; which received Caerite rights, but the former were called Latin colonies: Romans might settle in them, but they thereby stepped out of their tribes, though they might re-enter them whenever they pleased. Afterwards these colonies joined the Latin towns, and the thirty Latin places mentioned by Dionysius before the battle of the lake Regillus, were unquestionably the places named in the treaty of peace between Rome and Latium; some of them were those towns which are said to have been founded by Tarquinius Superbus as Latin colonies, and which occur as such in the Hannibalian war. Now there can be no question that the Romans who had thus joined the Latins, obtained the equal franchise. The number of citizens in the Latin colonies was much greater than in the Roman ones. At a later time the Italians were admitted to a share in these colonies, and they sometimes obtained a portion of the domain land, so that the colonies became the great means of spreading the Roman dominion; and the Latin language, being the political language of the Romans, suppressed and supplanted that of the ancient inhabitants. They were from the first dependent upon Rome, and without any bond of union among themselves. Until the downfall of Latium the number of Latin colonies was insignificant, but from that time they began to increase. The inhabitants of all these places were bound to serve in the Roman armies, and Rome prescribed to them what numbers they had to furnish; they were one of the principal means of the success of the Romans in the wars against the Samnites, for the Romans surrounded themselves with these colonies as with frontier fortresses. Several thousand men had a district assigned to them with the obligation of maintaining it; any Roman who wished to go out as a colonist, might do so, and others were added from Latium and other districts. The laws to be observed were prescribed by the Romans: the ancient inhabitants remained as a commonalty and undoubtedly formed the majority of tradespeople, but in a comparatively short time, they became amalgamated with the colonists, and these germs grew into a lofty tree. At first Rome etablished such colonies on the Liris in Campania, they were then extended into Umbria, and continued to be pushed onwards. This two-fold manner of founding colonies and conferring the franchise, sometimes with and sometimes without the suffrage, was the means whereby Rome, from being a city, became a state comprising all Italy. The colonists paid no personal taxes, which devolved entirely upon strangers, they only paid the tax of the ager *ex formula*.

The revolution which arose out of the conquest of the Latins was immense in regard to its consequences: even two years before, the destruction of Rome by the Latins was not an impossibility, but now her power was strengthened by those resources of Latium which had not perished in the struggle: but for the reasons already mentioned, the period which now followed, was for most of the Latin towns, a period of decay.

Among the Campanians, likewise, the Romans produced divisions: they distinguished the Campanian populus (the equites who received compensation) from the plebes. The relation in which they stood to the Hernicans was not altered, or if it was altered, the latter had received a compensation in money in the victories of the Romans. Capua, Cumae, Suessulla, Atella, Fundi and Formiae became free municipia, that is, isopolite towns, and the Romans accordingly recognised, at least nominally, their perfect equality.

LECTURE XXXIX.

OUR accounts do not enable us to form a clear idea of the internal condition of Rome: the war had cost her such heavy sacrifices, that, though her dominion extended from Sutrium and Nepet as far as Campania, the bleeding and exhaustion still continued for a long time: this renders the tranquillity which now followed quite intelligible, for all felt the want of peace.

In the year after the decisive victory over the Latins (A.U. 418) the praetorship was divided between patricians and plebeians, on condition that certain forms should be observed, and from this time forward the praetorship, generally speaking, alterna ted between patricians and plebeians. This can be historically demonstrated: deviations from the law do indeed occur, but only serve to explain the rule. Q. Publilius Philo was the first plebeian praetor, and there may perhaps have been some connection between this law and the three which bear his name. When the second praetorship, commonly called the *praetura peregrina*, was added, one was always held by a patrician, and the other by a plebeian, just as afterwards when the number of praetors was increased to four, two were taken from each order. But when their number was raised to six, the equal division could no longer be kept up, because the number of the patricians was ever decreasing. This law was the completion of the legislation of Licinius, for now the two orders were really placed on a footing of equality: great was the progress which had thus been made; for the fact that the patricians still continued to choose the *interreges* exclusively from among themselves was a matter of no consequence. The repetition of the *interregna* at this time shows indeed, that the patricians still indulged in dreams of evading the law, for the charms of what they wished to gain increased as the number of those who laid claim to it diminished; but these attempts do not appear to have called forth any violent reaction: the power of circumstances and truth were irresistible.

Abroad Rome had no important wars to carry on; a trifling one which broke out at this time was welcome to them, its object being to complete the compactness of their state as far as the Liris and Campania. The two banks of the Liris were

inhabited by Auruncans (the Greeks call them Ausonians, and
so also does Livy when he follows Greek authorities, such as
Fabius or Dionysius), an Oscan people.   During the Latin war
they had sided with the enemies of Rome, but afterwards they
had submitted as subjects, and now were under the protection
of Rome.   The conquest of the Sidicines had been left by the
Romans to the Samnites, but an arrangement seems to have
been entered into, by which the Samnites allowed the Sidicines
to continue to exist, in order not to lose the barrier between
themselves and the Romans.   This created a jealousy between
the Romans and Samnites, and it could not in fact be otherwise: the Samnite conquests in those districts had been the
main cause why the Volscians attached themselves to the Latins
and afterwards to the Romans; for at that time the Samnites
were more dangerous to them than the Romans.   Napoleon
once said in a diplomatic discussion: *"il faut de petits états entre
les grands,"* and on the same principle the large states allowed
the small ones to make war upon one another, because this
might lead to events calling for their powerful interference.
These small states were, so to speak, *"pour les coups d'épingles
qui précèdent les coups de canons."*   The Sidicines united with
the Auruncans of Cales attacked the other Auruncans, and this
led the Romans to march against them.   The latter carried on
the war with great prudence ; they conducted it with luke-
warmness, for it was anything but their interest to press the
Sidicines, lest they should throw themselves into the arms of
the Samnites.   They took Cales, which is situated between
Teanum and Casilinum, and established a strong colony in the
place.   Their system now was to establish themselves by means
of such colonies in the country between the Liris and Vulturnus, so far as it was not already occupied by the Samnites; and
this system they followed out with great zeal and success: the
colony of Cales connected the ever suspected Campania with
the dominion of Rome herself.   A second colony was founded
soon after at Fregellae, which became so remarkable in the
seventh century for its pride and its misfortunes; it was situated on the spot where the Liris is crossed by the Latin road
which leads through Tusculum to the towns of the Hernicans,
and thence by Teanum to Capua.   The establishment of this
colony was a true usurpation: the Samnites were masters of
the country as far as Monte Casino, they had there subdued

the Volscians and destroyed Fregellae; by their treaty with Rome they were permitted to make conquests in those districts, and even on their abandoning them the Romans had no right to take possession of them. The Samnites had also taken Sora, and they had undoubtedly established themselves there with intentions just as ambitious as those of Rome. The Romans concluded a treaty of isopolity with the Caudines, and yet both nations were convinced that a war between them was unavoidable. Under these circumstances, the Romans unquestionably adopted the same fluctuating policy which renders the history of the sixteenth century so interesting; the truth being: "*il y a trois sortes d'amis, ceux qui nous aiment, des amis indifférens, et des amis qui nous détestent.*"

It is certainly not a mere accident, when we observe in history that at certain times similar changes take place in countries far distant from each other: these changes in the one which produce a new state of things, cannot be the result of the changes in the other, because they occur simultaneously and in different countries; we recognise in them the hand of Providence which guides the fate of men and the development of all nations as one great whole. The destruction of the Latin confederacy and the extension of the power of Rome is an epoch of that kind, and is quite similar to the period about the close of the fifteenth century. It is of great interest to compare the two periods: it is as if the stages of development through which particular countries and nations can pass by themselves had come to an end, and as if all their circumstances were to be changed by new relations; for on such occasions we find nations joining one another which had never before been in contact, and states which till then had been most prosperous, begin to decay as if the autumn of their existence had set in; the spirit of the most eminent nations becomes extinct never to return: a change manifests itself in inclinations and tastes, and in the whole of the ordinary and daily habits of life; nay even the physical nature of man undergoes alterations, for new forms of disease make their appearance. Such was the case about the end of the fifteenth century, for then the prosperity of the Italian cities disappeared, just as at the time of which we are now speaking, the states of Greece fell into decay. The very things which had been the cause of the prosperity of Greece, the equilibrium of the many small states, became the cause of her decay, no one single state being powerful enough to maintain the independence of the whole. The circumstances of Italy in the fifteenth century were of precisely the same kind, for Florence and Venice stood by the side of each other with equal power, and if Venice had been strong enough to rule, a new and more beautiful order of things would have been the result. The battle of Chaeronea and the destruction of the Latin league occurred in the same year; and this simultaneously shows us the hand of Providence that rules the affairs of the world according to its own counsels.

The Romans and Samnites were apparently equal to each other, and there were reasons for believing that a struggle between them would lead to the destruction of both, so that foreigners or barbarians would reap the advantages; for in the north the Gauls were already masters of a great part of Italy, and in the south the Carthaginians were threatening. Timoleon, it is true, had a short time before checked the extension of their power in Sicily, but they were already masters of Sardinia with the exception of one mountain, and it was impossible to prevent them from acquiring sooner or later the islands of Sicily and Corsica. There was accordingly every appearance that after the mutual destruction of the Romans and the Samnites, Italy would be divided between the Gauls and Carthaginians.

Until then no political relation had existed between the Greeks and Romans; but an intercourse with the inhabitants of Magna Graecia and the Siceliots seems to have been maintained: I believe that even the literature of Magna Graecia exercised a much greater influence upon the Romans than is commonly supposed, and at that time a knowledge of Greek was probably nothing extraordinary at Rome. Granting that Pythagoras did not become a Roman citizen, since, perhaps, he is not even an historical personage, yet the Romans were at an early period acquainted with the Pythagorean philosophy and entertained a veneration for it. Connections with the Greeks of neighbouring places are often mentioned; Cumae afforded ample opportunities, and the Sibylline books existed at Rome as well as at Cumae. The first embassies to the oracle of Delphi are fabulous, but there can be no doubt that the Romans did consult that oracle. The connection of the Romans with Massilia at the time of the Gallic conquest, and with the

Lipariots, the guardians of the Tyrrhenian sea against the pirates, are the only other facts relating to the intercourse of the Greeks and Romans which we know for certain: all the rest is fabulous. But the first political affair in which the Romans as a state came in contact with the Greeks, belongs to this time; for the treaty with Massilia was probably nothing but a commercial treaty, as I conclude, more particularly from the circumstance that Massilia and Carthage were hostile to each other on account of the fisheries, as Justin relates; by which we must understand either the coral fisheries on the coasts of Africa, or the tunny fisheries on the Italian shores. The inhabitants of Provence, throughout the middle ages, were in possession of the coral fisheries on the coast of Africa. The first political connection between the Romans and the Greeks was the treaty between Rome and Alexander, king of Epirus; for the Epirots may be regarded as Greeks, since notwithstanding their Pelasgian origin they had become Hellenised. Alexander had been invited to come to Italy by the Tarentines in the year A.U. 420, or Olymp. 112.

The glory of Magna Graecia had already disappeared; and most of the Greek towns, as Posidonia, Pyxus, Caulonia, Hipponium, Terina and others, had been conquered by the Lucanians and Bruttians, some of them remained in the possession of the conquerors, others were abandoned: only a few maintained their independence, but had to fight for their existence. Rhegium, Locri, and the once flourishing Croton, had been laid waste by the Dionysii of Syracuse, who had abandoned those places indeed, but they were lying half in ruins and were but partially restored, as Delhi and Ispahan are at the present time. Thurii and Metapontum defended themselves with difficulty against the Lucanians; their territory was almost entirely lost, and they were struggling like the Italian towns in the sixth and seventh centuries against the Longobards. The only Greek town which, notwithstanding the general misfortune, was still in the enjoyment of the highest state of prosperity, was Tarentum; this city too, soon after the period of the expedition of Xerxes, had suffered a great defeat from the neighbouring Messapians, but had soon recovered from it; and at the time when the tyrants of Syracuse and the Lucanians threatened the other towns, Tarentum was in a thriving condition; it was undoubtedly increasing by the immigration of numerous Greeks

from the other towns, which were either destroyed or threatened.
A parallel to this occurs in the growing prosperity of the Netherlands and Switzerland in the time of the Thirty Years' War;
the flourishing condition of those countries arose mainly from
the distressing state of Germany, industry and commerce taking
refuge in them. In this manner, Tarentum became wealthy
and powerful; it had, moreover, the additional advantages
which a neutral state between two belligerent parties always
has, and the rulers of the Tarentine state must have been men
of great wisdom.

The Tarentines had acquired great wealth through their
industry, commerce, wool-manufactures, their skill as dyers, and
also from their salt works; they had a powerful navy: and with
the exception of Syracuse, no one of all the Greek cities, not
even Rhodes, was as wealthy as Tarentum. Its inhabitants,
according to their circumstances, were perfectly peaceable, and
consisted of excellent seamen. There is no doubt that, as is the
case with the people of the modern Taranto, navigation and
fishing were their principal pursuits, a kind of idle busy life
which is the delight of the Greeks and southern Italians: a
Neapolitan is perfectly happy when he is rocking on the waves
in his fishing boat. Nature has blessed the country about
Tarentum with every thing in abundance. There is perhaps
no part of the European seas so rich in fish and shell-fish as the
bay of Tarentum; and the poor Tarentine leads a truly princely
life in idleness, for he requires only bread, salt, and olives,
which he can always easily procure. The territory of Tarentum was not so large as to lead the people to devote themselves
much to agriculture. The tribes of the Latin race, the Etruscans, Umbrians, and Sabellians, on the other hand, were born
husbandmen; and an Italian husbandman, who has an hereditary piece of land is thoroughly good, honest and respectable,
while the people who live in towns are good for nothing.
Those Italians who are not descended from Greeks are not at all
fit for a seafaring life, and the Roman coasts were provided
with fish by the southern towns, which continued to be Greek
even in the middle ages. The Greeks are bad husbandmen,
and were so even in antiquity; they cannot be compared to the
Italians as agriculturists; the work of Theophrastus indeed
shews great knowledge of agriculture, but the Greeks did not
feel happy in that occupation; they liked to cultivate the olive

and vine but not corn. The soil of Greece, too, is in a great many parts almost unfit for the growth of corn, being better suited for the cultivation of olives. A Greek is cheerful and happy as a fisherman, and makes an excellent sailor.

The Tarentines were quite a democratic people like the Athenians in Piraeus, as is observed by Aristotle; and the state was very rich through the variety of its revenues. With these large means they were enabled to raise armies of mercenaries, as was then the custom throughout Greece, and as was the case in Holland in the seventeenth century. General opinion is not favorable towards the Tarentines: it is true that at the time when they became involved in war with the Romans, they were an effeminate and unwarlike people; but the censure which is usually thrown upon them arises from a peculiarity of human nature, which leads us, when a powerful state or individual falls, to seek for the cause of the fall in the conduct of the unfortunate, instead of feeling sympathy. I am convinced that next to Athens, Tarentum produced the wisest and most intellectual men in antiquity, and that the state made excellent use of them. A city that produced an Archytas, the Leibnitz of his time, a man who possessed all knowledge then attainable, and was at the same time a great general and statesman,—and neither envied nor banished him (as the Ephesians did with their Hermodorus) but raised him seven times to the office of supreme commander, should not be censured: the spirit of Greece must have dwelt in it in all its beauty. The miserable anecdotes which Athenaeus for instance relates of the Tarentines, are refuted by that one fact alone. They do not deserve blame any more than the great characters who are reviled in Schiller's *Maria Stuart;* a fact for which I cannot excuse Schiller, notwithstanding the beautiful poetry. It is certainly possible that Archytas and the other Tarentine statesmen looked more to the interests of their own city than to those of the Greeks in general (the Athenians alone rose to the moral height which enabled them to feel for all Greece); he may have kept up a good understanding with the tyrants of Syracuse, with more regard to the advantage than to the dignity of his native city; but these are faults which the noblest men when placed at the helm of a state in unfortunate times have been unable to avoid. The Tarentines are blamed for having made use of foreign soldiers and armies, first of Archidamus

of Sparta, next of Alexander of Epirus, then of Cleonymus,
Agathocles, and at last of Pyrrhus; which Strabo considers
a sign of cowardice and imprudence; and he at the same time
adds the remark, that the Tarentines were ungrateful towards
their protectors. But during the period that followed the Peloponnesian war, it was a general evil that wars were no longer
carried on by armies of citizens, but by hired mercenaries: and
this circumstance must be accounted for by the fact that wars
had become more extensive and bloody, whereby the ancient
race of citizens was destroyed. The ravages of war had made
large numbers of men homeless, who wandered about, especially
in Greece (as in modern times in Switzerland), by thousands,
and were one of the greatest of plagues. It had long been
a fair custom in Greece to leave the inhabitants of a town
taken or destroyed in the enjoyment of their freedom, and not
to sell them as slaves; but as all their property was taken from
them, they were forced to gain their living in any way
they could: in the Thirty Years' War likewise, it became from
year to year easier to find troops[1]; such soldiers being constantly in arms were far superior to the militia, and when once
they had begun to be employed, the militia soon became
unable to resist the enemy. A city like Tarentum could not
raise legions; which can be formed only where there exists a
respectable and numerous class of husbandmen, and hence
there are countries where absolutely nothing can be done but
to hire mercenaries, as was the case at Florence when the
militia had got out of practice: but the same system would
be destructive to other states. Tarentum therefore was under
the necessity of making use of mercenaries, and it would have
been contrary to their notion of freedom to keep up a standing
army; they acted wisely in confining themselves to their city
militia when they could do without other troops. Whenever
there was a necessity for enlisting troops, numbers of homeless
persons[2] were always to be got in Greece about Taenarus;
they were however untrustworthy and faithless, since they
followed him who paid best, like the condotti in the fifteenth
and sixteenth centuries; and a condottiere might easily act the
part of a traitor or set himself up as tyrant. Hence it was
much more prudent to engage the services of princes with

Πόλεμος πόλεμον τρέφει.   [2] *Latrones*, μισθοφόροι

their disciplined armies, for the honor of such a prince afforded at least some guarantee. Why should the Tarentines have disturbed their commerce and trade, as they were enabled to manage things differently? Such a hired army might indeed become dangerous, but so long as it was possible they took wise precautions: Alexander of Epirus afforded them real advantages, but Pyrrhus did not. The English system of levying armies has likewise been censured, but only by persons who had no knowledge of the circumstances of the country. There is nothing that deserves censure in the conduct of the Tarentines except the insolent manner in which they drew upon themselves the war with Rome, but we shall assuredly have no reason to be severe towards them, if we consider the exasperation which drove them to it.

About this time they became involved in a war with the Lucanians, who had attacked Heraclea and Metapontum, which towns were under their protection. The Lucanians had already lost that part of Calabria, which was afterwards called Bruttium, for its inhabitants consisting of the Pelasgian serfs of the Greek towns had united into one people, and refused to obey the Lucanians, who were wise enough to recognise their independence and remain their friends. But in order to indemnify themselves, the Lucanians turned their arms against Tarentum, attempting to subdue Heraclea. In these circumstances the Tarentines invited to their assistance Archidamus of Sparta, who with the unhappy Phocian exiles had gone to Crete; but he fell in an engagement against the Lucanians, on the same day on which the battle of Chaeronea was lost. A few years afterwards they took into their pay Alexander the Molossian, of Epirus, a brother of Olympias, the wife of Philip. Philip had given him his daughter Cleopatra in marriage, and had allowed him an appanage: his kingdom was very small; Philip who everywhere contrived to gain strong positions, kept the fortress of Ambracia for himself, and at first gave to Alexander only three small towns in Cassopia, on the Thesprotian coast; afterwards, when Philip had extended his empire and every where put himself in possession of the fortified places, he raised Alexander to the throne of the Molossians, among whom he found but little to do. Philip followed the same policy in regard to his relations, as Napoleon did in reference to his brothers: they were to be kings, but

without power; so that they were nothing else than satraps
without paying tribute. It was for this reason that Philip
retained Ambracia for himself. During the time that Alexander of Macedonia was engaged in his Eastern expedition,
Alexander the Molossian was under the authority of the insolent old Antipater; he was not on good terms with the
Macedonian king, and according to the accounts of the ancients,
it was jealousy of the glory of his nephew, that induced him
to go to Italy; he is said to have complained bitterly that fate
had made him fight against men, while his nephew was opposed
only by women. As the Macedonian was not inclined to allow
our Alexander to extend his dominion in Epirus, the latter
received the invitation of the Tarentines with great pleasure.
He accordingly went to Italy, but with intentions quite different from those with which the Tarentines had invited him:
they expected that he, as a small prince, with a well trained
army, would protect them, but Alexander went over with a
desire of conquering a kingdom for himself.   He was successful;
subdued the Messapians and Sallentines, made a diversion to
Posidonia, delivered the Greek towns, and united them into a
confederacy, of which, he of course, became the στρατηγός
and ἡγεμών. Being in the service of the Tarentines, he was
never in want of subsidies, like the nations who in the
last century were in the service of England under Walpole;
but the history of his exploits is almost entirely lost, and it is
only in the Greek grammarians such as Tzetzes, that a few
interesting statements are preserved.   His success was brilliant,
so long as he acted in concord with the Tarentines; but when
he betrayed his ulterior intentions, and wished to assume the
title of king of Italy (of course in the narrower sense of the
term), the Tarentines were exasperated and dispensed with his
services.   Whether they concluded a separate peace with the
Lucanians is uncertain; but as the diet of the Greek towns
met at Heraclea, although Tarentum was the most powerful
and illustrious of those towns, the diet seems to have been
transferred by Alexander, which clearly indicates a rupture
between him and the Tarentines. However, as his power was
now too small, he seems to have carried on the war as a mere
adventurer like Charles XII.: he made predatory excursions,
and Pandosia in the heart of Lucania became his Pultawa;
there he was surrounded by the Lucanians and Bruttians: his

army was divided, both parts were annihilated, and he himself was slain. He had previously concluded a treaty with the Romans, which is incidentally mentioned by Livy, but uudoubtedly on the authority of Roman annals, and this treaty is a proof of the manner in which the Romans made their calculations: they had nothing to fear from him, and sought his alliance only for the purpose of overawing the Samnites, who had concluded a treaty with Tarentum. A real alliance, however, did not exist between Rome and Alexander, for the treaty between Rome and the Samnites was still in force. So far as we know the circumstances, we must blame the Romans for having favoured a foreigner in preference to kindred people of their own peninsula. The Samnites indeed are not mentioned among those who in the end waged war against Alexander, but his predatory excursions had brought him into contact with them: at Posidonia they fought against each other. It is interesting to speculate on what would have been the probable consequences, if Alexander had established a kingdom in Italy; it is likely that he would only have facilitated the victories of the Romans, and hence their treaty with him was very prudent, though not praiseworthy.

LECTURE XL.

THE ancient historians had no difficulty in forming a clear conception of the relations then existing between Rome and Samnium, as we see especially in the excerpts *de Legationibus* from Dionysius: each nation saw in the measures of the other, nothing but fraud and hostility, and on the whole they may not have been very wrong in these suspicions. The Romans had kept the nations that dwelt about Campania, partly in the condition of isopolites, such as the Fundanians and Formians, and partly in a state of dependence, as the Privernatans. These latter endeavoured to shake off the yoke; for the franchise without the suffrage was only a burthen for them, and the advantages which they enjoyed were small in proportion to what they cost; the right of acquiring landed property within the Roman dominion, was no benefit to a city which had itself a fertile territory. The Romans imagined that this insurrection had been stirred up by the Samnites; and there can be no doubt that every one dissatisfied with the government of Rome met with sympathy from the Samnites. The Privernatans were joined by the Fundanians, one of whose nobles, Vitruvius Vaccus, was the leader in this movement; but the Fundanians did not persevere, and withdrew from the contest. The Privernatans were severely judged by the Romans, of which a very interesting account is given by Livy and Valerius Maximus: the ambassadors of the Privernatans were asked to state conscientiously what punishment they had deserved; they answered that they deserved the punishment due to those who struggled for liberty. The consuls received this answer favorably, and then asked whether they would keep peace if they were pardoned, whereupon they replied: "If you give us an honorable peace we will keep it, but if you give us a degrading one we shall break it." The consuls then said, that men like these deserved to be Roman citizens, and the franchise was accordingly conferred upon them. The same story occurs in the excerpts *de Legationibus* of Dionysius, but many years earlier, and there is perhaps no foundation at all for it. It is related by Valerius Maximus indeed, but he is no authority whatever, being only an echo of Livy. The story is perhaps an invention of the gens Aemilia or Plautia which had the patronage of Privernum, and bore the surname of Privernas, the annalists having afterwards inserted it where they thought fit.[1] A few years afterwards, the Privernatans, according to an unequivocal expression in a *plebiscitum*[2], were again in a state of insurrection; but this has been effaced from history in order to preserve the interest of the old story. At a later time, Privernum was in possession of the franchise, and that of a higher kind than the mere Caerite franchise, for they formed the *tribus Ufentina*. Fundi and Formiae too were severely punished. This is the natural connection of the events so pathetically narrated by Livy: the generosity which he ascribes

---

[1] The Plautii preserved upon their coins the recollection of the conquest of Privernum as the most glorious event in the history of their family. *Rom. Hist.* III, p. 175. L. Aemilius Mamercinus Privernas, and C. Plautius Decianus triumphed over the Privernatans.—Ed.   [2] Liv. VIII. 37.

to the senate is quite incredible, and his account of it a piece of mere declamation.

There is no doubt that the Samnites secretly promoted the disturbances among the subjects of Rome, and they openly demanded the evacuation of Fregellae. Justice was unquestionably on their side, for the Romans had no right to establish a colony in a place which had been conquered by the Samnites, although at the time when Rome sent her colony thither, it was not in the hands of the Samnites; for otherwise they would, perhaps, after all not have sent it. But in such cases justice cannot always be done : wrong and injustice are often very different things. On this occasion, I should not like to cast a stone at the leaders of the Romans for not giving up a place which they had taken in a deserted district, even if their taking it was an act of positive injustice. The Samnites were rapidly spreading in that district; and Fregellae, at the head of a bridge on the upper Liris, was a strong point for defending the country against them; and the advantage which the Romans might derive from its possession was much less than the disadvantage to them of Fregellae being in the hands of the Samnites. As soon as Rome gave it up, the Latin road would have been opened, and her allies, the Hernicans, Latins, and undoubtedly the Aequians also, would have been exposed to imminent danger. The case was similar to that of 1803, after the peace of Amiens, when the evacuation of Malta by the English was demanded by everybody: the English could not give it up, though they had promised it, which surely they ought not to have done. The slow movements of the Samnite senate might, perhaps, have been some security against any abuse that might be made of Fregellae.

The outbreak of the war was so anxiously looked forward to, that even two years before it took place, a Roman army was encamped on the frontier, it being expected that the Samnites would make an attack upon Fregellae. By the treaty with Alexander of Epirus the Romans hoped to secure a friend, and they now tried to protect themselves against the enemy, still more by a peace with the Gauls. The latter had now been settled in Italy for upwards of sixty years, the migrations across the Alps became every year less numerous, the commotion among those nations had ceased, and the Gauls who were never an entirely savage people did not fail to acquire a certain civilisation; they devoted themselves to agriculture and became a harmless agricultural race, just like the Goths under Vitigis, who were likewise a defenceless host of peasants, whom Totilas was obliged to prepare for war by special training. The Gauls had before them two roads to the South of Italy,—the marshes about the Arno and the wild part of the Apennines protected Etruria;—the one down the Tiber through Umbria towards Latium and Campania, and the other through Picenum along the coast of the Adriatic towards Apulia. Upon this latter road they must have repeatedly attempted to advance southward: but it was more difficult than the other road, because they were opposed by the Sabellians in the Abruzzo. Now the Romans, in order not be disturbed by an attack of the Gauls, which the Samnites might easily have brought about, concluded a formal peace with them, which Livy passes over in silence, but which is expressly mentioned by Polybius, and which the Romans undoubtedly purchased with money, for why should the Gauls have promised the Romans to remain at peace?

This anxiety of the Romans to protect themselves for the future, renders it highly probable to me that the old statement of their having, in conjunction with the other Italian nations, sent an embassy to Alexander at Babylon, is not a mere fiction. Alexander had put a limit to his conquests in the East, and to march Southward against the Ethiopian nations would have been senseless. It was naturally expected, when he returned from India that he would direct his arms against the West; for no one was so foolish as to believe that he would all at once put a stop to his conquests. Many persons are of opinion, that the people in the West knew nothing at all of the Eastern conquests of Alexander; but the Western nations were not so much isolated from the rest of the world as is generally thought: the Romans must have known of the expedition of Alexander, just as Clapperton and Denham found people in the interior of Soudan, acquainted with the insurrection of Greece and with the co-operation of individual Europeans in it. During the Seven Years' War, when my father was in Sana, people there had a very distinct knowledge of the great war that was being carried on in Europe, and especially of the war between the English and French; nay, one intelligent Arab of Sana brought forward a map, and made enquiries about the geographical position of those European states. This happened in the very heart of Arabia; and we must remember that the modern Arabs are a degraded and ignorant people, which cannot be said of the nations of antiquity. The means of communication, moreover, were far more easy at that time than in the twelfth and thirteenth centuries, when, nevertheless, there existed communications with the remotest parts of Asia. I believe that the Romans had accurate information about Persia and India: it is true they did not yet possess geographical works, but they undoubtedly had maps of the world like those which existed in Greece, and it is certain that at that time some Romans received a Greek education, as seems to be proved by the very surname of P. Sempronius Sophus. No one doubts that the Samnites and Lucanians sent ambassadors to Alexander, although later writers call in question the statement that the Romans did go; the Lucanians sent their embassy in order to avert his wrath on account of the death of his uncle; the Samnites, in order to secure his friendship if he should come to Italy; and in like manner the Romans were anxious not to offend him at least, though they might not hope to win his friendship. Even the Iberians sent an embassy to him as soon as they heard of his preparations against Carthage. Livy hits upon the singular idea that the Romans had perhaps never heard of him. It is possible that the Romans concealed the embassy from pride, or that the Greeks invented it from vanity; but it would be necessary to suppose that the latter was done at a time when the Romans were already so powerful that the homage of Rome could increase the glory of Alexander. But Clitarchus, through whom the account of the embassy has come down to us, was an elegant author; he wrote immediately after the death of Alexander, at the time when the Romans were still engaged in the doubtful contest with the Samnites. Aristobulus and Ptolemaeus Lagi, who far surpass him in historical fidelity, speak of Tyrrhenian and Samnite ambassadors, and the former of these names comprises the Romans also, just as the name of the Samnites applies to all the Sabellian nations. If Alexander's life had been spared, he would have first directed his arms against Sicily, and thence against Carthage, which would certainly have fallen before him: in Italy the Greeks would have received him with the same enthusiasm as in Asia Minor, for he was δεινὸς παρέλκειν; he would have won them, concluded treaties with them, and have weakened those who opposed him so much, that the whole peninsula would have been his. Livy has a discussion upon this point which is very beautifully written, but a complete failure: his national vanity entirely blinds him, and he is egregiously mistaken in his calculation of the military resources of Italy, as well as in his belief that all Italy would have united against Alexander. If he had come to Italy, Rome would certainly have fallen; and his death was a necessary ordinance of Providence in order that Rome might become great.

This was the state of affairs at the time when the war broke out between Rome and Samnium. The immediate occasion of the war was the conduct of Neapolis and Palaepolis, the ancient Parthenope. Palaepolis is mentioned only by Livy: it was an ancient Cumaean colony, the Cumaeans having taken refuge there across the sea. Neapolis derives its name from being a much later settlement of different Greek tribes, and was perhaps not founded till Olymp. 91, about the time of the Athenian expedition to Sicily, and as a fortress of the Greeks against the Sabellians. It is not impossible that the Athenians also may have had a share in it. Both towns, however, were of Chalcidian origin and formed one united state, which at that time may have been in possession of Ischia. Many absurdities have been written about the site of Palaepolis, and most of all by Italian antiquaries. We have no data to go upon except the two statements in Livy, that Palaepolis was situated by the side of Neapolis, and that the Romans had pitched their camp batween the two towns. The ancient Neapolis was undoubtedly situated in the centre of the modern city of Naples above the church of Sta. Rosa; the coast is now considerably advanced. People have sought for Palaepolis likewise within the compass of the modern city, without asking themselves whether there would have been room for an army to encamp between the two places. I alone should never have discovered its true site, but my friend, the Count de Serre, a French statesman, who in his early life had been in the army and had thus acquired a quick and certain military eye, discovered it in a walk which I took with him. The town was situated on the outer side of Mount Posilipo, where the quarantine now is; it is an excellent and healthy situation facing the islands of Nisida and Limon: it may be that in antiquity there was a port at Palaepolis, and the two islands still have very good harbours. That point moreover

had a natural communication with Ischia. Mount Posilipo
with its ramifications lay between the towns at a distance of
about two miles, so that there was sufficient room for the
Roman army to encamp on the hills and thus to cut off the
communication between the two towns. There exist neither
monuments nor coins of Palaepolis. According to the common
supposition, the two towns would have been so near to each
other, that darts thrown from their walls would have met in
their course.

LECTURE XLI.

The war was occasioned by piracy or at least by hostilities
committed at sea against the defenceless merchant vessels of
the Romans, who had then no fleet, and strangely enough pretended not to care for the sea, as if such things could be
neglected with impunity. Complaints respecting the division
of the Falernian territory may likewise have contributed to
the outbreak of the war. Such a division was always a great
event: many persons sold their lots, while others settled upon
their farms; and that district became a sore point in the dominion of Rome. If, however, this was the cause of the disruption between the Palaepolitans and Romans, the complaint
of piracy which Dionysius introduces in so declamatory a manner is entirely out of place, since it would be no more than
natural for them to endeavour to disturb the commerce of the
hostile people. The Neapolitans, trusting to their alliance
with the Samnites and Nolanians, refused the reparation which
the Romans demanded of them. The Oscan population had
gradually become predominant at Nola, though it had undoubtedly Chalcidean *epoeci,* who formed a considerable part of the
population. How much its inhabitants had become Hellenised
may be seen from the Greek symbols on the coins of Nola with
the inscription *NΩΛΛΑΙΩN.* It is in general remarkable, how
easily the Samnites amalgamated with the Greeks; Strabo calls
them φιλέλληνες, and the Samnites, without a literature of
their own, were undoubtedly open to that of the Greeks, and

endeavoured to speak like the Greeks themselves. The Romans never agreed well with the Greeks, to whom the Lucanians also were hostile although their civilisation was Greek; and it certainly cannot be questioned that the Pythagorean philosophy was established among them. The statement that Pythagoras was a native of one of the Tyrrhenian islands must mean, that the roots of the theological parts of his philosophy must principally be sought for among the Pelasgians and in the religion of Samothrace.

An auxiliary corps of 4000 Samnites and 2000 Nolanians threw themselves into the towns of Palaepolis and Neapolis; the Tarentines are likewise said to have stirred up Palaepolis, for the Tarentines who were very well disposed towards the Samnites employed their money to involve the Romans in war at a distance. The Romans looked upon the occupation of Palaepolis by the Samnites as an act of hostility, and brought their complaints before the diet of Samnium. The evacuation of the place was a moral impossibility, and the answer which the Samnites returned was, that as the Romans wished for war, war they should have, and there was no need to dispute about trifles. This answer was confirmed by the assembly of the Samnite people. In the meanwhile the siege of Palaepolis had already been going on for some time, and the Romans had no prospect of success, for their art of besieging was still in its first infancy, and the Greeks opposed them with great technical skill; the attacks of the Romans therefore produced no effect, and the sea was left open to the Greeks. But treason did what force was unable to accomplish. Neapolis possessed ships of war with which they may frequently have made predatory excursions against the Roman coasts, which the Romans were unable to protect. The Samnite garrison, at least the greater part of it, appears to have been stationed at Palaepolis, and the Greeks at Neapolis. Two Greeks Charilaus and Nympheus now betrayed the Samnites to the Roman consul Publilius Philo: they proposed to the Samnites to make an expedition against the Roman coast, and the Samnites quitted the city ready to embark. As the town on the side of the harbour was protected by a wall, the conspirators closed the gate after the Samnites had gone out, and admitted the Romans by another gate. The Samnites found that the ships had been drawn away from the coast, and were obliged to save themselves as well as they could. Palaepolis now disappears from history, and there can be no doubt that it was destroyed on that occasion. Neapolis obtained a favourable alliance with Rome, from which we may perhaps infer that the conspirators were Neapolitans. The acquisition of Neapolis was extremely important to Rome; for thus the two harbours of Nisida and Naples, from which alone expeditions by sea could be undertaken against their territory fell into their hands. At that time Naples was not, as at present, a city of 400,000 inhabitants, but must have been somewhat like our town of Bonn. This conquest was made by Q. Publilius Philo *pro consule ;* he was the first to whom the consular power was prolonged (A. U. 429) by a senatus-consultum and a plebiscitum, on the proposal of a tribune, so that his own law concerning plebiscita was applied to him. The fact of a new magistracy being thus created in substance though not in form, was a great change in the constitution. Up to that time no one had celebrated a triumph except during the period of his magistracy, but Publilius triumphed as proconsul.

This was the beginning of the second Samnite war which, if we except the Hannibalian, is the greatest, most attractive and most noble in all the history of antiquity. It is to be lamented that we know so little about it, for the places where the battles were fought are mostly passed over in silence; but we should not be ungrateful; with some pains we may yet obtain a satisfactory knowledge of the war. Livy had described some parts of it with great pleasure, but others with evident weariness, which was the result of his mode of writing: he entered on his task without preparation, whence he wrote with freshness and vigour indeed, but had neither a clear insight into the history nor a command of his subject. If he had made better use of the annals, we should see our way more clearly. It is to be regretted that the books of Dionysius on this war are lost, for the few fragments in Appian, who copied from him, and in Constantine Porphyrogenitus, throw much light upon many points; Dionysius' account of that period must have been excellent, for the annals were already sufficient to enable a diligent searcher like him to make out a real history. There existed some nameless chronicles as early as that time, though they may have been dry and obscure in their details: the fact that isochronistic history does not commence till a hundred years later, is here of no consequence. Livy has unfortunately made no use at all of the ancient materials which formed the foundation of the annals whence he makes his choice quite arbitrarily when the annals contradicted one another, and in most cases prefers that which is wrong. He affords us no means of gaining a general view of this war which lasted twenty-two years; and it was only after many years' study that I succeeded in forming a clear conception of it.

The war must be divided into several periods: the first extends from the year A.U. 429 to 433. During this period the Samnites appear to us in a strange light; for although they had wished for the war, yet they were evidently unprepared, and seem to have had the conviction that they would not be able to hold out. The instigators of the war must have lost their popularity, and the war itself was disagreeable and troublesome to the people. Such a state of things may appear surprising; but those who have witnessed the great war of the revolution must remember quite similar circumstances. The case of the Athenians in the Peloponnesian war also resembles that of the Samnites, for after the first and second campaigns they wished for peace; and so did the Venetians after the battle of Ghiera d'Adda. In the year 1793, the war against France was quite popular in England (I was myself in England about that time), for the English remembered the interference of France in the American war, and still had great expectations from their colonies: the national hatred too was generally speaking very great, although a few were in favour of the revolution; but when the war was carried on badly, when no objects, at least no important ones, were gained, and when the power of France was ever increasing, the war became thoroughly unpopular, and the general outcry was for peace, so that in order to maintain themselves, the ministers were obliged to yield and enter into negotiations. When, however, the nation became aware that peace was impossible, they rose in a brilliant manner, and in 1798 and 1799, the war was again extremely popular. This observation is very humiliating to those who attach so much importance to public opinion. Such also was the case with the Samnites, for when it was proved that the Romans carried on the war quite differently from what had been expected, the Samnites were disappointed and wished for peace. Afterwards, however, a complete change took place in their minds, for as the war was protracted, they began to feel as if they could not live without it, especially when it was carried on unsuccessfully, for, as in gambling, men will rather perish than withdraw from a contest, and thus give themselves up to the enemy; and this feeling changed the war into one of guerillas. In the midst of the war, when these misfortunes were much greater than at the beginning, the Samnites had arrived at the conviction that peace was impossible.

The Samnites, as has already been remarked, consisted of four states, which took the supreme command in turn. This was a very great disadvantage, for when one general was elected, the other leaders probably hated and envied him, for such is always the case among allied states, as we see in the history of the German empire and the United States: may God prevent this ever happening in the army of our German confederacy! The unhappy war of the revolution likewise arose from the fact, that in the campaign of 1799 one general rejoiced in the defeat of the other. When a great man like Pontius had the command, and it so happened that the other praetors were honest men and acted with him, a great advantage might indeed be gained; but in the year following every thing was altered again. If the Samnites had been united, they would have been more than a match for the Romans; but as it was, the Romans overcame them through the excellence of their institutions, for various and even most hostile elements were all firmly concentrated under the one power of the spirit of Rome. In the art of war, the Samnites undoubtedly equalled the Romans, for, according to Sallust, the Romans had adopted their armour and perhaps their whole mode of warfare from the Samnites, at least we find that in the battles the armies were drawn up in exactly the same manner, and the reports of the battles attest that they fought against each other as equals against equals. I must here contradict the opinion of General Vandoucourt, who asserts that the Italian, Spanish and African nations fought their battles drawn up in the phalanx. Their strength consisted in the sword: the Italicans had cohorts, and undoubtedly used the pila like the Romans.

The Samnites it appears, had allies; the district from Frentenum to Luceria being either an allied country or a distinct canton; but the alliance was so loose that the Frentenians kept entirely aloof during the war. To the north of the Samnites there existed the confederacy of the Marsians, Marrucinians, Vestinians and Pelignians; and of these the Vestinians were on friendly terms with the Samnites, while the others were indifferent to them and even attached to the Romans. The situation of the Samnites was thus very perilous, but if they had carried on the war on the Liris as far as Capua, which seems in fact to have been their plan, they would have been able to have maintained themselves against the Romans; but the latter had a far bolder plan: for, as in the Latin war, they again formed a semicircle round Samnium, a plan which now involved much more danger and was on a greater scale than in the Latin war. The Samnites were cordially hated by the Apulians, among whom the ruling class consisted of Oscans, who may either have subdued the ancient Pelasgian population and amalgamated with them, or have expelled them. The country of Apulia is surrounded by mountains which form a horse-shoe, so that the country presents the aspect of a theatre; the mountains themselves form a part of Apulia, but the real country below these mountains is a table land of a chalky soil, and almost as hot as Leon in Spain. The Apulians had two principal towns, Arpi and Canusium, each of which was the mistress of a large territory and jealous of the other. The Samnites had conquered the eastern hills of Luceria; and the plain, too, may have been threatened by them. As Tarentum was allied with the Samnites, the Apulians applied to the Romans, and much may have been gained by their mediation. It was a gigantic resolution of the Romans to transfer their army to Apulia: there were two roads, the one passing through the country of the Aequians, who were friends of the Romans, along the lake of Celano, by Sulmona and through the narrow country of Samnium; the other led through the country of the Sabines to Reate, Civita Ducale, and the fearful passes of Antrodoco (the ancient Interocrea) which are of such a kind that a gallant people may there resist an enemy for a very long time, but which were so disgracefully abandoned by the Neapolitans in 1821; the road then proceeds to Pescara on the eastern coast, and thus reaches Apulia by an enormous circuit. The two roads were probably taken by the Romans at different times, but at first they marched along the former; now as long as they were not sure of the Vestinians, but were on good terms with the other nations, they certainly could take the former road; for on the latter, the Vestinians were the only one of the four northern Sabellian tribes through whose country they were obliged to pass in order to reach Apulia; in addition to which they would have had to fight their way through the territory of the Frentenians. But if they had chosen the former road, the Marsians and Pelignians would, unquestionably, have opposed them as much as the Vestinians, since it was their interest not to allow the Romans to march into Apulia. Now, as on that occasion the Vestinians are called peaceful, it is clear that the Romans marched through the passes of Antrodoco. Had the Samnites been united, they ought to have made every effort to support the Vestinians; but this was not done, in consequence of which the Romans defeated and compelled them to submit. They therefore established themselves in Apulia, and thereby obliged the northern confederates to keep up a good understanding with one another. It was a great advantage to be in possession of Apulia: the country of the four Sabellian people as well as that of the northern Samnites, the Pentrians, Bovianians and even of the Frentenians, is a mountainous and pasture country in the Abruzzo. During the winter those districts are covered with snow, and it is impossible to keep sheep there; whence during the winter they are sent into Apulia, which is then covered with beautiful and excellent grass: in the spring the shepherd drives his flock again into the mountains. In southern countries the great features of nature always remain the same, and they are at the present day just what they were in antiquity. The establishments at Tarentum for dyeing wools show that the breeding of sheep was very extensive as early as that time. The use of those pastures was of the highest importance to the Marsians, Marrucinians, Pelignians, etc., and the Romans, being in possession of Apulia and protecting the pastures for their allies, obliged them to maintain a friendly understanding, and at the same time pressed hard upon the northern Samnites. Hence we see that the Romans did not undertake that formidable expedition at random, but that their course was thoroughly justified by the nature of the country; nevertheless, they did not venture upon the hazardous undertaking, until they saw that it was unavoidable; and that this was the only way in which the war could be brought to a close.

LECTURE XLII.

THE Romans had formed an alliance with the Lucanians as
well as with the Apulians. The Lucanians are called a Samnite colony, which must be understood in a different sense
from what we mean by a colonial city. It is certain that the
Lucanians were an offshoot from the Samnites, from whom
they had separated themselves. They dwelt among the
Oenotrians (the ancient Pelasgians) and Greeks; and as the
Samnites were Sabellians who had become Oscans, so the
Lucanians were Oenotrians who had become Samnites: they
had commenced extending themselves about Olymp. 80, that
is, at the time of the fall of Sybaris, which opened those
districts to the Italian nations. We have no information
respecting the relation in which the Lucanians at first stood
to the Samnites. The territory of Lucania is larger than that
of Samnium; but there was not a corresponding proportion in
the powers of the two nations, as we see from the census lists.
The Lucanians were never powerful, not even in much later
times, when the Samnites were greatly reduced; the number
of their capita did not amount to 30,000, that is much less
than half that of the Samnites. This shews that the greatest
part of the Lucanian population had no share in the sovereignty,
which was concentrated in a few places only, such as Petelia;
the country was distracted by parties. One portion of the
people resolved to join the Romans; but this can have been
only a small majority; for soon afterwards a revolution took
place in which that alliance was broken, and the Samnites were invited to occupy their fortified places. We are
acquainted with the treaty of the Lucanians and Romans from
Livy, but all the rest of his narrative relative to these events
must be greatly modified, as for example when he says, that
the Tarentines, frightened by the power of the Romans, prevailed upon the Lucanian nobles to tell the people that the
Lucanian ambassadors had been cruelly treated by the Romans,
at which the people are said to have been enraged, and actuated
by this feeling, to have thrown themselves into the arms of
the Samnites. This is the same story as is related of Zopyrus
and Sextus Tarquinius. We here see that treacherous blind-

ness of party spirit, which is so saddening in the history of the later Greek states. The Samnites thus unexpectedly became masters of Lucania, and availed themselves of its resources, both in men and money, for their own advantage.

These wars, as far as we can survey them, are from the beginning extremely interesting, on account of the determination, skill, and firmness with which they were conducted. They resemble a single combat between two excellent champions, for the two parties aimed at each other's life, directing their blow with the greatest boldness at each other's heart. They fought with the same resolution as in modern times has been shewn in attacks upon particular places. If after the battle of Cannae, Hannibal, with his enormous talent, had had the same resolution—if he had not been too cautious, but had followed the same plan against Rome as the Samnites did, he would decidedly have triumphed over his enemies. Each of the belligerent parties calculated very much upon the disaffection of those who were dependent upon the other. The frontier of the Samnites was in the Abruzzo above Sora, and Casinum was their city. The course of their operations seems always to have been determined by those mountains. Thence also they acted on the offensive, and that with the definite object of causing an insurrection among the Latins, who fourteen years before had been independent, and were therefore inclined to rebel. The traces of a partial insurrection are obscured in Livy, but are nevertheless discernible; and we find, that even Tusculum, in conjunction with Privernum and Velitrae, rose in arms; but the Romans always quelled these insurrections, and the consequence was the destruction of many of the Latin towns. All this can be inferred also from certain allusions; for example, from the proposal of a tribune (which, however, was not carried), to destroy the Tusculans altogether. To the same circumstances must be referred the strange story in Livy of a sudden nocturnal alarm in the city, as if the enemy were within the walls; for as the armies were at a great distance, an insurrection of the Latins naturally produced terror up to the very walls of Rome.

The Samnites endeavoured to penetrate through the Apennines to the sources of the Liris, and straightway to advance towards Rome. The Romans at the same time crossed the Vulturnus, and tried to reach Saticula in Campania, and

thence to invade Samnium. Each was little concerned where
the blows of the other fell, provided it could itself inflict a
deep wound. This method of carrying on the war had peculiar advantages for both. For the Romans it was an advantage
that the Samnites ravaged only the territory of their allies,
whereas the Romans inflicted sufferings on the Samnites
themselves. This, however, could not have the same evil
effect as the ravages of the Samnites produced upon the disposition of the Roman allies. It is a mere accident that we
know that the seat of this war was in the neighbourhood of
the modern abbey of Subiaco, on the frontier of the Aequians
and Hernicans, among the high mountains which separate the
valleys of the Liris and the Anio. Livy states, that the
enemies faced each other near Imbrinium, in Samnium; but
even the early Italian commentators, such as Sigonius and
Hermolaus Barbarus, justly remark that Imbrivium must be
meant; and they identify the place with that from which the
emperor Claudius constructed his aqueducts, in the country of
the Aequians, near Subiaco. Livy shews too few traces of
accuracy and care to prevent us adopting this correction,
which is commended not only by probability, but by positive
necessity. There the Samnites established themselves, and
thus cut off the Romans from the road to Apulia, whereby
the latter were obliged to keep up the communication on the
road by Antrodoco. That district is very important in military history. Circumstances wore so dangerous an aspect,
that in the third year of the war, the Romans appointed
L. Papirius Cursor to the dictatorship, the consul L. Furius
Camillus being ill. Papirius Cursor is remembered among
the first generals of his nation. By his side stood M. Valerius
Corvus, who was of about the same age, and the younger
Q. Fabius Maximus, whom Valerius Corvus probably survived.

M. Valerius Corvus was the most popular man of his age.
He was free from all political party spirit; he loved the
people, and was beloved by them, and the soldiers had
unlimited confidence in him. In his leisure hours he felt as
happy among his soldiers as in the midst of his family; he
shared his labours and his pleasures with them: his popularity
was the inheritance of the Valerii. It was his personal
character that enabled him to quell the insurrection of the
year A.U. 413, which no one else would have been able to
accomplish.

L. Papirius Cursor was a rough, and properly speaking a barbarous man, who had somewhat of the character of Suwarow, except that the latter was a far more educated man, for he was well acquainted with German, French, and English literature, and possessed great judgment. Cursor had enormous bodily strength; and, like the emperor Maximinus, kept it up by eating and drinking like an athlete. He tormented and annoyed the soldiers by excessive severity, and rendered their service as hard and difficult as possible, thinking that the soldiers would thereby become all the more useful. Towards the officers and commanders of the allies he was equally severe. It was his delight to see those around him tremble; and he would not pardon the slightest neglect, but inflicted corporal and even capital punishment upon those who were guilty of it. He was generally hated, and looked upon as a demon, in whom, however, the republic possessed an invincible bulwark, which in case of need might afford a last refuge.

Q. Fabius was a different man from Valerius Corvus. He does not appear to have been so cheerful and loveable a character as Valerius; but he was withal *comis*, a gentle commander, and a mild and wise man. Great reliance was placed on his wisdom and good fortune; in the latter, Papirius was inferior to him. He too was highly popular, but not in the same manner as M. Valerius; for it seems to have been owing more to the respect than to the love which was felt for him. He was regarded as the first man of his age, whence he received the surname Maximus. He was no less great as a statesman than as a general, and was a rallying point for all parties. By birth and rank he was an aristocrat, but a very sensible one, and in many cases he was able as arbitrator to bend the oligarchy. His whole life shews that he was in earnest in everything, and able to control his own feelings, and sacrifice them to the good of the commonwealth. It is these three men who give to the history of that period its peculiar interest.

The dictator faced the Samnites in the neighbourhood of Subiaco, but at the same time another army was stationed in the neighbourhood of Capua to protect Campania against the inroads of the enemy. The dictator is said to have perceived that the auspices had not been correctly observed. It was impossible for him to take new ones where he was, the auspices differing according to the localities, some being valid at Rome, others in the enemy's country; hence he was obliged to return to Rome to take fresh auspices on the Capitol. Whether it really was for this, or any other reason, he left the camp and went to Rome, leaving the command to Q. Fabius, his master of the horse, expressly enjoining him not to act on the offensive. This injunction may have been well founded; but it is not impossible that it arose from a want of confidence in the younger man, or from a desire not to allow him an opportunity of distinguishing himself. The Samnites very soon observed, that the Romans were not permitted to fight, and they therefore provoked and pressed them all the more: the inactivity of the Romans was dangerous, for the Latins in their rear were ever ready to revolt, if the Samnites should offer them support, though by themselves they were unable to undertake anything. Under these circumstances, Fabius with youthful confidence resolved to give battle to the Samnites: he gained the victory, and according to some authorities even defeated the enemy twice. As the army regarded the dictator's order only as the result of his ill-will and envy, the master of the horse sent his report, not to Papirius Cursor, but direct to the senate, disregarding him who had the auspices, and through whom alone the report ought to have been sent. He then burnt the booty, in order to deprive the dictator of the spoils for his triumph. In the city the fear of the consequences was undoubtedly not less than the joy at the victory. Papirius forthwith returned to the camp; and his speedy arrival there shews that the army cannot have been far away from Rome. Surrounded by his twenty-four lictors, he summoned the master of the horse before his tribunal, and only asked him whether he had fought against his orders or not. When every thing was ready for the execution of Fabius, the whole army assumed so threatening an attitude, and the general indignation at Papirius was so great, that he himself began to hesitate, and at the urgent request of the soldiers, granted a respite until the following day. In the night Fabius fled to Rome and applied to the senate; but during its meeting, and while Fabius was standing in the midst of the hall, Papirius himself also appeared, and demanded his victim. Although the senate afterwards shewed on several occasions that it was not favourable to Fabius, yet sympathy for the youthful hero was then very general, and it was resolved to protect him. Papirius did not dare to use force: the situation of Fabius, however, was not so desperate as Livy describes it, for we know from Verrius Flaccus, that the patricians had the right of appeal from the verdict of the dictator to the curies. Livy's statement that he invoked the tribunes, is either a confusion caused by the expression, *provocatio ad populum*, or it was a sanction of the decree of the curies by the plebes, in which case the whole people would have granted an amnesty to Fabius. Papirius even now refused to yield, but the determination of the two orders snatched his victim from him. Livy's statement, that he became reconciled to Fabius, is impossible. Fabius resigned his magistracy, and Papirius took another master of the horse. The object of general hatred, he returned to the army, and the unfortunate issue of an engagement was attributed to him. This happened in the year A.U. 430.

Fabius is said to have gained his victory chiefly by having ordered the *frena* to be taken from the horses, and thus caused the cavalry to dash upon the enemy. If by *frena* we understand reins, the statement would be absurd: and the difficulty may be explained by the bits which have been discovered at Herculaneum and Pompeii. The bridles and bits of the horses used by the Romans were extremely cruel; if therefore instead of these, the Roman general ordered the gentler ones of the Greeks described by Xenophon to be used, it is natural that the horses, thus eased, should have pressed forward with greater cheerfulness and vigour.

The war took such a turn that the Samnites were in great difficulty, and regretted having undertaken it. They concluded a truce on condition of their giving pay and clothing to the Roman soldiers, and then began to negociate for peace, which they thought they might obtain by yielding to the first demands of the Romans in reference to the garrison at Neapolis and the recognition of the colony at Fregellae. But the Romans now undoubtedly made quite different claims, demanding, in addition, that Lucania and Apulia should be evacuated, and, what was always done in such a peace, that the Samnites should be reduced to the same position as if they had been entirely subdued: this was one of the maxims which contributed to the greatness of the Romans. The attempt to conclude a

peace was unsuccessful, the war was renewed, and the Romans
now conducted it with great energy. Fabius, who was made
consul, led his army into Apulia and took Luceria and many
other towns of the Apulians and Samnites. His repeated victories compelled the Samnites to withdraw from Fregellae in
order to oppose his progress. The other Roman army was also
successful, and as the Romans gained great advantages in the
whole of the following campaign, the Samnites came to the
determination to seek peace at any cost. They now vented all
their indignation upon Papius Brutulus, the man whom they
regarded as the soul of the whole war, and who belonged to
the family which, two hundred years later, produced C. Papius
Mutilus. The Romans again concluded a truce, for which the
Samnites made great sacrifices. We are indebted to the excerpts from Dionysius for a knowledge of these transactions:
the Samnites were ready to do every thing in their power to
punish the authors of the hostilities; but the Romans unquestionably demanded the surrender of Papius Brutulus, and the
resolution which he took shews that he was a great man. He
had lived for his countrymen, and served them as long as they
wished to be great, but now that they were desponding, life
had no value in his estimation, and he made away with himself,
in order that his fellow-citizens might be able to say that the
author of the war had atoned for his offence. This is one of
the most heroic acts in all antiquity, and is greater even than
the similar deed of Cato. The Samnites, to their own disgrace,
sent his body to Rome.

As the Romans had, on the first application for peace gone
beyond the demands they had made before the war, so they
now again exceeded the terms they had last proposed, demanding that the Samnites should recognise the supremacy of Rome
(*majestatem populi Romani comiter colere*). The Samnite
ambassadors had appealed to the humanity of the Romans,
they had declared that they would accept any terms, if the
Romans were resolved not to give up a single point, but that
they could not consent to recognise the Roman supremacy,
since upon this point the national diet alone could decide.
The consequence of such a recognition would have been a
state of perfect dependence in all their relations with foreign
states: they would have been obliged to give up their alliance
with the Tarentines and Lucanians; and Roman commissioners

would have appeared among them with the right to enquire
whether the treaty was duly observed. Such terms were
intolerable to the Samnite people: they had lost their leader,
humbled themselves, and imploringly prayed for a suitable
peace; but all was now in vain; they resolved to perish to a
man rather than conclude such a peace as was offered to them.
This time the Romans had carried their maxim too far: the
Samnites exerted their utmost power, and commenced the war
in Apulia on account of the physical importance of that country. Luceria with its Roman garrison was besieged: it had
originally been a Samnite town, but had been conquered by
the Apulians. The Romans also changed their mode of warfare,
and as the main army of the Samnites was stationed in Apulia,
resolved to concentrate all their forces too in that country:
they had before directed their attention to Apulia, and had
indeed found some allies there, but without gaining a firm
footing. They would accordingly have been obliged to compel
the Vestinians to allow them to march through their territory,
a plan which seemed to be dangerous, because they might thus
become involved in a war with the Marsians, Marrucinians,
and Pelignians. But there the unfortunate jealousy among
the Samnite tribes would have come to their assistance; other
nations also to whom the Romans were troublesome, such as
the Aequians and even the Campanians, sided in their hearts
with the Samnites, though they did not wish the latter to gain
a decided victory: those little petty nations imagined that the
Romans and Samnites would mutually weaken each other, and
that they themselves might derive advantages from this state
of things.

When it was known that Luceria was besieged, both consular armies wanted to march to Apulia, and resolved to take
the nearest way, forcing their road through the midst of
Samnium, for the Samnites had become contemptible in their
eyes. They perhaps took the road by which A. Cornelius
Cossus had gone, viz. the one from Capua by Beneventum to
Luceria. C. Pontius, the general of the Samnites and one of
the greatest men of antiquity, who had foreseen this, left at
Luceria only as many of his troops as were necessary to con-
tinue the blockade, and encamped on the road which the
Romans had to pass, near Caudium, the capital of the Caudine
Samnites: that town afterwards disappeared from the face of

the earth, that there might be no trace of the disgrace of the
Romans. The Romans descended a defile into a valley, on
the opposite side of which another pass formed a steep ascent
up the mountain: they had not yet met the enemy anywhere,
and therefore advanced very carelessly. The army, forming a
long column, had descended the one pass, and the first part of
the column was beginning to ascend the opposite defile, but
found it completely barricaded with stones and trees. The
Samnites had probably made preparations of the same kind as
the Tyrolese in the year 1809, who had placed on the heights
large trunks of trees fastened together with ropes, and behind
them huge blocks of stone, so that when they cut the ropes
the enemy in the valley below were crushed under the falling
masses: this seems to be suggested by the mention of stones
in Livy. According to his account, the Romans behaved on
this occasion in a most cowardly manner, for they are said to
have attempted to return, and finding that the opposite path
was likewise obstructed, they made up their minds to encamp
in the valley. This is an absurdity, for an army thus shut in
would under all circumstances fight with the courage of despair
and endeavour to escape. There can be no doubt that a
pitched battle was fought in which the Romans were defeated,
as is clearly stated by Cicero (*cum male pugnatum ad Caudium
esset*). Appian, of whose work we have only fragments relative to those events, states that the superior officers who
survived with the consuls, signed the peace; he mentions
twelve tribunes, but as the complete army contained twenty-
four tribunes, twelve must have fallen, or at least have been
severely wounded. Zonaras, also, speaks of a lost battle and
the conquest of the Roman camp. In urging the point that
there was no engagement at Caudium, Livy displays a truly
strange kind of vanity: he describes the Romans as cowards
in order to conceal the disgrace of a defeat. The particulars
of this affair are buried in great obscurity, but the result of
my investigations is as follows. According to Livy's account
the consuls only *promised* that the Roman people would conclude peace, and that beyond this nothing was agreed to; so
that he represents the Romans as not having been faithless;
but that half of the Roman equites (six hundred) were given
as hostages. But the affair was in reality quite different:
Appian, who derived his information from Dionysius, says that

the hostages were given, ἕως ἅπας ὁ δῆμος τὴν εἰρήνην ἐπιψη-
φίσῃ, that is, until the curies and tribes should have ratified
the peace. Its terms were fair; C. Pontius, not knowing, in
the extreme joy of success, what use to make of it, summoned
his father Herennius Pontius, a friend of the Tarentines and
especially of Archytas[1] into his camp, to ask him how he
should treat the Romans. Herennius answered that all should
be cut to pieces; and when the son replied, that this was inhuman, the father is reported to have advised his son to dismiss
them all without injury, in order to place the Romans under
an obligation by this act of grace. But the Romans of that
time would have laughed at such an εὐήθεια. The meaning
of the story can only be this:—Herennius meant to say "The
only thing that can be done, is to destroy the enemy; how
can you have any doubt about that? If you are at all in
doubt, you had better dismiss them at once." But C. Pontius
was a high-minded man, he had a great Italian feeling, and it
was impossible for him to annihilate the army of a nation
which protected Italy against invading foreigners, especially
Gauls and Carthaginians; he did not doubt that a lasting
peace might be concluded with the Romans, if they could
be secured; we fortunately know its terms from the fragments. The consuls and all the commanders pledged their
word of honour that the people would ratify the peace; and
until then the equites, the sons of the most distinguished families, were to remain as hostages, the *status quo ante bellum* was
to be restored, all conquered places were to be given back to
the Samnites, the colonists were of course to be withdrawn
from Fregellae, and the ancient equal alliance between the Romans and Samnites was to be renewed. Compensations in
money or any humiliating conditions are not mentioned at all;
the Romans were to depart, but leave behind all their arms,

---

[1] Herennius appears to have been altogether a model of wisdom among the
Samnites. According to a passage in Cicero, *de Senectute,* he was one of the
interlocutors with Archytas in a philosophical dialogue of some Pythagorean
philosopher,—a remarkable proof to what extent those Italiote towns were
familiar with the Sabellian people, and how little they looked upon them as
barbarians. For the Opicans they had a great contempt, and probably made a
marked distinction between them and the Samnites. The intercourse with the
Greeks explains how it came to pass, that Numa, the source of all Sabellian
wisdom, was regarded as a Pythagorean: this is a genuine Sabine tradition.
They went so far in their friendly feeling, that the Greeks insisted upon the
Samnites being a Spartan colony.—N.

money, waggons, horses, etc. This is in accordance with
the general Italian law of nations. The passing of the
Romans under the yoke is described as *superbia* on the part
of the Samnites, but was quite in the natural course of things:
the Samnites had completely surrounded the Romans with
palisades: some of these were taken out, and a gate was formed,
through which the Romans were allowed to pass one by one
unarmed. The same thing had often been done before, and
was perfectly natural. It should be remarked, that Pontius
was so far from being cruel, that, according to Appian, he
granted to those who departed, sumpter horses to carry the
wounded to Rome and provisions for their journey. Never
has a great victory been more nobly used. The question now
is whether the peace was ratified by the Roman people, for
here lies the cause of so grave a charge, that Livy places it in
the back ground. The fact of the peace having been ratified
is attested by the circumstance that the tribunes of the people
were delivered up to the Samnites; they accordingly must
either have sanctioned the decree of the curies regarding the
peace, or have made a formal proposal to the plebes for that
purpose. A tribune of the people was not allowed to spend a
night out of the city; and therefore could not have been among
those who had concluded the peace with the enemy in the
camp. The only other possible way of explaining the circumstance would be to suppose, that by a formal decree, a tribune
was sent to the army; but even this can be conceived only on
the supposition that he was sent thither for the purpose of
ratifying the peace. This was necessary in order to recover
the hostages, and therefore the peace was ratified, to be afterwards broken, under the pretext that the consul and tribunes
who had brought the motion before the senate and the plebes,
were traitors and ought to be delivered up to the Samnites. This
is the most detestable act in Roman history, and surely the
Romans had good reason to conceal it; in order to do this,
Livy has corrupted and distorted the history of the whole of
the year following, by stating that in it the Romans, at the
conquest of Lucretia, recovered their hostages, who considering
that the peace had been so shamefully broken, would certainly
have been massacred long before.

LECTURE XLIII.

THE existence of the peace is further attested by the events which took place afterwards; for in the very next year we find the Samnites in possession of Luceria and Fregellae: it is said, indeed, that the latter place was conquered, but this may be a forgery, or the colonists were unwilling to quit their homes, and the Romans may then have left the place to be taken by the Samnites. At any rate the latter occupied Fregellae, which was a matter of great importance, if the war should break out again; for Fregellae commands the Latin road leading from Tusculum through the country of the Hernicans to the upper Liris and Campania. The Romans therefore now had only the road by Terracina, Lautulae and the lower Liris in the neighbourhood of Minturnae: moreover when a Roman army was stationed in Campania, and another marched by Subiaco into Apulia, the communication between the two was cut off. Of still more importance was the subsequent occupation of Sora by the Samnites, not only for the reasons already mentioned, but because they thereby acquired a basis for their operations. The calamity of Caudium belongs to the year of the city 433, according to Cato; and this forms the conclusion of the first period of the war.[1]

The Romans now cancelled the peace, and delivered up to the Samnites the consuls and other commanders who had sworn to it: by this means they endeavoured to escape the punishment for their perjury, and it was perhaps for this purpose that they had carried their hypocrisy so far as to cause the peace to be decreed by the tribes and not by the centuries, in order to exclude the auspices, and thus to avoid coming into collision with the law of religion. Livy, on the occasion of the surrender of the tribunes, indulges in a perfectly senseless piece of declamation: the tribunes had to meet their fate as well as the consuls, and in so deep a humiliation of their people, they could hardly look upon their personal misfortunes as anything extraordinary. It is further related, that the consul Postumius kicked the fetialis who delivered him up to the Caudines, with

[1] In the Lectures of 1826–7, Niebuhr fixed the end of the first period *before* the defeat of Caudium, so that the second period would be that of the success of the Samnite arms. —ED.

these words: "Now the Romans may carry on the war with justice, for I am a Samnite citizen and have violated the law of nations." This sounds quite absurd, but it is nevertheless possible, for we know from Velleius Paterculus, that previously to the outbreak of the war isopolity had been established with a portion of the Samnites, and these Samnites may have been those very Caudines; now as every Roman on going into exile might assume the franchise of such a state, Postumius, according to the forms of the law of nations, may have claimed for himself the franchise of the Caudines. By such a detestable farce he imagined that he was drawing the punishment of heaven upon the Samnites. But however this may be, the peace was broken in a most unprincipled manner, and this act forms a glaring contrast with the noble generosity of C. Pontius, who sent back all the prisoners, saying, that if this principle was to be followed, the Romans ought to send all their legions back to Caudium, in order that the affair might be restored *in integrum*, and that the individuals were not his enemies. This shews Caius Pontius to have been an extraordinary man, and the Samnite people to have possessed great moral worth.

The Samnites continued to gain great advantages, but none that were lasting, and the Romans, who made immense efforts, returned to their former plan of operation, that is, they conducted the war against Samnium from Apulia and on the western frontier. Publilius Philo and L. Papirius Cursor were elected consuls: the latter went to Apulia; the former is said to have fought on the road which was so unfortunate for the Romans in the year 433, and to have forced his way to Papirius who was stationed near Arpi. This is not very probable, but we cannot speak with any certainty about it. The Romans established themselves at Arpi which was friendly to them, and from it they carried on the siege of Luceria. There Pontius is said to have been blockaded with 7000 Samnites and the 600 Roman hostages, to have been obliged to capitulate, and to have been dismissed after having passed under the yoke. But the whole story is nothing but an invention of vanity.

Diodorus' accounts of these times deserve great attention; we know not whence he derived his materials, it may be from Fabius or from Timaeus; that he made use of the latter at least, is very possible, for Timaeus may have written the history of this period as an introduction to his history of Pyrrhus, or in his histories of Sicily and Italy. The statements of Diodorus are very remarkable though they are extremely fragmentary and unequal. He sometimes drops the thread of his narrative and takes it up again at random; he is on the whole a very miserable historian; his work contains names of places which are now quite lost: some are evidently mistakes and perhaps of the author himself, but others are simply unknown to us. Livy's account of the year 434 (the consuls at that time entered upon their office in September, so that what he relates belongs to the spring of 435) occurs in Diodorus under the year 439, which is far more probable, for it is not likely that Luceria was conquered twice. The consuls undoubtedly confined themselves to making preparations, and reducing to obedience those of the allies who had become rebellious. The Romans now made the greatest exertions in Apulia, most of whose inhabitants they subdued; for in A.U. 436 and 437 there was a truce between them and the Samnites, which had been effected by the mediation of the Tarentines, who were greatly concerned about the restoration of peace, since they dreaded lest the Romans should permanently establish themselves in their neighbourhood. The truce at this period was a misfortune for the Samnites; and there can be no doubt that C. Pontius was not invested with the supreme command, owing to the jealousy of the other cantons. The Romans already began to assume an imposing attitude, but in A.U. 438, the war again burst forth with extreme violence. It is full of the most remarkable vicissitudes of fortune; the ever memorable campaign of the year 1757 indeed is more brilliant, but we might also compare it with that of the Samnites. They conquered Sora by treachery, whence we see that, pursuing the same plan as they had adopted at the beginning of the war, they again endeavoured to extend their sway on the Upper Liris. The Romans, on the other hand, with that lionlike intrepidity which characterises both nations in this war, laid siege to Saticula in the neighbourhood of Capua, for the purpose of gaining ground against Samnium, and disturbing the Samnites by a diversion. I may here pass over the detail. One Roman army was already in the interior of Samnium, and the other in Apulia, but both were almost surrounded, so that a report of the danger reached Rome. The Samnites had strengthened themselves on the Liris, and the Romans, perceiving that it was the object of all their movements to cut off Campania from Rome, sent a detachment under the dictator Q. Fabius, with the greatest haste, to the pass of Lautulae, whence he was to join the army in Campania. But even Fabius was not invincible. The Samnites came across the mountains behind Fundi and occupied the narrow pass, the Thermopylae of that country. The Romans, who seem to have fallen in with them unexpectedly, were completely defeated and put to flight, as is clearly stated by Diodorus (A.U. 438 or 439); Q. Aulius, the master of the horse, allowed himself to be cut to pieces. This victory produced a mighty revolution, for the Samnites now spread into Latium. Satricum joined them, and the nations, far and wide, either actually revolted, or showed a hostile disposition. In what manner fortune turned is a point on which Livy leaves us in the dark, because the preceding defeats are only slightly alluded to by him. The Samnites were besieging a place which Diodorus calls Kinna (we do not know what place is meant). The Romans, in relieving it, completely defeated the enemy, and then again subdued the revolted towns. One of the revolted people were the Ausonians or Auruncans, about the mouth of the Liris, who had probably intended to remain neutral. Some of those who may have been most compromised now displayed features of baseness which one would hardly think possible. Twelve Auruncans came and surrendered their towns to the Romans, who destroyed them; which Livy, with his kindly feeling, relates with horror, but in a political point of view the destruction was quite right. The more difficult the circumstances were, the more necessary was it for them to strike terror into their subjects, for they could not calculate upon any attachment. Livy says *Deleta Ausonum gens vix certo defectionis crimine*, an expression we cannot perhaps take in its strict sense. The disposition to rebel extended as far as Praeneste, the revolt of which place in this very year may be inferred from Livy, for under A.U. 449, in speaking of the Praenestine Q. Anicius, who was then plebeian aedile, he says, *qui paucis annis ante hostis fuerat.* But most of these people, in going thus far, only injured themselves without benefiting the Samnites. None of them wished that the sovereignty of Rome should pass into the hands of the Samnites, but all were anxious to remain separate between the two in their miserable independence. If they had been prudent they would have endeavoured to unite with Rome, and Rome would readily have received them. It is a pity that Livy passes over these painful reports, and does not explain in what manner the two Roman armies contrived to escape from their perilous situation. This must have taken place, and deprived the Samnites of their advantage. Livy himself says, *omnes circa populi defecerant.* We are indebted to Diodorus for our knowledge that the army of Fabius saved the Romans. By dint of a careful examination, we can in some measure determine the whole extent of the insurrection. According to Diodorus, Capua actually revolted; while according to Livy it was only suspected, and the leaders of the conspiracy made away with themselves. The former statement is more probable; and the consequence was, that a Roman army under C. Maenius, who was appointed *praetor rei gerendae causa,* marched into Campania and re-conquered the city.

In the year 440, which is the turning point, the second period of the war came to its close. The battle of Lautulae and its consequences had raised the Samnites to the summit of prosperity; but the Romans now again succeeded in drawing fortune over to their side, as in general they always shewed themselves greatest after a misfortune. Horace says, *merses profundo pulchrior evenit;* the Romans never lost their presence of mind except after the battle on the Alia. With such a determination they could not fail to conquer the world. He who is at one with himself, able, conscious of his power, and who resolutely resists his opponent, is always sure to win. Even the very next year, Rome paralysed her enemies by her invincibleness, though materially she suffered fearfully from such exertions; but in the field she was indomitable.

The year 440 was the twelfth of the war, and the Samnites had not yet lost any thing except the insignificant towns of Saticula and Luceria; Fregellae was still theirs. After this time, however, though they were successful in some undertakings, fortune soon decided in favour of Rome. This is the third period of the war. In A.U. 441, the Romans conquered Fregellae, Atina, Nola (a very important conquest, not so much in a military as in a political and financial point of view, for they thus obtained possession of the fertile country east and north of Mount Vesuvius), and Sora. Nuceria, between Mount Vesuvius and Salernum, likewise surrendered, but soon after revolted again. They now carried on the war against Samnium as if it had been a siege, advancing nearer and nearer until the main wall was reached. According to Livy, Luceria, which had previously revolted, was now retaken; but I believe that it had never been conquered before, and that the first account of its capture is a mere fiction made to cast back the disgrace of Caudium upon the Samnites. That account, however, is here repeated. The Romans now determined to leave a garrison at Luceria, and sent 2,500 colonists to the place. They had to defend the territory assigned to them, their persons, and property: they were a permanent garrison, which was kept complete by the succession of their children, and thus formed a safer defence than cohorts. Even the boldest must have felt giddy at the resolution to establish a colony at so great a distance: but boldness here was the right thing; the colony maintained itself, and the passes of Apulia were now in the hands of the Romans. They also established themselves on the Liris, and conducted their sieges with regular parallels which they continued to push onward. They restored Sora, built quite a new town called Interamnum, fortified Fregellae, Casinum, Saticula, and Suessa Aurunca, in order to make an imposing impression: Cales had been occupied by them even before this time. Every access on the Latin road was thus closed, and the series of fortresses was like those of Vauban on the French frontier. There are some obscure traces that the Romans now began seriously to dread the participation of the Tarentines in the war. Tarentum was a maritime power, though not like Athens in ancient times. Hitherto the Tarentines had only given subsidies, but now they sent a fleet under a Spartan prince to Agrigentum, in order, as the Greek writers say, to regulate the affairs of Syracuse (Olymp. 116. 3.); but it was either actually destined to act against the Romans, or the Romans expected that it would do so. Hence they built a fleet, and appointed *duumviri navales classis ornandae reficiendaeque causa*, independent of the consuls, and founded a colony in the Pontian islands, which had a good harbour. These islands were very conveniently situated for harassing the coasts; and hence the Romans were afraid lest the Tarentines should there establish themselves. The same circumspection was shewn by the Romans in all things. Their fortresses now afforded them a safe basis, and they transferred the war into the country of the Pentrians, in the northern part of Samnium.

In this campaign, the army of the consul Junius Bubulcus came into great danger. Guerillas were formed, and his communications were cut off, so that his army, in a hostile and deserted country had great difficulty in providing itself with the means of subsistence; the Romans learned that the Samnites had driven their cattle into the mountains, and when they set out to take possession of the animals they were surprised by the Samnites and escaped only after sustaining great losses. In this battle, the consul had vowed a temple to Salus, for which C. Fabius Pictor made a picture which according to the judgment of a lover and connoiseur of art was an excellent painting.[2] I have discovered this opinion in a fragment where no one would be likely to look for it.[3] It may be remarked generally that this was the age of the fine arts at Rome, for to this period belongs the exquisite statue of the she-wolf (A.U. 457), and we know that in other temples also pictures were dedicated at that time; statues were erected to C. Maenius and C. Marcius, and Sp. Carvilius ordered a colossus to be erected on the Capitoline hill, which could be seen from the Alban mount. This circumstance shews with certainty upon which hill the temple of the Capitoline Jupiter was situated. Rome afterwards sank down to a mere imitation of Grecian art, and lost her original productive powers. These facts throw great light on the history of art, which no one can learn from books, but which, like the military art, must be acquired by personal observation. A person who should take Pliny alone as his guide would not be able to understand it. It is further necessary to be acquainted with modern art, for he who knows how and under what circumstances art arose, flourished and decayed in Italy, is almost able to prophecy what will be the career of art among ourselves in future; and a perfect parallel occurs in the history of Greek art.

The Romans had conquered a great part of the Samnite

---

[2] The Romans therefore were not annihilated as Zonaras says.—N.

[3] This probably refers to the passage in Mai's Exc. XVI. 6. from Dionysius, cited in *History of Rome*, III. p. 356. n 604.—ED.

country; and if the war had been continued in this manner, they would in all probability have attained their object, and have concluded a peace with the Samnites, on the terms refused by the latter before the battle of Caudium. But here we have the remarkable spectacle of the isolation of the nations of ancient Italy: it was now the fourteenth year of the war, and, with the exception of the Tarentines, no people had yet joined the Samnites; the northern confederacy until then had been hostile to them, or at least neutral, and the Etruscans had not moved a hand perhaps from fear of the Gauls. According to a statement in Polybius, the Romans about that time concluded a treaty with the Gauls, probably with a view of employing them in case of need against the Etruscans. Under these circumstances Samnium had become quite reduced; but now the Etruscans, led by the Vulsinians, at length declared against Rome, which was thus compelled to carry on a twofold war. It was certainly not a mere accident, as Livy would make us believe, that the rise of Etruria coincided with the end of the Samnite war; that event was brought about by the Samnites themselves. The Etruscan war was a relief to the Samnites; the Romans nevertheless did not leave them alone, but continued the war on the offensive. These occurrences are worthy of notice indeed, but it would lead me too far to enter into the detail of those operations. In order not to interrupt the narrative of the Samnite war, I shall defer speaking of the Etruscan war, until I have concluded my account of that against the Samnites. The duration of the Etruscan war, which was interrupted by truces, was different with the different towns; with Vulsinii it lasted thirty years.

LECTURE XLIV.

How low the Samnites had sunk is clear, from the fact that even one consular army was too much for them: this army took by storm Bovianum, next to Maleventum, the most prosperous town of the Samnites, but which, like all Samnite places (in contrast with those of Etruria), was fortified only by nature, and provided with an arx. The fate of Bovianum may serve as an example of the sufferings of the Samnite towns: it was thrice taken by the Romans, and we may easily conceive how it could become so insignificant a place as it was in the days of Strabo. Magdeburg experienced the same fate in the Thirty Years' War for in its capture and destruction by Tilly, its population was reduced from 30,000 to 3000, and only the cathedral and a few houses were left, huts being erected on the ruins. While the Romans were fighting in Etruria, the Samnites evidently had the intention of carrying out the great scheme which renders the third Samnite war so remarkable, namely, to transfer their forces to that country, and to meet the Romans on foreign ground. What the Etruscans wanted, was a courageous army trained in war, and with this the Samnites wished to provide them. But even in the third year of the war, the Etruscan towns concluded a truce with the Romans, and thus destroyed the hope of such a diversion. The expeditions of the Romans into Samnium now became real wars of destruction, for they had no hope of establishing themselves there, so long as a single Samnite was alive: the armies had possession of only the ground on which they stood, and suffered from want of everything necessary for the support of life, the population fleeing into the forest wherever they came. It was in one of these expeditions, that, as before mentioned, the consul, C. Junius Bubulcus fell into such imminent danger. Afterwards, when Q. Fabius was stationed in Etruria, another Roman army was surrounded in Samnium, and the consul wounded: the distress of the Romans was so great, that a reserve army was formed at Rome, and it was thought necessary to appoint a dictator. The senate had to determine upon the person to be appointed, the curies to sanction his appointment, and to grant him the imperium, and then the consul had to proclaim him. Papirius Cursor was elected, and as one consul was blockaded in Samnium, it devolved upon Fabius, his mortal enemy, to proclaim him. The senate sent a deputation to Fabius, to request him to undertake the proclamation, for it was expected that he would oppose the appointment to the last: Fabius had a severe struggle with himself, which is well described by Livy; but he showed himself to be a man above the desire of revenge. Papirius answered the expectations which the senate entertained of him, he delivered the blockaded army, and defeated the Samnites.

When after three years' fighting, the Romans had made
peace with at least a portion of the Etruscans, they again
directed all their forces against the Samnites, and now the
petty nations began to perceive what would be the consequences
of the victories of Rome. The northern confederacy perhaps,
with the exception of the Vestinians, was gained over to the
interests of the Samnites, but it was too late; twelve years
earlier, it would have led to the destruction of Rome: similar
things occurred in the history of the French revolution. Those
nations thought their kinsmen now sufficiently weakened to
assist them without risk or danger. The Hernicans also took
part with the Samnites, and the Aequians seem to have done
the same, or at least to have favoured them. In A. U. 446,
Fabius marched into Samnium, and gained a great victory
near Allifae. The exertions of the Samnites had been most
extraordinary, for they had availed themselves of the years of
the Etruscan war to reconquer Sora, and thereby to re-establish
themselves on the Latin road, and to influence the tribes in
that neighbourhood. Their efforts were not exclusively directed to the raising of large armies; but we also hear of special
ornaments being bestowed upon their troops, of gold and silver
shields; by which, however, we must understand brass shields
with gold and silver emblems, like those which have been
found at Pompeii, among the armour of Campanian gladiators,
which are evidently of Greek workmanship. This circumstance
allows us to infer, that the Samnites had received subsidies
from the Tarentines, for Samnium had been too much ravaged
to permit any such lavish expenditure; the Tarentines probably clothed and paid the soldiers, and we may therefore conclude
that the Samnites employed mercenaries. The Tarentines
might do this the more readily, as the Samnites kept the
Lucanians in submission.

After the battle of Allifae, some Hernicans also were found
among the prisoners, and this was regarded by the Romans as
high treason; they demanded the surrender of the guilty, and
severe punishment was inflicted on the prisoners. Hannibal
treated his enemies cruelly, with the view to extirpate them,
but he was mild towards allies in order to win them: the
Romans followed the opposite system, their object being to
force their enemies to recognise their supremacy, and when
they succeeded in this, they did not by any means intend to

extirpate them, their object at that time being rather to subdue all the Italians, and then gradually to raise them to the rank of Romans. But while they were unwilling to destroy their rivals, they adopted the system of terrifying the small revolted tribes in such a manner as to prevent their attempting to revolt again. Hence they dismissed the Samnite prisoners for a certain ransom, for the Italian law of nations permitted a prisoner to ransom himself; but those who were not Samnites were sold as slaves, and the Hernicans, being guilty of high treason, were distributed amongst the municipia until they could be tried. Three towns do not seem to have taken any part in the war, but Anagnia, Frusino, and the other towns, did not, as Livy says, accept the terms dictated to them; which were to submit, and ransom their prisoners. The word *caeteri*, in Livy, shews that the Hernicans must then have been a greater people than in the early times, when they consisted of only five tribes. Most of the Hernican towns now took up arms; this was very convenient for Rome, since owing to her excellent system of fortification, matters were in such a state that the fortresses in the south occasioned to the Samnites the greasest difficulties in communicating with the Hernicans, who being thus cut off, were so little able to cope with their enemies, that after a battle they purchased a truce for thirty days. This came most opportunely for the Romans, the other army under Postumius being blockaded in Samnium and in great distress. Marcius, therefore, hastened thither, and arrived before matters had come to extremities; the Samnites fought bravely, but the blockaded consul forced his way through the enemy, conquered the Samnite camp, and thereby gained the victory. After this battle and another, a truce was concluded for three months, whereby the Romans gained time to subdue the Hernicans. The proud Anagnia which then formed a separate state, like Thebes in Boeotia, lost its political existence and became a municipium of the second order; it lost its right to transact business with other states on its own account, but retained the rights of sympolity, that is connubium and commercium; this place and Frusino lost moreover the more important of their magistracies, and annually received a praetor from Rome to administer justice. The other Hernicans, who submitted to the laws of Rome, retained their political existence, but became subjects. This conquest was of the utmost

importance to Rome, for the alliance with the Hernicans had
become very troublesome. It is probable that the Romans had
even previously made attempts to bring about a change, and
that these very attempts drove the Hernicans to their insurrection.

As the truce with the Samnites did not lead to a peace, the
Romans traversed Samnium for five months, and, according to
Diodorus, destroyed and annihilated with the utmost fury
every living thing that came in their way, just as Ibrahim
Pasha did in the unhappy Morea. On the part of the
Samnites the war became a mere guerilla war. After such
devastations, the Romans themselves were compelled to withdraw from the wilderness they had created; but the power of
the Samnites was not yet broken. In the following year, both
Roman armies again entered the heart of Samnium, where
they were opposed by two strong Samnite armies. The Roman
consul Postumius had fought an unsuccessful battle near Tifer-
num, and his colleague likewise engaged in a battle in the
neighbourhood of Bovianum. This campaign greatly resembles
that of 1815; Postumius, instead of retreating to his basis,
broke up as soon as he heard of the other battle, and in the
evening, after the engagement had lasted the whole day, he
arrived in right time to gain a complete victory, which
decided the war: the Samnite commander, Statius Gellius,
was taken prisoner. It was now impossible to raise another
Samnite army; the Romans reconquered Nuceria and the
towns in the country of the Volscians, Sora, Arpinum, and
others. The following year passed away under a truce, during
which the Samnites were obliged to keep a Roman army in
their own country. At the end of this year; when, according
to Diodorus, the war had lasted for twenty-two years and a
half, reckoning its beginning from the commencement of the
war against Palaepolis, a peace was at length concluded.

The terms of this peace are preserved in a fragment of Dionysius. The Samnites recognised the majority of the Roman
people, so that they were not allowed to conclude any treaties,
and they withdrew their garrisons from the countries which
had before been subject to them. How far their boundaries
were altered it is difficult to ascertain; the country of the Volscians of course remained in the hands of the Romans, but
whether Salernum and Buxentum became Roman, cannot be

positively asserted, though it is probable; since henceforth the
Romans appear to be in direct communication with Lucania;
the Frentenians also seem to have been quite separated, and if
this was the case, the territory of Samnium would have been
considerably diminished on both coasts, and completely cut off
also from Tarentum. The claims of the Samnites to the places
on the Liris, such as Fregellae and others, were of course given
up. Lucania henceforth again appears independent; during
the war it had been under Samnium; but now the Roman party
gained the upper hand, and the country thus gradually became
entirely subject to Rome.

This peace, however, did not last quite five years, for like
those of Amiens and Luneville, the very nature of its terms
rendered its continuance impossible. The Samnite war was
followed by the subjugation of the Aequians, who still clung
to their independence. The Romans wished to unite them
with their own state, which they effected by a short but fierce
war, for the Aequians dwelt in villages on the hills and it was
difficult to reach them. The consequence was that they obtained the Roman franchise on favourable terms. The Romans
now established a colony at Carseoli, in the country of the
Aequians, and another at Alba, on lake Fucinus; the former
was directed against Samnium, while the latter revealed to the
Marsians and other northern cantons the secret, that they too
were to become subjects of Rome. All the passes leading
through the Apennines were now closed. The Marsians rose
against the Romans, but a peace was very soon concluded, in
which the Romans prudently granted very favourable terms,
whereby that brave and warlike people was completely won,
and became the most faithful ally of Rome. This happened
in A.U. 451.

In the mean time, the Etruscan war had broken out in A.U.
444. It is a distinguishing feature of the Etruscans, that they
observed their truces with the greatest fidelity; and it was in
consequence of this feeling that the Tarquinians did not avail
themselves of the circumstances of the Samnite war. The victory of the Samnites at Lautulae, however, appears to have
given them the first impulse. It was difficult to bring about
a union among the Etruscan cities, for with the exception of
Caere, which had concluded a peace for one hundred years with
Rome, there were at that time, nine states which were to unite

for the war, although each had quite different interests.[1]   The
Tarquinians, for example, had nothing to fear from the Gauls,
while other states were threatened by them.   In the mean time
while they were deliberating, the crisis had already taken place,
victory having returned to the Romans, which was another
reason for the Etruscans to begin the war.   Thus the Romans
as early as A.U. 442, regarded an Etruscan war as unavoidable,
and appointed a dictator; but the preparations of the Etruscans
occupied so long a time, that even the whole of the year following passed away undisturbed.   It was not till the second
year after, that they commenced hostilities, but they found the
Romans prepared; their army was considerable, and they conducted the campaign on the offensive, a boldness which they
may have acquired through their fierce wars with the Gauls.
As the Etruscans were besieging the Roman frontier fortress of
Sutrium, the Romans sent Q. Aemilius into Etruria.   Ever
since the Gallic war, the mountains of Viterbo had been the
frontier towards Etruria; they are now a barren ridge of hills,
but at that time they were covered with a thick forest, the
silva Ciminia of which Livy gives so romantic a description: it
was, however, nothing but a natural division between two nations which were not connected by friendship, and wished to
have little to do with each other.   Such a frontier is often
intentionally allowed to become wild by the growth of a forest,
as the frontier between the Austrian Croatia and the Turkish
Bosnia, where from time immemorial the forest has been left
to itself, with the exception of a few necessary roads.   This
forest was by no means like the *silva Hercynia* with which
Livy compares it, but was just of such an extent that, according to his own account, the Romans only wanted a couple of
hours to march through it.   Sutrium and Nepet were the real
frontier fortresses of the Romans, but always against Vulsinii,
and not against Tarquinii and Falerii, for there the country
was quite open and in constant intercourse with Rome.   The
Roman consul set out to relieve Sutrium, and the battle which
ensued is well described by Livy, from whom we learn that for
a long time the Romans kept back their strong reserve.   This
they often did till the very last moment, allowing their regi-
ments to fight as long as they could, and in this way they

---

[1] Comp. *Hist. of Rome* III. p. 276. ED.

gained many a victory. Such also was the case on this occasion: after fighting the whole day with the Etruscans, they gained the victory in the evening by bringing up their reserve. Livy states that in this battle the Etruscans lost more lives than the Romans, but that the number of the wounded was greater among the Romans; this arose from the circumstance that the Romans fought with the pilum and the sword, whereas the Etruscans, who wore Greek armour, used the lance, and employed a number of light armed troops. Although we may acquiesce in this statement of Livy, yet we cannot admit the conclusion that the Etruscans were completely defeated, for in the year after they were still encamped before Sutrium, and Fabius went to its relief. The army of the Etruscans was very numerous, and Fabius considered it either dangerous or unnecessary to attack the Etruscans, as in general the Romans were not so much bold as circumspect, and disliked to open a campaign with a battle.

Livy's account of these wars abounds in great exaggerations, which is the more surprising, as otherwise his history of the Fabian gens is very accurate. Fabius Pictor wrote only a hundred years after the war, and he was so excellent an author, that we cannot ascribe the fault to him; he was unquestionably followed by Diodorus, whose description of these wars is quite plain and credible, and altogether irreconcilable with that of Livy: no one knows what authority the latter may have followed. According to him the Etruscans must have lost 400,000 men in the battles, but, even apart from numbers, his account of the siege of Sutrium is wholly incredible. The account of the first battle of Fabius mentioned by Livy is probably founded upon nothing else than the fact, that by a very close march, Fabius succeeded in introducing Roman troops and provisions into Sutrium. When notwithstanding this, the Etruscans did not raise the siege, Fabius determined to invade Etruria itself through the Ciminian forest, a resolution which the Romans looked upon as fool-hardy. The news of it filled Rome with alarm, and it was believed, that the army would necessarily fall between two Etruscan armies; the Etruscans of Sutrium might have cut off his direct retreat, and then he would not have been able to return except by a round-about way through Umbria, which it was likewise difficult to pass. The senate thought his design so rash that five ambassadors and two tribunes of the people were sent to dissuade him from it : the tribunes accompanied the embassy evidently for the purpose of arresting him if he should refuse to obey; but Fabius had hastily broken up, and when the commissioners arrived in his camp, he already stood victorious in the heart of Etruria, like prince Eugene who did not read the orders not to fight, till the battle was over.   Fabius had pushed his army onward, but he himself remained behind with his cavalry.   He left the camp standing, undertook a great reconnoitering expedition, and thereby deceived the Etruscans during the day; but towards sunset he followed his army and thus unexpectedly crossed the mountain. But according to Diodorus, if rightly understood[2], Fabius invaded Etruria by a circuitous route through Umbria, and thus attacked the Etruscans in their rear: in this case the march through the Ciminian forest would be a mere invention.

The rich country satisfied the desire of the Romans for booty; for within the last hundred years no enemy had entered the district, not even the Gauls.   The Etruscans now raised the siege of Sutrium, and withdrew towards Perusia, where Fabius gained so decisive a victory over them, that Perusia, Cortona and Arretium immediately sued for a truce, and then concluded a peace for a series of years.   The western towns, Tarquinii, Vulsinii and Volaterrae were thus left unsupported and sued for a treaty on tolerable terms.[3]   The Romans were perhaps not inclined to conclude a formal peace, and both parties were satisfied with renewing the truces from year to year.   Vulsinii alone resisted for a period of thirty years, always drawing into the war some of the other towns; but the hostilities were constantly interrupted by truces.   At Vulsinii, the clients had acquired the sovereignty, but afterwards the proud Vulsinians attempted by a counter-revolution to cast the new plebes into a state of clientship: and as they did not succeed, they preferred seeing their city destroyed by the Romans to sharing the honours of the government with the commonalty.   But this very insurrection of their subjects enabled Vulsinii to hold out so long while other places, far more favorably situated, were obliged to

---

[2] That is, if 'Ομβρίκων is read for ὁμόρων. See *Hist. of Rome*, III. p. 282, note 488.—Ed.

[3] In the Lectures of 1826-7 Niebuhr here also mentioned the battle of Lake Vadimo, which he afterwards seems to have rejected, as may be also inferred from *Hist. of Rome*, III. p. 284.—Ed.

submit in the very first campaign, for their own subjects were
their enemies.[4]

The Romans had also formed connections with Umbria: they
had concluded a treaty with Camers, and taken Nequinum,
a very strong place on the Nera, near the northern frontier of
the ancient country of the Sabines: they changed this place
into a Latin colony under the name of Narnia. By extending
their line of colonies to that point, they cut off the communication between Etruria and Samnium: at the same time they
established similar fortresses near the mouth of the Liris at
Minturnae and Suessa. At Narni, Samnite auxiliaries seem to
have been posted; for it is stated in the Fasti that Q. Fabius
in his fifth, and P. Decius in his fourth consulship, triumphed
over the Umbrians and Samnites; the peace was already
concluded with Samnium, but it was very common with the
Samnites to serve in the armies of foreign nations.

An obvious consequence of the peace with the Samnites is
manifested in the relation between the Tarentines and Lucanians.
During the war we do not perceive a trace of a hostile feeling
between the two people; but from the moment that peace is
concluded, hostility breaks out, so that the Tarentines were
obliged to seek assistance. This is accounted for by the fact,
that until then the Samnites had had the supremacy over the
Lucanians and employed them against the Romans. The
Tarentines now invited Cleonymus, because, as our Greek
authorities say, they were at war with the Lucanians and
Romans; whence we must infer, that the Romans were allied
with the Lucanians. Cleonymus was a prince of Sparta, son
of the aged king Cleomenes; as the succession at Sparta was
disputed and he might possibly be excluded, he readily accepted
the invitation of the Tarentines: he was not an insignificant
man; but from this time he became an adventurer, and sold his
services to several nations. He brought 5000 men with him to
Tarentum, there enlisted a still greater number, and compelled
the Lucanians to accept a peace. Hereupon he took Metapontum,
either in his own name or in that of Tarentum, but oppressed
it by exorbitant imposts, and acted there as a real tyrant. His
conduct towards the Tarentines was so base, that they broke
off their connection with him; they got rid of him by his being
taken into the service of one of the parties that opposed

[4] See above p. 66.

Agathocles at Syracuse. The undertaking failed, and on his return, Cleonymus found the territory of Tarentum shut against him; hereupon he took possession of Corcyra which he made his head-quarters for further undertakings. Thence he made an expedition against the Sallentines, but was defeated by a Roman general; he then proceeded to Venetia and through the lagunes against Padua; but having gone astray into the muddy marshes, he was obliged to retreat with considerable loss. He thus continued to wander about for more than twenty years longer, after which he returned to Sparta and yielded to circumstances: but still he was deeply mortified. Afterwards he tempted Pyrrhus to his unfortunate expedition against Sparta, and must have died soon after at an advanced age.

From these facts, we must infer things which were passed over in the Roman annals. Not long before, the Romans carried on a war in Apulia against the Sallentines, who were always on good terms with Tarentum; now as we find the Romans united with the Sallentines against Cleonymus, it is probable that throughout the Samnite war the Tarentines were hostile towards Rome, and that they concluded peace with her at the same time as the Lucanians. The subsequent existence of a treaty between Rome and Tarentum is quite certain, since twenty years later the breach of a treaty is alleged as the cause of the war between them; one of the conditions of that treaty was, that no Roman ships of war should sail north of the Lacinian promontory. This treaty, indeed, is called by Livy an ancient one, but a writer who pays so little attention to precision in the use of words, may easily call a treaty ancient which has been in existence for no more than twenty years; it cannot have been concluded at an earlier time, since until then the Tarentines always appear as hostile towards the Romans.

LECTURE XLV.

AMONG the great men of this period whom I have already spoken of, we must not omit to mention Appius Claudius, who is celebrated in history under the name of The Blind, having had the misfortune to lose his sight. He is quite a peculiar character; and his actions seem to stand in the strongest contradiction to one another, unless we clearly represent to ourselves the time in which he lived. Being born and bred in the pride of a patrician party, he, as interrex went so far as to refuse votes for a plebeian candidate for the consulship: this we know from Cicero, and yet he was the first who, setting aside men of distinction, introduced the sons of freedmen into the senate. Contrary to custom and usage, he attempted to usurp the censorship beyond the time which had long been fixed by law; and in his old age he appears again as the deliverer of the state, who in time of need roused the senate which had become pusillanimous.

Such a character seems to be a real mystery. To men like Dionysius and the moderns, who believe that at Rome, as in Greece, the struggle was between the wealthy and the ὄχλος, it could not be surprising that Appius should admit the libertini into all the tribes, and even raise them to the rank of senators. But the matter must be looked at from a different point of view, and we must bring vividly before our minds the party feelings of that period. During the fifty years which had elapsed from the time of the Licinian law, a nobility had been formed among the plebeians which already comprised a considerable number of families, and many of them already possessed the *jus imaginum*. The number of illustrious patrician families had become greatly reduced; and it is by no means certain whether the noble plebeian families were not already as numerous as the patricians; most of the latter had become extinct or impoverished, and the names which constantly recur are the Claudii, Cornelii, Sulpicii, and Furii. The plebeians stood to the patricians in the same relation as the nobili of the terra firma stood to the nobility of the city of Venice; if those nobili had become a corporation, as Maffei proposed, they would have formed a plebes, but the nobility of Venice hated no other men so much as those very nobili of Padua, Verona, etc., while they were familiar and condescending towards the common people of Venice. A Roman patrician entertained similar feelings towards his clients, while he hated the order of free plebeians; and a proud patrician like Appius Claudius saw in a Licinius or a Genucius nothing but a detested rival. Such an aristocracy feels the greatest hatred against those families to which it cannot deny an equal rank, and it usually tries to ally itself with those who are furthest removed from all aristocracy. Such alliances occur very frequently in the south of Europe, where history often shews us the aristocracy leagued with the mob, in order to maintain itself; the Santafedists at Naples were Lazaroni, from the very dregs of the people, and the royal volunteers in Spain consist of the lowest rabble. Appius appears on the one hand as a man of great historical reputation, and on the other, Livy speaks of him as a *homo vafer*, a crafty intriguer, an opinion which does not seem to be quite unfounded. Appius Claudius and other patricians seem to have still entertained the idea of depriving the plebeian nobility of its authority by calling in the assistance of a party which by itself could lay no claim to honorable distinction. Such sentiments were unfortunate in every respect, and disturbed the development of the consti-tution. But Appius Claudius was nevertheless a highly distinguished man, and motives may be mentioned to account for his innovations which to a certain extent even justify them. He admitted the sons of freedmen into the senate, and distri-buted the freedmen themselves among the tribes: we must start from the latter point.

The peculiar characteristics of the plebeian order were landed property, and a free and independent existence, in con-tradistinction to the condition of clients. It was necessary for a plebeian, as well as for a patrician, to be well-born (εὐγενής, *ingenuus*); hence he, like a patrician, added to his name that of his father and grandfather. A freedman could not mention such a pedigree, for if he himself had been a slave, he could not mention any father at all; and if his father had been released from slavery, he could mention him alone: but if his grandfather had been emancipated, there was no barrier, for he was then perfectly *ingenuus*, and he might be admitted into the tribes. In so protracted a war as that against the Samnites, the number of those bound to military service must have been very much reduced, and the levies must have been felt very severely. It is a remark of Aristotle, that the character of the Athenian demos was greatly altered during the Peloponnesian war, because its numbers were reduced, and the gaps were filled up with freedmen and others. As the Romans adhered to their system of adding only entire tribes, while the gaps in the old ones were filled

up but very scantily, and as the levies were nevertheless made
in the same proportion as before, the citizens of those ancient
tribes naturally were sorely oppressed. It was therefore a
natural idea to increase the number of those bound to serve
in the legions; but among the Romans, rights and burthens
were inseparably connected: whence it is not surprising that a
censor should have wished to fill up the tribe, since he who
had to bear the burthen of war, should also enjoy the advantage of belonging to the commonalty. The undoubted right
of the censors to enrol people in a tribe, or among the equites
and senators, as well as to eject them, obliges us to suppose
that the absence of two ancestors was, after all, not an insurmountable obstacle to being entered in a tribe; and it therefore
cannot have been a thing so absolutely novel for freedmen to
be admitted into the tribes; but there can be no doubt, that
up to this time such cases had occurred very rarely, and the
innovation of Appius consisted in his distributing the whole
body of freedmen among the tribes. This measure had in
itself something to recommend it; but the development of
circumstances also had to be considered, which must always
be conceived as in a state of motion, and in the new state
of affairs commerce and trade might acquire a much greater
importance than before. If instead of slaves, a large number
of aerarii had carried on the trades and enriched themselves,
all relations would have been changed, and the state would
have been obliged to take into consideration any fair demands
those persons might have made. No immoderate advantages
ought to be given to them, and at the same time it would
have been necessary to afford protection to that which actually
existed against that which was new and in luxuriant growth.
With such principles, free states can always maintain themselves. It was in this manner that a class of men, who are
now mentioned for the first time, had been formed at Rome, I
mean the notaries or *scribae*, who were even more numerous
than the *tabelliones* under the emperors. They formed a
corporation, which in the time of Cicero was a close one,
persons being admitted into it by purchase, and it contained
people of very different kinds. The business of administration, according to the Roman constitution, required no other
knowledge than the *artes liberales*, which comprised every
thing that a well-educated person had to learn; but the whole

mass of business, the transaction of which constitutes the principal duty of officials, was performed by the scribes. The praetorship, for example, required a vast quantity of writing, but neither the praetor himself, nor any other *homo ingenuus*, had any thing to do with it, for it all devolved upon the scribes. This occupation was very lucrative, and all transactions were recorded by them according to certain formularies. These scribes were employed not only by the magistrates, but in all imaginable circumstances, as the Romans committed every thing to writing. They kept all the accounts of the aediles, the laborious registers of the censors, and many other similar things, the magistrates themselves only superintending such records. The scribae were also employed by the bankers (*negotiatores, equites*), for every Roman was obliged to keep accurate accounts of his income and expenditure, which was demanded even by public opinion, for a person who neglected to do so would have been considered a *homo levis*, and many Romans kept a scribe for that purpose.

This class of men now appeared for the first time, and became at once a body of great importance through Cn. Flavius. If Appius wished to deprive the plebeians of the position they had gained, it was no longer the time to take up arms along with clients and isopolites. He was obliged to act with cunning, and this he did by connecting a large mass of men with the patricians, and introducing the libertini among the tribes; for by this means he secured a majority in the decision of the plebes. In like manner, the municipes might be useful to his plans, and even in the senate he might carry things which would formerly have been utterly impossible, by removing, in his capacity of censor, the independent plebeians from it, and by introducing in their stead persons of low birth. Something similar was done by Sulla, who in his legislation likewise went back more than two centuries, and, ostensibly for the good of the aristocracy, introduced a number of proletarians, or people of the lowest orders into the senate. Such also has been the case in France, where at this day there are many people, who during the revolution rose from the lowest ranks. Some of them endeavoured to conceal their low origin by titles and the like, and of others the descent is forgotten by the public. From the censorship of Appius we find in Livy a distinction between *plebs sincera* and the *forensis factio*. The former are manifestly the ancient plebeians, and the latter the libertini and isopolites.

Those who were newly introduced into the senate were of course only to be the creatures of Appius Claudius and his party. He assuredly never thought of making himself tyrant; he had too much good sense for that: his son indeed is said to have contemplated it, but he must have been a madman. His plan therefore can only have been to further the interests of the aristocracy. His enrolling the libertini in the lists of the senate, however, created such indignation, that the consuls in defiance of him called up the senators according to the previous lists, for Appius seems also to have struck out some names of senators, probably of plebeian ones: and his list of senators never acquired legal validity.

The duration of the censorship had long since been reduced from five years to eighteen months; but Appius claimed the office for full five years, and gained his end until he wished to be consul and censor at once. This was contrary to the Genucian law, and the tribunes had resolved to arrest him if he should attempt to carry his plan by force: this induced him to give up the censorship. It is possible, however, that he wished to prolong his office, not so much from a desire to rule, as because the execution of the great works which he had commenced required it. He constructed the Appian road, the queen of roads, because the Latin road, passing by Tusculum, and through the country of the Hernicans, was so much endangered, and had not yet been quite recovered by the Romans: the Appian road, passing by Terracina, Fundi, and Mola, to Capua, was intended to be a shorter and safer one. He first made the road as far as Velitrae, and then as far as Setia round the Pomptine marshes, for the road leading through these marshes was not made by him — that which was afterwards made there for the Roman troops was of little use, — but he made a canal through them in order to drain them to some extent, for it was not possible then, and probably never will be, to drain them completely. The object of this canal was to convey warlike stores from Cisterna to Terracina, which was very necessary, as the Romans had no fleet, so that the Tarentines might easily prevent their communication with Campania by sea. The main road for the troops passing over the mountains and past Setia, was called *Via Setina*, which for this reason is specially mentioned in the list of roads; it is the same as that which throughout the middle ages down to the time of Pius VI. was again the ordinary road, when the Pomptine marshes were abandoned. The Romans chose this road, because the distance between Cisterna and Terracina through the marshes was too great for one day's march. Forum Appii it is true was situated on the canal between those two towns; but it was probably inhabited only in winter: on the Via Vetina, on the other hand, the armies might in summer nights bivouac on the hills. Had they attempted to spend a night in the Pomptine marshes, they would have been destroyed by virulent fevers; this shews the necessity for the Via Vetina. The Appian road, even if Appius did carry it as far as Capua, was not executed by him with that splendour for which we still admire it in those parts which have not been destroyed intentionally: the closely joined polygons of basalt, which thousands of years have not been able to displace, are of a somewhat later origin. Appius commenced the road because there was actual need for it; in the year A.U. 457, peperino, and some years later basalt (*silex*), was first used for paving roads, and at the beginning, only on the small distance from the Porta Capena to the temple of Mars, as we are distinctly told by Livy. Roads constructed according to artistic principles had previously existed, and along both sides of them there ran footpaths paved with square blocks of peperino (*saxo quadrato*). It was especially the money raised by fines that was employed for paving the roads with basalt.

Appius was also the first who built an aqueduct to provide Rome with water, the *Aqua Appia*. The Roman aqueducts of later times were of immense extent, but that of Appius was only a small beginning, and made merely to supply the actual want. The Romans obtained their water from wells, but principally from cisterns (*plutei*), as the water of the Tiber is not fit to drink. The districts situated in low and marshy ground, as the Velabrum and Forum Olitorium, had of course no wells, and were therefore limited to cisterns, and it was the object of the Aqua Appia to provide those districts with water, which was brought from a distance of eight Roman miles. It was built after the year A.U. 440, during the war against the Samnites, when fortune began to turn in favour of the Romans.

It ran, as Frontinus says, under ground, that it might not be destroyed in war, or during the many insurrections of the Latins; for a structure of arches above the ground might easily have been destroyed, as was done by the Goths in the time of Belisarius. It passed by the Caelian hill, below the Porta Capena to the spot near the Aventine, where it was discovered by Piranesi, near the Clivus Sublicius at the corner of the hill. Its issue is now obstructed, the water having in the course of time become corrupted by the numerous stalactites, as has happened in many other aqueducts. This supply of water was a blessing to Rome, such as was not known in any part of Greece.

It is said that a wish to complete these two works induced Appius not to lay down his censorship. Much is written about the contest between him and the tribunes: if it was only his intention to complete his works, it would certainly have been mean on the part of the tribunes to oppose him, but the works were perhaps undertaken on too large a scale for the circumstances of those times, and the question is, did he not overburden the generation of his own time for the good of posterity. According to an account of Fabius who, although himself a patrician, was opposed to the oligarchy, and from whom Diodorus here derives his information, Appius undertook those works even without the authority of the senate, and if so, his mode of acting was certainly audacious, though not inconsistent with his character. He seems also to have sold portions of the *ager publicus* for that purpose; by this measure the plebes suffered, it is true, but his own order likewise sustained a loss.

His real agent in all these matters seems to have been Cn. Flavius, the son of a freedman, who therefore could mention only his father whose name was Annius. This is an Etruscan name, whence we may infer that he was probably an Etruscan prisoner, though in his own country he may have been a man of distinction, who by his captivity lost his *ingenuitas*. Cn. Flavius became the benefactor of the people in a manner which we cannot easily comprehend. According to the earliest Roman custom, the year of ten months contained thirty-eight court days, i.e. every eighth day was a court day, so that the kings, and subsequently the consuls, held their courts on the nundines. This was afterwards altered, it being intended that the nundines should no longer coincide with the court days, as on the ＿undines the plebeian country people assembled in the city in large numbers, so that a tumult might easily break out. Those thirty-eight days therefore were distributed over the whole year of twelve months; and as their number was too small, some other days were added on which likewise *lege agebatur*. But there now arose a double difficulty, of which the patricians made use for the purpose of keeping the plebeians in a state of dependence: the thirty-eight days were distributed over the whole year without any regular order; and if, for example, a person wished to bring forward a *vindicatio*, he, not knowing when the praetor was to hold a court, had to make enquiries in the forum or of the pontiffs on what day a *legis actio* could take place. It may indeed be said that persons might have marked for their own use those thirty-eight days; but there were other days which were half *fasti* and half *nefasti* on which also *lege agebatur;* and others again on which comitia might be held, but still not *lege agebatur*. Now it is related, that Appius Claudius ordered his scribe Cn. Flavius, to inquire continually of the jurists on which days *lege agi posset*; and in this manner he is said to have drawn up a calendar on a table covered with gypsum (*album*), and to have set it up in public; many copies were then taken of it, and the plebeians were full of gratitude towards him. But in order to secure their independence still further, he also published the *formulae actionum;* according to Cicero, this was done after the time of Flavius, because the formulae themselves are said to have been devised subsequently, but the statement of others that Flavius was the author of this measure is more probable. We must not consider this to have been a system of law, though it is commonly called jus Flavianum; it merely contained the formula for each particular case. The influence of the nobles over the lower orders received a severe blow by this measure, for until then no one had been able to transact any business without the assistance of a lawyer; certain kinds of business could be transacted only on certain days, etc. The publication of these formulae was a great step towards civil freedom.

The gratitude of the plebeians for these benefits secured Cn. Flavius their votes, when he came forward as a candidate for the aedileship: it was said against him that he could not become aedile *quia scriptum faceret*, but he promised on his oath that he would give up his profession as a notary; from which we see that at that time the occupation of a scribe was still incompatible with *ingenuitas*. Along with him was elected Q. Anicius of Praeneste, who only a few years before had been an enemy of Rome, and who may have been the founder of the family of the Anicii, so illustrious during the latter period of the Western empire; their competitors had been two distinguished plebeians, Poetelius and Domitius, which shews that isopolites and libertini, the *factio forensis*, here united to decide the election. Pliny tells us that Flavius made a vow, *si populo reconciliasset ordines* (*populus* here are the patricians); and as he performed what he had then named, he must have accomplished the reconciliation. It seems to me not improbable that in the subsequent censorship of Fabius and Decius, Flavius acted as mediator, and induced the libertini to allow their own rights to be curtailed as much as the good of the republic required. For the enrolment of the libertini among the tribes caused great disturbances down to the censorship of Q. Fabius Maximus and P. Decius, when (A.U. 449) a reconciliation was brought about: it was impossible to deprive the libertini of all their rights, but they were thrown together by Fabius into four tribes, the *tribus urbanae*, which henceforth remained the *tribus libertinorum* and hence *minus honestae*. This measure was followed by the most salutary consequences; for if we consider that the votes were taken in each tribe separately, and that in each the majority decided, we may easily imagine that if the libertini, who carried on trade in the city, were distributed among all the tribes, they, being always on the spot, would naturally form the majority in assemblies convoked on a sudden so that only a few of the country plebeians of each tribe could come to the city. In this manner all the power would have fallen into their hands, whenever the commonalty had to assemble on any sudden emergency; and without the wholesome reform made by Fabius, the system of Appius would have been highly pernicious.

Another change, the abolition of the *nexum*, likewise belongs to the period of the second Samnite war; Livy places it in the consulship of C. Poetelius and L. Papirius, but Varro, according to a correction founded upon a manuscript, states that it took place in the dictatorship of Poetelius in A.U. 441. This also agrees with the statement, that the poverty of the families of those who were in bondage for debt was a consequence of the defeat at Caudium. We here see till how late a period certain occurrences, which do not actually belong to the political history, continued to be arbitrarily inserted in the annals. A young man who was ill-used, ran to the forum, and a tumult arose, and this is said to have brought about the abolition of the *nexum*, so that henceforth neither the persons of debtors nor their children were answerable for debt. This exhibits to us a state of things, in which the multitude has already acquired great power; there can be no doubt that even as early as that time, persons in fact pledged themselves by *fiducia*, when they had quiritarian property; and this system of pledging may have become more general, in proportion as quiritarian property increased among the plebeians; henceforth this was the only pledge that was legally allowed, and it was forbidden to pledge one's person. But if a man became involved in debt by a *delictum*, the *addictio* still remained in force, and he had to remain in it, until he ransomed himself; examples of it occur even as late as the Hannibalian war. The continuance of this relation has deceived many, and raised doubts in regard to the law of Poetelius, but *addictio* is something quite different from *nexum*. Livy calls this law *novum initium libertatis plebis Romanae*.

After the close of the second Samnite war, in A.U. 452, the Ogulnian law raised the number of *pontifices majores* from four to eight, and that of the augurs from four to nine, the additional priests being taken from among the plebeians. The ninth pontiff was the Pontifex Maximus, who was undoubtedly chosen indifferently from both orders. Afterwards *cooptatio* was established, but whether this was so from the beginning, is uncertain. Twenty years later Ti. Coruncanius was the first plebeian Pontifex Maximus. Livy gives us the *suasoria* of Decius on the occasion of the Ogulnian law, but the speech is not quite in character with the age, for the patricians themselves then knew right well, that they could no longer maintain their privileges. This change in their convictions appears very clearly in the circumstance, that although the appointments to those priestly offices were undoubtedly made by the curies or by the *cooptatio* of the colleges themselves, yet the law was not violated at all, and the plebeians were at once admitted to those offices. Thus the reality of circumstances had conquered the mere letter of the old institutions; nominally the distinction between patricians and plebeians was still kept up, but the parties of the nobility and non-nobility were already in existence, and the former comprised all distinguished patrician and plebeian families.

Admission to the priestly offices was a matter of great interest to the plebeians, as the pontiffs were the keepers of the civil law and of the whole *jus sacrum;* and the augurs, whose words were still received in good faith, exerted much influence upon all matters of importance.

LECTURE XLVI.

THE peace between the Romans and the Samnites lasted scarcely four years: during that interval the Samnites had prepared for the continuation of the war by the defence of Nequinum or Narnia, for they only wanted rest to recover themselves. According to the terms of their peace with Rome, they were obliged to abstain from every kind of hostility against the neighbouring states; but this was impossible. In Lucania, disputes between the two parties soon broke out; that country had recovered its independence and commenced hostilities against Tarentum; the Samnites then declared war against Lucania, and the Lucanians being thus threatened placed themselves under the protection of Rome. As the Romans did not like to see the Samnites recovering strength they required them to give up their Lucanian conquests in accordance with the terms of the peace. The Samnites returned a haughty answer, and cautioned the Roman ambassadors against their appearing in Samnium. In A.U. 454, while the war was still going on in Etruria with some towns, though interrupted by truces, a fresh war broke out with the Samnites. The Apulians were allied with Samnium, for Apulia was too distant for the Romans to maintain their dominion in that quarter; the Sabines also were favourably disposed towards the Samnites, with whom some of them were even in alliance. Circumstances were thus somewhat more favorable to Samnium than before; but Rome's power, on the other hand, had been so much enlarged, that she was now a far more formidable enemy.

This war took a very different turn from that of the earlier ones, whence we must infer that circumstances also were different. The Romans did not now transfer the war to Apulia, either because the Apulians had revolted from them, or because other considerations prevented them. They attacked the Samnites right in their front, and the latter did not enter the Aequian country, but proceeded to the Falernian district, in the neighbourhood of Vescia. The war lasted eight years, and was even more destructive to the Samnites than the earlier ones; but they conducted it with great vigour, and their whole plan, though not crowned with success, is one of the grandest recorded in history: but *victrix causa Diis placuit*. In the very first campaign the Romans appeared in the interior of Samnium, and penetrated into Lucania to assist the Lucanians; the same campaign, however, was at times unfavourable to the Romans, though they did not lose any great battle.

In the year 455, both the Roman armies commanded by Fabius and Decius were in Samnium and carried on a destructive war, the accounts of which in Livy appear to be perfectly authentic: he made use of genuine memoirs, and yet they often contain statements which are quite irreconcilable. The Romans moved from place to place, and wherever they pitched their camp, they destroyed all around every trace of cultivation. Fabius encamped in eighty-six, and Decius in forty-five places: few towns were taken, because the Samnites on their heights defended themselves with such undaunted courage that the Romans were unable to take them. In A. U. 456 Volumnius and Appius Claudius were consuls, and Decius proconsul; Volumnius is said to have defeated the Samnites again and again, and to have finally compelled their army to take refuge in Etruria: this is a disgraceful misrepresentation of the heroic courage and the great design of the Samnites. Their army was so far from having been driven from the country, that Gellius Egnatius fought in Etruria for several years, and even after the destruction of his army, the Samnites maintained themselves during a long time in Samnium: their great idea was to abandon their own country to the enemy, and to transfer the war to Etruria. Within the last hundred years, the Etruscans had become better acquainted with the Gauls, of whom those who were settled in Romagna had no desire to emigrate, and were engaged in peaceful agricultural

pursuits; few only allowed themselves to be prevailed upon to
serve as soldiers in the armies of other nations. But as the
commotion among the tribes north of the Alps still continued,
the Transalpine hosts from time to time crossed over into Italy,
and then created new commotions among the Gauls. Such a
commotion must have taken place about this time, and the
Etruscans availed themselves of it to take the Gauls into their
pay against Rome: it must have been very difficult for them
to make up their minds to such a measure, for if the Gauls had
settled on the Lower Tiber on the ruins of Rome, Etruria
would have been surrounded by them and destroyed. But
passion and hatred against Rome were stronger than prudence.
The Etruscans, with the exception of a few places, had again
taken up arms, trusting to the aid of the Gauls, and they violated even their wonted fidelity in keeping their truces;
Perusia, for instance, did not observe its peace of thirty years.
As the Etruscans were a wealthy people, and when assisted by
their serfs, also a strong one, but were in want of able generals,
the Samnites resolved to march through the country of the
Pentrians, Marsians, Sabines and Umbrians into Etruria.
This does not form a parallel to the heroic conduct of the
Vendeans, who in October 1793 with their whole population
crossed the Loire abandoning their country to the enemy,
because they could not defend it. The Samnites were a mere
army, and the Romans did not oppose them in their passage.
This march of the Samnites is one of the most brilliant feats
in ancient history, and created no little consternation at Rome.

It was difficult for Gellius Egnatius to unite with the Etruscans, on account of the new Roman colonies. The Samnites
were obliged to pass by Antrodoco; and Volumnius followed
them, but was unable to prevent their reaching and joining
the Etruscans. This happened in A.U. 456, and so far were
the Romans from regarding the Samnites as fugitives, that
the consul Volumnius was commanded by the senate to
transfer the war from Samnium to Etruria, where Appius
Claudius did not seem able to cope with the enemy. The
latter, in his patrician pride, regarded this as an insult, and
demanded that Volumnius should quit the province; and this
great and insolent folly might have placed the very existence
of the republic in danger. Volumnius was willing to return,
and only the entreaties of his army prevailed on him to remain.

In this year the Gauls did not stir; and it is possible that the expected hosts had not yet come across the Alps.

The campaign of the year 457 decided the fate of Italy, and the Romans made enormous efforts. One detachment remained behind on the frontier of Samnium, in order to prevent the Samnites from acting on the offensive against Rome; it perhaps consisted mainly of Campanians and Lucanians, but it acted only on the defensive. The army under the proconsul Volumnius marched against the Gauls, and the old consular army of Appius, which was stationed in the neighbourhood of Foligno, was reinforced by two new legions which Fabius had levied. There were, moreover, two reserve armies, consisting of such men as took up arms only in times of need, probably nothing but a militia, armed with spears: one was stationed on the Vatican hill outside the city; the other had advanced as far as Falerii for the purpose of keeping up the communications. The consul Decius proceeded to the army to undertake the command of the legions, and Fabius brought him reinforcements. The Romans had established themselves among the Umbrian mountains in the neighbourhood of Nuceria, where they were encamped, and one detachment proceeded to Camerinum[1] on the northernmost slope of the Apennines, in order to prevent the Gauls from marching through the passes to Spoleto in the rear of the Romans. The Gauls, it must be conceived, came by way of Ariminum and Sena and crossed the Apennines. Polybius here assists us in forming a clear idea of these movements. The legion which had been pushed on as far as Camerinum, was taken by surprise and entirely cut to pieces, so that the Romans knew nothing of the defeat until the Gallic horsemen came up and exhibited the heads of the slain on their spears.

The Etruscans, Samnites, and Umbrians, who had hitherto remained on the defensive, now drew close together, and the two Roman commanders again ventured upon an extremely bold enterprise: ἀσφάλεια, or caution, is commonly the prevailing feature in Roman tactics, but in circumstances like these, they were obliged to risk every thing in order to gain every thing. They marched sideways against an enemy

---

[1] Not *Clusium*, as Livy says, for this was called in Umbrian *Camers*. Polybius has the right name, and even a mere consideration of the nature of the country might shew us that Clusium cannot be meant.—N.

immeasurably superior to them in numbers: the main army proceeded from Nuceria, across the Apennines, which are not very high there, to Sentinum; the Gauls and Samnites were stationed on the right, the Etruscans and Umbrians on the left. Between these armies they marched onwards until they came to the district where the Apennines sink down into mere hills towards the Adriatic; it appeared as if they intended to invade the country of the Senones, but the latter instead of coming forward returned to their frontier, and the Romans drew themselves up *en échelons*. The consuls then ordered the reserve armies to advance; and Cn. Fulvius marched from Falerii (Civita Castellana) into the position which the main army had abandoned, and was sent to Assisium in the neighbourhood of Perusia. The mountain there is very high and strong, so that he could make inroads into the country, and tempt the Etruscans to separate themselves from the Gauls. All this must be looked upon as certain; but I suspect that the second reserve army which had been stationed on the Vatican also followed as far as Falerii. There can be no doubt that at Rome, all preparations were so far completed, as to enable the citizens to resist any sudden attack which might be made from Samnium. There is another point which can scarcely be doubted, although Polybius only supposes it: the Romans must also have withdrawn Volumnius who opposed the Samnites in their own country, so that he arrived on the decisive day, after a hasty march through the country of the Sabines, on the road leading by Terni. Samnium was thus left to its fate.

The diversion of Fulvius towards Perusia was crowned with the most complete success. The Etruscans and Umbrians sent considerable detachments of their main army to their respective countries, in order to protect their frontiers from the ravages of the Romans: these were the best troops of the Etruscans, whereas the Romans under Fulvius were the worst. The two consuls, Q. Fabius V., and P. Decius IV., are the only commanders mentioned in the battle; but there can be no doubt, as I have already mentioned, that Volumnius also was present as proconsul: the Roman forces amounted to about fifty or sixty thousand men, who were opposed to an infinitely more numerous enemy. There were many reasons for proceeding to Sentinum which are not mentioned by the historians, but which can be distinctly perceived: the first was to draw the

Etruscans away from their country, so that in case of their being obliged to retreat, they would be separated from their allies, and have to march along the curve of which the Romans had intersected the chord: the second object was, to alarm the Gauls for their own country, and it was to be expected that a great number of them would disperse to protect their open villages: lastly the Romans dreaded the ἀπόνοια of the Gauls. If they had cut off the retreat of the Gauls in the south, they would have compelled them to fight with the courage of despair, but now the retreat into their own country was left open, though they had not yet crossed the mountains.

We here see how thoughtfully and energetically the Roman commanders acted: their wisdom was rewarded with success. But the numbers of the enemy were so overwhelming, that the Romans did not rely on the efforts of human valour alone: Decius on quitting Rome had resolved, in case of need, to devote himself to the infernal gods, and for this purpose he had induced the plebeian pontiff M. Livius to accompany him and to perform the solemn ceremony in the midst of the battle. Decius faced the Gauls, Fabius the Etruscans, Umbrians, and Samnites, and the legions of Volumnius were probably stationed between them. The Samnites were by far the most formidable among these enemies. Fabius, like every other great general[2], had something peculiar in his mode of conducting a battle: he spared the reserve till the very last moment—a manoeuvre the practicability of which entirely depends upon the nature of the army; for it can be done with a very well disciplined army; but it would expose one consisting of young soldiers to the danger of being completely defeated: when the battalions in front were almost cut to pieces, he brought up his fresh reserve, with which he almost always gained the victory. Such also was his plan now against the Samnites. But Decius who faced the Gauls necessarily pursued a different method: the fact that the Romans fought against every enemy in a peculiar manner, constitutes their greatness in battles. The wars of the

[2] A general is an artist in the highest sense of the word, and may always be distinguished from others by the peculiarities of his movements. During the wars of the revolution, I acquired so accurate a knowledge of the peculiar manner of each general, that in very important cases I was able to predict how Napoleon, for instance, would act: many of my friends did not believe what I said, but my prophecies usually turned out to be true.—N.

Greeks are infinitely less attractive than those of the Romans; for with the former the phalanxes attacked one another as inflexible masses, whereas the whole of the Roman tactics were light and elastic; and Polybius who was himself a great tactician considered it suitable under all circumstances. Fabius endeavoured to wear out the Samnites, because it was summer, the heat of which was much more easily endured by the husbandmen of a warm climate, than by the Samnites who lived in the mountains and cold valleys. It would certainly have been very easy to exhaust the Gauls also in the heat of the sun, but they formed an innumerable host which threw itself upon the enemy with the utmost vehemence: the first shock was the worst, but if that was successfully resisted, victory was tolerably certain. Decius did every thing he could to stand against that first shock, but in vain: the numerous cavalry of the Gauls although at first repulsed, again pressed forward with irresistible force, and then the Gauls brought up their thousand war-chariots, which were a frightful sight for the horses of the Romans. The horses were terrified and took to flight notwithstanding the efforts of the horsemen to prevent it. The armies faced each other for two days, and on the morning of the third the Romans had an omen which promised them the victory: a hind was chased down the mountains by a wolf, which overtook and tore her to pieces. Nevertheless the day seemed to be lost, when Decius, following the example of his father, devoted himself to death: he rushed among the Gallic hosts, adding to the form of devotion the prayer that terror and death might go before him. A panic is said to have seized the hostile army, which checked them in their pursuit of the Romans. Be this as it may; it is one of the stories which might make one believe in miracles; but these are things which we can only touch upon gently, and which may easily be abused. The death of Decius decided the battle: the Romans rallied, collected the pila upon the field of battle, and hurled them against the Gauls. The Gallic cavalry had advanced too far: it was surrounded and cut to pieces, and Fabius who had already conquered the Samnites, sent his troops as a reinforcement, and then brought up the reserve also. The Gauls now stood together in a dense and immovable mass like the Russians in the battles of Zorndorf and Austerlitz, and dispersed only to take to flight; the Samnites, Etruscans, and Umbrians, retreated to their camp with less confusion. The Romans are said to have lost 7000 men of the one army and 1200 of the other; the Gauls lost 25,000, and from 7000 to 8000 are said to have been taken prisoners. After the battle the Gauls withdrew to their own country, quite unconcerned about the further progress of the war, just as if they had been mercenaries. The Samnites again executed an exceedingly bold undertaking: Gellius Egnatius himself had fallen in the battle or during the retreat; and the Samnite army was again obliged to march round that of the Romans or through the midst of it, pursued by Volumnius, and attacked by the people through whose territory they passed, and which' they were obliged to plunder in order to obtain subsistence. When they reached Samnium their number was reduced to 5000 or 6000. Thus ended a campaign which, in regard to achievements, battles and design, is the greatest known in the early history of Rome. The statements of the numbers of the armies are corrupt in most manuscripts: Livy mentions 40,330 Gallic foot and 46,000 horse; the first number has been left unaltered, but the 46,000 have been reduced to 6,000; whereas the numbers should be 1,000,000 foot and 46,000 horse.[3] These however are not historical numbers, but such as belong to the chronicles. The battle of Sentinum was so glorious that even the Greeks heard of it; and Duris of Samos, in his history, mentioned that 100,000 Gauls had been slain, a number which shews the standard by which the victory was measured, and rendered it conceivable how the chronicles could speak of an army of 1,000,000 foot soldiers.

LECTURE XLVII.

A CAMPAIGN of such historical importance, greatness and artistic excellence, as that of the year 457, fills our hearts with grief, and at the same time with the highest respect. The end

---

[3] For the reasons in support of this assertion see *Hist. of Rome*, III. p. 385. n. 647.—ED.

of the third Samnite war brought sufferings and destruction
upon Samnium, and however miscalculated the exertions of
the Samnites may appear, yet they were great and noble. I
shall relate the end of the war very briefly. It was continued
in the same manner as before till the year 461, when it was
brought to a close (peace was not concluded till A.U. 462).
The Samnites renewed their attempts to penetrate into Etruria,
but in vain. The Romans clung to the heart of Samnium,
where they destroyed all cultivation; and the Samnites took
vengeance by acting in the same manner in the Falernian district between the Liris and Vulturnus. It must be remarked
in general that during the last years of the war immense exertions continued to be made, and in the very year of the battle
of Sentinum, the Samnites made a predatory excursion through
Campania. In the second year[1] after the battle, we hear of
two great armies which they sent into the field and one of
which pledged itself by a most solemn oath to fight to the last
man. The marvel is, where the Samnites found their forces,
and how they could afford to equip their soldiers so richly; for
Livy mentions that their shields were covered with gold and
silver. Such magnificence among a people which had been
subjected to so much suffering sounds fabulous[2]; but it is an
historical fact that the consuls Postumius and Carvilius, in their
victories over the Samnites, obtained spoils of extraordinary
splendour, and that out of one portion of them a colossus of
brass was erected in front of the Capitol.

The war was in reality decided as early as A.U. 459, by the
consuls L. Papirius and Sp. Carvilius. It is characteristic of
the mode of warfare that the Samnite towns, both at this time

---

[1] Throughout this period, I follow the Catonian era; in Varro and in the
Capitoline Fasti entire years are interpolated. The difference arises from an
immense blunder which Varro makes in the interval between the taking of
Rome by the Gauls and the Licinian law. According to him the taking of
Rome falls three years earlier than is stated in all the other accounts; from the
foundation of the city to the conquest, Varro and Cato agree with each other.
Varro's calculation is connected with that of the Greeks whence the Varronian
era is sometimes used for synchronistic purposes. But not one ancient historian
has adopted this patchwork; and Polybius in particular uses the Catonian era,
which must be preferred for this reason also, that we can always state with certainty why Cato calculated in this manner and not otherwise. A perfectly
satisfactory chronology of Roman history is an impossibility, for it was not till
the first Punic war, that the commencement of the year was fixed.—N.

[2] See above p. 376.

and afterwards in the Sullanian wars, disappear so entirely from the face of the earth, that in the geography of later times they are entirely unknown, and that, as I have been assured by competent persons, no Samnite monuments are to be found in those districts. The last great battle was fought in the year 460, when Q. Fabius Gurges, the son of the great Fabius, marched into the country of the Pentrians. The Samnites were commanded by C. Pontius, the hero of Caudium, whence we must infer that the Caudines also took part in the war. The Romans were defeated and lost all their baggage: they fought their way through the enemies indeed, but were unable to continue the campaign. When the news of this defeat arrived at Rome, Fabius entreated the senate not to deprive his son of the imperium as had been resolved; and he not only succeeded in his petition; but was permitted, in the capacity of a legate, to go to his son with reinforcements: this was the noblest reward which the republic could give to that great man. He now gained quite a decisive victory, by which, as Orosius correctly remarks, the war was brought to a close, for Eutropius, who states that the war lasted one year longer, is so careless a writer that no weight can be attached to his assertion. The result of the victory was horrible: C. Pontius was taken prisoner, led to Rome in triumph and then executed. Roman history has no greater stain than this: the fate of Pontius even at this day deserves our tears, and the conduct of Rome towards her generous enemy, our curse. His native city must have been destroyed about that time, to efface every memorial of the deeds of which it was the scene.

At the end of this war, when it was too late to give events a different turn, new allies came forward in support of the Samnites. These were the Sabines, whose peace with Rome had then lasted one century and a half, and in such a manner that we must believe they had the Roman franchise, as is in fact stated by an otherwise untrustworthy author. This may have induced the Romans to grant peace to the Samnites, although they were not annihilated. The terms of the peace are unknown, because the books of Livy and Diodorus relating to this period are lost; but it is self-evident that the Samnites were obliged to give up their alliance with Apulia, and that the boundaries of the Roman dominion were extended. By this peace the Romans were enabled to establish the great colony of Venusia, the birth-place of Horace, on the frontier of Apulia; 20,000 colonists are said to have been sent thither; and if this be true, the colony must have received a large territory. It separated Samnium from Tarentum, and its importance gives some probability to the statement of the great number of colonists: in the war against Pyrrhus it saved Rome; but for it the army of Laevinus would have been completely destroyed after the battle of Heraclea. At a somewhat later time, the Romans founded another colony at Aesernia, in Samnium.

The Sabines were chastised by M. Curius. They consisted of several loosely connected tribes: Amiternum had been allied with the Samnites even before, and was taken in the third Samnite war. There can be no doubt that until then the Sabines were protected by the dread with which the Romans looked upon the Gauls; but now the Sabines seem to have been required by the Romans to accept of the Caerite franchise (sympolity), and as they declined to do so, a war broke out. As nearly all the Sabine towns were open places, the contest was short and occasioned little bloodshed, and the conquest easy; the booty was immense, owing to the long period of peace which the Sabines had enjoyed.

This Sabine war led to a great assignment of public lands, for their numerous and important wars had thrown the Roman people into great distress. Something similar is mentioned by the excellent bishop Massillon in his funeral oration on Louis XIV. All those great victories appear to us to be brilliant in a political point of view, and the whole period is a splendid one; every one must feel that if he had been a Roman he would have liked to live at that time and amongst those men; but all this splendour was only a cover of very great misery: such circumstances have too often been overlooked in ancient history; for men are generally so much dazzled by brilliant exploits, that they do not perceive the misery that lies behind them. However much St. Augustine and his friend Orosius may exaggerate, yet in reality they are not very far wrong. Before the battle of Sentinum, a miracle had happened: the statue of Victoria was found taken down from its pedestal and turned towards the north, and milk, blood, and honey, flowed from her altar. This gave a wide scope to interpreters, who said that as the goddess was turned towards the enemy, she promised

victory to the Romans; the blood was supposed to denote
the war; the honey to be a sign of the plague, because honey
was usually given to persons suffering from that disease; and
the milk was interpreted to mean scarcity, as indicating the
necessity of dispensing with corn, and of making use of that
which was produced spontaneously. This interpretation is so
forced, that we see at once that it cannot be very ancient; but
it is a poetical exposition of what actually happened. A plague
was then extending its ravages, far and wide: it probably did
not originate at Rome, but in Umbria or Samnium; it may
have been the consequence of the calamities of war, but it is
possible also that it was connected with other occurrences.
That period, in general, was one of great physical revolutions,
and there are traces which shew that all nature throughout
Italy was then in a convulsed state. Earthquakes began to be
frequent in this century, and continued to be so till the end of
it, when they became dreadful; the winters were extremely
cold, and there was an eruption of the volcano in the island of
Ischia. Epidemics must have raged all over Europe, and
according to Pausanias, a fearful plague, which completed the
depopulation of Greece, raged in that country at the time of
Antigonus Gonatas. In A.U. 460, according to Livy, it was
raging at Rome, already for the third year. There can be no
doubt that Latium was also visited by famine, in consequence
of the devastation of Campania, the granary of Rome. By
the command of the Sibylline books, the Romans sent an embassy to Epidaurus for the purpose of fetching Aesculapius to
Rome. It consisted of Q. Ogulnius and another person, who
having arrived with their trireme, explained their request to
the people of Epidaurus. The senate of the city referred them
to the god himself, who during the *incubation* promised to
follow them, and a gigantic serpent crept forward from the
adytum and remained on the deck of the trireme. When, on
its return, the ship arrived at the mouth of the Tiber, the
serpent leapt into the water, and swam up the river till it
reached the island opposite the city, where the temple of Aesculapius was afterwards built. This embassy to Epidaurus
cannot be doubted at all, nor can it be disputed that a sacred
serpent was brought to Rome from that city. Harmless serpents were kept in the temple of Aesculapius at Epidaurus;
and at an earlier period such a serpent had been conveyed from

Epidaurus to Sicyon in a waggon drawn by oxen. The groundwork of this legend is true, but all the detail is a poetical addition: we are here on ground quite different from that of former times. The story is further remarkable, because it shews the Greek ideas were then by no means foreign to the Romans.

During this great distress, there arose at Rome on the one hand, great debts, and on the other, a desire for a better state of things. The booty which Curius brought with him after his victory over the Sabines, was so great, that the historian Fabius (quoted by Strabo), says that through this victory, the Romans for the first time became acquainted with wealth; most of it, independently of money, undoubtedly consisted of cattle and land: of the latter, Curius declared there was so much, that it would be necessary to let it lie waste, if he had not so many prisoners.

This is one of the obscurest periods in Roman history, owing to the loss of the eleventh book of Livy. During my investigations, I have gained firmer and firmer ground to stand upon; and I may perhaps still be so fortunate as to clear up every obscurity. It is certain that Curius was involved in the most violent disputes with the senate, undoubtedly on account of the distribution of the domain land, for Curius insisted on an assignment on a larger scale to the people (this is now the right term, and we can no longer speak of the commonalty), and also to the libertini, because they were contained in the tribes. The popular indignation therefore was directed against the plebeian nobility, as well as against the patricians, the former being as much interested in preventing the assignment as the latter. The ferment was so violent, that a band of 800 young men united, for the purpose of defending the life of Curius, just as the equites united to protect Cicero. During these tumults the assignment of lands was decreed, and on that occasion the triumvirs wished to give to Curius seven times the amount of the seven jugera, that is, an entire centuria of that time; but Curius refused it, saying, that he should be a bad citizen if he were not satisfied with his legal share. We may readily believe that Agrippa Menenius was poor, but we can hardly suppose that Valerius Poplicola was so, as he was able to build a splendid house for himself; it is however well attested, that M'. Curius was not rich, and yet was cheerful with his limited means. It

is equally well known that the Samnite ambassadors found him
sitting at the hearth of his Samnite farm when he rejected their
presents, and that the senate assisted him in the management
of his domestic affairs during his consulship.   Curius was one
of those proud characters, who feeling no wants, are much
happier than others who roll in wealth.

In his censorship, which falls two years later, he executed
one of the most magnificent works that the world contains,
and in comparison with which the pyramids of Egypt sink
into insignificance.   I allude to the draining of lake Velinus,
whereby the falls of Terni were formed, the height of which is
140 feet: it is the most beautiful waterfall in the world, and
yet is the work of human hands.   Livy calls the Via Appia,
a *monumentum gentis Appiae*; this is a *monumentum Curii*.   Lake
Velinus filled a large mountain-valley without any outlet,
because a range of not very high rocks separated it from the
river Nar (Nera).   Curius cut through the rock, gave an
outlet to lakes Pie de Luna and Velino, and thus rendered
available many square miles of the most excellent soil in all
Italy, the territory of Rieti, the *prata rosea*, which Cicero calls a
Tempé.   We are indebted for our knowledge of the fact that
Curius executed this work, to a very accidental mention of it
by Cicero.   The water is calcareous, as is universally the case
in the Apennines, whence stalactites are formed, which, as the
work had been neglected during the middle ages, have rendered
it necessary, ever since the sixteenth century, to alter the course
of the river from time to time.   The lake has changed its bed
in such a manner, that a bridge built in the middle ages, is
now entirely covered with limestone, and was only discovered
a few years ago.   An excellent Roman bridge over the canal
is still visible, but is never visited by strangers, because the
access to it is rather difficult: there can be no doubt that that
bridge is likewise a work of Curius.   It was shown to me by
an intelligent peasant: it is built in the ancient Etruscan fashion,
in the form of an arch, of large blocks of stone, and without
cement; although it is covered with earth and trees to nearly
the height of a house, still the stones are not displaced in the
least.   Thousands of travellers visit the falls of Terni, but few
know that they are not the work of nature.

LECTURE XLVIII.

THE period from the third Samnite war down to the time when Pyrrhus was called into Italy, though it embraces scarcely ten years, is one of the most important in all ancient history, whence it is to be greatly regretted that we have no accurate knowledge of it. In the sixteenth century people are said to have conjured up spirits for the purpose of recovering the lost works of ancient authors: if such a thing were possible, or if by any sacrifice a lost work could be recovered, I should not hesitate, as far as information goes, to choose the eleventh book of Livy in preference to any other work: it is possible however that sooner or later the history of that period may yet be discovered. I have collected much, but it does not suffice to furnish a complete historical view; and the following is all that I can here give as the results of my enquiries. In the year 642 (according to Cato) the Maenian law was passed; it is only a few days since that I found a passage relating to this law, which I had read indeed very often, but the importance of which I, as well as all others, had overlooked; the law is otherwise known to us only from a hasty remark of Cicero, who says that it was a great thing that Maenius when tribune compelled the interreges to accept the votes for a plebeian consul, because the Maenian law did not yet exist. The context shews that this law can have had no other meaning, than that the *auctoritas* of the patres in regard to curule elections was abolished, as had been done forty-six years before by the Publilian law, in regard to legislation by the centuries. This law was absolutely necessary, for the sanction in cases of election was absurd and a mere source of annoyance, since the patricians had already given their votes. Henceforward the senate gave its assent beforehand; the imperium was conferred by a mere *simulacrum* of the curies, that is, by the lictors who represented the curies, as the five witnesses at sales, etc., represented the classes of the centuries. The curies accordingly were not abolished. The law must have been carried after great struggles; and the passing of it was one of the stormy events in the consulship of M'. Curius.

The Hortensian law, of which I should like exceedingly to

have an accurate knowledge, was of quite a different kind.
Until very recently, we merely knew from Zonaras that disturbances arose in consequence of the state of debtors. The
tribunes proposed to cancel all debts, and as they did not
succeed, the plebeians established themselves on the Janiculum, whence, after a long secession, they were at length led
back by the dictator Q. Hortensius. This dictatorship produced the Hortensian law, which is known from Gaius and
the Institutes, and the terms of which were *ut plebiscita omnes
Quirites tenerent.* Last year [1828] something more was
discovered in the *Excerpta de sententiis*, published by A. Mai;
it is a fragment from Dion Cassius, but extremely mutilated.
I have endeavoured, in the *Rhenish Museum*[1], to restore the
connection, and I have no doubt as to the correctness of the
meaning in general. According to this passage, the tribunes,
in consequence of the great distress[2], proposed the cancelling
of debts (*tabulae novae*): distress and debts are most severely
felt during the first years after a peace. The tribunes made
the proposal according to the Publilian law[3], by which the
resolution of the plebes was only a bill which still required
the sanction of the curies. The senate could only introduce
measures to the curies, and the latter could not transact any
business which had not previously passed through the senate:
the senate therefore might reject the bill, but if not, it was
brought before the curies. The plebeians were delighted
with the proposal of their tribunes, and passed it; but it had
to be brought before the senate; and when this was done, the
senate rejected it. Circumstances were already the same as
those which present themselves so glaringly in the time of
the Gracchi. It was a struggle between the people and the
nobility: the plebeian nobility screened themselves behind
the curies, and were very glad to see the proposal rejected by
them. The tribunes now made a further proposal. As the

---

[1] The essay here alluded to is reprinted in Niebuhr's *Kleine Hist. und Philol.
Schrift.* II. p. 241, etc. — ED.

[2] " The advantage of an assignment of lands came at a time when the people
were in urgent want of an improvement in their domestic affairs, but too late
to secure it." *Hist. of Rome*, vol. III. p. 416. — ED.

[3] It is evidently a mistake that the Publilian law is here mentioned instead
of the Horatian, since the former affected only matters connected with the
administration, but the latter was still the only valid form for actual legislation.
See above, p. 215. — ED.

cancelling of debts appeared too much, they referred the creditors to the Licinian law, and proposed that the interest already paid should be deducted from the principal, and that the rest should be paid off in three instalments. At that time usury was forbidden, and the creditors therefore had to evade the law by means of foreigners. When any money business was to be transacted, they went to Praeneste or Tibur, and a Tiburtine nominally lent the money on interest, and any disputes arising from it were decided in his forum. Thus we can reconcile the law forbidding usury, with the fact that interest was nevertheless paid.

The curies refused to sanction the law even with these modifications; and after each refusal the bill could not be brought forward again except in *trinum nundinum :* the people would have been quite satisfied with the modified proposal, but the curies said, No. This infuriated the people: they quitted the city, and established themselves on the Janiculum; we can hardly suppose that the plebes was headed by a magistrate, as had been the case in former secessions. The heads of the democratical party intended to make use of these circumstances for their own advantage, and allowed the people to go on, though they were probably not as harmless as the plebeians had been in their earlier secessions. As the multitude gathered on the Janiculum did not disperse, but continued to increase in numbers, the rulers of the republic began to be alarmed, and were ready to come to an understanding. But now the leaders of the insurgents would not agree to the terms proposed, but demanded more and more. What this was we cannot say, but they probably required an assignment of lands, and a much greater reduction of the debts. At last they came forward with the demand, that as the opposition of the senate and the curies had shaken the peace of the republic, they should forego their *veto ;* and this was obtained. The curies for the last time met in the *Aesculetum*, and decreed their own dissolution. An analogous case occurred in the *ordinanza della giustizia* of Florence, whereby a great part of the noble families were excluded from all civil offices, and that through their own fault, since they had indulged in every profligacy, and refused to submit to the demands of justice.

On these terms Hortensius succeeded in restoring peace.

His law embraced other matters also, and it is a mistake to
speak of several laws.   What are thus called were only clauses
of one and the same law.   Down to the time of Cicero, there
had been only one dictator, Hortensius, and one Hortensian
law.

This decree is an extraordinary event; and it cannot but be
admitted that the Hortensian law was the first step towards
the dissolution of the Roman state.   On the whole, however,
the political condition of Rome was so healthy, that 150 years
passed away without any injurious consequences becoming
manifest; but at last they did come.   From the distance at
which we are placed, we can survey the entire history, and
see how and when the injuries arising from the abolition of
the *veto* became visible in the republic.   I do not mean to say
that the veto ought to have remained as it was, for it was no
longer suited to circumstances; but what ought to have been
done was this: the curiae ought to have been completed by
plebeian nobles, and a number of gentes ought to have been
formed of the principal allies.   It is one of the disadvantages
of free constitutions, that remedies which are not applied in
proper time, afterwards often become utterly useless.   Even if
the Roman senate had retained the right to put its veto on
plebiscita, still it would have been too weak in numbers, and
could not have had the same weight as a strong and well-
organised aristocracy.   It is evident that the *sincera plebes*,
or the ancient and excellent country population, was gradually
disappearing in the assemblies at Rome; and that the *factio
forensis* was gaining the ascendancy: the elements which had
made the Roman commonalty so excellent, died away by
degrees, and ought to have been renewed.   When we look
back upon the history of the periods that had passed, it seems
strange that this idea should not have occurred to any one;
but I believe that the wise and aged Fabius, if he was still
alive, must have been aware of it.   The alternative seems
to have been, either to keep up the old phantom, and to
leave the curies in the possession of their power, or to abolish
it.   The true political wisdom is to construct something new
in the place of that which is decayed; and Montesquieu justly
observes, that the art of preserving a state, is to lead it back
to its *principia*.   If he had written nothing but this single
idea, he would still be one of the greatest and wisest men, for

this is really the great art which unfortunately is hardly ever practised. Whoever in a free state should say, "Recollect what was the principle of our forefathers," would be looked upon as a traitor, and gain no hearing. I am not acquainted with any example in history, where, in an important question, this principle has been adopted. I might in some sense mention the legislation of Andrea Doria; but that is a sad phenomenon, which, however, will be constantly repeated, and entail the destruction of states.

Sp. Carvilius, a son or grandson of the conqueror of the Samnites, proposed in the Hannibalian war, that two members from each of the senates of the allied states should be admitted into the Roman senate—Scipio Maffei made a similar proposal at Venice,—but he found no hearing, and was almost torn to pieces in the senate. Sallust says, that the most peaceful and orderly period in Roman history was that between the second and third punic wars: this is true, but it was only the peaceful condition which marks the beginning of dissolution, just as previously to the revolution in France, when the government had lost its power, and when, in the absence of violent conflicts, the revolution was preparing itself. Some few evil consequences of the failure of Carvilius' plan appeared even at an early time; one of them was, that the admission of the Italians to the full franchise became more and more difficult, since their admission would have lessened the influence of the old citizens. This afterwards gave rise to a coalition between the allies and the nobility; but the mischief was, that the nobility did not form a corporation, while that of the patricians was crumbling away, and nothing was put in its place.

It was in many respects an unfortunate period. A single individual is often sufficient, by insolence and arrogance to drive the people into madness. The French revolution was greatly accelerated by the foolish ordinance of the aged Marshal Ségur, who was otherwise a sensible man: but he made it a law, that commoners should be appointed officers only in the artillery, and that all other officers in the army should be noblemen. This enraged all the soldiers, even those who themselves did not in the least desire to rise. This great offence was one of the main causes of the revolution: few people are aware of this, but I have repeatedly been assured of it by Frenchmen, who had witnessed the outbreak of the revolution. A similar

provocation was given at Rome, by L. Postumius, a strange
character, who was thrice invested with the consulship, which
was then a rare occurrence, and was also employed in the decisive embassy to Tarentum: he must therefore have been a
man of consequence but he behaved like a madman. In his
consulship, he insulted the aged Q. Fabius, who commanded
the army as proconsul, for Postumius drove him from the army
and sent him home with threats: the cause of this must have
been the oligarchical party spirit, for Fabius, although an aristocrat, was free from all oligarchical feelings. After the war,
Postumius took possession of immense tracts of country, and
employed 2000 soldiers to clear away a forest. For these repeated acts of insolence, he was accused by the tribunes, and
sentenced to pay a fine of 500,000 *asses*. Such circumstances
were more provoking than anything else, and the more so, because the party of the oligarchs was weak in numbers.

To this period belongs the appointment of the *triumviri
capitales*. The form triumviri is properly a solecism, and a
proof that the oblique cases already began to predominate, as
in the modern languages derived from the Latin: people often
heard the form *triumvirorum*, and from it they made a nominative *triumviri*, which was generally used as early as the time of
Cicero. The *triumviri capitales* correspond to the Attic ἕνδεκα
for they had the superintendence of prisons, but otherwise their
office is involved in great obscurity. They received the functions which had been transferred from the ancient *quaestores
parricidii* to the curule aediles. There were many cases, namely,
those of a *delictum manifestum*, which admitted of no trial; but
the praetor had not time to investigate in every instance,
whether a person was a *reus manifestus*, and there was accordingly a need for officers to declare to the praetor, that this or
that case was a *delictum manifestum*: this must formerly have
been done by the quaestors, but now became the function of
the *triumviri capitales*. They were moreover judges in cases
where the praetor could not act, as for foreigners, slaves, etc.,
and also superintended their punishment, because they were
not under the protection of the tribunes: but whenever there
were any doubts, it was necessary to assign a judex. These
functionaries therefore were a mixture of police and criminal
officers.

According to Zonaras, it was the Tarentines who stirred up

the people far and wide against Rome; they first roused the Lucanians, and then the Etruscans; and even the Samnites, whose power was broken, were prevailed upon once more to take up arms and try the fortunes of war. The Greek towns were no longer exclusively the friends of Tarentum; they now looked to their own advantage, and were ready to sacrifice Tarentum to the Lucanians and Bruttians. A peace had been concluded between Rome and Tarentum, after the third or even after the second Samnite war, and in A.U. 451 or 452 they already appear on terms of friendship; the Greek writers also speak of this peace as an ancient treaty. They seem to have mutually fixed their boundaries, the Romans pledging themselves not to appear in the bay of Tarentum with any ship of war, north of the Lacinian promontory; and the Tarentines must have made a similar promise.

LECTURE XLIX.

AFTER the close of the third Samnite war, every unbiassed observer ought to have seen that the fate of Italy was decided, and the Italian nations should have hastened to ally themselves with Rome on terms as favourable as they could obtain. But passion is not possessed of such wisdom; and people always expect that a *deus ex machina* will come to alter everything. One nation after another entered the ranks of Rome's enemies; and the Lucanians, who in the third Samnite war had been allied with her, employed their independence to accomplish their own objects, and to subdue the few Greek towns which yet remained free. The Bruttians likewise joined the enemies of Rome; but the Greek towns being abandoned by the Tarentines solicited its aid. The Etruscan nation, though in a state of complete dissolution, still continued alternately at peace and at war; the Vulsinians alone seem to have carried on a contest without interruption. The power of the Samnites was completely shattered, yet they endeavoured to recover their strength in order to take up arms again, as soon as they could hope to do so with any success; for the present they kept aloof, and gave the Romans no cause for hostilities. The Tarentines strove to stir up even the Gauls, and according to Dion Cassius (in Zonaras), they were the soul of all these movements; but they could act only by means of subsidies; they themselves did not come forward, and there was every appearance that the amicable relation between them and the Romans was going on undisturbed. It must have been great distress which induced the Romans to dissimulate: we merely know that they assisted Thurii against the Lucanians, according to their system of supporting the weak against the powerful. On that occasion, we find the first instance of a Greek city erecting a statue to a Roman (C. Fabricius): the assistance of the Romans saved Thurii.

In Etruria the contest now took a different turn, and the Etruscans appear to have been so divided among themselves, that the war party invited the Gauls to fight against their opponents. The Gauls laid siege to Arretium in the north-eastern corner of Tuscany, which was governed by the Cilnii, and was connected with Rome by friendship. In A.U. 469 (according to Cato the birth of Christ falls in the year 752 and not 754), the Romans sent two legions and about 20,000 auxiliaries under the praetor L. Caecilius Metellus to the assistance of Arretium. But the Senonian Gauls, although they dwelt on the other side of the impassable Apeninnes, forced their way through them and defeated the Romans so completely, that Metellus himself and 11,000 Romans remained dead on the field of battle, and the whole army seems to have been annihilated. M'. Curius was now sent with an army into Etruria, and at the same time ambassadors went to the Senones to ransom the Roman prisoners. But the Senones were fired by a desire to take vengeance for their loss in the battle of Sentinum, and Britomaris, a young chief whose father had fallen in that battle, caused the ambassadors to be murdered. This breach of the law of nations exasperated the Romans so much that they resolved to employ every means to punish it. The consul P. Cornelius Dolabella, instead of attacking the army of the Gauls, who were perhaps already thinking of conquering Rome a second time, determined to invade the deserted country of the Senones; and there with the utmost cruelty, massacred or carried away the population which had remained at home. The army of the Senones, maddened by the news of this calamity returned to their own country, but were completely defeated by the Romans; and it is probably no exaggeration to say that the whole nation was extirpated. The gold of the Etruscans and Tarentines attracted other swarms of Gauls, and the Boians who now crossed the mountains and united with the Etruscans, were defeated on Lake Vadimo, but the Romans were not able to invade their country, which extended from the river Trebia to the Romagna. In the following year, all the Boians capable of bearing arms returned to Etruria, but were not more fortunate than before: few escaped, but the nation was not extirpated, for the women and children had remained at home, and thus the Boians recovered from their misfortunes. It was not till fifty years later, that the Romans entered their country and destroyed the nation. The Gallic emigrants henceforth no longer invaded Italy, but turned towards Thrace and Macedonia.

The scanty history of this period entirely passes over the further proceedings in Etruria, nor does it tell us which towns submitted, and which concluded separate treaties with Rome.

While fearful wars were thus waged upon the northern frontiers, the city itself was quiet, in consequence of the peace concluded on the Janiculum and in the Aesculetum; but in Lucania the Romans continued their war uninterruptedly, and in it C. Fabricius Luscinus appears for the first time in history. The aged heroes of this period were still alive: Valerius Corvus was at a very advanced age, and had withdrawn from public life; Appius Claudius was blind, but still exerted very great influence; Fabius was probably dead. M'. Curius Dentatus, a great military hero, and in politics decidedly democratical without being a demagogue, was younger than Appius, but older than Fabricius. Curius and Fabricius are remarkable characters and of similar temperaments: it is a well established fact that both were really poor; both were proud characters, and both *novi homines*, who were raised by their personal greatness in war and by the respect they commanded. Fabricius has at all times been held up as the model of a virtuous citizen. By the side of these men we must notice a few other important but opposite characters: L. Postumius was energetic but not noble; and P. Cornelius Rufinus was as avaricious as Fabricius was disinterested, and the latter in conjunction with his colleague Q. Aemilius Papus expelled him from the senate on account of his love of luxuries. These are the most distinguished men of the period, but Rome seems to have been rich in other great characters, and I believe that even in its peculiar intellectual culture, Rome was far above the best periods of the middle ages, and that even in its literature.

Ti. Coruncanius was another great man; he was great as a wise politician, although no distinct recollection of him was perpetuated in the state; he was the first plebeian Pontifex Maximus, and enjoyed great reputation for his wisdom and profound knowledge of the law. He was always looked upon as the *beau ideal* of a Pontifex.

In the course of time the Romans became better aware of their true relation to Tarentum: the peace continued only because they were separated by other countries, and the wealth of the Tarentines, their navy, and their facility in obtaining Greek mercenaries rendered the Romans very much disinclined to engage in a contest with them. As the Roman army was carrying on the war in Lucania, surrounded on all sides by guerillas, every thing that was wanted for the army had to be sent by sea. The treaty respecting the mutual maritime frontier which had been concluded about twenty years before, must under the present circumstances have appeared unnatural to the Romans: they might have said that at the time the treaty was made they were not in possession of Venusia, and that by the establishment of that colony, they had tacitly acquired the right of sailing beyond the Lacinian promontory: but it appears that the Romans wanted to see how long the Tarentines would allow matters to go on without a war. This is the more probable, as according to a statement from one of the lost books of Livy, which is confirmed by Zonaras, the Tarentines endeavoured to form a great coalition against the Romans, with which even the expedition of the Gauls against Arretium is said to have been connected. Certain it is, that they wished for such a coalition, but the various nations joined it with hesitation. The Romans sent a squadron of ten triremes under the *duumvir navalis*[1], L. Valerius, to the road of Tarentum. In all Greek cities the theatre was, if possible, built in such a place as to have a view of the sea, or at least

---

[1] This office must have been abolished previously to the Punic war, between A.U. 471 and A.U. 489.—N.

the spectators were turned towards the sea; such was the case not only in really Greek towns, but also in those which were built in a similar manner, as at Tusculum and even at Faesulae; the people assembled in those theatres, as at Rome in the Forum. The agora, in Greek towns, was not so much a place of meeting for the people, as for transacting real business: the theatres were much more convenient, they were open all day, and the people might sit down while listening, for any one who wished to address them, might step upon the stage for that purpose. When the Roman ships were steering towards the harbour of Tarentum, it unfortunately happened that the people were assembled in the theatre: had this not been the case, the whole history of the world would have taken a different turn, for it is probable that the strategi would have requested the Romans to withdraw, and the whole undertaking would have remained without any consequences. But as it was, the people excited one another, and without coming to any definite resolution every body ran to the harbour, dragged the galleys into the water, sprang into them, and attacked the Romans, who were unprepared for such a reception; a few only of the ships escaped, the rest were sunk, and Valerius himself was killed. The populace of Tarentum, who had never yet seen a Roman army, were delighted with their victory.

At Rome this occurrence produced great consternation. It was known that all Italy was in a state of ferment, and that the Tarentines were calculating upon a general insurrection. There are distinct traces which prove that the Romans did not even trust the Latin people; and the Praenestines in particular were on the point of revolting. The affair, therefore, was very dangerous for Rome, so that instead of at once declaring war, they sent an embassy to Tarentum to protest in the face of the whole world, in order that every one might see that vengeance was only postponed, and not given up. Ambassadors were also sent to several of the allies north of the Tarentines, partly in order to keep them in good humour, but partly also to demand hostages to secure their fidelity. Among these latter ambassadors was C. Fabricius, who, by a breach of the law of nations, was arrested, apparently among the Samnites. The Romans now made the greatest efforts, for they wished to make an imposing impression without beginning the war at once. L. Postumius headed an embassy to Tarentum. A light-headed, unsteady, and giddy people like that of Tarentum would have grown intolerably insolent, if the hated Romans had shown any symptoms of fear. The demand of Postumius that the guilty should be delivered up had no effect, as had undoubtedly been foreseen by the Romans. It unfortunately happened that the Tarentines were celebrating the Dionysia or vintage-feast, and the democratic Tarentines did not take the ambassadors into the senate, but into the orchestra before the people, where they had to speak up to the audience, whereas at Rome they had been accustomed to stand on an elevated place when addressing the people. This circumstance alone must have made them nervous and confused. The inhabitants of the city were in a state of intoxication, and drunkards and insolent fellows laughed at every mistake which the ambassadors made in speaking Greek; and one even went so far as to soil the *toga praetexta* of Postumius. The Roman lost his composure; he showed the affront which he had received to the Tarentines, and loudly complained of it; but at this sight the intoxicated populace burst out in shouts of laughter. Postumius then shook his garment, saying, " I prophesy that you Tarentines will wash out this blot with your best life-blood." Hereupon the populace became so infuriated, that he escaped with great difficulty.

The ambassadors returned without the reparation they had demanded, nay without any answer at all, and impressed upon the Roman senate the necessity of immediate punishment. Many senators however advised caution and patience, till they should be in more favourable circumstances. The people also, who were suffering great distress, had at that time an aversion to war, and hence the first proposal to declare war was rejected. Fresh negotiations were to be commenced, but supported by an army. Afterwards, however, it was decreed by the people that an army should be sent to the frontier of Tarentum; and the consul, L. Aemilius Barbula, received orders also to make an attack upon Tarentum, in his expedition into Lucania. At Tarentum, likewise, there were two parties, one mad for war, the other more thoughtful and cautious. The former, however, perceived that the contest could not be carried on otherwise than by calling a foreign prince into the country, and that this could be no other than Pyrrhus of Epirus, who had an army quite ready for action. But it was to be foreseen that if Pyrrhus should be victorious, he would set himself up as king of Italy, and he was far more powerful than Alexander of Epirus. The aristocracy of Tarentum wished for an alliance with Rome, in order to control the unbridled populace; but the rulers had lost their senses to such an extent, that instead of protecting the Italiot towns, as they had done until then, they made common cause with the Lucanians, withdrew their protection from Thurii, a colony common to all Greece, and abandoned it to its enemies. This important city, venerable on account of the great men it had produced, was now conquered and plundered by the Lucanians; the Romans afterwards re-conquered it, but it never recovered from the blow. When Aemilius Barbula appeared before Tarentum, a peace would probably have been concluded, had not the Tarentines already commenced their negotiations with Pyrrhus. When the Romans laid waste the country about Tarentum, those negotiations had not yet led to any certain result; and now Apis, a proxenus of the Romans, offered himself as a candidate for the office of strategus, for the purpose of opening negotiations with them; but just at the moment when they were to commence, the intelligence arrived that Pyrrhus had accepted the proposals which had been made to him. Apis was dismissed, and the war began.

Pyrrhus was then in his thirty-seventh year, the happiest period of a man's life. Although he lived at a time when no right nor property was safe, yet none of his contemporaries experienced so many changes of fortune as he. For a great man nothing has such charms as an active and busy life. A man can call his own only that which he himself has acquired, and there is no greatness in spending a quiet life in the peaceful possession of what fortune has given us; but activity also may be carried to excess, if a man entirely overlooks the calm happiness of possession. Characters of the latter kind are Charles XII. and Pyrrhus, men who, when they occupy a throne, are a misfortune to their subjects, and dangerous to their neighbours.

LECTURE L.

THE kingdom of the Molossians was first drawn forth from its obscurity in the time of the Peloponnesian war, by Tharyps, who had been educated at Athens. From the time of Philip, the kingly family of the Molossians was divided into two branches, that of Arymbas, and that of Neoptolemus, the father of Olympias; and the latter, or younger branch, being supported by the influence of Macedonia, ascended the throne. Philip, to favour his wife's relations, extended the kingdom, and Thesprotia and Chaonia seem to have belonged to it as early as that time. Afterwards, however, Aeacidas, the father of Pyrrhus, who belonged to the elder branch, succeeded to the throne. The legitimate power of those Epirot kings was very limited, like that of the kings in the middle ages. Aristotle compares them to the Lacedaemonian kings; but the train of soldiers whom they had at their command was certainly not always insignificant; and misled by this source of power, Aeacidas, in opposition to the general opinion of his subjects, interfered in many occurrences of his time. He was a partizan of Olympias, although he had before been expelled from his kingdom by the arrogance of his cousin Alexander of Epirus, and with peculiar generosity he involved himself in the fate of that fury of a woman. By this means he drew upon himself the hatred of Cassander, by whose assistance he was expelled from Epirus. Pyrrhus was then only two years old, and it was with the greatest difficulty that he was saved by faithful servants, for Cassander was bent upon destroying the whole family. He was brought up by Glaucias, a prince of the Taulantians, although the latter had been hostile to Aeacidas. Glaucias formed so great an attachment to the boy, that he did everything to protect him against Cassander. No sooner had Pyrrhus grown up, than he went to the court of Demetrius Poliorcetes and the aged Antigonus, the one-eyed; amd it was in that school that he developed his extraordinary talents as a general, although Demetrius was a spoiled genius. Pyrrhus there maintained his moral dignity in the midst of the most profligate society. Demetrius nominally restored to him the kingdom of the Molossians; but, according to the custom of the times, Pyrrhus was in the service of the greater king, and like the other petty Epirot princes, held a post in his army. He thus accompanied Demetrius and Antigonus to the battle of Ipsus (Olymp. 119. 4), in which the kingdom of Antigonus was destroyed, and he himself perished. Pyrrhus was then sixteen years old. When this battle was gained by the allies, they began to dispute among themselves; and the cunning Demetrius soon found an opportunity of forming a connection with Ptolemy Soter, who had quarrelled about the booty with his old friend Seleucus, and with Cassander whom he had always hated, as well as with Lysimachus. Pyrrhus was sent to Alexandria, for the purpose of carrying on the negotiations, and served at the same time as a hostage for the fulfilment of the conditions. His personal appearance had a peculiar charm; his wonderful talents were of the most varied description: nature had endowed him with the most fascinating amiability and beauty. These qualities he employed to the greatest advantage, both for his patron and for himself.

In the mean time the Epirot towns were lost, and the kingdom of Pyrrhus had in all probability fallen into the hands of Neoptolemus, a son of Alexander the Molossian; but Pyrrhus won the favour of Ptolemy and Berenice, and married Antigone, a daughter of Berenice by a former marriage. By means of Egyptian money he was restored to the throne, and his favour with the people soon delivered him from his rival Neoptolemus, for which purpose, however, he made use of unjustifiable means, as was the common practice in the sixteenth century also. He now tried to establish himself firmly, and his good fortune soon afforded him an opportunity. Cassander died, and his surviving sons were hostile towards one another; one of them who wanted the protection of Pyrrhus ceded to him Ambracia, Amphilochia, and those Epirot districts which until then had been united with Macedonia. This was of the greatest importance to Pyrrhus, for now Epirus really deserved the name of a state. Pyrrhus faithfully supported his new ally, but the latter fell through his own fault, and Pyrrhus remained in the possession of the newly acquired territories. Demetrius Poliorcetes also now again ascended the throne of Macedonia, and at first Pyrrhus kept up the old friendly relation with him; but Demetrius was an arrogant and aggrandising prince, in consequence of which a war soon broke out between them. The oriental haughtiness of Demetrius was offensive to the Macedonians, who revolted against him; Pyrrhus allied himself with Lysimachus; and as the people favoured them, they divided the country between themselves. This division, however, again provoked the Macedonians, and as Lysimachus was a native of Macedonia, and Pyrrhus a stranger, the inhabitants of the portion assigned to the latter deserted him. The time at which Pyrrhus lost Macedonia is usually placed too early by several years.

Pyrrhus was not obstinate in the pursuit of fortune: he practised war as an art, and when fortune was unfavourable, he gave it up. War was the happiness and delight of his life; he brought the art of a general to the highest pitch of perfection, and was also a great master in the art of conducting a battle. A fragment from Livy preserved in Servius, states, according to a correct emendation: *Pyrrhus unicus bellandi artifex magisque in proelio quam in bello bonus;* the result of a campaign was less interesting to him. Some generals display their talent in making the dispositions for a battle, but either do not know how to manage a campaign, or after gaining a battle, grow tired of the war; others show an eminent talent in forming the plan for a whole campaign, but are less successful in battles. The archduke Charles of Austria was a general of the former kind, as he himself owns in his military writings. Pyrrhus also took so great a delight in winning the game of war, that he scarcely ever followed up a victory which he had gained: it may perhaps have been even painful to him, when he had defeated an enemy, to annihilate him, since art was no longer required. This is a feature of a noble soul, but by it the object of war is lost.

Pyrrhus now took up his residence at Ambracia, and embellished it so as to raise it to the rank of really royal city. There the Tarentine ambassador appeared, and concluded with him a treaty of subsidies, in which many points undoubtedly remained unsettled. Pyrrhus quickly sent over Cineas with 3,000 men, in order to gain a firm footing, and to prevent the outbreak of a revolution in consequence of the devastations committed by the Romans. Cineas, like his royal friend, was an extraordinary man: his connection with Pyrrhus was perfectly free; he had attached himself to the king from inclination, and clung to him with all his heart. He belonged to a people which has never produced any man of note, for he was a native of Larissa, in Thessaly, and probably belonged to the illustrious family of the Aleuadae. He is called a disciple of Demosthenes, but this is hardly conceivable, for Demosthenes had died forty years before this time, and the statement is perhaps based upon a misunderstanding; but he may have really been a *sectator Demosthenis*. Few persons were then in a condition rightly to appreciate Demosthenes; but a man like Cineas would understand him, and be inspired by his orations. We know nothing of the manner in which Cineas became the friend of Pyrrhus, although it is a question a satisfactory answer to which would be worth more than a knowledge of a whole series of wars.

When Cineas landed in Italy, the Tarentines delivered up their citadel to him, and he skilfully regulated his conduct towards them in such a manner, as to keep them in good humour and to deceive them in regard to the designs of Pyrrhus: he allowed them to do as they pleased, and thereby gained their full confidence; they made very few preparations, thinking that others would bleed for them. Pyrrhus' own resources were not great, but he procured succour from several neighbouring princes, who provided him with elephants, military engines, ships and other things necessary for the war, and Ptolemy Ceraunus supplied him with 5000 Macedonian soldiers. He was a thorn in the side of all his neighbours, who were glad that he was going to so distant a country. He is said to have crossed over with 20,000 foot, from 4000 to 5000 horse, and a number of elephants, which is not distinctly stated. He was ready early in the year, but the passage was unfortunate, partly because the art of managing ships was yet in its infancy, and partly because the Epirots in particular were less skilled in it than the Greeks. The sea near the Ceraunian cliffs, moreover, was then, as it still is, notorious for sudden storms: the current from the Adriatic towards the Syrtes, which may almost be compared to the great Mexican current, rendered the communication by water extremely difficult. Several ships of his fleet were lost, others were cast on shore, and he himself with great difficulty reached the Sallentine coast, where he collected all that had escaped from the sea. He quickly proceeded to Tarentum, which opened its gates to him; and no sooner was his scattered fleet re-assembled than he began to take serious measures at Tarentum. He saw that his army alone was not sufficient for his object, and that it was too expensive to engage mercenaries; he therefore ordered the gates to be closed, made a levy among the Tarentines themselves, and incorporated them with his phalanx. This measure displeased the people in the highest degree, and many were anxious to escape; but he increased the rigour of his proceedings, abolished the gymnasia and other places of amusement, and appeared to the Tarentines in the light of a tyrannical ruler. They were indeed greatly disappointed in their expectations, for they wished to treat Pyrrhus like the princes whose services they had engaged before, intending to remain at home, while he was to carry on their war; but Pyrrhus could not adopt such a plan, his kingdom was but small, and the war threatened to become bloody: for which reasons he was obliged to demand the co-operation of the Tarentines. They murmured, but were quite powerless, as he was in possession of the citadel; and the consequence was that he had recourse to dictatorial measures.

Pyrrhus was opposed by only one consular army under P. Valerius Laevinus. The history of this period, if we except the campaigns of Pyrrhus, is very little known; but Rome was probably employing a great part of her forces against Etruria, in order to obtain a definite peace in that quarter. All Italy was in a state of ferment; the Romans, although they made their wavering allies give hostages, endeavoured every where to conceal their fear, and raised great military forces; but it is inconceivable how they could venture to send only one consular army against Pyrrhus, whose personal character drew towards him all the nations far and wide. Among all the barbarian kings of that time, he alone was surrounded by the lustre of ancient Greece; and although he was not without faults, yet he was a being of a higher order, and could effect much with little means. The Samnites and Lucanians had sent ambassadors to him even while he was in Epirus; and the Apulians and several other Italian nations joined him immediately on his arrival; but this did not at once increase his forces. The proconsul L. Aemilius Barbula, was engaged in Samnium which he ravaged fearfully, in order to prevent the Samnites conceiving the idea of joining Pyrrhus against the army of Laevinus. A correspondence took place between Pyrrhus and Laevinus, in which the king offered to mediate between Rome and Tarentum. He had a high opinion of the Romans, but

still he did not know them sufficiently, for the tone of his letters, so far as we are acquainted with them, was not the right
one, and hence nothing was effected. The Romans required
him to atone for having, as a foreigner, entered Italy; and this
seems to have been their national view. Valerius now proceeded to Lucania; wishing to fight a battle before the king
was joined by an army of his Samnite and Lucanian allies,
since they were as yet probably prevented by the other consular
army. Pyrrhus had likewise gone to meet him, intending to
offer battle before the two Roman armies should have united.
He advanced across the Siris, in the neighbourhood of Heraclea,
the most beautiful country in that part of Italy, which in fertility and wealth equals Campania. He was confident of victory, and he wished to humble his Italian allies by defeating
the Romans without their assistance. The Romans seem to
have made slow progress in their preparations; Pyrrhus threw
great difficulties in the way of their obtaining provisions, and
they were obliged to fight that they might not be compelled to
quit that country and withdraw to Venusia, which would
have been dangerous on account of the allies. On the eve of
the battle, while Pyrrhus was reconnoitering the position of
the Romans, their order filled him with amazement: he was
accustomed to fight against Macedonians and Greeks or Illyrians, but when he saw the elasticity and training of the individual Roman soldier, the thought of the approaching battle
made him very serious. The opposite tactics of two excellent
armies were to contend for victory: the Macedonians whose
tactics had then reached their highest point, fought in masses[1],
but the Romans fought in lines far outflanking the enemy. If
the Epirot phalanx waited for the Romans in its immoveable
position, the latter could do nothing, but it would have required
a great deal of courage, coolly to sustain the furious attack of
the Romans, the showers of pila and the vehement onset with
swords. But as the Roman cavalry was badly mounted and

[1] We must not imagine that a whole phalanx, consisting of 16,000 men,
always formed a single mass sixteen men deep; the Macedonians advanced in
smaller divisions of about 420 men as is mostly done in our own times. They
were therefore moveable masses, and could find openings to pass through,
which would have been impossible for the great phalanx if it had formed one
mass of men. The drawing together of the different divisions was a manœuvre
to which recourse was had only in extreme cases, and such a mass was impenetrable.—N.

badly armed, Pyrrhus had a great advantage in his Thessalian horse. The Roman army, to the amazement of Pyrrhus, marched through the Siris, and made the attack; both armies fought with great vigour. The Romans had never yet contended with a Macedonian phalanx: seven attacks were repulsed, and like Arnold of Winkelried, they threw themselves like madmen upon the sarissae in order to break through the phalanx: the day was not yet gained, but the Roman cavalry at the beginning of the battle was very successful, and the Epirots were already wavering, so that in an instant they might have been routed. At that moment Pyrrhus brought up his cavalry, which contrary to all expectation had before been repelled by the Romans[2], and along with it came about twenty elephants: the Roman cavalry was startled, and the horses being frightened took to flight. The Thessalian horse now cut to pieces the flanks of the legions and made fearful havoc: many Romans, especially horsemen, were taken prisoners. The defeat was complete, the camp could not be maintained, and every one fled as best he could. If Pyrrhus had pursued them, the whole Roman army would have been destroyed, like that of the French at Waterloo. But the Romans, and especially Laevinus, here again showed their excellent spirit: like Frederic the Great after the battle of Kunnersdorf, they rallied and withdrew to Venusia, for this must be the place in Apulia of which Zonaras speaks on this occasion. If it had not been for that fortress, they would have been obliged to march across the mountains as far as Luceria. It now became evident what an excellent idea it had been to make Venusia a colony, since without it, no Roman would have escaped, for the Samnites and Lucanians would have destroyed them.

The Italian allies did not arrive in the camp of Pyrrhus until the battle was over. The king at first expected Roman ambassadors, but as he heard nothing of the Romans, except that they were making fresh preparations, he broke up. The straight road to Rome was open to him, and he accordingly left the Romans armies on one side and began his march towards the city: he rightly intended to bring the war to a speedy termination. But as he advanced, he was terribly disappointed by the condition of the country: Rufinus had taken up the

[2] We see from this what firm determination can do, as the cavalry of Pyrrhus was excellently trained and far superior in numbers.—N.

remnants of the army of Laevinus, and they had either fought their way through Samnium, or had marched to Rome across the country of the Marsians and Marrucinians. Pyrrhus had expected that his army would find provisions everywhere, but he was horrified at seeing the state of Lucania and especially of Samnium. According to a recently discovered fragment, he told the Samnites that they had deceived him, for that their country was a desert. His advance was therefore necessarily slow. As he approached Capua, that city with praiseworthy fidelity closed its gates against him. He must have crossed the Vulturnus in the neighbourhood of Casilinum, and he now endeavoured to gain the Latin road, in order to reach the discontented towns of Praeneste, Tibur and others. He at the same time reckoned upon the Etruscans, and perhaps even on the Gauls. Here again we clearly see the hand of Providence, for had not the Boians been destroyed, the year before, they would undoubtedly have marched into Etruria to assist the Etruscans; but as it was, the Etruscans were confined to their own resources and were also divided among themselves. On that occasion the Romans seem to have shewn great adroitness: they must have concluded the συνθῆκαι εὐδοκούμεναι with the Etruscans at that very moment, whereby only slight burthens were imposed upon the latter.

Pyrrhus availed himself of the time occupied in his slow progress towards Rome with, it is said, 70,000 men, to negociate for peace, and sent Cineas to Rome. At first sight, the terms which he proposed seemed alluring, but when closely looked at, they were found to be very harsh. He demanded that the Romans should conclude a peace with Tarentum, Samnium, Lucania, Apulia and Bruttium, as though those states were their equals, and that they should give up whatever they had taken from them, namely Luceria, Fregellae and Venusia; that is, that everything should be restored to the state which had existed forty years before. These terms were unreasonably severe: we know them from Appian, who must have taken them from Dionysius, but our histories represent Pyrrhus as begging for a peace with Tarentum. However, the impression of the defeat was terrific, and Rome was deeply shaken; the majority already began to give way to the idea of concluding peace. This is the celebrated negociation of Cineas, which proves his extraordinary skill: he did not at all hasten the matter, but endeavoured to win the minds of the Romans by shewing attention to every one, and in this he was greatly assisted by his astonishing memory, for he called every Roman by his name, and treated each person according to his peculiar character. But Appius Claudius decided the question, and thereby made amends for whatever faults he had previously committed. He inspired the senate with courage to reject the proposals of Cineas, and to order him to quit Rome within twenty-four hours. After these negociations, Pyrrhus appeared before Rome.

LECTURE LI.

THE history of this war has been transmitted to us in such meagre accounts that we know only by an accidental allusion, that Pyrrhus took the important town of Fregellae by storm, and advanced on the Latin road as far as Praeneste, whose citadel he conquered. Thence he could survey the territory of Rome, but he found himself completely disappointed in his hopes. The Etruscans had concluded peace, and the army which had fought against them was in the city, where all men capable of bearing arms were called upon to enlist. The troops of Laevinus who had been reinforced, had closely followed Pyrrhus' footsteps, and had advanced from Capua on the Appian road; the allies who had remained faithful to Rome were exerting all their powers. Under these circumstances, he was stationed at an advanced season of the year on the lofty Aequian hills: one army was before him within the walls of Rome; another was at his side; a reserve was forming in his rear, and all this occurred in a country which could not support him, and from which a retreat during the winter would have been impossible. He therefore with a heavy heart resolved to return to Campania; one Roman army followed him and another under Laevinus marched at his side. He wished to fight a battle with Laevinus before the two Roman armies could unite; but the courage and cheerfulness of the Romans and the demoralized condition of his own troops, who already

showed their ill-will towards his allies, affected him so much
that he lost his spirits, and satisfied with a large mass of booty
and a great number of prisoners, he returned to Tarentum.

Although this campaign terminated without any permanent
evil consequences for the Romans, yet they were greatly weakened, the number of prisoners taken by Pyrrhus being far
greater than that which the Romans had taken in the battle
near Heraclea. They accordingly despatched an embassy to
negociate the ransom of their prisoners or their exchange for
those of Tarentum and the Italicans. It was on that occasion,
that the celebrated conversation between Pyrrhus and Fabricius occurred, which the Romans were certainly not the first
to record. Timaeus wrote a separate work on this war:
Pyrrhus himself left memoirs, and it is undoubtedly from these
that later accounts were taken; they show what a high opinion
the Greeks entertained of the Romans. The embassy was
unsuccessful; but, in accordance with the noble generosity of
his soul, and with a view to produce an effect upon a people
like the Romans, Pyrrhus permitted the Roman prisoners to
go to the city to celebrate the Saturnalia, binding them by an
oath that after the festival they would return to him. It is
stated that not one ventured to break his oath, and the senate
and consuls had issued a strict command that none should
commit a breach of faith. These acts on both sides are a
proof the noble spirit of those times, and we may say in general that this war is one of the most beautiful in history, on
account of the mutual respect of the belligerents, for although
both were fighting for life and death yet both felt attracted
towards each other. The history of the embassy of Fabricius,
Rufinus and Dolabella, and that of Pyrrhus trying to persuade
Fabricius to remain with him, and share his kingdom, has
been repeated in innumerable moral tales. I believe indeed
that the king wished to make Fabricius his friend and companion; the account is so perfectly in harmony with the
character of Pyrrhus, that we cannot but believe it, although
the details may be the embellishments of rhetoricians, and
especially of Dionysius of Halicarnassus. It is a peculiar
feature of the genius of Pyrrhus that he felt a passionate admiration for the Romans, and courted their friendship. Although
there are some actions of his life we cannot justify, still the
ensemble of his character is so great, and so beautiful, that I

do not know any period of history on which I could dwell
with more delight. He wished for peace, but insisted on a fair
peace for his Italian allies, whom he would not abandon.

The negotiations during the winter did not produce peace,
and Pyrrhus now clearly saw that by such attempts upon the
heart of Rome, he could effect nothing, and that it was necessary to take the places in Apulia, Venusia and Luceria, from
the enemy by force of arms. In the mean time a circumstance
occurred which rendered the war more difficult for him, as in
consequence of it he could no longer draw reinforcements from
Macedonia: this was the inroad of the Gauls into that country,
in which Ptolemy Ceraunus, who had hitherto supported Pyrrhus, was slain. Pyrrhus seems to have been embroiled with
his Italian allies, so that he was obliged to carry on the war
with much smaller forces than before. The Romans were in
Apulia with both their armies: it is stated that Pyrrhus was
besieging a place in Apulia, when one of the Roman armies
appeared, but its name is not mentioned; it is probable, however, that it was Venusia. The battle of Asculum is the only
event in the campaign of this year with which we are acquainted, but the different accounts of it in Plutarch are very
confused; and we must be guided by the statement of Hiero-
nymus of Cardia, who derived his information from the
memoirs of Pyrrhus himself. On the first day there was a
preliminary engagement between the two armies: the Romans
were afraid to descend into the plain, lest they should be crushed
by the elephants and cavalry; as, however, the phalanx with
its sarissae would labour under great disadvantages on broken
ground, Pyrrhus with great adroitness drove the Romans to a
position which suited him. There the Romans were beaten,
and are said to have lost 7,000 men; but they were so near
their camp, and had fortified it so well, that they withdrew to
it in perfect order: it was not a defeat, but only a lost engagement. The Apulians in the army of Pyrrhus seem to have
prevented his gaining a complete victory, for while the Romans
were retreating, they plundered the camp of their own allies,
so that it was necessary to send off troops to keep them in
order. The fact that he had gained no more than a mere
victory was sufficient to make Pyrrhus look upon the battle as
lost. Meantime winter was approaching, and the Romans
became more and more confident that they should conquer,

while Pyrrhus had no prospects. He could not recruit his own troops, for the Gauls were penetrating into Macedonia and threatened the frontier of Epirus; his kingdom was very limited, and the people showed the greatest disinclination to cross the sea for their ambitious king, while the barbarians stood on the frontiers. Pyrrhus, moreover, did not trust the Italicans: and in order to retain his control over them he placed together one Italian moveable cohort and a phalangitic battalion, alternately; the former fighting with the pilum. This may have been more appropriate theoretically, than it actually turned out to be: it is clear from Polybius, that Pyrrhus observed this order of battle, and he made use of it at Beneventum, perhaps even at Asculum.

It is probable that long before this time the Romans had subdued the revolted places on the Liris, and public opinion throughout Italy declared in favour of Rome. Both parties tried to negotiate: the Romans wished to drive Pyrrhus out of Italy, because they were sure of then becoming masters of the whole peninsula. Pyrrhus, on the other hand, who began to be weary and wished to give up the undertaking, made repeated overtures to the Romans, but they resolutely refused to negotiate so long as any foreign troops were in Italy. New consuls was now appointed, one of whom is called Fabricius; and a noble Epirot, or according to others, the king's physician or cup-bearer (his name also is not the same in all authorities, some calling him Timochares, Nicias, etc.) is said to have offered to the Roman consuls to poison the king. The story itself is not at all incredible: but it is related in all the versions in so contradictory a manner, that it cannot possibly have been publicly known. It seems to me to be nothing else than a preconcerted farce, devised by Pyrrhus, in order to obtain a pretext for quitting Italy: we should hardly venture to express such a suspicion, had not similar things happened in our own time; for the negotiation between Napoleon and Fox in 1806 is quite a parallel case. The intention was to conclude a truce, and when the Romans delivered up the traitor to him, Pyrrhus restored all his Roman prisoners without ransom, and the Romans, in return, probably sent him an equal number of Tarentines and Italicans. Pyrrhus now declared to his allies that he would go to Sicily whither he was invited, and that there he would find the means of affording them more effectual assistance. In this manner he obtained from the Romans a preliminary truce, by which however they did not renounce their right to continue the war against the Italicans; and unhappy Samnium was left to its fate. Pyrrhus had now been in Italy for two years and two months, and he remained in Sicily upwards of three years.

After the death of Agathocles, the Greek portion of the inhabitants of Sicily was divided into factions, and tyrants ravaged the island, while the Carthaginians extended their dominion, and the Mamertines (Oscan mercenaries) treacherously took possession of Messana. Pyrrhus was looked upon as a deliverer, especially as he had married Lanassa, a daughter of Agathocles: he took his son with him to Syracuse, and homage was there paid to the young man as king. Pyrrhus expelled the Carthaginians from the island, except from the impregnable Lilybaeum, and closely blockaded the Mamertines within their walls. His friend Cineas must have died before that time; for we find him surrounded by a different set of men, who were his evil genii and led him to ruin. His good sense induced him to conclude peace with the Carthaginians on most excellent terms, for they retained only Lilybaeum; the cowardly Siceliots, however, were dissatisfied, thinking that they were none the better, so long as the Carthaginians remained in any part of their island; though in reality their situation, under the present circumstances, would have greatly improved. Pyrrhus had conquered the Mamertines and united all Sicily under the strong monarchy of an Aeacide; but he now yielded to the unfortunate counsels of others, which were the more unsafe as he was wanting in perseverance. The siege of Lilybaeum was an enormous undertaking, for the fortifications of that city were among the wonders of the ancient world; and the fleet of the Carthaginians constantly supplied it with fresh troops and provisions. The consequence was that Pyrrhus was obliged to raise the siege, whereby he lost credit with the fickle Siceliots: this led him to tyrannical measures; and he was not a little pleased when the Italian allies requested him to return at all hazards, since otherwise they would be compelled by the Romans to conclude a most disadvantageous peace. He landed at Locri, for it was impossible for him to cross the straits, Messana being in the hands of the Mamertines, and Rhegium in those of a rebellious Campanian legion. During his passage to Italy he was attacked by a Carthaginian fleet, which destroyed a great many of his ships, so that he saved scarcely any of the treasures which he had collected in Sicily, and had lost a great part of his men and money when he arrived on the coast of Italy.

During his absence of more than three years, the Romans had continued the war with extreme cruelty: the people against whom they fought could form only guerillas, who did much injury to the Roman armies, but yet were unable to resist them in open warfare; and consequently they became weaker and weaker. I will not speak of the particular places which were then destroyed: the ancient city of Croton, which was twelve miles in circumference, now received its death-blow, and became quite deserted; the Romans conquered one place after another and changed the country into a wilderness. On his return to Italy in A.U. 477, Pyrrhus restored his army in the most wonderful manner; he had a great many veterans from the army of Agathocles, Punic deserters and others, and he now called upon the Tarentines and all the Italians to take up arms: his army is said to have consisted of 80,000 men, but this is probably an exaggeration. He pitched his camp in the neighbourhood of Taurasia not far from Beneventum, and was met by Curius, who seems to have had only a single army. Pyrrhus was already dejected, for he had lost faith in his invincible powers, and mysterious forebodings and dreams made him uneasy: he had not indeed become quite desponding, but his cheerfulness was no longer the same as before. His plans for attacking Curius were excellent, but many points were left to fortune, and Fortune had turned her back upon him. His intention was to march with a numerous detachment round the Roman camp which was situated on an eminence, and at the dawn of day to rush down upon the enemy from the heights, while another attack was to be made at the same time from below. But by night-marches an army always arrives later than is anticipated: the detachment which he had sent up the heights mistook its road; the king waited for the preconceived signal that he might advance even during the night, but it was already broad daylight, and no signal was seen or heard, when the Romans learned that the enemy was behind them in the mountains. They immediately prepared for a battle, and their camp being easily defensible, their main army marched out against that of Pyrrhus. The Romans were already familiar with fighting against elephants; they used burning arrows wrapped up in hemp, which when thrown with sufficient force penetrated the skin of the animals while the burning hemp and pitch infuriated them. They had previously made a similar attempt at Asculum; but they now employed this device on a much larger scale. Great mischief was done by a female elephant whose young one was wounded in this manner, for she rushed upon her masters with the utmost fury. The Epirots were overwhelmed, their phalanx was completely broken, and the defeat was so decisive, that Pyrrhus could not even maintain his camp, but retreated to Tarentum. The Romans, besides other booty, took eight elephants.

The contest was now decided, and Pyrrhus' only thought was how to give up the whole undertaking, though he was unwilling altogether to abandon his possessions in Italy. He accordingly left Milo at Tarentum with a considerable force, which was sufficient to prevent the Romans from venturing upon a siege, but at the same time a fearful scourge for Tarentum itself. The Romans now directed their arms against each separate nation which they had to subdue, while Pyrrhus had recourse to a stratagem for the purpose of getting away from Italy. He caused a report to be spread among the Tarentines that he was going to settle the affairs of Macedonia, and that he would then return with all the forces of that kingdom. It is possible, however, that he actually entertained some belief of this kind. After an absence of six years, he now returned with a reduced army to Epirus. He there found ample scope for enterprises. Antigonus Gonatas, who had just been raised to the throne of Macedonia, was deserted by his troops, and all the country proclaimed Pyrrhus their king; but soon afterwards the Macedonians were exasperated by the licentious conduct of his Gallic mercenaries, and again revolted to Antigonus. Pyrrhus then transferred the war to Peloponnesus, and undertook an expedition against Sparta, in which he nearly gained his object, but his success was thwarted at the very moment when the Epirots were entering the city. Fortune was always unfair to him, placing success within his reach merely in order to snatch it away. From Sparta he proceeded to Argos, being invited thither by the republican party to assist them against the aristocracy and the tyrant Aristippus, who had called in the assistance of Antigonus. During an engagement with the latter within the walls of the city, Pyrrhus was killed by a woman, who threw a slate from a roof on to his head. The history of Greece during that period is so obscure, that we do not even know the year in which the great Pyrrhus died.

LECTURE LII.

Two years after Pyrrhus had quitted Italy (A.U. 480), L. Papirius the younger and Sp. Carvilius completed the subjugation of Samnium. Both had been appointed to the command with the full confidence that they would accomplish this object, because twenty or twenty-five years before they had conducted the most decisive campaign in the third Samnite war. The Samnites had now come to the conviction that they could not struggle against fate, and saved themselves by a peace, which, painful as it was, cannot be called disgraceful: it was in reality a submission to Rome, rather than a peace. We know none of the particular terms of this peace; but it is clear that the bonds of the confederacy, of which, however, only three cantons remained, were broken. The Samnite cantons continued to exist separately, and had to pledge themselves *ad majestatem populi Romani comiter colendam.*

The same Papirius, either as consul or as proconsul, gained possession of Tarentum. Milo had remained behind in that city with a few thousand Epirot troops. He behaved altogether as a rough warrior, or in reality as the captain of a band of robbers, like the Spanish generals in the Netherlands. The soldiers thought themselves entitled to do anything they

pleased, and the name of *latro* is perfectly appropriate for
them.   Milo must have been a man like Ali, pasha of Janina,
and his associates capable of the deepest dissimulation, and no
word or oath was sacred with him.   We can scarcely form an
idea of what such a garrison (φρουρά) was in those times,
even when it belonged to an allied nation.   We may form
some notion of the truth, if we know the history of the Thirty
Years' War, and of that of the Netherlands, when such garrisons were like bands of robbers that took up their quarters in
the cities.   The discipline of the Romans was infinitely better.
Milo was a perfect scoundrel.   He made the Tarentines believe
that he would negotiate peace for them, and then quit their
city; but instead of this he sold the town, and delivered the
citadel up to the Romans, while the Tarentines were firmly
believing that peace was going to be proclaimed.   One morning when they awoke, they learned with horror that Milo had
opened the gates of the Acropolis to the Romans, and that he
himself had embarked and was gone.   The Romans must
have carried away many costly treasures even on that occasion.
The walls of Tarentum were razed to the ground, and all
those who had been alive at the time when the insult was
offered to Postumius, were massacred.   The Romans boast of
having restored Tarentum to freedom; but the meaning of
this is, that they allowed the town to exist, and permitted the
inhabitants to retain their landed property, and to have their
own magistrates; but for a long time a Roman legion was
stationed at Tarentum, which, like all the Greek towns south
of Naples, had to pay a tax (unless as was the case with Heraclea, they were particularly fortunate), to distinguish them
from the Italian towns, from which the Romans demanded
military services.   The Greek towns, however, had to furnish
Rome with ships.

The Lucanians, Bruttians, Sallentines, Picentians, Sarsina-
tans, and Umbrians, now one after another acknowledged the
supremacy of Rome, though for the most part not until they
had made a last attempt, whereby their fate only became
worse.   The terms of submission were various.   Bruttium,
for example, had to give up to the Romans half of the Sila-
Forest, which was of great importance for ship-building; but
the Romans acquired the sovereignty and revenues of all those

countries. They now established a new chain of fortresses, the first, which had been made during the Samnite war being no longer sufficient; on the Adriatic, Brundusium, and on the Lower sea, Pyrgi, and others.

Ten years after the departure of Pyrrhus, Rome was the mistress of Italy, from Romagna, Ferrara, Ravenna, the marshes of Pisa and the river Macra, down to the Iapygian promontory: it thus became the most powerful and compact state that then existed: it had a large number of free allies, and behaved in such a manner, that there must evidently have existed a general law which regulated its relations with the Italian allies: we clearly see the tendency to form by degrees all those elements into one Roman people. The allies had in reality to blame themselves for having fought so long against the will of fate. The nations retained their own administrations, laws, languages and dialects; but Rome was their central point, and they were gradually to rub off what was foreign to, and irreconcilable with that centre. Italy was divided for the purpose of taxation, and placed under a definite number of quaestors, who raised the revenues. Hence the increase in the number of quaestors from four to eight. It would almost seem that isopolity was established for all the people of the Oscan and Sabellian races; the Etruscans had a separate constitution. In these regulations, it was determined what part the separate nations were to take in each war, and there must have been a sort of gradation in the services they had to perform, although the consuls were at liberty, on entering upon their office, to announce to the commissioners of the allies, who had then to come to Rome, what number of soldiers each state had to furnish. At this time, regulations must also have been made to determine what share the allies were to have in the public land of the Romans, and in what proportion they might take part in the foundation of colonies; rules were laid down, moreover, for all Roman allies, on what conditions they might acquire the Roman franchise, and in order that too many might not be drawn from their homes to Rome, it was determined, that whoever should migrate to Rome, should be obliged to leave one member of his family behind in his native place. The obligation to serve in the Roman armies was regulated by general laws. If we compare the relations in which the allies of other ancient states stood to the states which had the supremacy, the comparison will be found to be extremely creditable to the Romans, who treated their allies in a very honourable manner. The Roman allies, for instance, had only to furnish pay for their own soldiers, and Rome supplied them with provisions. There was no new legislation; the ancient constitution was only consolidated, and fixed in matters of detail.*

* The remainder of this Lecture has already appeared in Vol. I. of Niebuhr's *Lectures on Rom. Hist.* p. 95, etc. (London, 1844), where the history of Rome is continued from the point at which it here breaks off. Comp. the preface to the present volume.—ED.

INDEX.

uation of that of the Tribunus Celerum, 107

Magister populi, meaning of, 126

Magna Græcia, disappearance of its glory, 337

Maleventum the most prosperous town of the Samnites, 374

Maniples, origin of the, 105; combination of the Roman and Latin centuries into, 121

Manlius roused by the screaming of geese, 269; his name of Capitolinus not derived from saving the capitol, 279; charged with aiming at kingly power, ib.; plebes put on mourning on his accusation, 280; his conduct accounted for, ib.; points to the capitol, 281; thrown down the Tarpeian rock, ib.

—— Torquatus, his combat with a Gaul, 294; his opposition to the Latins appearing in the senate, 318; orders his son to be put to death, 320; his unprecedented arming of the accensi, 323

Manutius' commentary on Cicero's letters indispensable, 169 n.

Marcius Rutilus C. first plebeian censor and dictator, 299, 326

Marriages, mixed, the children of, followed the baser side, 179

Marsians, colony at Alba to intimidate the, 379; rise against the Romans, ib.; won by the favourable terms of peace granted by the Romans, ib.

Mastarna, original name of Servius Tullius, 67; criticism on the tradition about, 99

Maxims, one of the, which contributed to the greatness of the Romans, 361

Melpum destroyed by the Gauls, possibly on the site afterwards occupied by Milan, 254

Mensian law, the, relating to marriages, 82

Mercenaries, origin of, 340

Mettius Fuffetius torn to pieces, 43

Mezentius probably the Etruscan Conqueror of Cære, 61

Migrating people, only known instance of the return of the torrent of a, 258

Military arrangements, Roman contrasted with Greek, 322

—— constitution under Tarquinius Superbus, 105

—— rank, Roman mode of determining the grades of, 316

—— tribunes, their usual number, six, 101; instead of the consuls, 221; remarkable change in their number, 221; a majority of plebeians among them, 225; the first called

triumviri reipublicæ constituendæ, 292

Milo left at Tarentum by Pyrrhus, 436; behaves like the captain of a band of robbers, 437; betrays the Tarentines, 438; his departure, ib.

Molossians, two branches of the kingly family of the, 422

Mons Sacer, secession to, 139

Months, truce with the Veientines for forty years of ten each, 165

Monument of Porsena, its fabulous construction, 116

Mound, the great, constructed by Servius Tullius, 98

Mourning, period of, 244

Mucius P. orders his nine colleagues in the tribuneship to be burnt alive, 193

Municipia, 327

Mutius Scævola, his mistake inconceivable in history, 117

Næniæ, songs at funerals and afterwards inscribed on the tombs, 10; laudationes and, sources of the earliest history, 11

Names of nations, a fallacious criterion of their history, 17

National vanity, 12

Neapolis, origin of its name, 348; site of the ancient city, ib.; conquered by Q. Publilius Philo, 351

Nequinum taken by the Romans, 383; its name changed to Narnia, ib.

Newton assigns seventeen years as a mean number to the reign of a king, 4

Nexum, the, 133; abolition of the, 393; different from addictio, 394

Nola, importance of the Roman conquest of, 371

Nomentum obtains the franchise, 328

Noricans in Austria of the Celtic race, 259

Numa Pompilius born on the day of the foundation of Rome, 5; his reign, 41; peace during his reign of forty years historically impossible, ib.

Numerical schemes in the early chronological statements, 3; systems, the Etruscan different from the Greek or Tyrrhenian, 24

Nummi restituti, 289

Nundines, courts held on the, 391

Oenotrians and Peucetians, names of the earliest inhabitants of the south of Italy, 16

—— —— the ancient Pelasgians, 356

Ogulnian law relating to the Augurs, 45, 394

Omen in a battle with the Samnites, 401

Samnite war, the first, 306; the first in Roman history worthy of being related, 308; except the Hannibalian, the greatest, most attractive, and most noble in all the history of antiquity, 351; second war lasted 22 years, 352

Samnites, the, resisted Rome for 70 years, 66; admitted as *epoeci* at Capua, 235; alliance with the, 296; probable motives of the Roman alliance with the, *ib.*; duration of the war with the, 300; descended from the Sabines, 302; superseded Oscans, *ib.*; conquer Cumæ, 303; consisted of a confederacy of four cantons, 304; their extension towards the Liris involves them in war with the Romans, 306; a nation greater than the Romans and Latins put together. *ib.*; great battle with the, 310; peace with the, 317; betrayed by Charilaus and Nympheus, 350; consisted of four states which took the supreme command in turn, 352; equal to the Romans in the art of war, *ib.*; conditions of the truce with them, 361; withdraw from Fregellæ, 362; promises made to them by the consuls after the defeat of Caudium, 365; the consuls and tribunes pronounced traitors for making stipulations with the, 366; this act of breaking the peace with them the most detestable in Roman history, *ib.*; the consuls delivered up to them, 367; defeat the Romans and put them to flight, 370; revolution produced by this victory, *ib.*; gold and silver shields of their soldiers, 376; their country made a wilderness, 378; recognise the superiority of the Roman people, *ib.*; their junction with the Etruscans, 397; their march to Etruria one of the most brilliant feats of history, *ib.*; defeat the Romans under Q. Fabius Gurges, 404; their soldiers swear to fight to the last man, *ib.*; their towns disappear from the face of the earth, *ib.*

Samnium, relations between Rome and, 343; occasion of the war with, 348; completion of the subjugation of, 549

Samothrace, temple, and mysteries of, 15; Dodona and, were to the Pelasgian nations what Delphi and Delos were to the Hellenic world, *ib.*

Sanction, sham, given by the lictors representing the curies, 327

Saturnian verse used by the Romans before their adoption of Greek poetry, 9; prevailing character of it, *ib.*; developed in Plautus with great beauty, 10; two poems of this kind still extant on the tombs of the Scipios, 71; specimen of the verse, *ib.*

Scævolæ, the family of, origin of their name, from a circumstance different from that commonly supposed, 117

Scribes, first mentioned in history, 387; nature of their occupation, 388; their office inconsistent with *ingenuitas*, 393

Secession to Mons Sacer, 139; duration commonly assigned to it erroneous, 141; lasted only about a fortnight, *ib.*; its permanent result the establishment of the tribunes, 142; its result not a decided victory of the plebeians, 146; to the Janiculum, 411

Sempronius Sophus, inference from his surname, 347

Senate, filling up vacancies in the, 228

Senators, plebeian, 233

Seniores, duty of the, 91

Senonian Gauls, their first appearance, 293; defeat the Romans, 523; the Romans march into the country of the, 416; extirpation of their whole nation. *ib.*

Sentinum, campaign ending with the battle of, the greatest known in the early history of Rome, 402; number of the Gauls at the battle, one million of foot-soldiers according to the chronicles, *ib.*

Serpent, a sacred, brought to Rome, 406

Servilius Ahala exiled for the murder of Sp. Mælius, 231

Servius Tullius, the whole account of his descent a fable, 52: traditions respecting him, 67; important in three respects, 68; Etruscan tradition respecting, 99; murder of, 102

Setina via, the, 390

Sewers, their direction, 98

Sibylline books kept by decemvirs, 287; existed at Rome as well as at Cumæ, 336

Siccius L., his story, 206

Sicinius, leader of the soldiers in the secession, 139

Siculians or Itali, a race inhabiting Epirus, and the south of Italy, 15; in Latium from a period which cannot be chronologically defined, 18; existed in the south of Italy in Homer's time, 19; the same as those whom Cato calls Aborigines, *ib.*

She-wolf, statue of the, when erected, 29; exquisite statue of the, 373

END OF VOLUME I.

J. Wertheimer and Co., Printers, Circus Place, Finsbury Circus.

A School Dictionary of Antiquities.

Selected and Abridged from the "Dictionary of Greek and Roman Antiquities." By WILLIAM SMITH, LL.D. One small volume, Two Hundred Wood-cuts. 10s. 6d. cloth.

THIS work, abridged from the large "Dictionary of Greek and Roman Antiquities," exhibits, in a form adapted to the use of junior pupils, the results of the labours of modern scholars in the various subjects included under the general term of Greek and Roman Antiquities.

A New Classical Dictionary

OF ANCIENT BIOGRAPHY, MYTHOLOGY, and GEOGRAPHY. Edited by Dr. WM. SMITH. One vol. 8vo. 1l. 1s.

THIS work comprises the same subjects as are contained in the well-known Dictionary of Lemprière, avoiding its errors, supplying its deficiencies, and exhibiting in a concise form the *results* of the labours of modern scholars.

Niebuhr's History of Rome,

From the earliest times to the Fall of the Western Empire. Fourth Edition. Five vols. 8vo. 3l. 6s. 6d. Vols. I. and II, Translated by BISHOP THIRLWALL and ARCHDEACON HARE. 16s. each. Vol. III. Translated by Dr. SMITH and Dr. SCHMITZ. 18s. 6d. Vols. IV. and V. Lectures. Second Ed. (Vols. II. and III. of the Lectures). Edited by Dr. SCHMITZ. Two vols. 16s.

THE great work of Niebuhr stands unrivalled among all ancient and modern histories of the Roman people, for the extent and profundity of the investigations on which it is founded, and for the singular vigour of mind by which the author elicits a true narrative of events from the masses of fable, contradiction, and absurdity, under which it lay buried till his time. The author does not content himself with detailing the results he has arrived at, but gives at full length the researches themselves which led to them; so that the reader, who devotes adequate study to this profound work, will not only acquire sounder views of Roman history than could be derived from any other source whatever, but will acquire a knowledge of the critical methods by which the haze of remote antiquity has been so happily penetrated.

Niebuhr's Lectures on the History of Rome.

Edited by Dr. SCHMITZ. Second Edition enlarged and greatly improved. Three Volumes 8vo. Portrait. 1l. 4s. cloth. Or, sold separately, Vol. I. 8s. Vols. II. and III. 16s.

THESE Lectures form a history of Rome from the earliest ages to the overthrow of the Western Empire. Their subjects are concurrent (up to the first Punic war) with those of Niebuhr's great work "The History of Rome," and comprehend discussions on the sources of Roman history, with the criticism and analysis of those materials. The Lectures differ from the History, in presenting a more popular and familiar exposition of the various topics of investigation, which are treated in the History in a more severe style.

Among the subjects most elaborately treated, are the geographical positions of the ancient races of Italy, which are traced through all their migrations; the political, military, a[...]stitution and the domestic life of the Romans; the state of literatur[...] e nations that gradually came with[...]

The last two volumes are an [...]hr's *History of Rome*, from the point where that History terminates.

Poetical Works of John Keats.

In One Vol. Fcap., with a Portrait from a Drawing by HILTON. Price 5s. cloth. Also published in Royal 8vo., price 2s.

Confessions of an Opium Eater.

Royal 8vo. Price 1s. 6d.